THERAPLAY

INNOVATIONS IN ATTACHMENT–ENHANCING PLAY THERAPY

EDITED BY

Dr. Evangeline Munns

JASON ARONSON INC.
Northvale, New Jersey
London

This book was set in 10 pt. Carmina Light by Alpha Graphics of Pittsfield, NH, and printed and bound by Book-mart Press, Inc. of North Bergen, NJ.

Library of Congress Cataloging-in-Publication Data

Innovations in theraplay : attachment enhancing play therapy / edited by Evangeline Munns.
    p. cm.
  Includes bibliographical references.
  ISBN 0-7657-0227-4
  1. Play therapy. 2. School children—Mental health. 3. Family psychotherapy. I. Munns, Evangeline.
  RJ505.P6 I56 1999
  618.92'891653—dc21   99-34329

Printed in the United States of America on acid-free paper. For information and catalog write to Jason Aronson Inc., 230 Livingston Street, Northvale, NJ 07647-1726, or visit our website: www.aronson.com

To Ann Jernberg
for her inspiration

To Phyllis Booth
for her guidance

To my mother and father, Vera and Nickolas Scraba,
for giving me such good beginnings

To my husband, Tom, and my daughter, Catherine,
who are the anchors in my life

Contents

Preface

Theraplay is a form of play therapy that is gaining wide recognition as a treatment method for attachment-disordered individuals. It is congruent with the keen interest in attachment theory and research around the world today and is supported by the latter in its findings that early attachment is a crucial factor in one's ability to relate to others in later life. Its founder, Dr. Ann Jernberg, first used it in the late 1960s in her effort to increase the attachment between Head Start mothers and their children. Since then, it has grown so that now it is practiced around the world. Mental health practitioners come from all parts of the globe to be trained in Theraplay at the Theraplay Institute in Chicago, Illinois. As well, certified trainers teach Theraplay throughout the United States, Canada, and Europe. There is a growing interest in this treatment method for a number of reasons: it is short term, cost-effective, and applicable to a wide age range and a broad spectrum of mental health problems. It is simple in theory, action oriented, and visual, so that parents of any educational level can understand it easily. Because of its emphasis on building up an individual's self-esteem and confidence, and its playful engagement of those involved, clients soon learn to relax and enjoy it. It is a method that creates feelings of unconditional acceptance and joyfulness, and it is fun. In the therapeutic process children learn to feel cared for and valued for who they are. Their ability to trust and to relate to others grows.

One of the exciting things about Theraplay, is that it is highly adaptable, not only to various populations, but within various formats. It can be used individually, with dyads (parent–child, marital Theraplay), with siblings, with whole families, with multifamilies, with groups, and within school and health systems. This book discusses many of the ways of using Theraplay.

The innovations of Theraplay described in this book came partly from a situation of necessity. In our children's mental health center (Blue Hills Child and Family Services in Aurora, Ontario, Canada) in 1992, a

new department, Play Therapy Services, was established. Soon there-
after, to our surprise, we had a three-year waiting list for clients, and
a two-year waiting list for professionals who wanted to be trained in
Theraplay or in more traditional nondirective play therapy, which we
also used in our center. But because of government funding cutbacks,
we were unable to expand our services. Somehow, more children and
more trainees had to be seen in shorter periods of time. So we began
seeing two identified siblings (both siblings had been diagnosed as having emotional and behavioral difficulties) at the same time and then
three, four, and even five. We also started working with two families
simultaneously. As well, various Theraplay groups were started—from
troubled preschoolers, including autistic children, to acting-out latency
and teenaged children. We also started a Theraplay group with mothers and their teenage sons who had attachment issues and later formed
father/son and mother/daughter groups. This book describes some of
our efforts and some of the innovations of other therapists at centers
in the United States.

Part I introduces the concept of Theraplay, and gives the history
of its development. This is followed by a summary of the theory, underlying dimensions, and techniques of Theraplay in its traditional format—with one child and his or her parents.

Part IIA discusses the adaptation of Theraplay to varied populations and describes different ways of using Theraplay, but still within
the single-family format. The chapters describe work done with attachment-disordered children, with an acting-out child, with abusive parents, with failure-to-thrive infants, and with a sexually abused child
and her sibling.

Part IIB discusses Theraplay within a multifamily format. A case
study of two electively mute little girls, coming from a culture where
physical contact and emotional expression were often carefully controlled, presented a challenge to therapists using Theraplay, in which
spontaneity of positive feelings is often modeled and encouraged.
Theraplay with homeless mothers and their children in a shelter setting is discussed. The multifamily format is described in two chapters
focusing on adoptive families and family Theraplay in a school setting.

Part III focuses on group Theraplay where children are included
without their parents. The cases described include work with autistic
children, who often can be significantly helped by Theraplay, and physically handicapped and developmentally delayed children, who respond

so beautifully to the self-esteem enhancement of Theraplay. Other chapters describe the use of Theraplay on a broader basis within a school system and a primary health care system.

To accommodate the readers of this book who will not read the chapters sequentially, there is a short summary of the main dimensions of Theraplay in some of the chapters. This results in some repetition of material, but it has been kept to a minimum.

Theraplay therapists will find this book helpful in stretching their own horizons in the use of Theraplay. In addition, play therapists, counselors, social workers, psychologists, psychiatrists, and other mental health practitioners will find stimulating ideas and new ways of helping children, parents, families, and other adults.

Evangeline Munns, Ph.D., C. Psych.
King City, Ontario, Canada
December 1999

Acknowledgments

So many people have contributed in some way to this book. First, to the children and parents whom I have had the privilege of knowing in ways that are rarely granted to most people, thank you for teaching me and allowing me to share in your pain, your joy, and your growth, for I have grown with you.

Thank you to all of the authors who contributed to this book, for their ideas and their hard work.

Thank you to the interns and externs in our play therapy training program at Blue Hills for their dedication and caring. Special thanks to Janet MacQuarrie, a supervisor of the training program, for her warmth and willingness to help, no matter what was asked of her.

Thank you to Peter Rossborough, executive director of Blue Hills, for his support of the play therapy program, and to Elizabeth Morocco-Burns, my co-director, for her help in the administrative area.

My gratitude to Phyllis Booth, director of training at the Theraplay Institute in Chicago, for her wise counsel and support, and to Ann Jernberg, who founded Theraplay and encouraged me to become a Theraplay therapist and trainer.

I want to thank my husband, Tom, who taught me how to use a computer, often corrected my mistakes, and pitched in to help me in my more desperate moments.

My gratitude extends as well to the staff at Jason Aronson Inc. for their faith in this book, and particularly to the editors Anne Marie Dooley, Judy Cohen, and Norma Pomerantz, whose cheerful support made my job so much easier.

Contributors

Deborah Azoulay, M.A., C. Psych. Assoc., is currently completing a doctoral degree in clinical psychology at the Adler School of Professional Psychology in Chicago. She has more than twenty years of experience in school psychology and is a former Theraplay extern at the Blue Hills Play Therapy Services Training Program. Mrs. Azoulay has published articles on the Adlerian approach to child training and education and on Adlerian treatment for posttraumatic stress disorder. She has also given presentations on Theraplay. At present, Mrs. Azoulay is a doctoral psychology intern at Whitby Mental Health Centre, Whitby, Ontario.

Connie Bernt, Psy.D., is a licensed clinical psychologist specializing in child and adolescent psychotherapy. She has worked for the last ten years at DePaul University Community Mental Health, where she supervises graduate students in clinical psychology. In addition, she works at the Barr-Harris Children's Grief Center of the Chicago Institute for Psychoanalysis, which treats children and families following a parental death. Dr. Bernt has a private practice in Oak Park, Illinois.

Sherri Blanchard, L.S.W., has a private practice in the Ottawa region of Ontario, Canada, where she devises programs for children with special needs. She has a Social Service Worker diploma and has completed much of her training toward certification in Theraplay through the Blue Hills Play Therapy Training Program. Previously, Ms. Blanchard was employed at a children's mental health agency as a group and family counselor.

John Breuer, M.S., Ed.S., is a behavior management consultant at the Toronto Association for Community Living and is certified as a Theraplay therapist. He uses Theraplay on home visits as a way of helping parents who are experiencing behavioral challenges raising preschool-age children with developmental disabilities. Mr. Breuer also leads Theraplay groups in day-care centers.

Susan Bundy-Myrow, Ph.D., is a counseling psychologist practicing in West Seneca, New York. She brings her background in special education and rehabilitation counseling to her work with both normal and developmentally challenged children and adults. Dr. Bundy-Myrow, who trained with Ann Jernberg, Phyllis Booth, and other Theraplay Institute staff, is a Registered Association for Play Therapy Supervisor and certified Supervisor of Child Psychotherapists and Play Therapists. She is a consultant to several agencies and teaches psychiatry residents and counseling psychology students at the State University of New York at Buffalo.

Lisbeth DiPasquale, D.C.S., C. Psych. Assoc., is a registered psychological associate and is employed by the York Region District School Board in Ontario, Canada. She provides psychological assessments for students from junior kindergarten through high school to determine special learning difficulties, acts as a consultant to teachers and parents regarding educational programming needs, and advises on behavioral and social/emotional issues. She also works part-time as an extern at Blue Hills Child and Family Services as a therapist-in-training to become a qualified Theraplay therapist.

Norma Finnel, M.A., is a licensed professional counselor and a licensed marriage and family therapist in South Dakota, as well as a clinical member of the America Association of Marriage and Family Therapists. She was trained and certified as a Theraplay therapist and a Theraplay trainer at the Theraplay Institute in Chicago. Ms. Finnell has worked with children and families since 1973, in inpatient and outpatient settings, specializing in attachment problems and work with adoptive families. She also provides training for other professionals through seminars and case consultations.

Richard P. Hollingsworth, Ph.D., received his doctorate from Florida State University in clinical psychology, interned at Vanderbilt University, and was clinical services coordinator for a children's residential facility for seventeen years. He has published in the areas of research methodology, program evaluation, and community mental health.

Doug Loweth, M.S.W., specializes in counseling families with younger children. He is a social worker with Peel Children's Centre in Mississauga, Ontario, and has recently started a private practice. Mr. Loweth has led many parent education and support groups and has provided training workshops and consultation to child care providers and teachers. He is an extern in the Blue Hills Play Therapy Services training program and has almost completed his certification in Theraplay.

Janet MacQuarrie, B.A., is a certified Theraplay therapist, a supervisor of play therapy services at Blue Hills Child and Family Services, and a child and youth worker for the York Region District School Board. Ms. MacQuarrie has an extensive background working with children and families in social service and school settings. She has been a presenter at national and international play therapy conferences.

Anita Mahy, M.A., is a psycho educational consultant for the York District Catholic School Board as well as community child/family clinics. She conducts workshops and consultations for business and university communities on stress management, achievement, and motivation. Mrs. Mahy is an extern in the Blue Hills Play Therapy Services training program.

Glen Manery, B.A. (honors), has worked with autistic children, adolescents, and adults at Thistletown Regional Centre in Toronto. He is a certified Theraplay therapist. Mr. Manery is currently working as a special education assistant with the Vancouver School Board and is enrolled at the University of British Columbia in the master's program in counseling psychology.

Doris Martin, Ph.D., has a doctorate in family and child development. She began her career as a teacher in Head Start and has since worked with infants through primary-school children in various contexts, including teaching and directing in child care centers and laboratory schools. She has taught at the School of Education at James Madison University in Virginia. Her work and research on social development has been presented at national conferences and has been published in professional journals.

Charles O. Matthews, Ph.D., received an A.B. from Davidson College, an M.A.T. from Harvard University, and a doctorate from Duke University. He is an associate professor of counseling in the School of Education at the College of William and Mary. In addition, he is a nationally certified counselor with a private practice as a licensed professional counselor in Virginia. Dr. Matthews has published articles and book chapters on topics such as parent education, self-esteem, the application of general system theory to group therapy, counselor education, and transpersonal psychology.

Evangeline Munns, Ph.D., C. Psych., RPT/S, is a certified clinical psychologist and the clinical director of Blue Hills Play Therapy Services, which is part of a children's mental health agency (Blue Hills Child and Family Services) in Aurora, Ontario. At Blue Hills she has organized and leads the largest training school in Theraplay in Canada. She also has a small private practice. Dr. Munns is a registered trainer/supervisor with the Theraplay Institute in Chicago, the Association for Play Therapy in the United States, and the Canadian Association for Child and Play Therapy. In the latter, she serves on the ethics and certification committees. She has given numerous workshops on play therapy across Canada and the United States. In recent years, much of her time has been spent in training and supervising therapists in Theraplay and/or nondirective play therapy, including teaching at Western University in London, Ontario. She has also served as a consultant to numerous agencies. In May, 1999, she received the Monica Herbert award from the Canadian Association for Child and Play Therapy for making an outstanding contribution in the field of play therapy in Canada.

David L. Myrow, Ph.D., is a clinical psychologist in private practice. He has been involved in Theraplay since its inception, working for the Theraplay Institute as a college student and, after earning his doctorate at the University of Illinois (Urbana), becoming a certified Theraplay therapist. Dr. Myrow has utilized Theraplay in work with children manifesting a variety of concerns, notably attachment issues. He trained with Ann Jernberg, Phyllis Booth, Ernestine Thomas, and Terrence Koller, among others, at the Theraplay Institute. Dr. Myrow is a registered Association for Play Therapy supervisor, and a certified supervisor of child psychotherapists and play therapists by the International Board of Examiners of Certified Play Therapists. He teaches psychiatry residents at the State University of New York at Buffalo, and has presented workshops on Theraplay in the United States and Canada.

Phyllis B. Rubin, Psy.D. (clinical psychology), is a certified Theraplay therapist and group Theraplay trainer, and a licensed speech and language pathologist. Dr. Rubin developed the present group Theraplay format. She is an affiliate of the Theraplay Institute and practices psychotherapy and speech/language therapy in the Chicago area.

Jamie Sherman, B.Ed., is a special education teacher and the head of special education at Zareinu Educational Centre in Toronto. He received a specialized honors degree in psychology in 1992, a bachelor's of education in 1993, and a specialist in special education in 1997, all from York University. He is currently completing studies toward a master's in education, specializing in special education, at the Ontario Institute for Studies in Education. He is also completing certification toward becoming a Theraplay therapist.

Mary R. Talen, Ph.D., is a clinical psychologist and associate professor at Wright State University in Dayton, Ohio, where she teaches in the Schools of Professional Psychology, Medicine, and Nursing and Health. She also has a private practice in individual, marital, child, and family therapy. Dr. Talen has published extensively and has given presentations throughout the United States and abroad. Her most recent works are in the areas of interdisciplinary health care teams, community-based primary health care, adoptive families, and the teaching of supervision.

Susan Wood, M.S.W., is a social worker and a member of the Ontario College of Certified Social Workers. Ms. Wood works at Kinark Child and Family Services. Her experience in Theraplay was obtained in the Theraplay Extern program at Blue Hills Child and Family Services.

Janet Zanetti, Ed.D., L.P.C., is a professional counselor in private practice in Virginia Beach, Virginia. In her work as an educator, family counselor, and adjunct faculty member of undergraduate and master's-level students, Dr. Zanetti has developed several training programs. She has presented at many local and national conventions.

PART I

Introduction and Background

Theraplay is a treatment method that fosters healthy attachment, self-esteem, and trust, using preverbal interactions. It has proven to be a remarkably powerful intervention with significant changes apparent over a short period of time. Since parents are directly involved in Theraplay, there is more generalization of positive outcomes into the home and school. It is validated in its basic premises not only by research on attachment and the importance of touch, but also by the exciting new research of psychobiologists and psychoneurologists, which suggests greater use of nonverbal or preverbal therapies, particularly in cases of deprivation or neglect, poor attachment, and trauma. Furthermore, this research verifies that we should be using intervention methods as early as possible (from birth to age 3) to take advantage of the period of greatest plasticity of the brain. Theraplay is applicable to this age range but is also helpful for all ages—infants, preschoolers, latency-aged children, adolescents, adults, and the elderly. It is also widely adaptable to many formats: individual, family, and group. This book exemplifies many of the innovative ways that Theraplay has been adapted in Canada and the United States.

1

Theraplay:
The Early Years

DAVID L. MYROW

I was 19 years old, finishing my freshman year at the University of Illinois in Urbana, when Ted Hurst hired me to be a clerk for the Head Start project, under the aegis of Worthington, Hurst and Associates. WHA had just gotten the first contract for psychological services to Chicago's Head Start summer program, and there were 5,000 pre-schoolers enrolled. Ted was trying to determine how to provide psychological help for these children—and for their teachers, many of whom taught third to seventh grade and were unfamiliar with preschoolers. Head Start was one program in President Lyndon Johnson's Great Society; there was a fair amount of optimism and excitement about it, and a little anxiety. Ted hired Ann Jernberg to be the clinical director of this project, and Viola Brody (who later developed Developmental Play, a close cousin of Theraplay) came around a few times in the early stages.

WHA was a psychological consulting firm; its usual clients were large corporations. However, Ted Hurst was a man of great intuition and many talents. He also had a wide range of colleagues, several of whom were associated with the University of Chicago, including Ann Jernberg, whose graduate studies were at the Human Development Program. The four summers I spent with WHA and the Theraplay Institute brought me close to these talented people and inspired my eventual career direction. By the time I completed my senior thesis, I had developed enough skills to do some informal research on the Head Start project, and even to take a role in writing the annual report to the federal agency that funded it.

In 1967, when Ted Hurst first proposed providing psychological services to Head Start, he made a decision that demonstrated his brilliant sensibilities in applied psychology. He proposed that psychologists in Head Start serve as consultants to the teachers. His was a radical departure at the time, when psychologists typically were called in to evaluate specific children, usually devoting all their time to psychological testing. The resources provided to Head Start psychologists would be quite limited, and the teachers faced a multitude of stressors, in that the children were poor, malnourished, and mentally unstimulated, and their parents were young and immature. Some children were abused. One child had been dropped head first out of a second-story apartment—and survived. Another child had been locked in his apartment for two days with his dead mother, after witnessing her murder. In addition, many of the teachers had no experience with young children.

Ted determined that the most productive role for Head Start psychologists would be as "teachers' psychologists." The strategy turned out to be quite successful, and, by the time a national conference of Head Start psychological consultants was held in 1969, the "Chicago Format" was proposed as a model for all other Head Start programs.

In the beginning, we had groups of psychologists, social workers, and others coming in for recruitment and training. Ann Jernberg was concerned about making sure people were well received and treated sensitively. One of the trainers was Bruno Bettelheim's daughter, a social worker, who briefed the staff on the complexities of working in the inner city. She told the women to dress down and not wear a lot of makeup.

Ann Jernberg's main contributions to the early Chicago Head Start Psychological Services program were in the clinical area. She began to formulate the strategies that would become Theraplay, and she offered to everyone she touched a positive, hopeful view of people that pervaded the whole program. She brought on board other clinicians of great talent, especially Phyllis Booth, who became director of clinical training and who advanced the theory of Theraplay. She recently rewrote the original text of *Theraplay* (Jernberg and Booth 1999). This revised version shows how twenty years of advances in research and theory on attachment both validate the original premise and set the stage for further development of the approach.

Together, Ann and Ted defined the psychologist's role as multifaceted. In the 1969–70 annual report, they cited examples of the psychologists' interventions: "Helping a child build self-confidence, helping a parent to understand her child, helping out a teacher in a tough moment and using the chance to interact with the children, reinforcing a good teacher in a critical moment, providing much-needed advice to parents about child development, parental roles, [and] offering specific suggestions for a teacher eager to improve her relationship with a little boy."

While the psychological services component of the Chicago Head Start program served the teachers, it became evident that many children were in need of therapeutic services. The psychologists and teachers began to identify children in trouble, most of whom were 4 years old, but there were few resources available to offer them more intensive help. One or two children per class were considered to be in dire need of services because they were withdrawn, overactive, or demonstrated bizarre behavior. They could not be engaged constructively in the preschool program. These children were at a point in development where they could benefit significantly from treatment, but the wait for admission to mental health clinics was often more than a year. Failure to treat could be considered a crime.

In the face of this challenge, Ann worked with Ted to develop the mental health aide program, the predecessor to Theraplay, in which paraprofessionals were trained to do a very specific intervention that it was hoped, would be powerful, quick, and effective. The intention was to develop, on short notice, more resources for children in need. Basing much of her thinking on the work of Austin Deslauriers, a psychiatrist with whom Ann worked at Michael Reese Hospital, Ann developed a therapy that the 1969–70 annual report described as "providing vigorous, pleasurable, physical, direct, and highly personal contact between the therapist and the child." As the approach evolved, Ann and Ted gave it the name Theraplay, and trademarked the name to distinguish it from other approaches that lacked the theoretical base and the disciplined respect for children. Ernestine Thomas was also a key figure in the development of Theraplay, especially in its belief in the positive potential growth in the child.

Mental health aide candidates were recruited from many walks of life, and included suburban housewives, high school dropouts, college students, and Head Start sisters and mothers. In the spirit of President Johnson's Great Society, efforts were made to train people as child therapists (with supervision) who might otherwise be disenfranchised. The successful candidates were homemakers or professionals, and it was the professionals—psychologists and social workers, speech therapists, and special educators—who went on to become Theraplay therapists and to develop the art. All candidates were put through a rigorous training course before working independently with children, and were closely supervised by professional staff, even after training. Ann was especially concerned that the therapists be competent and ethical. This was a new treatment, it required physical contact with clients, and it raised a lot of anxiety in other mental health professionals! Coming from a largely analytic frame of reference, Ann was particularly concerned that the therapists' personal issues not spill over into treatment. As a result of this concern, the current requirement for Theraplay trainees is certification in a mental health or educational profession.

The training itself was ambitious, consisting of a minimum of 500 hours of work. It typically started by meeting with a mother who was struggling with her Head Start–age child, and the training group would focus on the parent–child interaction. Later, there were systematic observations of individual family members in different settings (a zoo, a playground, a beach). Later still, the focus was on the trainees' reactions to various children, parents, and teachers, in an effort to increase the trainees' self-awareness so as to help the children more sensitively.

The mental health aide program was evaluated on an ongoing basis. Teachers' evaluations of the work were requested. A WHA field psychologist interviewed twenty-three teachers at their Head Start sites. These teachers had a total of forty-one children with whom mental health aides had worked during the school year. The average length of treatment was about fifteen sessions, usually one a week. The teacher interviews produced the following findings:

1. *Reason for referrals*: About one-third of the children were referred because of withdrawn behavior, about one-third because of

hyperactive behavior, and the rest for bizarre, immature, or other difficult-to-handle classroom behavior.

2. *Social relationships*: After treatment, 73 percent were seen to have improved peer relationships and 87 percent were seen to have improved relationships with adults.

3. *Overall behavior*: 87 percent of the children were described as manifesting some or much improvement; 13 percent were seen as showing no improvement.

4. *Teachers' ratings of the mental health aide program*: On three different rating scales, a majority of teachers described the program as helpful, and many expressed a wish for more availability of services.

5. *Special contribution of the mental health aide program*: Of the 23 teachers, 21 indicated that the mental health aide program offered help that was not otherwise available in Head Start.

6. *Teachers' predictions of children's success in kindergarten the next year*: On separate before and after scales, teachers' predictions of the children's success in kindergarten rose markedly.

Another way in which Ann and Ted endeavored to establish the efficacy of Theraplay was by creating demonstration movies to show to professional and nonprofessional audiences. WHA hired a professional film production company to produce the first movie, "Here I Am." This film depicted Theraplay sessions with two withdrawn children. The therapists met with the children in a corner of a Head Start classroom. Typically, a blanket defined the therapy space. The movie shows the children at various stages of treatment; the positive changes are easily observable. The children progress from being pathetically withdrawn to being actively engaged with other children and adults. WHA was not sure in the beginning that these particular children would experience a good outcome from treatment, but the resources to make the movie were committed on the basis of the awareness that most children were benefiting from the intervention. "Here I Am" won the Chris, a major award roughly equivalent to an Emmy, in the educational film field. Three years later a follow-up sequence was added to the film, showing how these youngsters had gone on to lead normal lives.

Another movie, "There He Goes," shows the course of treatment for an overactive boy. This movie clarifies the hypothesized dynamic for these children of experiencing unmet nurturing needs that become manifested as overactive and aggressive behavior in the classroom. Posttreatment footage shows the enduring effects of treatment.

"Here I Am" and "There He Goes" remain compelling testaments to the power of Theraplay. The creative spirit of Theraplay interventions is clear, and the follow-up sequences documenting the long-term positive outcomes are convincing.

Over the next twenty-five years, Ann Jernberg and her many colleagues continued to refine the techniques, strategies, and theoretical basis for Theraplay. Theraplay is now being used throughout the United States, and in Canada, Japan, Germany, Australia, and Finland. In addition to the Theraplay Institute in Chicago (under the leadership of Phyllis Booth and Sandra Lindaman), there are now training centers in other locations in the United States, in Canada (under the leadership of Dr. Evangeline Munns), and in Germany (led by Ulriche Franke).

REFERENCE

Jernberg, A., and Booth, P. (1999). *Theraplay: Helping Parents and Children Build Better Relationships through Attachment-Based Play.* San Francisco: Jossey-Bass.

2

Traditional Family and Group Theraplay

EVANGELINE MUNNS

Theraplay is a short-term, structured form of play therapy whose prime objective is to enhance healthy attachment, self-esteem, and trust in others. It is based on replicating normal parent–child interactions, which include a lot of physical contact, joyfulness, and fun. No interpretations are made. Bizarre behavior is ignored. It is not a talking therapy that dwells on the problems of the client. Rather, it concentrates on the healthy, positive aspects of the child with the underlying belief that everyone has the potential for inner healing and growth.

No toys are used. Treatment concentrates on playful interactions between child, therapist, and parent. Simple, inexpensive materials such as baby powder or lotion, band-aids, cotton balls, nerf balls, balloons, bean bags, pillows, a blanket, snacks such as potato chips, popcorn, slices of watermelon, apples or other fruit, lollipops, and so on, are often used.

Each session of Theraplay is preplanned according to the needs of the individual child. The therapist follows the session's agenda, which is usually posted on a wall within the therapist's visual range. The therapist leads the session, playfully engaging and directing the child while parents first observe a few sessions through a one-way mirror or from a corner of the room, and then actively participate in the activities with their child under the guidance of the therapist in later sessions. Parents who have a personal history of neglect or deprivation are often brought into the sessions early so that they can receive Theraplay. Such parents often need to receive nurturing themselves before they can give it to their children.

In my work I often feel that clients sense they have a chance to start afresh in Theraplay—a new beginning where people see them as attractive and delightful in some way. This comes about because the therapist, right from the start, gives a feeling to the client of unconditional acceptance, of being glad to be with him or her. The sense of new beginnings also comes from the therapist's deliberate use of regression where the child is fed, perhaps cradled and rocked, or soothed in a way one might a very young child, giving an unspoken message of "In here we will take good care of you—you are accepted for who you are—for just being you." This is often an unfamiliar but profound experience for a child or an adult. Children usually respond beautifully to this unpressured atmosphere in Theraplay and in the end, comments such as the following are often heard: "I wish I could come here every day" (from a 7-year-old tyrant); "I wish I could come here forever"(from an acting-out, aggressive teenager).

THEORY

Theraplay is based on attachment theory, which proposes that the first relationship a child has is the most important one in his/her life, as it forms the prototype for all other relationships. If that relationship is not a strong or a positive one, then subsequent relationships can go awry, resulting in difficulties in relating to others in adult life. Theraplay goes back to the original relationship and tries to make it a healthier, more secure one. This is done by deliberately evoking the feelings and memories of an earlier time by replicating what a normal mother and father typically do with their young child. It is this aspect of Theraplay that is unique and powerful. Interactions are replicated that touch on the roots of interpersonal connectedness. Early emotions are relived and reexperienced in an atmosphere of caring and acceptance, provided first by the therapist and later by the parent under the coaching of the therapist. As treatment progresses, there is less emphasis on regression and more focus on age-appropriate activities. Because Theraplay builds up the child's and parent's self-esteem, both end up feeling valued and important. Once they start feeling good about themselves, they are more ready to be sensitive to the cues of others and to be in affective attunement with each other. This empathic, attuned, responsiveness on the part of the parents is crucial for the child to develop an inner sense of a strong, competent self, of feeling worthy, of feeling securely attached to his/her caregivers (Jernberg and Booth 1999, Stern 1995).

RESEARCH

Attachment theory is well grounded in research and many studies are devoted to this topic around the world today (Rutter 1994, Van Ijzendoorn 1994). Attachment research is more fully described in other chapters of this book, but a few landmarks should be mentioned here. Bowlby's observations in orphanages and studies on the effects of maternal separation and deprivation, coupled with his association with ethologists Lorenz and Tinbergen in the 1950s, led him to postulate that humans have an instinct for attachment to a caregiver, in the interest of self-survival. If this attachment is a good one, the child develops a secure base from which he/she can explore the world (Bowlby 1973, 1988, Holmes 1996). Mary Ainsworth, a colleague of Bowlby's, developed the "strange situation" (see Chapter 4) as a measure of early patterns of attachment (Ainsworth and Bell 1970, Ainsworth, et al. 1978) and their effect on the later ability to relate (Bretherton 1985, Crittenden 1994, Karen 1994). Mary Main developed the Adult Attachment Interview (Main and Goldwyn 1985), which has been used extensively in researching the intergenerational transmission of secure and insecure attachment patterns (Fonagy 1994, Main et al. 1989, Zeanah 1994, (Zeanah and Zeanah 1989). All of this research supports the idea that our early relationships have a tremendous influence on our emotional adjustment and responsiveness to others in later life.

Theraplay includes a lot of physical contact, which characterizes normal interactions between parents and their baby. The research supporting the importance of touch is gaining momentum today (Field 1995, Smith et al. 1998). Even in treating physically or sexually abused children, where touch used to be taboo, there is a growing realization of how necessary positive touch is to the healing process (Ford 1993, Hindman 1991, James 1994, Smith-Lawry 1998).

The recent research of psychobiologists and psychoneurologists is giving us hard data that help us understand the development of the human brain and how it is affected by environmental conditions. Specifically, it has been found that deprivation, trauma, and poor attachment can have profound effects on the developing brain (Marcellus 1998, Schore 1998). Research in this area validates the Theraplay approach, which is nonverbal, multisensory (including touch), relationship based, and ideally suited for enhancing attachment at all ages, but especially with the very young. Theraplay has also been used successfully with deprived and/or traumatized children (with emphasis on gentle nurturing).

In infancy there is tremendous neuronal growth in the human brain so that by the age of 3, nine-tenths of the brain is developed (Marcellus 1998, Schore 1998). Particularly in the first year, there is a spurt in the growth of neuronal connections, followed by a "pruning" period after the first year, where neuronal pathways that are not stimulated or used tend to fade out. In young children who are not stimulated (such as in conditions of deprivation or neglect), this process results in areas of the brain that do not show as much activity as compared to similar areas in the brains of normal children. As well, if the child is in a situation where there is poor attachment or trauma, resulting in the child being left in a chronically high arousal state over time, the neurotransmitters, such as norepinephrine or the stress hormone cortisol, are produced in such strength that they become toxic to the brain (Marcellus 1998). This may result in cell death (Schore 1998) and /or inhibition of the growth of the dendritic fields in the brain. As Schore (1998) states:

- Limbic connections that are in the process of developing are exposed to heightened levels of excitotoxic neurotransmitters and stress hormones.
- Adverse social experiences during early critical periods result in permanent alterations in opiate, cortico-steroid, corticotropin releasing factor, dopamine, noradrenaline, and serotonin receptors.
- Such receptor alterations are a central mechanism by which early adverse developmental experiences may leave behind

a permanent physiological reactivity in the limbic areas of
the brain. [p. 7]

Not all researchers would agree as to the specificity of areas of the
brain that are affected, but there seems to be a general agreement that
there is a significant negative effect on the developing brain from chronic
high arousal states in the infant. What this means is that it is crucial
for mental health practitioners to treat children at a younger age (from
infancy to age 3). Treatment methods for poor attachment or trauma
(such as Theraplay) should be put into place at an early age before more
damage is done and while the brain is most plastic.

Another finding of current research in the psychobiology field is
that the right hemisphere, which controls sensorimotor perception and
integration and processes social emotional input, is dominant in the first
three years of life. Memories of trauma and poor attachment experiences in the early years are processed in the right side of the brain. These
memories are "indelibly imprinted in the brain stem and mid brain"
(Marcellus 1998, p. 1). This suggests that since these experiences are
processed and stored in a part of the brain that is preverbal or nonverbal, it makes sense to pay more attention to nonverbal methods of
treatment (Schore 1998), such as Theraplay, sandplay therapy, dance
and movement therapy, touch therapy, eye movement therapy, nondirective play therapy, and others.

Zeanah (1998) and Osofsky (1998) advocate relationship-based
therapies where child and parent are treated together when there are
trauma or attachment issues, since the latter issues always involve more
than one person. Theraplay is clearly a relationship-based therapy in
that the direct participation of parents interacting with their child is
encouraged, guided, and supported.

In addition, because there is a growing concern over the rise of violence in the United States (which has been described as "the most violent developed country in the world. . . . Homicide is the third leading
cause of death for all children between the ages of five and fourteen"
[Osofsky 1998, p.6]), there is an urgent need to address the roots of
violence and the transmission of violent family patterns of interaction
from one generation to the next. Theraplay is ideally suited for changing negative family interactions into more positive ones where violence
is replaced by caring, nurturing interactions, first modeled by the thera-

pists and then learned by the direct participation of the parents with their children (see chapter 7).

One of the clinical observations often noted by therapists, teachers, and parents is that aggression is diminished in children receiving Theraplay. This was supported by a study on twenty-five children (Munns et al. 1997) using pre- and post scores on the Auchenbach Child Problem Checklist, on which the aggressive factor was significantly lowered.

The research pertaining to the direct use of Theraplay is not extensive and clearly needs attention. (Chapters 8, 12, 14, and 18 are based on research studies using Theraplay.) A controlled study conducted in Germany (Ritterfeld, personal communication), using three matched groups of language-disabled children, found some surprising results. The group receiving Theraplay had significantly higher scores not only on social-emotional tests as expected, but also, surprisingly, on language expression as well, in contrast to a group that received speech and language therapy (from professional speech therapists) and a control group that received arts and crafts activities. It was postulated that although the Theraplay group did not receive any speech therapy, the children increased their expressive language skills because they became freer emotionally and consequently more verbal. This has also been observed on a clinical level when working with autistic children, who often begin talking more spontaneously and appropriately when receiving Theraplay.

Morgan (1989), in her study using Theraplay, found that two-thirds of her subjects, after receiving Theraplay, improved in four factors—self-confidence, self-control, self-esteem, and trust—as assessed by parents, teachers, observers of the program, and the therapists.

DIMENSIONS UNDERLYING THERAPLAY

In Jernberg's observations of normal parents with their babies, she noted many warm and delightful interchanges. She categorized her observations under four dimensions: structure, challenge, intrusion (later called stimulation or engagement), and nurture. She later added another dimension—playfulness. These are the dimensions that underlie the activities that are chosen for each Theraplay session.

Structure

There is an orderliness and rhythm to a baby's life in terms of regular feedings and nap times in the normal situation. As the child matures there are emerging rules on what is or is not permitted; for example, a child can throw a toy but not a cup of milk, and the child can explore the world but not touch a hot stove or an electrical socket. The child's world is structured in terms of time and space by the parent, giving the child a sense of predictability and safety. So it is in Theraplay. The therapist plans the activities and leads them. The therapist is in charge. There is a definite beginning and end to the sessions, and there are rules, such as that no one gets hurt. This dimension is particularly stressed for impulsive children who lack inner controls, or for tyrants who try to control everyone in their environment.

Challenge

Challenges come early in life. Taking risks and mastering skills build a sense of competence and self-confidence. The parent may have the baby sit without the support of pillows, or take that first step without a helping hand. The important thing is that the steps for mastery of a new skill be within the capability of the child so that he or she does not experience failure, but rather an accomplishment. In Theraplay, the child is given age-appropriate risks—for example, to jump a little higher, to remember a clap pattern in a progressively more difficult sequence, to thumb or arm wrestle, and so on. Challenging activities should be fun and should allow for a lot of tension release. Such activities are particularly good for timid, fearful, withdrawn children who have been overprotected, and for aggressive children so that they can let off steam.

Engagement

Parents do not normally leave their baby lying for hours alone in a crib (unless the baby is sleeping). They engage their baby in many playful ways and, in doing so, intrude in their child's world. When this is done in tune with the baby's needs, it is usually mutually enjoyable for both and often accompanied by laughter and pure joy. The parent may play Peekaboo, may blow on the baby's tummy, or may softly whisper in the baby's ear. Babies gradually learn who they are, their body boundaries, and a sense that they are a source of delight and pleasure for the parents. In Theraplay sessions, the therapist engages the child in many stimulating ways, often with an element of surprise, and so the child learns that life can be adventuresome and fun. This dimension is frequently used with very withdrawn, rigid, or avoidant children who have high protective barriers, such as autistic children.

Nurture

Nurture is necessary for every child. Parents demonstrate their love and caring for a child in many ways: feeding, bathing, powdering, cradling, rocking, singing, caressing, hugging, kissing, and praising. But it is especially through nurturing that children learn to feel valued, loved, wanted, and secure. If children are to thrive, they must have good nurturing, and so all children in Theraplay receive nurturing in every session. This nurturing includes feeding the child a snack at every session (sometimes giving a lollipop or a bottle while the therapist gently rocks the child), powdering or lotioning his hurts on hands or feet, making hand prints, cradling or rocking the child while singing a special song about him, rocking him in a blanket, and so on. Even with older children, these activities, although regressive, give a sense of caring and emotional nourishment that many children lack. This is often especially true of aggressive, acting-out children who rarely are nurtured, or superachieving, pseudomature children who have lost their childhood.

Playfulness

Children love to play. All activities in Theraplay are done through games or in a playful way that easily engages the child.

APPROPRIATE CLIENTS

Theraplay is suitable for clients of all ages—infants, preschool, and latency-aged children; and adolescents, adults, and the elderly—and for a wide range of problems—from acting out, impulsive, aggressive children, to those who are timid, fearful, and withdrawn. This has included homicidal and suicidal children. It is particularly helpful for children with attachment issues, such as autistic children and adopted, foster, or stepchildren. It has been successfully used for those with low self-esteem or socialization difficulties (learning disabled, developmentally delayed, or physically disabled), and for children with depression. The fun and surprises inherent in Theraplay have helped children with obsessive-compulsive disorder and the superachiever or tyrant. Sexually or physically abused children have also benefited from the gentle nurturing and feelings of acceptance they so urgently need.

INAPPROPRIATE CLIENTS

Children who have been recently traumatized, such as those grieving from the loss of a close family member or friend, or those recovering from recent hospitalization or illness, need a quiet time to recuperate, not the playful exuberance of Theraplay. Children who have been recently traumatized sexually or physically need the nurturing that Theraplay can give them, but they also need special considerations (see Chapter 9). Intrusion should be very gentle and their refusals to do an activity should be heeded. These children need to be empowered, not overwhelmed. If a child is frightened, then the trusted parent or friend may need to be in the Theraplay room until the child has learned to be more comfortable with the therapist alone. These children usually also need more traditional forms of play therapy to work through their trauma. Children who are very fragile and panic at the approach of an adult also may benefit more from nondirective play therapy.

TRADITIONAL FORMAT FOR FAMILY THERAPLAY

After a thorough family and developmental history, plus an assessment of family interactions using the Marschak Interaction Method described in Chapter 3 of this book, the child and parents are seen generally for eight (or more) half-hour sessions, once or several times a week. Treatment usually extends over a period of three months and is followed by four follow-up sessions over the course of a year. In the first four sessions the parents observe either through a one-way mirror or from a corner of the room as the therapist plays with their child. An interpreting therapist is with them to answer their questions and to explain the therapeutic interventions and role modeling of the therapists. In the following four sessions they watch for only about ten or fifteen minutes and then enter the room and are directly involved in interacting with their child under the guidance of the therapist. As treatment progresses, the parents may be asked to lead some of the activities. As well, parents are encouraged to practice Theraplay activities at home every week and are allowed to include siblings if this is appropriate. At about three sessions before termination, the child is informed that the Theraplay sessions will soon end, and a party is planned for the last session, featuring the family's favorite activities and food, which the parents bring. A small present is often given to the child at the end.

If the parents are unable to participate because of work or for other valid reasons, individual Theraplay is then carried out with just the child, in which he learns to relate positively to the therapist and to feel better about himself.

Example of a Family Theraplay Session's Agenda

All sessions are preplanned by the therapists according to the needs and goals of the family. While the parents observe from the sidelines, or through a one-way mirror, with an interpreting therapist beside them, the activities may include the following:

Entrance (e.g., Follow the leader)
Welcome song
Checkup or inventory (point out child's positive features: sparkly eyes, rosy cheeks, beautiful smile, "let's measure it")
Lotion or powder hurts (powder rubbed gently on scratches or bruises)
Play-Doh trophies (Play-Doh imprints of various body parts such as fingers, elbows, ears)
Silly Bones (Silly Bones says: Touch hands together, elbows, feet, noses, etc.)

When the parents join the session, the following activities are done:

Hide under blanket (parents come in and find the hidden child)
Rock child in blanket (while singing a special song about the child)
Motorboat song (everyone joins hands in circle for this action song)
Duck duck goose (as "it" and "chaser" pass each other they give
  each other a hug and then continue to race to the empty spot)
Lotion hands (family members lotion one another's hands)
Hand stack up and down (everyone in group participates in a circle)
Feeding (leader feeds everyone a chip and then others take turns)
Goodbye song
*See appendix at the back of the book for a description of these
  activities.

At our center, the Blue Hills Child and Family Services, in Aurora, Ontario, each Theraplay session is followed by a half hour of parent counseling. This is not traditionally done in Theraplay.

TRADITIONAL FORMAT FOR GROUP THERAPLAY

Group Theraplay was spearheaded by Dr. Phyllis Rubin, a speech pathologist, with the assistance of Jeanine Tregay, a special education teacher (Rubin and Tregay 1989), in the 1980s, when they formed a Theraplay group with special-needs children with behavior disorders. A goal of this group was to form a cohesive, family atmosphere where the children could feel a sense of belonging and acceptance, as well as learn to relate to each other in a more positive fashion. This was accomplished, and group Theraplay evolved from a school setting to other settings such as hospitals, day-care centers, mental and public health centers, and other institutions. Group Theraplay has been used for a wide age range, from babies with high-risk teenage mothers to the elderly. At our center we have used Theraplay groups with emotionally troubled preschoolers, including autistic children, latency-aged and adolescent boys from our residential treatment setting, high-risk teenage pregnant mothers, and mother/son, father/son, and mother/daughter groups. In the near future we plan to do a father/daughter group.

Group Theraplay focuses on the four basic dimensions of structure, challenge, engagement, and nurture. The children are engaged through a variety of active, sometimes boisterous, games, where they can release underlying tensions, interspersed with quiet, restful, more intimate activities, where they can calm down. This way things do not get out of control. The co-leaders are in charge and preplan the agenda of activities. There is a designated leader who takes the lead role, especially in initiating the welcome song at the beginning, the goodbye song at the end, and the feeding of a snack, which is included in every session. As well, the leader, especially in the first few sessions, reminds the children of three rules:

1. No hurts
2. We stick together (follow the directions of the leader)
3. We have fun

Starting a Group

Parents must give their written consent for their child's participation in the group. Permission must also be obtained from school or agency administrators if the group is held in either of those places. Videotaping (with parental consent) is recommended for supervision purposes as well as for safeguarding the therapists from any accusations of sexual abuse, as there is a lot of physical contact in Theraplay.

The general goals for clients in group theraplay are the following:

1. To enhance self-esteem and self-confidence
2. To increase trust in others
3. To increase one's awareness of others and the needs of others
4. To promote feelings of care and concern for others
5. To increase the ability to wait and take turns
6. To increase inner controls for those who are too impulsive or who act out
7. To promote a feeling of safety with others
8. To promote feelings of acceptance and belonging
9. To enhance the ability to relate to others
10. To experience joy, laughter, and fun with others

Makeup of Group, Size, and Frequency

Sessions are held usually for a half hour at least once or twice a week, or daily in some settings. Groups may last three months or longer, are then evaluated, and become ongoing if successful. There is a main leader and one or more co-leaders, depending on the size and makeup of the group.

The number of children in a group can vary from four to thirty (the larger groups have been conducted with normal children in a day-care setting). If there are highly disturbed children, the group size should be four to eight children usually. It is prudent not to have too many acting-out children in one group, as they can sabotage it. The larger the group, the more structure it needs. This is especially true for adolescent groups, where more challenging activities are undertaken.

Example of a Group Theraplay Session

A group session can include the following activities:

Entrance (stepping stones)
Welcome song (The children and coleaders sit or stand in a circle with their shoes off while the welcome song is sung; the leader tries to maintain frequent eye contact with everyone and is warm and welcoming)
Special welcome to each child ("John, you've brought your bright smile, Mary your nice curly hair," etc.)
Three rules: No hurts, stick together, have fun!
Powdering or lotioning of hurts by leaders or by peers
Tracing shapes, letters, or numbers on the back of a neighbor, who guesses what it is
Red Light, Green Light (children move forward on "green light" but freeze when leader calls out "red light."
One Potato, Two Potato, Hug (traditional chant but on the word *more* give person a hug)
"Row, Row, Row Your Boat" song, with hands on shoulders
Cotton Ball Guess (one child closes eyes and guesses where the other child is touching him with a cotton ball)

Cotton Ball Soothe (one child gently moves a cotton ball over the
   forehead, nose, cheeks, etc. of another child, and then the chil-
   dren switch partners)
Feeding (leader feeds chips to everyone and others can take turns
   doing the feeding)
Say one nice thing you like about your neighbor
Goodbye song
*See Appendix for description of activities.

Discipline Problems

If a child is hurt, the leader immediately stops the activity, soothes the
injured child, and ascertains what happened. If there has been an aggressive act by one of the children, that child is asked to make a form
of restitution by helping to soothe the hurts of the injured child by either putting a Band-Aid on the hurt or gently rubbing lotion or powder around the hurt. The injured child is also encouraged to tell the
aggressor: "Don't hurt me anymore." This has proven to be an extremely powerful technique in helping children gain an awareness of
the consequences of their aggressive actions and allows the aggressor
to make some form of restitution to the child he has hurt. Both children end up feeling better.

If a child refuses to participate in an activity, he may just sit quietly
in the circle with a co-leader beside him, and wait until he feels more comfortable joining in (this is especially true for abused children, who should
never be forced to participate). However, if a child starts acting out or
displays negative behavior as a way of getting attention, then the child is
warned in a nonpunitive but firm manner that he is wanted as part of
the group; however, he must manage his behavior. Another warning is
given if necessary, but a third infraction results in the child being removed
from the group with an adult sitting next to him until he can calm down
and participate again. The co-leader decides when this should occur, and
the child is warmly welcomed back into the group when he returns.

Benefits

Group Theraplay increases attachment among peers and between children and their leaders. Participants become familiar with each other

quickly and learn each other's names easily. The group encourages cooperation, spontaneous sharing, affection, trust, and a heightened sense of self-respect, and it reduces aggression.

REFERENCES

Ainsworth, M. D. S., and Bell, S. M. (1970). Attachment, exploration and separation: illustrated by the behavior of one year olds in a strange situation. *Child Development* 41:49–67.

Ainsworth, M. D. S., Blehar, M. C., Waters, E., and Wall, S. (1978). *Patterns of Attachment: A Psychological Study of the Strange Situation*. Hillsdale, NJ: Lawrence Erlbaum.

Bowlby, J. (1973). *Attachment and Loss, Vol. 2: Separation, Anxiety, and Anger*. London: Hogarth Press.

——— (1988). *A Secure Base, Parent–Child Attachment and Healthy Human Development*. New York: Basic Books.

Bretherton, I. (1985). Attachment theory: retrospect and prospect. In *Growing Points in Attachment Theory and Research*, ed. I. Bretherton and E. Waters, pp. 3–35. Monographs of the Society for Research in Child Development, vol. 50, no. 209.

Crittenden, P. (1994). *The A/C pattern of attachment: risk of dysfunction versus opportunity for creative integration*. Paper presented at the International Conference on Attachment and Psychopathology, Toronto, Ontario, October.

Field, T. M. (1995). *Touch in Early Development*. Hillsdale, NJ: Lawrence Erlbaum.

Fonagy, P. (1994). *Crime and attachment: representation of attachment relationships in a severely personality disordered prisoner group*. Paper presented at the International Conference on Attachment and Psychopathology, Toronto, Ontario, October.

Ford, C. W. (1993). *Compassionate Touch: The Role of Human Touch in Healing and Recovery*. New York: Simon and Schuster.

Hindman, J. (1991). *The Mourning Breaks*. Ontario, OR: AlexAndria Associates.

Holmes, J. (1996). *Attachment, Intimacy, Autonomy*. Northvale, NJ: Jason Aronson.

James, B. (1994). *Handbook for the Treatment of Attachment-Trauma Problems in Children*. New York: Lexington.

Jernberg, A. (1979). *Theraplay*. San Francisco: Jossey-Bass.

Jernberg, A., and Booth, P. (1999). *Theraplay: Helping Parents and Children Build Better Relationships through attachment-Based Play*, 2nd ed. San Francisco: Jossey-Bass.

Karen, R. (1994). *Becoming Attached*. New York: Warner.

Main, M., and Goldwyn, R. (1985). *Adult Attachment Classification and Rating System*. Unpublished manuscript, University of California, Berkeley.

Main, M., Kaplan, N., and Cassidy, J. (1989). Security in infancy, childhood and adulthood: a move to the level of representation. In *Growing Points in Attachment Theory and Research*, ed. I. Bretherton and E. Waters, pp. 66–106. Monographs of the Society for Research in Child Development, vol. 50, no. 29.

Marcellus, J. (1998). *The neurodevelopmental sequelae of child maltreatment: implications for assessment and treatment*. Paper presented at the Post-Conference Institute of The Long Shadows of Trauma Conference, Toronto, Canada, November.

Morgan, C. (1989). *Theraplay: an evaluation of the effect of short-term structured play on self confidence, self-esteem, trust and self-control*. Unpublished research, York Centre for Children, Youth and Families, Richmond Hill, Ontario.

Munns, E., Jensen, D., and Berger, L. (1997). *Theraplay and the reduction of aggression*. Unpublished research, Blue Hills Child and Family Services, Aurora, Ontario.

Osofsky, J. (1998). *Trauma and recovery in infants: the importance of early intervention*. Paper presented at the conference on the Long Shadows of Trauma, Toronto, Ontario, November.

Rubin, P., and Tregay, J. (1989). *Play with Them: Theraplay Groups in the Classroom*. Springfield, IL: Charles C Thomas.

Rutter, M. (1994). *Clinical implications of attachment concepts: retrospect and prospect*. Paper presented at the International Conference on Attachment and Psychopathology, Toronto, Ontario, October.

Schore, A. (1998). *Early trauma and the development of the right side of the brain*. Paper presented at the conference on the Long Shadows of Trauma, Toronto, Ontario, November.

Smith, E., Clance, P., and Imes, S., eds. (1998). *Touch in Psychotherapy*. New York: Guilford.

Smith-Lawry, S. (1998). Touch and clients who have been sexually abused. In *Touch in Psychotherapy*, ed. E. Smith, P. Clance, and S. Imes, pp. 201–210. New York: Guilford.

Stern, D. (1995). *The Motherhood Constellation*. New York: Basic Books.

Van Ijzendoorn, M. (1994). *The Adult Attachment Interview: review and meta-analysis of psychometric, developmental, and clinical studies*. Paper presented at the International Conference on Attachment and Psychopathology, Toronto, Ontario, October.

Zeanah, C. (1994). *Intergenerational transmission of relationship psychopathology: a mother–infant case study*. Paper presented at the International Conference on Attachment and Psychopathology, Toronto, Ontario, September.

——— (1998). *The relationship content of trauma in infancy*. Paper presented at the conference on the Long Shadows of Trauma, Toronto, Ontario, November.

Zeanah, C., and Zeanah, P. (1989). Intergenerational transmission of maltreatment: insights from attachment theory and research. *Psychiatry* 52:171–196.

3

The Marschak Interaction Method

LISBETH DIPASQUALE

The Marschak Interaction Method (MIM) is a technique developed to provide a structured way of measuring various aspects of the relationship between a parent and a child. Human behavior is formed or influenced by the social environment. Every family member influences and is influenced by everyone else in the family, and the way they interact often has more impact than the words they use to communicate (Minuchin and Nichols 1993). When problems occur in a family, assumptions can be made about the cause, based on experience with similar difficulties in other families. However, these assumptions may not be accurate or complete.

Hypotheses generated to help explain the cause of problems within a family might be tested if it were possible to observe the members interacting in everyday activities. The MIM was developed to create this opportunity. It is a powerful tool, providing a "bonding assessment" that identifies both positive and negative aspects of the interactions between parent and child. This can be used as a basis for diagnosis, intervention, or therapy. In a therapeutic setting, which is the focus of this chapter, it is used to help plan the course of treatment, and when

administered before and after therapy it can provide a gauge to measure the effectiveness of the treatment.

HISTORY

Early interest in behavioral responses tended to concentrate on the individual, focusing internally on the psyche, through psychoanalysis,
to explain why a behavior developed, or externally on the observed behavior and what in the environment might have triggered and reinforced it. In the late 1940s, the focus shifted, in some quarters, to the
family as a whole. With the development of the general systems theory
of family dynamics, from which current family theory has evolved,
the symptoms of the identified patient were viewed as signs of problems within the family as a whole. The individual was believed to alter
his behavior as a way of trying to help stabilize the family unit (Satir
1967, as reported in Goldenberg and Goldenberg 1991). Study of the
kinds of interactions that were typical in these troubled families was
originally restricted to either clinical observation of everyday life in the
home setting or analysis of the verbal communications between family members in a clinical setting. Situations were not contrived or designed to focus on or evoke any specific behaviors.

While at the Yale Child Study Center, Marianne Marschak became
interested in developing a way of measuring aspects of child–parent
interaction. She wanted to identify the degree of imitation and identification of preschool children to either parent (Marschak 1960). She accomplished this through in-home observations of parents interacting
with their small children, but, in contrast to the normal routine of
observing whatever situation occurred naturally, she controlled the
situations to be observed by devising a series of specific tasks. These tasks
were designed to measure the child's desire to imitate the parent, to
gauge behavioral similarity and the child's fantasy of being like the
parent, as well as to identify parental attitudes that might influence
the assimilation by the child of parental interests, values, and preferences. The activities were structured and administered in the same way
to each family, in order to provide a structured measure of the behaviors relevant to the identification process. This preliminary observation
method was first called the Controlled Interaction Schedule (CIS) and
was copyrighted in 1961 (Marschak 1960). Since its inception, there

have been some additions and modifications to the format and activities, but the design of today's MIM basically follows the original CIS guidelines.

The MIM was used by Marschak in a number of research studies to analyze parental behavior and to help explain the observed behavior in the child. She compared the interactions of normal Head Start children with their mothers versus children referred to by their teachers as "difficult." She found the "difficult" children to have mothers who were more intrusive. She also studied the interactions of Kibbutz-reared versus home-reared children in Israel and found family-reared children to be more engaged with their parents (Marschak 1973). In collaboration with Call, of the Department of Child Psychiatry at the University of California at Los Angeles, she studied schizophrenic and autistic children in interaction with both parents (Marschak and Call 1966), and she introduced the use of the MIM for longitudinal studies. Through her research, she concluded that a child's readiness to imitate or identify with the parent is encouraged or hindered by three aspects of the parenting style: the quality of the affection shown by the parent, the way the parent directs or controls the child's behavior, and the parent's perception of the child (Marschak 1980).

METHOD OF ADMINISTRATION

General Description

The Marschak Interaction Method incorporates Theraplay-like activities to provide insight into the relationship between a parent and child (Jernberg 1979). The tasks are structured to introduce situations that are likely to evoke the kinds of responses that represent the problems occurring in the family, thus providing a window into the family's customary patterns of response, such as how the child takes direction, who has control, how family members respond to affection from each other, and whether they are having fun. This assessment helps the therapist plan the focus for treatment.

The standard method of administration has engendered subsequent innovations and adaptations. In the traditional format, the MIM is conducted with one parent one week, and the other the following week, so as not to tire very young children. The parent and child are brought

into the room and are asked to sit at a low table that has a line down
the center. The chairs are placed on the same side of the table, on either
side of the line, which is used as a guide to indicate when one family
member approaches the other, that is, when one moves toward the other
crossing over the line. An example of this might occur when a parent
leans toward the child to put powder on him. The child, on the other
hand, may pull back, suggesting fear or rejection of the nurturing. (With
an infant or toddler, the pair would sit on a mat or blanket on the floor.)
The parent and child are introduced to the session with the simple instructions that they will be engaging in a number of fun activities described on a series of cards that are placed face down on the table, in
sequence, with the first activity on top. All the materials needed for the
tasks are to be found close at hand, either beside the table or next to the
mat. They are told to proceed with the tasks at their own pace, beginning with the top card. If the session is to be videotaped, this would
have been discussed during the preliminary interview and the parent's
written permission received. Ideally the video camera should be in an
unobtrusive place to reduce interference with the session. In most cases,
the session will also be observed by the therapist through a one-way
mirror.

The parent reads the top card and the pair proceed with the task,
using the props provided, if appropriate. When this activity is completed, they continue with the next card until all the activities have
been performed. There are usually seven to ten tasks in total, selected
from a wide range of possible activities. The particular ones chosen
are designed to tap the four dimensions of parenting devised by Marschak (see below), as well as to test the hypotheses formulated during
the initial family interview, based on family history and the presenting problem.

Selection of Tasks

Four Dimensions

In her original research, Marschak was interested in investigating
four dimensions of parenting: promoting attachment, alerting to the
environment, guiding purposive behavior, and assisting in overcoming tension or reducing stress. A fifth dimension, playfulness, was subsequently added.

These original dimensions have been revised over time into the four current dimensions of interaction designed to assist in the planning of treatment for the family:

1. Structure: to assess the ability of the parent to direct or instruct the child, set limits, and have him follow this guidance. Examples of tasks designed to investigate this dimension include the following: adult teaches child something child doesn't know; adult gives instructions for taking care of the doll; and adult and child each take paper and pencil, and adult draws a quick picture and encourages child to copy.

2. Challenge: to assess the parent's awareness of age-appropriate expectations, the ability of the parent to provide stimulation and encouragement to grow and develop skills, and the parent's ability to enjoy and take pride in the accomplishments of the child. Examples of tasks: adult removes puzzle pieces and frame from envelope and asks child to make the puzzle; adult builds a pattern out of blocks and asks child to copy it; and adult composes quick tune on xylophone with sticks, and then puts sticks down and waits for child to copy.

3. Engagement/intrusion: to assess the ability of the parent to draw the child into an activity, to encourage involvement, interaction, and teamwork when appropriate, and, alternatively, to encourage independence and self-sufficiency when appropriate. It also provides an opportunity to see how alert the parent is to the child's level of stress and what method is used to help reduce stress. Examples of tasks: adult and child tell each other's fortunes; adult plays peek-a-boo with child; and adult and child each draw a picture. The first two tasks are done by the adult and child together, the third separately.

4. Nurture: to assess the parent's ability to provide care and support to the child, to meet the basic infantile needs and accept that the child may need to regress at times while also allowing him to grow up. Both the parent's ability to provide the necessary physical contact and the child's ability to accept this contact is observed. Examples of tasks: adult and child feed each other; adult and child powder each other; adult and child comb each other's hair; and adult tells child about when child was a baby, beginning "When you were a little baby . . . ."

When choosing the specific tasks to be performed by a family, these four dimensions are taken into account. At the same time, the ability of the parent to provide empathy, stress reduction, and playfulness is also observed. Playfulness is encouraged throughout the MIM, but activities designed specifically to evoke playful interaction might include playing a familiar game or playing with squeaky animals. Many of the MIM activities will tap into more than one of these dimensions, sometimes intentionally and sometimes based on the parent's interpretation. For example, a playful, engaging task such as putting hats on each other may become a very structured activity if the parent instructs or controls the sequence of events, while a task such as feeding each other is intended to be nurturing and engaging.

Other Selection Criteria

When selecting the specific MIM tasks for a particular family, it is important to choose activities that are age appropriate for the child. Some tasks are designed for very young children while others are more suitable for adolescents. Tasks are also divided into those that are performed by parent and child together and those that are performed individually. It is important to have a good mix to allow observation of the parent's response when the child is intended to perform a task by himself and to see how well they work as a team. In addition, some tasks challenge the child to strive while others encourage regressive behavior. The former group allows insight into the parent's level of expectation for the child, while the latter reveals how well the parent accepts or encourages the independence of the child, as well as the parent's degree of comfort with, and response to, the child's juvenile or dependent urges.

The particular tasks are selected to elicit the kinds of behaviors identified as the major problem during the initial family interview. Hypotheses are formed at that time, and the MIM is an opportunity to test these hypotheses and view the reactions first hand. For example, if a mother reveals that she had problems bonding with her infant after birth, activities would be selected to reveal the degree of attachment between mother and child, such as combing each other's hair or discussing baby memories. Attachment concerns might also be considered in families with foster or adoptive children, children who are autistic or have autistic-like tendencies, or children who have obsessive-compulsive disorder.

If the parents reveal during the interview that their child will listen to his father but will not do anything his mother asks, it is important to include tasks for both mother and father that require the child to follow their directions. This will provide an opportunity to observe the differences in the way the parents approach a structured situation and how the child responds to the directions of each. In this case, the instructional task selected may be identical for each parent.

If more than one MIM is conducted with a family, either to provide a measure of change before and after treatment or to provide longitudinal information for research purposes, the same activities are chosen and performed each time in the same sequence.

Order of Activities

The order of tasks to be performed is carefully considered. It is recommended that the session be introduced with a fun task that will engage the participants in a game and help them relax. An example might be the adult and child putting hats on each other. It is also important to avoid having two tasks in a row that are likely to cause stress for the child. Alternating a stressful or frustrating task, such as the adult leaves the room or puzzle-making, with a nurturing or engaging activity, such as the adult tells child about when the child was a little baby or playing piggyback, will help to keep the child involved and interested. The final activity should also be a satisfying, enjoyable task, to end the session on a positive note, such as the adult and child feed each other or the adult reads to the child.

Observations

It is important to take note of the responses of each individual since they influence each other. A positive initiation by a well-meaning parent may be rejected by the child, which in turn triggers a reaction by the parent. It may be that the parent has skills that might be successful with a child of a different temperament, but are not successful with this child. Instead of modifying the approach, the parent may tend to give up or become frustrated and angry. Things to watch for include how well attuned the parent is to the child and how responsive the child is to the parent, how capable the parent is of giving what is demanded by the task (instruction, control, encouragement, comfort, etc.) and how well the child accepts this from the parent. It is revealing of the problems in a family to observe the parent's repertoire of skills and responses when interacting with the child: which dimensions flow easily, which are avoided, which are pursued in spite of a child's initial rejection, and which are successful. When performing a nurturing task, a parent may tend to focus more on himself, for example, asking the child to put lotion on him first, or making assumptions about a child's emotions based on personal feelings. A parent or child may be able to receive nurturing but not reciprocate. When given direction by the parent, the child may comply, refuse, or take control of the situation and change the rules. Some activities may be extended, while others are shortened, or the family may race through the entire session with only a token effort on each task.

While observing, there are many things that will alert the therapist to potential problems. Does the parent allow the child to perform tasks on his own without interference? Does he/she offer guidance or encouragement when needed or praise upon completion? Is the parent aware of what causes stress for the child and how to help him cope better? Is he/she aware of the developmental level of the child and have reasonable expectations for what might interest or challenge him? Does the family seem to be enjoying their time together, or do they appear to be self-conscious or at a loss to know what to do with each other? Does the child listen to the parent and follow directions, or lose focus and become distracted by other things, or defy authority and do whatever he wants? Is the parent rigid and uncompromising, following the rules closely and not allowing himself to relax and have fun? Do parent and child make physical or eye contact and if so, at what times?

Decisions about what constitutes normal versus dysfunctional behavior within a family are based on clinical experience, as is the decision about the best way to approach treatment for a family. The MIM provides a tool to help identify the most critical problems.

Recording Methods

Observations of the session may be conducted at the time of the MIM, preferably from behind a one-way mirror, or at a later time by viewing a videotape of the session. It is important to record any verbal interchanges between family members, along with the accompanying nonverbal body language. Careful notes are made regarding nonverbal interactions, such as when or whether the individuals look at each other, when they smile, laugh, or frown, and whether this is at appropriate times. The observer also notes when or how family members touch, or if they lean toward or away from each other. The observer records the degree of involvement of the parent with the child: Does the parent do too much, not allowing the child to try things on his own, or perhaps leave the child struggling with something that is too difficult, not recognizing when it is appropriate to give a little help or a hint.

A shorthand method of coding the various types of nonverbal interactions, using symbols, has been developed. For the most commonly used symbols taken from the MIM manual, (Jernberg et al. 1991) see Figure 3–1. These symbols are used to indicate who initiated an interchange, what kind of interaction it was (e.g., body movement, eye contact, facial expression, etc.) and what response it evoked from the other party. A form devised for recording using these symbols is shown in Figure 3–2. The nonverbal symbols are used in the center columns, to indicate any physical action or facial expression of a family member with accompanying verbal comments recorded alongside in the verbal column. Inferences made by the observer may be added at the time of the MIM or later, upon review of the session. The feedback column is used to make notes as reminders to discuss a particular interchange during the feedback interview. The entire interchange can be recorded easily and chronologically, as it transpires.

Observations may be made by more than one person, allowing for different interpretations of the significance or implications of various interactions. This helps to keep the interpretation more objective and allows for collaboration when formulating a plan for treatment. If the observers are not the same individuals as the therapists who will be conducting or have conducted the treatment, it may help to increase objectivity, particularly in the posttreatment phase. However, this is not usually possible, due to time and manpower considerations.

Figure 3–1. MIM scoring symbols (reprinted with permission of the Theraplay Institute).

STRUCTURED BEHAVIOR SCORING METHODS

To make these observations more structured, particularly for use in research or for comparison before and after therapy, the Theraplay Institute has designed a form, using a seven-point scale, to evaluate frequency or quality of observed behaviors during the MIM. Most are rated as occurring from not at all to always. The behaviors are also

Figure 3–2. Sample MIM Recording Form (reprinted with permission of the Theraplay Institute).

	ADULT					CHILD		
Feedback	Inference	Verbal	Non-Verbal	Non-Verbal	Verbal	Inference	Feedback
You used a nice playful approach to get the game started.	playful, trying to engage him	C'mon, let me try this hat on you.	↑ ⌣	BC→ ⌣	No, I don't want that one! (pushes mom, moves away, selects another hat, begins to play by himself)	physical distancing from her	He didn't seem to want you to get too close. Does he prefer to keep his distance?
He was very aware that you weren't paying attention to him. He didn't like you ignoring him.	responds to his rejection by focusing on self	I like this one. Look how it goes with my shirt. (puts hat on self)	⊙	V		wants mom's attention	
You were willing to play his game.	accepts role but attempts to take back control	Okay. You're the sheriff. Let's catch the bad guys.	∧ ⌣	↓	Here, I like this one. You be my deputy. (gives her a cowboy cap)	child wants to deflect mom's attention back to himself— wants to lead	He made sure he kept your attention. How does he do this at home?

grouped according to the five dimensions of parenting—structure, challenge, engagement-intrusion, nurture, and playfulness—with empathy and stress reduction as added categories.

A second approach to structuring the results of the MIM for research purposes was developed by McKay, and colleagues (1996), called the Behavior Rating Scale for the MIM, to quantify the quality of parent–child interaction in their study on stress. Overall evaluation of behaviors, such as facial expression, degree of social involvement, tendency to offer help or guidance, and balance of control, were rated on a five-point scale as to how positive or negative each behavior appeared. Individual activities were not considered separately.

Debriefing Interview

Immediately following the MIM, the parents discuss their reactions to the session. During this time, the practice at the Blue Hills Child and Family Centre, Aurora, Ontario, is for the child to be taken to another room and asked to do projective drawings. Each parent is asked:

"What was your reaction to the session?"
"Were there any surprises for you and if so what?"
"Was your child's behavior typical of what you see at home? If not, in what way was it different?"
"Which activity did you like most? Why?"
"Which activity did you like least? Why?"
"Which activity do you think your child liked most? Why?"
"Which activity do you think your child liked least? Why?"

When the child returns, he is asked which activities he liked most and least, to provide a measure of the parents' attunement to their child. The answers to these questions can provide valuable insight into what was going through the parents' minds during the activities that might not be apparent to the observer. It will sometimes help to confirm a hypothesis and it will offer further insight into the problems and motivations of the individuals involved. For example, if a parent were of the opinion that his child did not enjoy an activity that in fact was a favorite, it would indicate a lack of awareness of what the child likes as well as a lack of attentiveness to the child's responses.

Feedback Interview

The feedback interview may immediately follow the debriefing questions, particularly if the session has not been videotaped. However, it is usually conducted one week later, particularly if the MIM has been videotaped, to allow the therapist time to review the session, decide on particular points to discuss with the parents, and consolidate the plan for therapy. During this part of the interview, the therapist has an opportunity to point out significant interactions observed during the MIM, both positive and negative, and discuss how representative these are of what occurs at home.

This session should begin with positive comments, even if the examples are few or brief, in order to help the parents feel that they are competent in some ways and to provide them a solid base from which to begin therapy. By having the therapist acknowledge that they demonstrate some positive parenting skills and explain that therapy can help increase the frequency of the effective moments, they will be more likely to accept the guidance for changing what is not working. It is important to empathize with parents who may be feeling discouraged or defeated by their child's negative reactions to genuine efforts at good parenting on their part. For example, the therapist might point out an instance where the child rejected the parent's attempts to engage him in a game, saying, "I like the way you tried to get Carolyn to play with the squeaky animals. You didn't give up easily, even when she wouldn't cooperate. It must have been discouraging to you when she threw hers away." If the parent feels understood, he/she will be less likely to become defensive and be more open to suggestions for an alternative course of action.

During this interview, the therapist should take care to narrow the focus for therapeutic change so as not to overwhelm the parents with a broad number of areas to improve. If they are left feeling crushed, they may become so discouraged that they see treatment as hopeless. Alternatively, they may feel angry, persecuted, and resentful that they, and not the child, are viewed as the problem. In either case, they may decide not to return for treatment.

Pointing out behaviors that may contribute to the current situation with the child should be done diplomatically, to avoid triggering a defensive response. For example, the therapist might say, "When Grant approached you with the hat, at first you pulled back from him. Were you aware that you did that? What might have been going through your mind?" or "When Mary finished matching your building blocks, you didn't look at her work. How do you think that made her feel?" thus enlisting the parent's help in interpreting the situation. There are times, however, when the direct approach is the best, in order to confront a parent about, for example, an inappropriate response, such as shouting or using physical force to control the child. The therapist might say, "When Jason did not do what you asked, you raised your voice and grabbed his arm. Was there any other way you could have handled this situation?" Although the overall approach is to be as positive as possible, it is important for the parents to acknowledge that they have played an active role in creating the current situation and will need to play an active role in making positive changes. Their willingness to do so is essential if therapy is to be successful.

The advantage of using a videotape of the MIM is that the parents can see first-hand examples of the responses they are discussing. This is a very powerful and effective tool to help break through personal defenses quickly. It can be very enlightening for parents to see themselves "caught in the act." They may not even have been aware of their own reactions prior to viewing the tape. The significance of what they are seeing might also not be apparent without the therapist's interpretation. While viewing the tape, for example, the therapist might say, "I like the way you reached out and patted Michael's shoulder there. That lets him know you care and are encouraging him" or "Do you see how Karen was looking at you when she finished the puzzle? She really seeks your approval." This method is especially effective with parents who need a more concrete, visual approach in order to gain insight rather than a strictly verbal one.

Throughout the interview, the parents are invited to comment and discuss their reactions to various situations during the MIM. The interview concludes with a discussion about the specific needs of the child revealed during the MIM and the focus for therapy. Details about the therapy are carefully explained so there will be no major surprises. It is essential that the parents are in agreement with and are supportive of the direction therapy will take and are encouraged to be part of the goal-setting process. They must also be willing to commit to being directly involved in the therapeutic process and doing what is needed of them. In effect, a verbal contract is made with them regarding their attendance and participation in the sessions.

THE MIM REPORT

When writing the report for the MIM session, it is important to record who was participating in the segment and what activities were performed by this pair or group of individuals in the correct chronological order. Any significant observations made should be indicated along with the clinical interpretation of the interchange. Following the description of the session, the responses of the parents to the debriefing questions are noted. A summary of the observations would include the overall interpretation of the needs of this family and the plan for treatment. The report should conclude with the specific goals for treatment. A sample MIM report follows. Note that this MIM included both parents together with the child in one session, which is a nontraditional way of administering the Marschak.

Sample MIM Report

Name of child: David Smith
Date of Birth: 02-10-93
Age: 6
Sex: Male
Date of assessment: 2-15-99

The first stage of the MIM consisted of the following activities:

David, Mom, and Dad:

1. Hats
2. Puzzle
3. Powdering
4. Play familiar game
5. Feeding

Mom read the instructions. David got a hat for his dad but when he approached his mom to put one on her, she jumped and pulled away, as though startled, then put it on herself. She took pains to find a hat that would hold the rose, since David had said he wanted this. Dad stood up for the entire activity. During the puzzle making, Mom misread the instructions and told David to take the pieces out first. Neither parent gave much reinforcement to David as he solved the puzzle, but they did guide him a little when he had trouble.

When Mom read the powdering instructions, she laughed and told Dad to powder his son. David really resisted this but finally allowed his dad to put some on his neck and chest. Dad then blew on his chest playfully. Mom put a little on his arm, but very quickly. David seemed to be very self-conscious during this activity. For the familiar game, Mom and Dad began listing possibilities for David to choose, but David jumped in to start one without indicating his preference first, interrupting them. He chose "I Spy." David kept ordering his parents to close their eyes when it wasn't their turn to pick something to spy. When it was one parent's turn, the other deferred to David to guess. When he had difficulty with one, Mom gave him hints to help him. He showed good persistence. The game was ended by Mom. At feeding time, Mom told David to feed them first, then they would feed him. David fed himself at one point. Mom did not feed Dad.

During both the powdering and feeding, there did not appear to be much nurturing toward each other. As well, there appeared to be emotional distance between David and his mother. Mom frequently gave eye contact to Dad, rather than to David, even when David was looking at her.

The second stage of the MIM involved mother and son.

David and Mom:

1. Squeaky animals
2. Block design
3. Hair combing
4. Leave the room
5. Baby memories

Mom deferred to David during "Squeaky animals," following his lead. He said, "I'm walking and you don't know me." He became aggressive, pouncing on her, and when she no longer followed along he abruptly ended the game. Mom confused the instructions for the block design and used most of the blocks during her turn, so he could not copy it. She then dismantled it and he tried to copy it from memory. He did very well. When the hair-combing activity began, David started to comb his own hair. When Mom told him to comb hers, the two started combing each other's hair simultaneously in a very awkward fashion, with no visible nurturing and there was distance between them. David stopped this activity quickly. When his mom left the room, David called out to his dad behind the one-way mirror, then began crawling around the floor until his mother returned. For "Baby memories," Mom again misread the instructions and began telling about when she was a baby. David seemed uninterested until she mentioned something he knew about. Then he asked a few questions. He was very aware of the observers behind the mirror and kept waving at Dad.

In this part of the MIM, it was felt that Mom and son were not comfortable with each other and felt awkward with any kind of physical contact or nurturing activity. In addition, there was some egocentricity on Mom's part and clear defensiveness on the child's part.

The final stage of the interaction was between father and son.

David and Dad:

1. Piggy back
2. Hampered movement
3. Teach something new
4. Leave the room
5. Read a story

The piggy back ride was quite short with little jouncing, perhaps because Dad had a bad back. David seemed to enjoy it. Dad didn't seem to know how to tie the legs for hampered movement and left them about one foot apart. When they tried to walk, they did not put arms around each other and Dad did not guide David. They did not appear to be having fun and walked only about ten feet, then stopped. Dad chose to teach David how to tell time. He moved his chair in closer to David and leaned in toward him as he taught patiently, using instructions at David's level. David listened intently. When it was time for Dad to leave the room, David seemed to be concerned about what his dad would be doing while he was gone: "Talking?" He began playing with the props to amuse himself and seemed unconcerned about being alone. When Dad returned and began reading him a story, David was inattentive, waving at Mom behind the glass.

Again there appeared to be some emotional and physical distancing between parent and child, although not as pronounced as with mother. Dad reached out to his son and seemed more empathic with him. However, Dad also seemed ill at ease with physical contact and was inhibited emotionally.

The parents were not surprised at how well behaved David was. They stated that he tends to behave better when his siblings aren't around. Mom felt David's favorite activity was the hats because he looked like he was having fun and put a different face on for each. She felt the least favorite was when she left the room. She said she could sense his apprehension. Dad chose Piggy back as David's favorite and felt he liked the story least, since he wasn't paying attention. Mom liked the feeding best because there was more personal interaction. At home, she finds it hard to get to the deeper level of affection. Her least favorite was telling about when she was a baby, because she was very self-conscious. Dad enjoyed the piggy back best because at home he finds it hard to roughhouse with David, now that he is so big. It is much easier to play actively with David's younger brothers, but David sometimes gets jealous, wanting to join in. Dad did not enjoy teaching something new because it was hard to think of something to teach.

Summary

Overall, the family did not seem to be having much fun together. All members seemed strained, ill at ease, and lacking in spontaneity. There were few smiles and most activities were brief, ended frequently by David. It seemed particularly difficult for Mom to nurture her son. Dad seemed more willing but did not seem to know how to have fun with his son or be close with him. David clearly had considerable control in his family, ordering his parents around ("I Spy"), selecting the activity or how it should proceed, and ending the game as soon as he lost interest.

The goals for this family are:

1. help facilitate Mom seeing the positive side of her son
2. help both parents use a positive approach with reinforcement for things David does right
3. help the parents take control, set limits, and follow through consistently
4. increase attachment between mother and son
5. build up David's self-esteem
6. build up parents' self-esteem and the ability to let go and have fun

VARIATIONS OF THE ORIGINAL MIM FORMAT

Over the years, the use of the MIM has been extended and modified for use with more than two participants at a time or with younger and older individuals. The tasks for children have been modified to extend the range from infancy to adolescence, with age-appropriate activities. The MIM has even been used to aid in marital therapy (Jernberg and Booth 1993) and with geriatric or Alzheimer patients in nursing homes. For infants, the MIM can be used therapeutically to help parents bond to their baby when this has not occurred naturally. The MIM has even been adapted for use before birth in high-risk pregnancies, to assess the attachment of mother and father to their unborn child and therapeutically to help them begin to view the child as a real person prior to birth (Jernberg, et al. 1985).

Family MIM

At the Blue Hills Child and Family Centre, in response to the increasing number of families with two working parents with less flexible schedules, as well as to increased demand for services, the original MIM format was changed. In the modified form, both parents and child(ren) are assessed during the same session. In addition to saving time, a benefit of the family format has been the opportunity to view mother and father interacting with the child(ren) together. This has provided a richness to the observation that was not anticipated, such as which parent takes charge and who defers, how the child responds when all three are together, and how the parents react to each other, giving insight into the marital relationship.

A major reason for originally conducting two sessions, one for each parent, was to keep the sessions relatively short so as not to tire the child. However, by reducing the number of tasks in each segment of the family MIM, according to the age and attention span of the child, it is possible to complete the full family MIM in one session, including both parents, without being too taxing on the child.

Order of Activities

The same general instructions for the MIM are given to the family together: to read the cards in sequence, beginning with the one on top, and to follow the instructions on each card. The cards are separated into groups, clearly marked according to who is to perform each section. Normally the family would do the first series of activities together, then one parent at a time would participate with each child individually.

Two Parents with One Child

The individual parent segments are the same as the traditional MIM administration, but the dual-parent segment offers a chance to observe how the parents interact with each other: Do they work together as a team and support each other? Do they make eye contact? Do they nurture each other? Do they make sure their partner is included? It also offers an opportunity to see how the interactions with the child may vary when the parent is alone with the child versus when the other parent is present: Does one parent defer to the other rather than take charge as he/she might if the other were not there? Does the child focus more on one parent or take directions from one better than the other? Does the child's behavior become more erratic or calmer? Does he/she play one parent against the other?

Single Parent with Two Children

When more than one child in a family is identified for therapy, it is essential to administer the MIM with each child, but this can be done in a single session. It is valuable to have an opportunity to observe all the family members together. Viewing the parent interacting with both children allows the chance to observe such things as who the parent focuses on more, is attention given more as a result of preference for that child or in response to demanding behavior, and is there an attempt to treat the children equally. This format for the MIM also provides the opportunity to see how the children react to each other: Do they try to include their sibling in activities? Does one child exhibit parental behavior toward the other? Is there animosity or jealousy of the parent's attention? Do they seem to enjoy each other's company?

Two-Parent Family with More Than One Child

When there are two parents and more than one child, the situation becomes a little more complex. Generally, all family members are first seen together for approximately four tasks, then one parent interacts with each child individually for a few tasks, followed by the other parent with each child individually for a few tasks. Another possible grouping might entail each parent interacting individually with all the children together. Because there are more people involved and therefore more combinations or groupings to assess, it is usually necessary to reduce the number of activities for each segment. However, fewer than three in any one grouping would not allow enough richness or variety of tasks to evaluate the interactions effectively.

This family MIM may also be used in a blended family situation to help identify problems in relationships between stepparent and child, between stepparent and natural parent when dealing with a particular child, or between stepsiblings.

Activities ideally suited to provide greater insight into the relationships between family members are those designed to encourage unstructured fun or to evoke nurturing of each other, such as adult(s) and child(ren) putting hats on each other, adult(s) and child(ren) feeding each other chips, and adult(s) and child(ren) putting lotion on each other.

Neonatal and Prenatal MIM

In cases where a parent is considered to be at high risk for developing problems bonding with and parenting the child, the neonatal MIM can be used both as an assessment and a therapeutic tool. It helps parents relate to and begin to communicate with their child as a separate human being. It also offers an opportunity to professionally evaluate the degree of bonding and the effort to do so. Activities include tasks such as talking and playing with the baby, teaching the baby something, and telling the baby about when he/she becomes a grownup. The session begins and ends with a drawing of parent and child together.

The prenatal MIM, developed by Jernberg, Wickersham, and Thomas in 1984, is used to evaluate parents' efforts toward bonding with their unborn child and as a therapeutic tool to help enhance feelings of attachment toward the child through communication with the fetus and open expression of hopes and fears for the child's future. It has been used with chemically dependent women to facilitate their viewing their baby as a person. Addicts often deny the impact of their dependency on the fetus, but by strengthening the mothers' attachment to the developing human life, it may provide the incentive needed to try to recover from their addiction (Chandler 1992).

The infant or prenatal format can also be adapted to help single mothers decide whether or not to keep their infant or psychologically prepare for separation from a baby who is to be put up for adoption.

Adolescent MIM

For adolescents, problems can be much more complex and the behavioral patterns within the same individual may range from immature, childish responses to independent, adult-like actions. As a result, some of the MIM activities chosen may be similar to those used for much younger children, while others may correspond to those used for adults. The dimensions may be modified somewhat to more appropriately evaluate adolescent development. The modified dimensions include reaffirmation of attachment, stress reduction, direction, preparation for adulthood, autonomy, and peer group affiliation.

Marital MIM

One of the most recent innovations of the MIM has been the Marital Marschak Interaction Method (MMIM) for use in marital therapy (Jernberg and Booth 1993). The MMIM is used for both structured observation and clinical intervention, with a focus on helping to evaluate the quality of the relationship, perhaps as a prelude to further therapy. It can help some couples decide if they are suited for marriage and others if they should divorce. Simply viewing the videotape and seeing themselves interacting can provide some individuals with tremendous insight into the nature of their relationship. When used for intervention, one MIM activity is viewed per session and provides a springboard for discussion and in-depth analysis.

OTHER USES OF THE MIM

Research

The MIM has become a tool for other researchers interested in evaluating parent–child interactions. It offers a structured measure of differences between experimental subjects and controls. When used in longitudinal studies, it can provide insight into changes over time.

Both Koller and Berndt used the infant MIM in their doctoral theses to investigate infant and toddler temperament and the effects on the parent–child relationship (as reported in Jernberg 1991). Berndt also used the MIM in her study on failure-to-thrive children. Jernberg and colleagues (1985) used a prenatal MIM (PMIM) to study the degree of bonding of new parents to their babies before birth. In drawings of the child done by the parent before and after participating in the MIM, the researchers found considerable change in the post-test drawings toward depicting the baby as more alive and engaged in activity with the parent. It proved effective for studying the quality of interactions between parents and their learning-disabled child (Bunge 1992). In a similar fashion, the MIM was used to study the interactions between a child with Tourette syndrome and his parents, to test the hypothesis that Tourette syndrome and its associated symptoms have a detrimental effect on the parent–child relationship (Steyn 1995). In addition, it has been studied for use as a short-term therapeutic medium to help a parent identify problems with the interactions with the child and formulate solutions to enhance the quality of the relationship (Wright 1994).

A number of studies by Booth and Jernberg are planned, including the comparison of performances on the MIM of cocaine using versus nonusing mothers, and a comparison of MIM behavior between custodial and noncustodial parents (Jernberg 1991).

Forensic Evaluations

The MIM has been used in court evaluations in cases of child abuse or failure to provide for the special needs of emotionally disturbed children (Safarjan 1992). Because these cases often result from the parents' emotional problems, it is important to determine the capacity of the parent, to identify the dynamics of the parent–child relationship, to determine what kinds of social services are needed to establish effective parenting, and to form recommendations for individual and/or family therapy. The goal is to protect the child(ren) and, if possible, keep the family together. The MIM is used to assess the parenting capacity and the bonding and attachment between each caregiver and the child(ren) to help determine the best placement. The recommendation can carry significant weight in the court decision.

SUMMARY

The MIM provides a structured method for evaluating the quality of the relationship between parent(s) and child(ren). It can be used as a diagnostic tool in a therapy situation, to help evaluate the effectiveness of treatment when used pre- and post-therapy, to help document any change between individuals in an experimental research situation, or to help provide a measure of change over time in longitudinal studies. There are very few other structured observation tools that provide such an opportunity to observe the kinds of problem behaviors that are encountered in typical family situations, along with a first-hand look at the way a parent triggers, responds to, or handles a situation as it emerges. In addition, it can be a powerful tool for providing insight to the parents into both their own behavior and that of their child.

The potential value of this tool is wide ranging, and the MIM is likely to gain greater use as it becomes more widely known.

REFERENCES

Chandler, J. (1992). The Prenatal Marschak Interaction Method (PMIM): a tool for bonding. *Theraplay Institute Newsletter* Winter, pp. 4–5.

Bunge, D. M. (1992). An analytical exposition of the interactional dynamics occurring between parents and their learning disabled child, utilizing the M.I.M. *Dissertation Abstracts*. MAI 32/02, p. 375, Summer, University of Pretoria, South Africa.

Goldenberg, I., and Goldenberg, H. (1991). *Family Therapy: An Overview*, 3rd ed. Belmont, CA: Brooks/Cole.

Jernberg, A. M. (1979). *Theraplay*. San Francisco: Jossey-Bass.

——— (1991). Assessing parent–child interactions with the Marschak Interaction Method (MIM). In *Play Diagnosis and Assessment*, ed. C. E. Schaefer, K. Gitlin, and A. Sandgrund, pp. 493–515. New York: Wiley.

Jernberg, A. M., and Booth, P. (1993). *The Marital Interaction: Structured Observation and Intervention*. Chicago: The Theraplay Institute.

Jernberg, A. M., Booth, P., Koller, T., and Allert, A. (1991). *Manual for the Administration and the Clinical Interpretation of the Marschak Interaction Method (MIM): Pre-school and School Age (revised)*. Chicago, IL: Theraplay Institute.

Jernberg, A. M., Wickersham, M., and Thomas, E. (1985). *Mothers' Behaviors and Attitudes Toward Their Unborn Children*. Chicago: Theraplay Institute.

Marschak, M. (1960). A method for evaluating child–parent interaction under controlled conditions. *Journal of Genetic Psychology* 97:3–22.

————— (1973). *Patterns of Parenting in Israel* (film and video). Chicago: Theraplay Institute.

————— (1980). *Parent–Child Interaction and Youth Rebellion*. New York: Gardner.

Marschak, M., and Call, J. D. (1966). Observing the disturbed child and his parents: class demonstrations for medical students. *Journal of the American Academy of Child Psychiatry* 5:686–692.

McKay, J. M., Pickens, J., and Stewart, A. L. (1996). Inventoried and observed stress in parent-child interaction. *Current Psychology* 15(3):223–234.

Minuchin, S., and Nichols, M. P. (1993). *Family Healing: Tales of Hope and Renewal from Family Therapy*. New York: The Free Press.

Safarjan, P. T. (1992). Use of Marschak Interaction Method (MIM) in forensic evaluation. *Theraplay Institute Newsletter* Winter:3.

Steyn, M. P. (1995). The interaction between a child suffering from Tourette Syndrome and his parents, with specific reference to the Marschak Interaction Method. *Dissertation Abstracts*. MAI 33/03, p. 990, June, University of Pretoria, South Africa.

Wright, S. U. (1994). The Marschak Interaction Method as a short term therapeutic medium for parent and child with interaction problems. *Dissertation Abstracts*. MAI 32/01, p. 348, February, University of Pretoria, South Africa.

PART II

Innovations
in Family Theraplay

A. Working with One Family

4

Applications for the Attachment-Fostering Aspects of Theraplay

DAVID L. MYROW

How does a therapist start a relationship with a child who has not attached well to other human beings? This is a tricky question, since the reason the child is seeing the therapist is also the reason it is hard to develop a relationship. The child may show all manner of avoidance, including physical avoidance—hiding in the playroom or refusing to recognize the therapist prior to the meeting. Or the child may be overtly amiable, perhaps even too friendly, considering that the therapist is a stranger. Yet there will be a sense that as the therapist gets to know the child, there will be more and more of a wall between them. The child's defensive posture is brought to bear in every important and potentially intimate relationship.

ATTACHMENT THEORY

Attachment theory has been influential in the field of mental health for the past five decades. As Karen (1994) states,

> Indeed, the great promise of attachment theory has been the pros-
> pect of finally answering some of the most fundamental questions
> in human emotional life: How do we learn what to expect from
> others? How do we come to feel the way we do about ourselves in
> the context of an intimate relationship? How do we come to use
> certain futile strategies in a vain effort to get the love we (often
> unconsciously) feel was denied to us as children? How do we pass
> on our own parenting style to our kids? [p. 5]

Theraplay rests on a foundation built by attachment theorists. To
Bowlby, Fairbairn, Ainsworth, Spitz, Main, and others, we owe a great
debt. The coherent system for explaining how babies come to relate to
their caregivers guides our thinking about how things can go wrong
at various stages of development, and how we can explain behavior that
otherwise would not make sense. Why, for example, does a later-adoption child insist on ignoring hundreds of interactional cues that would
indicate the interest, care, and affection of a new parent, and continue
to lie, steal, or destroy property of the very people who offer the love
he needs? Logic would suggest that a person who is hungry would take
food when offered. Yet the 7-year-old who has lost his biological parents (and perhaps one or two sets of foster parents as well) declines the
generous offers of his new parents. Attachment theory explains how
this is possible and paves the way for possible remedies.

Bowlby (1988) was the central player in the evolution of attachment theory, as described by Karen (1994). At a time when a number
of theorists were challenging Freud's drive-reduction theories, Bowlby
led the opposition by clarifying the human need for relatedness to others. He was probably influenced by Fairbairn, who declared that the
primary drive is not for pleasure (as Freud had postulated), but rather
for person. While Melanie Klein (a post-Freudian thinker known for
her work in child analysis) claimed that the child's first relationship
is with the breast (onto which the child projects both sides of its
ambivalence), Bowlby came to a broader understanding of the need
for attachment to the parent. In the course of five decades of thinking
about these concerns, a number of thinkers brought forth ideas and
data that permitted Bowlby and his successors to clarify the process
of attachment and the exigencies of inadequate and of traumatized
attachment. In the past decade, further research has extended those
ideas to our understanding of how early attachment experiences affect later development.

In brief, here are some of the kinds of work that led to our current thinking about attachment. Spitz showed, for the first time, the effects of maternal deprivation on children, in this case on hospitalized children. Bowlby's early work was with psychopathic children. He struggled with how these children had come to the point where they did not seem to care about other people, nor did they seem to experience any genuine feelings, even joyous ones. Bowlby was joined in his work by Robertson, a social worker who studied children who had had long hospitalizations—children who exhibited a similar detachment from others. It was Robertson who proposed the stages of grieving that these children experienced after a perceived loss of a caregiver—protest, despair, and detachment. Konrad Lorenz's studies of imprinting with birds provided Bowlby with a connection from basic scientific theory to understanding human psychology. (Most of us still chuckle at the image of young goslings following Lorenz around the laboratory grounds.) Harlow's brilliant work with rhesus monkeys suggested the instinctual need for tactile stimulation and also brought us closer to the awareness that, without early interactive experiences with the mothers, babies fail to develop social skills. Taken together, this line of thinking eventually led Bowlby to the following postulates about attachment in humans:

1. Attachment is instinctual, "a fundamental form of behavior with its own internal motivation distinct from feeding and sex, and of no less importance for survival" (Bowlby 1988, p. 27).
2. Separations from the caregiver thwart an instinctual need.
3. A significant function of attachment behavior is to relieve stress, which in infants is usually best accomplished with physical closeness (Lyons-Ruth 1996).

It was up to Ainsworth, who came to work with Bowlby, to detail the kinds and quality of attachments developed between child and parent. In the development of her "strange situation"* (a research proto-

---

*The Strange Situation is a research tool in which a series of scenarios that examine the child's secure and insecure attachment patterns with its mother are videotaped. The videotaped sequences are coded by researchers to determine the child's attachment patterns to its mother. The child's behaviors in a play room are observed during a series of separations and reunions, for

col, in which a child and mother play together, a stranger comes in, the mother leaves, the mother returns, the stranger leaves, the mother leaves again, the stranger returns, then the mother returns again—and the baby's reactions are studied), Ainsworth was able to develop some hypotheses about the quality of the child–mother attachment. Through this work and considerable succeeding research, some of it by Main (who extended the ideas), four categories of attachment were delineated (cf. Lyons-Ruth 1996):

1. Secure (54 percent of the population)
2. Insecure-avoidant (23 percent)
3. Insecure-ambivalent (8 percent)
4. Insecure-disorganized (15 percent)

Securely attached babies use the mother as a secure base, cry the least, and maintain healthy contact with her. Later on, in preschool, they tend to be popular and to manage stressful situations adaptively. They are comfortable with physical contact and, in elementary school, develop close friendships. Their mothers tend to be warm, in sync with the child's needs, and consistent in their interactions (Karen 1994).

Avoidantly attached babies seek little physical contact with the mother, do not respond to her attempts at comforting, and become angry. In preschool, they may stay close to teachers, but do not seem to expect to be calmed, and may become isolated. By school age, they show little enthusiasm in relationships, shun physical contact, and what friendships they do develop tend to be jealous and ambivalent. Their mothers tend to be emotionally distant and may encourage pseudo-independence.

As Karen (1994) characterizes it,

---

example, the child's reaction to the mother's departure and his coping with being left alone in the play room, his greeting of the mother upon her return and his exploration of the play room with the mother present. These same scenarios are enacted with a stranger. The child's behavior upon the stranger's departure and his manner of greeting and interaction upon the stranger's reappearance are compared to what took place in the child–mother scenarios. Clinicians also often find it useful to look at the mother's behavior during the Strange Situation, for example, her response to the child's distress as she leaves the room and her greeting and interaction with the child when she returns.

> With his bids for loving contact repeatedly frustrated and sometimes angrily rejected, the child with a history of avoidant attachment to his mother . . . finds himself in a special box. He doesn't feel he can be openly angry with her, despite the fact that anger, according to Bowlby, is the natural response when a child's attachment needs are thwarted. Experience has taught him that his anger will only cause her to become more rejecting. And so he has learned to turn himself off. At the slightest hint of pain or disappointment, he shuts down his attachment system and experiences himself as having no need for love. [p. 228]

Ambivalently attached babies cry a lot, are clingy and anxious, and have trouble with even brief separations. They are hard to calm. By preschool, they are clingy with teachers and often are seen as immature. When they enter elementary school, they continue to have difficulty with separations and do not develop close friendships. Their mothers tend to be inconsistently attentive, often poorly tuned in to the child's needs, and unpredictable.

Karen (1994) characterizes these children as follows:

> They are wildly addicted to [mother] and to their efforts to make her change, they become enmeshed with her in various unhealthy ways, and later in life they become similarly addicted to other potential attachment figures, such as teachers in the school years and, in all probability, romantic figures after that. But through it all they do not believe they have what it takes to get what they need from another person. [p. 225]

Babies who are characterized as insecure-disorganized do not display a consistent coping style at all. Sometimes they are clingy and anxious, sometimes they are ambivalent, and often they act in strange or bizarre ways, for example, approaching the mother walking backward. Research has begun to suggest that mothers of these children more frequently experienced highly traumatic childhoods themselves and are more likely to be struggling with serious concerns, such as alcoholism, teenage pregnancy, or depression (Lyons-Ruth 1966).

In recent years, the literature on attachment has expanded to include hypotheses about how children with attachment patterns appear as grown-ups. Main and Goldwyn (1985) developed the Adult Attachment Interview, a research technique in which adults' responses to questions about their early attachment figures are analyzed to assess such aspects as degree of idealization, coherence of speech, and feelings of love and rejection. Out of this line of inquiry, researchers have found patterns of adult attachment that are analogous to those revealed with children:

> The secure (or free-autonomous) adult can access a full range of feelings and memories, both positive and negative.
> The dismissing adult (analogous to the insecure-avoidant child) minimizes the importance of love and relationship. Parents are idealized, but there is little basis in specific memories.
> The preoccupied adult (analogous to the insecure-ambivalent child) continues to fear abandonment, maintains the angry/hurt posture toward parents, and takes little responsibility for her/ his own role in relationships.

There is also a rapidly growing literature examining attachment style and problematic behavior in school-age children. For example, Lyons-Ruth (1996) correlates patterns of attachment to aggressive behavior in children. DeKlyen (1996) examines mothers' responses on the Adult Attachment Interview and relates them to their children's disruptive behavior. Adam and colleagues (1996) show the relationship between disturbed attachment and adolescent suicidal behavior. Rosenstein and Horowitz (1996) detail the relationships between specific attachment disorders and personality disturbances, and show relationships between the parents' and teenagers' disorders. The data detailing and supporting the hypotheses of attachment theory are growing rapidly.

All of this work is important to our understanding of the development of the child, and therefore to our ideas about interventions in Theraplay. "According to Bowlby, early experiences are central in the formation of working models of the self, others, and self-other relationships. These models allow children to form expectations about the availability and probable actions of others with complementary models of how worthy and competent the self is" (Cicchetti et al. 1995, p. 9). The Theraplay therapist strives to understand the child's and parents' working models, and to develop strategies for encouraging the development of more effective models. The assumption is that the self and other perceptions and beliefs are developed in the first few years of life; it seems possible, if not likely, that nonverbal strategies may be essential to access these preverbal and early verbal experiences and reprogram them such as occurs through Theraplay. Instead of a nondirective model, the Theraplay therapist uses this understanding of developmental variables to provide largely nonverbal, playful interactions that meet the child (who, at the time of treatment, is often much older) at his emotional developmental level.

The nature–nurture debate, which finds itself at the heart of many philosophical and psychological questions, is also a central issue in attachment. Lyons-Ruth (1996) argues that there is much evidence addressing the issue of whether attachment patterns

> should be viewed as emerging from patterns of caregiver–infant interaction or from endogenous dispositions of the infant. . . . [First, the] attachment pattern strongly associated with one parent is not strongly associated with the attachment associated with the other parent. . . . [Second,] in a sizable majority of cases, the infant attachment strategy is predictable from the caregiver's state of mind with regard to attachment issues, even when assessed before the birth of the infant. . . . [Third,] the attachment strategy displayed toward the primary caregiver is more predictive of later social adaptation than the strategies shown toward other caregivers . . . even when the primary caregiver is not biologically related. . . . [Finally,] various measures of infant temperament have predicted distress to separation but have not predicted whether the distressed or nondistressed behavior pattern is classified secure or insecure. [p. 66]

As Karen (1994) reports, the proponents of the nature side of the argument had argued that children who appeared to have disturbed attachment patterns were actually children who had anxious temperaments. A study by van den Boom (as reported in Karen) gave strong support to the nurture side. Out of a pool of 588 children, van den Boom selected 100, "all highly irritable at birth, displaying a low threshold for the expression of negative feeling, as assessed on Berry Brazelton's Neonatal Behavioral Assessment Scale. These babies were irritable at birth." If these babies were "destined to be classified anxiously attached at one year regardless of how they are raised," then one would expect that the parents' caregiving efforts would have little effect on their irritability at one year. Van den Boom divided the infant-mother pairs into two groups. One group received three counseling sessions of two hours each when the babies were between 6 and 9 months old, "the purpose being to enhance the mother's sensitivity and effectiveness" (pp. 308–311). For example, the mothers were shown how to soothe a crying baby as soon as it became upset. The other group of mothers were given no intervention. The outcome was that, even with this very modest intervention, 68 percent of these very fussy babies were seen as securely attached at one year. Only 28 percent of the controls were seen as securely attached; they were still very fussy and easily stressed. This seems to provide a great deal of support to the nurture side of the argument. Therefore, it also gives credence to the view that preventative intervention—even in modest amounts—may make it possible for more children to have healthier and richer relationships throughout the life span.

In addition to the literature dealing with attachment, there is also a rapidly accumulating literature on the role of touch in development. This is significant because touch is seen as central to early attachment development. It is especially important to Theraplay therapists because, unlike many other child therapies, physical contact is intrinsic to the fun, intimate, and often regressive Theraplay interventions. This becomes extremely important when the central goal for a child and his family is to foster the attachment between them; the Theraplay strategies necessarily include nurturing activities comparable to those experienced by a young child with his parents.

Some of the earliest research demonstrating the importance of touch on development was done by Harlow with rhesus monkeys (Harlow and Harlow 1966). Monkeys reared in isolation consistently chose to cling to cloth rather than wire surrogates. The effect of being reared in isolation was profound; these monkeys were unable to relate in any functional way to monkeys reared socially, and spent their lives engaging in bizarre and meaningless behaviors. What is less well known, however, is the fascinating follow-up work by Harlow's student, Suomi. Suomi had young rhesus monkeys, reared socially, serve as monkey therapists to the older, isolated monkeys. The monkey therapists had to be at the stage where they were still clingy and not socially aware enough to be put off by the rejection cues given by the isolates (Suomi, personal communication, September 1997). The therapist monkeys approached the isolates with persistence and kindness. Within a few months of regular "treatment sessions," the isolates had begun to play and interact socially to the point that they were nearly indistinguishable from normal monkeys (Suomi and Harlow 1972).

More recent research continues to substantiate the critical role of physical contact in development. Field (1995b) presents work by authors from several perspectives, detailing some of the effects of touch on the developing organism (both animal and human). For example, Schanberg (1995) shows how maternal separation in rat pups during the time in which they suckle triggers hormonal changes in the pups. These hormonal changes correspond to behavioral changes analogous to failure-to-thrive behavior in humans. The effects on the pups were reversed when the mother was returned. On closer inspection, it was revealed that the specific behavior that was required to return to health was heavy stroking, like when the mothers lick the pups. In another study, Anderson (1995) reports on the kangaroo care method for neonates (both normal babies and preemies when they become stable). Mothers, and sometimes fathers, carried diaper-clad babies beneath their clothing in special carriers for periods of 30 minutes to five hours per day. Babies treated this way have a more regular heart rate, deeper sleep, less crying, and greater weight gain; the parents attach quickly and seem more confident. Field (1995a) also reports on some of her own research, in which preemie babies, after being released from intensive care, were given three 15–minute periods of massage daily for ten days. They gained 47 percent more weight than the control group, although caloric intake was identical; they were awake and active more of the time; they performed better on the Brazelton Scale on habituation, orientation, motor activity, and regulation of state behavior, and they averaged 6 days less in the hospital.

Since Theraplay looks first to the kinds of experiences that are associated with healthy development, it turns to the significant bodies of research on attachment and physical closeness to build its foundation. The magic is in the interactions between the caregivers and the child. As Wright (1991) states, "Starting from the beginning . . . the mother's face and the baby's smile soon become central features of a playful social interaction; this social interaction seems to be basic to the attachment process. The baby's responses become increasingly directed and specific; the mother's pleasure in and responsiveness to her baby increase as she feels that her baby recognizes her" (p. 11).

In helping to foster child–parent attachment, the Theraplay therapist's role includes finding ways for the child and parent to enjoy the healthy attachment-forming behaviors that happen ordinarily for most families. If the child has had past traumata or breaches in caregiving that interrupted this process, there may be a need to remediate the hurts and losses as well. Most of these children brought to treatment defend against closeness with their parents. In one way or another, the child avoids eye contact, physical closeness, sharing of loving feelings, or having fun. For the attachment to develop, the Theraplay therapist arranges situations and activities that make it more likely that there will be positive shared emotional experiences.

HOW THERAPLAY PRINCIPLES ARE ATTACHMENT-FOSTERING

The Theraplay therapist thinks developmentally. It is not the chronological age of the client that dictates the therapeutic strategies; it is the age at which the child is operating emotionally that dictates the intervention. So it is possible to "nurse" an 11-year-old if that child did not finish such work with his mother (Jernberg and Booth 1999).

The therapist attends to the child much like a mother to her infant. The therapist seeks eye contact, attends to physical hurts, engages the child when the child drifts off psychologically, and makes the child the center of her attention. The therapist attends to and recognizes the child's feelings and experience. The therapist provides physical closeness and provides a secure base from which the child can operate.

> Ten-year-old Carrie comes in for her first Theraplay session. She promptly shows the therapist the latest boo-boo on her arm. Dr. Z. gets some lotion to dab on the wound. The session starts from there by showing Carrie all the neat parts about her—he gently pats her long blond hair, remarks at the gold color in it, and points to her healthy pink fingernails. The therapist describes her big, round, green eyes and finds flecks of brown and gold in them. He has her try to touch her chin with her tongue and marvels at her newfound ability. Dr. Z. has her make muscles and then measures her biceps with his fingers held like a caliper.

An infant's caregiver shows the child her nose, her mouth, smooths her hair. The infant reaches out to the caregiver, touches her nose and the adult shows the child, "This is my nose. Here is your nose!" The infant giggles and kicks its legs. In a now-famous move familiar to many of us who have raised or worked with little ones, the child stretches out its arm, and with its cute, pudgy, pink hand snatches off the grown-up's eyeglasses with speed that would do a hungry viper proud! But the viper doesn't giggle. In much the same way, the Theraplay therapist finds ways to show the child his or her own personhood. In the safety of the Theraplay session, the child can accept his own regressive needs and allow them to be met.

A common concern of parents and therapists new to Theraplay is whether the invitation to allow regressive needs to be met results in the child "going backward," perhaps even permanently. It has always been interesting to me how children let us know what they need. A child who has unsatisfied regressive needs, no matter the age, will often behave in a way that signals to us that we are at his level. Often this will be in the form of laughs or vocalizations that sound more like those of an infant or toddler than those of a school-age child. And when I have misjudged a child's needs, the child usually indicates that he needs something a little more grown-up. The challenge comes in determining, in those cases, whether the child's reluctance is a resistance or whether his needs are for activities that are more developmentally advanced.

The attachment fostering aspects of Theraplay are useful even for children who are not in treatment because of attachment disturbances. Children who are securely attached to their caregivers also come to treatment when there have been stressors in their lives or when their families are not functioning smoothly. Stresses can include losses (e.g., loss of person, position, dreams), transitions (e.g., life stage, divorce, move to a new home), and illness. Of course, families present with manifold other concerns (habit problems, academic issues, failure to establish parental authority, etc.). Any of these issues can occur in a setting of an attachment disorder as well as where attachment issues are not central. Even when attachment is not a focus of treatment, Theraplay strategies can help by supporting the rapid development of a therapeutic alliance with the child. It might be argued, in fact, that the more securely attached a child, the more he or she will be able to enjoy Theraplay activities and move into a trusting relationship.

Six-year-old Robert was brought in by his parents because he was throwing tantrums at every frustration and ordering around the parents. Careful assessment of the family found Robert to be securely attached with his parents. However, the parents were woefully inconsistent in setting limits. Furthermore, they disagreed on the majority of the issues regarding limits, with mother attempting to set firmer rules and father dismissing the concerns ("Don't you think he'll grow out of it, Doctor?"). The parents were surprised to see themselves in action on the Marschak Interaction Method and were able to utilize the information constructively. A short course of Theraplay was prescribed, partly to demonstrate to the parents how they could set limits more consistently. During the first Theraplay session, Robert challenged the therapist subtly but frequently. The therapist responded by playfully sticking to the rules, and Robert went along. Robert laughed and played, and enjoyed the first session all the more with the consistent firmness. By the end of the first session, there were fewer challenges to the therapist and Robert began to accept little hugs. The fun activities (in this case, the slippery arm game, an eyeblinking contest, among others) drew Robert in to the treatment (see Appendix for description of activities).

How does Theraplay build trust quickly with a child? No doubt, the physical closeness and eye contact invite intimacy and feelings of trust. Recognizing the child ("What neat green eyes!" "That soccer shirt reminds me of how much you love soccer!" "Look how your muscles are getting bigger!") also lets him know that the therapist is genuinely interested in him. Games that invite a child to depend physically on the therapist (falling backward into the therapist's arms or jumping off the table into the therapist's arms) invite trust. Physical proximity—being in close body contact during much of the session—works toward more trust, but this will depend on the child's comfort with closeness, and may actually increase anxiety initially for tactile-defensive children. Any respectful therapist who meets with a child on a regular basis is likely to build a trusting relationship eventually; Theraplay strategies invite the trusting relationship to develop more quickly.

HOW THE STRUCTURE, CHALLENGE, ENGAGEMENT AND NURTURING DIMENSIONS FOSTER ATTACHMENT

In *Theraplay*, Jernberg (1979), describes four aspects of a child's needs for parenting: structure, challenge, intrusion (now also called engagement/stimulation), and nurturing. For healthy development, every child needs some of each of these, but the amounts and intensity vary for each person and at different stages of development. However, all of these aspects foster attachment, albeit in different ways.

A newborn needs the *structure* of being held, of regular times for sleeping and eating, of the comfort of dry diapers. The toddler needs to know it's okay to go off on his own to play a little while—and Mommy will still be there. He needs to be required to behave decently toward his peers. The first grader needs the structure of a regular bedtime, and to be required to complete his homework. A teenager needs Mom or Dad to help keep him from making seriously bad choices (when possible) and to have some expectations around when he needs to be home at night and around his commitments. All of these structures help a child know who he is, how to get along with other people, and how to negotiate getting needs met constructively. Yet there are attachment elements, too. There is a sense of security in knowing your parents will let you go only so far, and in knowing that they'll be there if you slip.

Challenge starts early in the child–parent relationship. We let the 4-month-old grab a hand and pull on it, or let a 6-month-old grab our eyeglasses off our face repeatedly. We hold the outstretched hand of the 11–month-old as he tries to walk across the room, and challenge the 2-year-old not to peek while we hide something. We challenge the 4-year-old to jump from the stairs into our arms or to hold on tight for a piggyback ride, and teach him to write his name. All of these activities challenge the child to grow, to learn, to discover new abilities and talents. They also have, intrinsic to their qualities of relatedness to other people, attachment-fostering elements. In the interest, caring, and recognition of the child required by these activities, there is an invitation to closeness and trust.

Engaging activities require attention and involvement. Eye contact requires interaction with another person.

> Six-year-old Josh, a rotund first-grader, takes the therapist's hand when they walk to the playroom, but then breaks away and leaps onto a pillow. When Dr. Z. reaches out his hand so that they can play a game that Dr. Z. knows Josh likes, Josh turns away and hides his eyes. The Therapist maneuvers around Josh in an attempt to make eye contact. Josh closes his eyes. Dr. Z. tells Josh that he blinks his eyes well, but that

he could probably do it even tighter. Josh squeezes tighter. Dr. Z. gives Josh a little poke in the ribs (he knows Josh likes tickles) and the boy opens his eyes. Finally, they make eye contact and Dr. Z. tells him how great it is to see those big, brown eyes.

More than the other three aspects of a child's needs, engagement intrusion must be utilized sparingly, and it must be used with great sensitivity.

When Dr. Z. first met Alan, a 12–year-old with pervasive developmental problems, Alan avoided contact by pacing around the room. It was necessary to find some less intimate activities to even begin building a relationship. Alan had a keen interest in remembering TV shows—when they were first shown and who the actors were—so they spent part of their time in a guessing game (guess who usually had the right answers!). But part of each session was spent in efforts to enjoy more engaging activities. It wasn't long before Alan was able to take up the challenge of an eyeblinking (staring) contest. When they played for "prizes" of getting to give the opponent a hug or a tickle, Alan at first recoiled at the gentle tickles that Dr. Z. gave him. Dr. Z. soon realized that these were actually painful to Alan. Knowing that it was possible that firmer contact might actually be perceived as more pleasant, Dr. Z. tried out the hunch, and discovered with Alan that he liked the occasional tickle if it was firm. The intrusiveness had to be used with great care to build the relationship.

Nurturing experiences are intuitively the most critical for fostering attachment. Without kindness, caring, and attention to needs, how can we convey our wish that this child grow and be happy? Unlike more child-directed play therapies, Theraplay actively nurtures the child. Nurturing activities include putting lotion on boo-boos (little bruises always seem to benefit from a little lotion), feeding and nursing activities, and giving hugs. These activities follow the lead of healthy infant–parent interactions. The parent and baby gaze into each other's eyes, the parent gently puts lotion on the baby after a bath, and holds her warmly while giving a bottle and humming a lullaby.

For older children, these activities sometimes need to be "dressed up" in the form of experiences that seem more age-typical. For example, with a 12–year-old who has developed in most spheres along age-appropriate lines, rather than drinking from a baby bottle it might be more comfortable for him to drink a soda pop from a can with a straw while trying to follow the therapist's eye signals ("one blink means drink, two blinks mean stop, alternating eyeblinks mean blow bubbles").

The therapist must look regularly to nonverbal cues to assess how the child experiences the nurturing efforts. Like the parent of the later-adoption child, the therapist may find her kindness rejected or ignored (leading to important countertransference considerations); over the course of the work, both the therapist and the parents need to provide the nurturance until the child accepts it.

CLINICAL PRESENTATION OF ATTACHMENT DISORDERS

Children are presented to us as therapists with a variety of concerns, for example, oppositional behavior, overactivity, poor peer relationships, habit problems, and so on. Rarely do parents bring in concerns that they label attachment disorders. Instead, we are told that the child is lying, stealing unimportant items from mother, clingy, resistant of hugs or emotional closeness, indiscriminate of strangers, oppositional, running away from home, engaging in dangerous behavior, or friendless. It is only via thoughtful assessment that we infer that an attachment disorder underlies the behaviors. Attachment theory offers a parsimonious explanation for apparently diverse behaviors; the explanatory value is indispensable in designing treatment strategies. While behavioral strategies can be helpful for specific behaviors, in my experience they often fail because they do not speak to the underlying developmental issues. The practical problem for behavioral schemes usually is that the child does not care enough about any potential reinforcers to work for them.

The *Diagnostic and Statistical Manual of Mental Disorders DSM-IV* accommodates attachment disorders primarily under the diagnosis of reactive attachment disorder of infancy or early childhood. Zeanah (1996) makes an important case for rethinking the common psychiatric classification of attachment disorders. "Defining attachment disorders by using criteria that are primarily drawn from children who have been physically abused, who have suffered extremes of deprivation, and who have been deprived in institutions limits the disorders to children in extreme situations and does not account for children who are in stable, albeit unhealthy, relationships without overt abuse or neglect" (p. 46). He argues for the need to focus on attachment-disordered behavior rather than the history of maltreatment.

Theraplay therapists often use the Marschak Interaction Method (MIM) to assess the quality of attachment of a child and his parents. (The MIM is discussed in Chapter 3.) With the aid of the MIM, we can observe actual parent–child behavior and find patterns that reflect on the quality of the relationship. One of the items, "Adult leaves room for one minute without child," has an obvious kinship with Ainsworth's "strange situation"; it is an attempt to provide a very mildly stressful situation and see how the child manages it. However, it is also an opportunity to see how the parent handles it. Will the child express anxiety? Will the parent offer some kind of support or a technique to reduce the anxiety ("Why don't you count to 60")? To get a flavor of some of the possibilities, here are a few of the actual responses to this stimulus that have been observed in my practice:

> Child starts to cry immediately after parent reads the instruction and insists that mother remain in the room.
> Child sits quietly, hands folded on the table, watching the door.
> Child immediately moves over into Dad's chair and watches the door.
> Child runs to the toys and plays with them in a random, poorly directed fashion.
> Child watches the clock and calls out to parent to return at the end of one minute.

These behaviors, and the parent's response to them, offer clues about the quality of the parent–child attachment, how secure it is, the kind of dance that the parent and child do around these issues. Can the child calm himself? How does he convey his needs to the parent? How does the parent respond? Is the parent sensitive to the child's anxiety—if it is apparent before the adult leaves, does the adult offer help ("Watch this hand on the clock. When it gets back here, I'll return.")?

THERAPLAY TECHNIQUES ESPECIALLY GEARED TOWARD FOSTERING ATTACHMENT

Theraplay strategies that work toward fostering attachment can be utilized with the therapist and also with the parents. Most often, the therapist develops an alliance with the child, and the parents are brought in later. When there have been highly disappointing relationships between the caregivers and the child, or when the caregivers feel that they can no longer manage the child's acting-out behavior, the therapist can fill the role of a new, neutral person, someone with whom the child can try out different behaviors and explore his experiences and concerns in a safe and less conflicted environment. Of course, it usually takes little time for the child to transfer onto the therapist the conflicts, hurts, and anger from his past that he displaces onto his caregivers at home. When this happens, the parents have a chance to observe the therapist model strategies for helping the child calm himself and/or provide structure and support.

As originally developed at the Theraplay Institute, in this model the child's therapist works with the child while an interpreting therapist talks with the parents as all three observe the child and his therapist through a one-way mirror. Later on in the work, after the child has started to let down defenses and becomes open to more closeness, the parents are brought into the playroom to enjoy activities with the child. For many of us, it is not practical to have two therapists working simultaneously with a family. In my practice, I play with the child and videotape the play session, and then show the tape to the parents afterward while the child waits. This format has the advantage of permitting us to review parts of the session on tape to clarify an issue or strategy ("Notice how Jeder responds when I give him a reassuring pat on the shoulder for trying a new activity"). The format has a potential disadvantage; some children find it difficult to wait while the grown-ups talk. It can also take the bloom off an especially warm and rewarding Theraplay session by postponing the family's departure while the adults meet. Nevertheless, the format has proven itself quite workable most of the time.

What kinds of Theraplay experiences lend themselves to promoting attachment? One might argue that most Theraplay activities do, because they are physical, fun, and intimate. Even so, certain activities seem more likely to promote closeness and attachment.

The attachment starts prenatally, when the prospective parents (whether biological or adoptive) start to fantasize about the baby. What will she be like? Who will she resemble? Will she share Mom's artistic bent? Dad's athletic proclivities? What kind of career will she choose? Will she get married? To whom? (Parents do get a bit carried away with this one!) So, one of the activities that works toward attachment is talking with the parents, pointing out the child's special qualities and strengths, and finding similarities between the parents and the child ("His eyes are almost the same shade of green as yours, Mom!").

In the playroom, the therapist will be emphasizing eye contact and physical contact by selecting experiences and activities where these are especially important components. This parallels the kinds of experiences mothers share with babies. Some examples :

1. *Mirroring:* The therapist and child sit facing each other. The child becomes the "boy in the mirror," moving hands, arms, body, and face opposite the therapist's.

2. *Pillow Ride:* The child sits on a large pillow with handles and holds on tight while the therapist pulls her around the room with fun twists and turns. The child is told that when she looks right into the therapist's eyes, the pillow "goes," and when she looks away, it "stops."

3. *Feeding activities:* There are many variations on ways to feed a child. For older children, when it may feel age-incongruent to be fed by an adult, it is possible to modify the activities to include a challenge. For example, in Guess the Goodies, the child is told to close his eyes while the therapist places different treats in his mouth; after the morsel is deposited, the child can open his eyes (to increase eye contact) and try to "guess the goody" (e.g., an M&M, a little pretzel, a grape, piece of carrot, a marshmallow, etc.). Another example is eating M&Ms with a straw: the child has to use the straw like a vacuum cleaner to lift candies out of an envelope or cup; when he is successful, the therapist feeds the candy to the child.

4. *Nursing activities:* Even older children will often take a baby bottle. It is important that this be done in context, however. I think the bottle has to be presented after the child has developed trust in and comfort with the therapist, and usually after there have been a few less intense feeding activities (as in those

noted above). Even then, with older children, I have made it a practice to present the bottle with a straw attached to it with a rubber band, so that a child who is uncomfortable with the nipple can make a choice that might seem more age appropriate. In practice, my experience has been that most older children will choose the nipple over the straw, and the assumption is that, when the child doesn't, he may not have needed to rework that aspect of his early attachment experience. In any event, most children who choose the nipple will utilize it for a few sessions and then indicate waning interest—much like a baby who starts weaning—by playing with the bottle, throwing it down, or asking to use the straw. Symbolic nursing activities also may be useful. The therapist can seat the child in her lap or across from her, and holding a juice box with a straw, have the child drink with "eye controls." When the therapist makes a sucking motion with her mouth, the child drinks; when she blinks her eyes tightly, the child stops drinking; signals are given in varied order to surprise the child and make it challenging. Or the therapist and child can share pop from a can with two straws ("We can only drink when both of us are looking right at each other"). (See Appendix for description of other activities.)

5. *Structuring to build a secure base:* A secure attachment depends on predictability and consistency. When a child who has had multiple caregivers comes to a new home, one of the first tasks is to establish the rules of the house—one way of structuring for the child. When parents have difficulty establishing limits, one of the therapist's jobs is to model for them how to do this. In the process of meeting with the child, the Theraplay therapist necessarily provides structure all along the way. Either by observing directly (e.g., via a one-way mirror) or indirectly (via videotape), the parents have an opportunity to observe the strategies and discuss them with the interpreting therapist. Later on, when the parents are brought into the playroom, they practice these skills, with the therapist's direction and encouragement.

Seven-year-old Tommy and Mom play an eyeblinking contest. Tommy wins the round and, as his prize, gets to give Mom a hug. He lunges at her and knocks her over with an overwhelming hug. Dr. Z. has Tommy practice the right amount of hug to give with Mom, and lets Mom know how to brace herself for potential future lunges. Dr. Z. gives Mom lots of support when she toughs it out on the next one and gives Tommy lots of support when he restrains himself.

SPECIAL CONSIDERATIONS FOR CHILDREN WHO HAVE BEEN TRAUMATIZED

Jernberg (1979) cautions against using Theraplay strategies, other than perhaps some nurturing, for children who have been recently traumatized. Traditional, child-centered, expressive strategies are the approaches of choice. As James (1994) notes, "Children with attachment disturbances resist feelings of belonging and being cared for because the feelings and the care can generate anxiety, depression and feelings of loss and uncertainty" (p. 83). The situation becomes complicated by the fact that children who are presented for treatment often were traumatized several years prior—and, presumably, have not resolved the hurts and anger. In these cases, the current crisis (perhaps some acting out, depression, or issue in the family) is not the traumatizing event, yet that may linger on the back burner as a core unresolved issue. James has made a compelling case for the need to deal with the unresolved trauma as well as providing for better experiences of physical and emotional closeness. "Children with histories of hurtful or inappropriate body contact are especially in need of positive intimate physical touch. The settings and structure for touching these children need to have clarity and be such that the child is not confused"(p.76).

It is possible to utilize a kind of hybrid model of Theraplay and child-centered strategies with these children. In my experience, with careful efforts to maintain clear boundaries, the gentler, "good touch" experiences of Theraplay nurturing (along with structuring and, when appropriate, some challenge) can help build a therapeutic alliance relatively quickly. As James (1994) suggests, part of each session can be set aside for "work," and part can be set aside for play. The play part can include Theraplay experiences that build the relationship and offer more positive physical closeness. As James suggests, family work, in these cases, should include helping parents provide "good touch" at home. For younger children in new homes, it is natural to have parents develop routines around grooming (shampooing hair, trimming nails) and rocking chair times—nurturing experiences that the child probably did not have with his family of origin. Even older children can benefit from grooming tasks and foot or shoulder massages with the caregivers.

CONTINUING CHALLENGES: PARENTS WHO CANNOT RESPOND, CHILDREN WHO CANNOT LET GO

Theraplay is an optimistic approach. It seeks the healthy in people and endeavors to help it grow. Nevertheless, there are situations where the clients are not ready or able to make changes that would improve their situations. In my practice, there have been cases—mostly with older-adoption children moving to their third or fourth placements—where the parents have not been able to get beyond the feelings of rejection, or the acting-out behavior never ceases to overwhelm them. Sometimes the children seem to be taking some chances at letting down their defenses, but the parents feel too depleted to respond. Other times the children just will not open their hearts to the parents (or sometimes to the therapist, either). If the parents are willing to readjust their hopes and expectations, the goals of treatment can be revised to develop more of a foster-parent arrangement. If things at home are so bad that the rest of the family seems to be sinking, it is justifiable to consider a trial, or even a permanent, separation. These decisions are best made, if necessary, after at least several months of consistent and concerted treatment efforts.

THERAPLAY AS A DIFFERENT TECHNIQUE FOR FOSTERING ATTACHMENT

Theraplay offers a different approach from traditional, child-centered strategies for fostering attachment. With its emphasis on physical closeness and warmth, Theraplay can expedite the building of a therapeutic alliance whether or not the primary treatment goals include improving child–parent attachment. When the attachment relationship is a central focus, Theraplay has special capabilities for addressing that need. Drawing on fifty years of research on the processes of attachment,

Theraplay is well rooted in contemporary thought about human development. A special contribution to work with children is the strategy of dealing directly with the child's skills in developing close relationships with adults.

REFERENCES

Adam, K. S., Sheldon-Keller, A. E., and West, M. (1996). Attachment organization and history of suicidal behavior in clinical adolescents. *Journal of Consulting and Clinical Psychology* 64(2): 254–263.

American Psychiatric Association. (1994). *Diagnostic and Statistical Manual of Mental Disorders*, (4th ed.) Washington, DC: Author.

Anderson, G. C. (1995). Touch and the kangaroo care method. In *Touch in Early Development*, ed. T. M. Field, pp. 35–51. Hillsdale, NJ: Lawrence Erlbaum.

Bowlby, J. (1988). *A Secure Base*. New York: Basic Books.

Cicchetti, D., Toth, S. L., and Lynch, M. (1995). Bowlby's dream comes full circle: the application of attachment theory to risk and psychopathology. In *Advances in Clinical Child Psychology*, vol. 17, ed. T. H. Ollendick and R. J. Prinz, pp. 1–75. New York: Plenum.

DeKlyen, M. (1996). Disruptive behavior disorder and intergenerational attachment patterns: a comparison of clinic-referred and normally functioning preschoolers and their mothers. *Journal of Consulting and Clinical Psychology* 64(2):357–365.

Field, T. M. (1995a). Infant massage therapy. In *Touch in Early Development*, ed. T. M. Field, pp. 105–114. Hillsdale, NJ: Lawrence Erlbaum.
——— (1995b). *Touch in Early Development*. Hillsdale, NJ: Lawrence Erlbaum.

Harlow, H. F., and Harlow, M. K. (1966). Learning to love. *American Scientist* 54:244–272.

James, B. (1994). *Handbook for Treatment of Attachment-Trauma Problems in Children*. New York: Lexington.

Jernberg, A. (1979). *Theraplay*. San Francisco: Jossey-Bass.

Jernberg, A., and Booth, P. (1999). *Theraplay: Helping Parents and Children Build Better Relationships through Attachment-Based Play*. San Francisco: Jossey-Bass.

Karen, R. (1994). *Becoming Attached*. New York: Warner.

Lyons-Ruth, K. (1996). Attachment relationships among children with aggressive behavior problems: the role of disorganized early attachment patterns. *Journal of Consulting and Clinical Psychology* 64(1):64–73.

Main, M., and Goldwyn, R. (1985). *Adult attachment classification system.* Unpublished manuscript. Berkeley: University of California.

Rosenstein, D. S., and Horowitz, H. A. (1996). Adolescent attachment and psychopathology. *Journal of Consulting and Clinical Psychology* 64(2):244–253.

Schanberg, S. (1995). The genetic basis for touch effects. In *Touch in Early Development*, ed. T. M. Field, pp. 67–79. Hillsdale, NJ: Lawrence Erlbaum.

Suomi, S. J., and Harlow, H. F. (1972). Social rehabilitation of isolate-reared monkeys. *Developmental Psychology* 6:487–496.

Wright, K. (1991). *Vision and Separation: Between Mother and Baby.* Northvale, NJ: Jason Aronson.

Zeanah, C. H. (1996). Beyond insecurity: a reconceptualization of attachment disorders of infancy. *Journal of Consulting and Clinical Psychology* 64(1):42–52.

5

Theraplay and Parent Counseling

ANITA MAHY
AND
JANET MACQUARRIE

Children experiencing emotional and/or behavioral difficulties and displaying overactive aggressive, withdrawn, hyperactive, or inattentive behaviors are often referred for Theraplay. Children with learning disabilities may develop associated emotiona difficulties that are often manifested as behavioral management concer. s. Parent counseling can be effective in the amelioration of many of these problems utilizing the goals advocated by Auerbach (1961) and Gold and Richmond (1979) for parents of the handicapped: to explore all aspects of the situation, to gain greater understanding of their child's development, to look at their roles as parents, and to become aware of parent–child relationships.

Parents involved in Theraplay receive information, role modeling, and support during Theraplay sessions; however, many of their concerns and personal needs cannot be fully addressed, particularly when their observation time with the interpreting therapist is limited. Therefore, our aim in parent counseling is to provide supportive therapy to reduce the intensity of presenting symptoms and distress, and to improve parents' adaptation and coping skills. Many parents have difficult, unstable, or limited interpersonal relationships, and are isolated socially. The strategy in supportive therapy focuses primarily upon conscious problems, symptoms, thoughts, and feelings. Identification with the therapists is encouraged, as they provide active teaching figures from whom the parents learn new methods of adaptation. Therapists provide information and responses to questions, suggest ways of resolving problems, and encourage alternative understanding of situations. Affective experience and expression of emotional responses are encouraged and accepted. It is hoped that if the parent can achieve appropriate behavioral and emotional patterns of interaction, the environment (e.g., the family, work, social interactions, etc.) will provide greater fulfillment and pleasure in response to their changes. The anticipation is that if, in response to their improvement in behavior, the environment is more supportive, fulfilling, and caring, the new behavior pattern may become self-sustaining and self-reinforcing as it becomes more solidly part of the parents' repertoire (Dewald 1994).

On the basis of the concepts of Anna Freud (1953) and Erikson's (1963) concept of ego development arising out of interactions between the instinctual drives and the environmental, it is possible to make intrapsychic modifications with children through the influence of their parents (Morrow 1974). As parents experience acceptance, respect, emotional support, and appropriate direction (i.e., supportive therapy), and as clear thinking and good sense take over, they automatically shift their approach and, in so doing, their relationship with their child is modified. As Benedek (1959) points out, the conflict between the child's own notion of the nature of things and his maturational urges may produce considerable conflict if the parent fails to recognize, respect, or support these notions and urges. A basic problem is often a breakdown in the social bond between the child and parents, as the child is locked in power struggles with adults.

Supportive therapy provides the opportunity for parents to experience strength-based interventions, for example, to learn to see their child from a different perspective, to focus on their child's strengths and positive potentials rather than on just their weaknesses, and to better understand their child's needs (Brendtro and Ness 1995). It is hoped that parents learn to interpret emotional behavior as a signal of the child's competence or lack of it in a specific situation. It is necessary to help parents identify the nonproductive behavior, the demands of the situation, and their child's skills (as compared with the skills needed). This focus is also applicable in working with parents, because what therapists may see as parental unconcern or instability may actually signal competence problems in handling their child's problematic behavior (Bricker 1967).

Families who have a child with disabilities and emotional and/or behavioral difficulties are at greater risk for stress and adjustment difficulties than families with a child developing normally (Walton 1993). Parenting a child who has attention deficit hyperactivity disorder places a massive strain on personal energy. Parents need assistance to become skillful stress managers (i.e., to develop physical, psychological, and emotional capabilities that facilitate health, and to develop appropriate coping skills). Parents are encouraged to share their feelings and not deny the stress they are experiencing. Establishing hope is important in therapy when dealing with issues of loss (of spouse, financial security, or social identity), and feelings of helplessness (regarding their child's behavior, social isolation, or the overwhelming responsibility of single parenting). Parents in therapy need to be asked what they can do to alter their thinking processes so they can become more rational, because irrational thought reduces their ability to handle stress. They need assistance in learning to use rational statements, such as "I can do it" and "I will do the best I can," and support in developing the ability to give themselves credit for things they accomplish with their child and with other responsibilities (Walton 1993). Furthermore, putting parents in touch with appropriate resources is important to strengthen their stress tolerance.

Termination of treatment occurs through a process of weaning to minimize the stress and loss of the treatment relationships. After termination there are four follow-up sessions. Active encouragement and reassurance are offered, maintaining the sense of continuity during the follow-up sessions.

THE TREATMENT SETTING

The Theraplay and parent counseling sessions that are described here were held at Blue Hills Child and Family Services, a treatment center for children and families in Aurora, Ontario. A formal play therapy room with a one-way mirror and an observation room was used. All sessions were recorded on videotape.

WHY THERAPLAY WAS CHOSEN
AS A TREATMENT METHOD

Theraplay provides the therapeutic opportunity to re-create the healthy interactions of normal parents with a normal young child, using activities involving structure, challenge, intrusion/engagement, nurture, and playfulness. In Theraplay the focus is on pleasurable activities that have one or more of these qualities and that create an active and affective connection between the child and the therapist and, ultimately, between the child and the parents. There are opportunities to enhance the parents' capacity to accept and practice self-nourishing behaviors, thus changing family interaction patterns (Jernberg 1979, Jernberg and Booth 1999).

The goals of Theraplay with the two families described below were providing basic physical nurturing, building self-esteem, and improving self-control. Nurturing dimensions of Theraplay were used, and proved successful because of the aggressive tendencies of the children and the parents in one family, and the emotional unavailability of the depressed mother in the other. Structuring dimensions of Theraplay were necessary and proved effective for the children to learn and observe clear, firm limits. The emphasis with these parents was to encourage gentle physical nurturing and joyful play with their sons, and to support limit setting and consistent follow-through in their parenting. This was accomplished through therapist role modeling, parent participation while receiving therapist support, and supportive parent counseling. An additional focus in parent counseling with the grieving mother in one family was affirmation of her sense of worth, and providing positive emotional support for her own personal development (e.g., social interaction, job search).

PARENT COUNSELING—A THERAPLAY INNOVATION
USED IN TREATMENT

A half hour of supportive parent counseling followed each Theraplay session and served the following purposes:

1. Provide a time for positive, undivided attention and support to parents regarding their own concerns such as feelings of helplessness, anger, depression, anxiety, and/or frustration pertain-

ing to their child, parenting, school, and marital and personal issues, thus encouraging improved adaptation, and increased self-esteem and self-confidence.

2. Provide suggestions, direction, and alternative perspectives, when appropriate.
3. Discuss the Theraplay sessions, both observed and participative, answer questions, acknowledge parental and child strengths and competencies, encourage insight, encourage gentle physical nurturing and joyful play with their children and each other as adults, and encourage consistent limit setting and follow-through in parenting.
4. Encourage ongoing, regular structure, gentleness, playfulness, nurturing of self-esteem, and physical affection at home, thus supporting the transfer of Theraplay principles into the home and everyday life.

SUBJECTS TREATED AND THEIR PROBLEMS

Family 1

The family consists of a grieving widowed mother and her aggressive 6½-year-old son Chris, who was diagnosed as attention deficit hyperactivity disordered (ADHD).

The Mother

The mother was a 43-year-old widow of one year who was moderately depressed. She was somewhat overwhelmed by the demands of her life as a widow and single parent. She acknowledged her loneliness, as she was without friends or colleagues and was unemployed. She was also without the support of nearby family. Her energy level was very low, as was her motivation to play with her son. She acknowledged feeling blue and needing to heal. Her self-esteem was poor, and her motivation and problem solving skills were limited regarding her son, her financial situation, and her personal needs for friendship and employment.

The mother's self-confidence as a parent was poor. Her parenting skills were limited, follow-through was inconsistent, and decisions were often deferred to her son. She was fearful and defensive regarding the perception of others, saying that she felt like she and her son were outcasts because of Chris's aggressive behavior. She reported that she was not enjoying her son, and that affection, fun, and positive times between them were rare.

The Son

Chris had idolized his busy and often absent father prior to the father's untimely death a year ago. The mother reported that her son had been affectionate, yet disobedient toward them. She described her current relationship with Chris as stormy, as he was uncooperative and regularly tested limits. Chris experienced mood swings (e.g., loving, caring, angry, upset, scared), frequent nightmares, and bed-wetting. At school he was reported to be aggressive (frequently involved in fights) with poor interpersonal skills (e.g., difficulty with sharing, turn taking, anger management), and impulsive, hyperactive, and inattentive.

Treatment Goals

The goals of Theraplay with Chris were as follows:

1. To increase gentleness
2. To decrease roughness toward his mother and aggressiveness toward his peers
3. To increase self-esteem
4. To improve compliance regarding adult direction, specifically his mother's requests, and to decrease his need for control
5. To improve the interpersonal skills of sharing, turn taking, anger management
6. To increase his experience of fun, gentle playfulness, and close physical nurturing
7. To increase healthy attachment to his mother

The goals of Theraplay and parent counseling with his mother were as follows:

1. To affirm her sense of worth and self-esteem
2. To build her self-confidence as the parent and person in charge

3. To support her in providing and following through with setting limits for her son
4. To encourage close physical nurturing and joyful play between them, and strengthen her attachment to her son
5. To provide positive emotional support for her own personal development in the areas of social interaction and job search

Treatment Progress

This mother and son participated in twelve Theraplay sessions, and the mother also participated in twelve parent counseling sessions. Pre- and posttreatment assessments of the family were conducted using the Marschak Interaction Method. Four follow-up Theraplay and parent counseling sessions took place during the year following the completion of treatment.

During Theraplay the mother observed the therapists' nurturing of Chris, their firm yet positive leadership in setting limits, their expectation and encouragement of his observing the limits, the son's cooperation with the therapists, and his having more fun than she had seen for a long time. His mother also participated actively in Theraplay with Chris and received support from the therapists for being the parent in charge and for following through with clear and firm instructions. Mother also received support in Theraplay in her encouraging gentleness, playfulness, and nurturing times together. Increased cooperation with less negotiation and increased fun, gentleness, and physical expressions of affection developed between the mother and son over the twelve weeks of Theraplay and parent counseling.

During weekly parent counseling immediately following Theraplay, this moderately depressed, isolated, and somewhat immobilized woman relaxed with the therapists over a cup of coffee while her son played close by or in a supervised playroom. She was not used to talking about herself and her situation, or to having someone listen, affirm, and support her. Initially she shared her feelings and concerns regarding her son, his acting-out behavior, his constant negotiation and testing of her limits, and how alienated and rejected by other parents she felt because of his behavior. Gradually she initiated conversation about her negative focus and effectiveness as a parent, her lack of motivation to play with Chris, the limited physical affection between them, and inconsistencies in limit setting and follow through, often allowing her son to have the last say regarding decisions. She also acknowledged her depression and her loneliness without her husband, friends, regular family support, and colleagues.

Parent counseling was important in supporting and effecting change in this family, particularly as the mother was needy of, and receptive to, individual positive attention, affirmation, and guidance. Her ability to keep facts straight, problem solve effectively, make decisions, develop plans, and follow through in many areas of their lives improved significantly. Parent counseling provided the ongoing opportunity to assist and support her in becoming mobilized and proactive in the life of her son and in her own personal development. As the mother's emotional availability, self-confidence, motivation, and energy increased, her sadness, sense of isolation, rejection, and helplessness decreased. Further successes were evident as she improved in providing parental leadership and affection. She was rewarded with increased cooperation and gentleness from her son, as his self-control and achievement improved at home and at school. These changes occurred by the fourth session, before Ritalin was prescribed for Chris.

Further improvements in Chris's school behavior were noticeable following the prescribing of Ritalin. Teacher reports indicated that he was playing well with his peers at school and walking away from fights, and that his behavior was not interfering with his ability to attend to and do his work. At home, however, where he did not have to concentrate as much and he was not on medication, he continued to resist limits and his mother continued to have difficulty with consistent follow-through.

Treatment Results

Several changes took place over the twelve sessions as the mother received positive modeling in the parenting of her son, and positive support for her own personal development. As she improved in her clear and firm parental leadership and decreased negotiation with Chris, she experienced more cooperation from him. She reported that she was more confident in her parenting, as she was better able to identify problems and manage herself and her son more effectively. Increased gentleness and physical expressions of affection were developing between them and were enjoyed. She became increasingly proactive and effective in her support of Chris at school through his difficulty with performance

anxiety, in sports with his soccer coach, and in her obtaining cooperation from her in-laws in supporting her in the consistent handling
of him.

During this time she also became increasingly proactive in other
areas of her life, as she enrolled in and completed a computer course in
preparation for working as a bookkeeper. Following a short job search,
she was hired. It was evident that she had benefited significantly from
the positive effects of Theraplay and supportive parent counseling. She
acknowledged that the clinical team helped and supported her through
a difficult time in her life, pointing her in the right direction.

Chris enjoyed the Theraplay sessions, and cooperated with his therapists and his mother throughout. He improved in self-control (e.g., turn
taking, sharing, waiting, increased gentleness, and decreased roughness
and aggression), and was able to relinquish the position of being in
charge. Interim school progress reports indicated that he was showing
slow yet steady improvement in his academic performance; that he was
assuming more responsibility for completion of his work; that he was
meeting school expectations regarding development, work habits, and
personal growth; and that he was interacting well with peers.

Family 2

This recently reunited family consists of a mother, a father, and a toddler son called Stevie.

The Mother

The mother, 26-years old, lacked confidence in herself as a person
and in her abilities as a parent. This was reflected in her low self-esteem and constant self-doubt. She was very strong willed and made all
household decisions for her family. She likened her stubbornness to a
bulldozer—if anyone got in her way, she would run him or her over.
She had an unpleasant childhood history of violence, failure, neglect,
and disrupted attachments. She experienced tremendous frustration
with school and in her interpersonal relations due to a learning disability that went undiagnosed until she was 15. Her lack of confidence and
low self-image as an adult resulted mostly from her lack of education.
She wanted only the best for her son and did not want him to "turn

out like me." She now held a job that allowed her to provide for Stevie in a manner that she hoped would ensure his success in life. Her job required her to work very long, odd hours, and she would not see her son for stretches of twelve hours to three days.

The Father

The father, 31-years old, had recently returned to the family after a separation of nine months. During his absence he had little contact with his son or his wife. He was currently unemployed. Since his return he worked doing household renovations in their home. He had completed high school and he was only a few credits short of completing a post-secondary diploma. He had a history of drug and alcohol abuse, and he served several terms in jail. Upon returning to the home, he and his wife were examining their commitment to each other and to their son.

The Son

Stevie, 2½ years old, was aggressive in most situations. He regularly bit others (both adults and children), often drawing blood. In his neighborhood and day-care center, other children, even those older and bigger than he was feared him. He was mean to his pet cat who often tried to avoid him. He was removed from day-care due to his aggression. There was rough play and verbal aggression between his parents, and this little boy was likewise physically aggressive. However, he appeared very bright, with a keen awareness of his environment and an eagerness to learn.

The family had several areas of need, including issues of separation, bonding, and loss; parenting issues such as limit setting, nurturing, establishing routine, sharing parental responsibilities, supporting each other to feel confident as parents; low self-image; and marriage issues, including commitment to the marriage, and kindness and gentleness toward each other.

Treatment Goals

The goals of Theraplay with Stevie were as follows:

1. To nurture his gentle, soft side
2. To diminish his aggressiveness
3. To eliminate his biting
4. To increase appropriate ways of expressing frustration
5. To improve his sharing and turn-taking skills in order to be less egocentric
6. To increase his self-esteem and self-image
7. To increase his self-control

The goals of Theraplay and parent counseling for the parents were as follows:

1. To increase physical affection and gentle nurturing of their son and of each other (e.g., affectionate touching, holding, less rough play, and increased gentleness)
2. To improve clear, firm communication, and follow through, that biting and hurting are not allowed, and to have their son be more obedient and cooperative in general
3. To improve self-esteem and self-confidence as parents
4. To improve their support of each other as parents
5. For mother to gain objectivity with her son

Treatment Progress

This family participated in twelve Theraplay sessions in combination with parent counseling. Pre- and posttreatment Marschak Interaction Method assessments were completed. Theraplay and parent counseling occurred twice a week for six weeks, and two follow-ups were scheduled. Several changes took place during the twelve sessions. Theraplay had focused on increasing nurturing and improving the self-esteem of each family member. Theraplay activities were directed toward being gentle with others as well as being able to receive nurturing from adults. This first began with the therapist and the child but also included the parents as they entered the playroom and participated in Theraplay sessions. Stevie struggled to allow the adults to be in control. He needed consistent structure and close nurturing to develop trust in the adults around him. During one Theraplay session, he looked up at the therapist and asked if he could bite her. This signaled the beginning of his increased gentleness and decreased aggression. The parents both had to experience the nurturing and structuring in Theraplay in order to realize their child's need for it. They then needed to process during parent counseling sessions how they could make it work at home. Emphasis was also placed on managing anger and frustration by learning and practicing acceptable ways of expressing negative emotion. This strategy proved successful.

Parent counseling supported the transfer of the newly learned behaviors to the day-care center and taught both parents how to provide structure and routine for their son. Within five sessions there was a noticeable increase in the frequency and spontaneity of gentleness within the family unit. The day-care staff as well as parents of other children remarked (without knowing of the family's involvement in Theraplay) how Stevie had stopped biting and was hitting others less often.

Parent counseling proved particularly valuable in promoting, supporting, and effecting change within the family. Weekly review of the events of the past week provided both reinforcement of successes and real-life opportunities to implement the philosophy and tenets of Theraplay in everyday life. Support for these parents to introduce both structure and routine into their daily activities was integral to their success. This opportunity to encourage insight into parenting styles and the resulting influence on their child's behavior was invaluable. Issues dealing with loss and separation (both Dad's absence from the family and Mom's long and extended working hours) were addressed.

These parents were particularly successful when they received verbal praise from therapists for their efforts at providing structure and routine and at practicing gentleness. Mom especially waited for praise from therapists and needed to tell everything she was doing to be sure that it was right.

The family practiced Theraplay activities during the week between Theraplay sessions. Family counseling encouraged this homework component. This gave the family the opportunity to use the Theraplay strategies of "no hurts" and soothing a hurt if it occurred (by using baby powder on the hurt) in their home life and in the day care. With support and encouragement the rule of "no hurts" became consistent at home, in the neighborhood and at the daycare.

The family reported that they were feeling good about the decrease in aggressive incidents. They could actually see the effects of anger management in their son. They were under less scrutiny from other parents because their son was not acting out. Mom said that she was feeling optimistic that her son would achieve those things she wanted for him in life.

Treatment Results

1. This family clearly developed increased structuring.
2. The parents' image of their son changed. He was more often seen as an enjoyable, fun, intelligent, and sensitive child.
3. Stevie was able to be at preschool without biting and hitting or throwing things. He was less controlling.
4. The family practiced saying "I'm mad," rather than using aggression.
5. The parents showed the capacity to be gentle, nurturing, and affectionate.
6. They were working to support each other with clear, consistent, and realistic expectations and consequences.
7. These parents saw that they could be effective parents; however, they needed much verbal praise and support, and their self-esteem needed continual boosting.

General Problems Encountered

How to provide uninterrupted parent counseling following Theraplay was an initial problem. We wanted the whole treatment team to be available to the parents during counseling. To occupy the child in a supervised manner, Stevie was given toys to play with in a corner of the room as his parents were counseled. This caused interruptions in the continuity of treatment and diminished the parents' ability to focus on the discussion. Assigning a therapist to play with the child either in the same room or in another alternate room was necessary.

How to nurture the parents during counseling, in an inviting manner, was addressed. With both families, creating a relaxed atmosphere by serving tea or coffee and cookies proved very successful.

FUTURE RECOMMENDATIONS

Parent counseling may be enhanced by formalizing the process of goal setting with the parents. This would ensure an agreed-upon focus, whereby the parents participate in creating the goals and evaluating weekly successes.

SUMMARY

Supportive parent counseling has been presented as an innovative technique in Theraplay, in support of significant family change. Supportive parent counseling provided the opportunity for the parents of the two families to talk about their own personal and family concerns and stresses, and to receive support, affirmation, counseling, and encouragement. In addition, they received assistance in incorporating techniques of Theraplay into their daily lives. Parent counseling provided for the needs of the parents at a separate time from the Theraplay sessions, thus allowing for uninterrupted observation of and involvement with their child in the process of Theraplay treatment.

REFERENCES

Auerbach, A. (1961). Group education for parents of the handicapped. *Children* 8:1365–1366.

Benedek, T. F. (1959). Parenthood as a developmental phase: a contribution to the libido theory. *Journal of American Psychoanalysis Association* 7:389–417.

Brendtro, L. and Ness, A. (1995). Fixing flaws or building strengths? *Reclaiming Children and Youth* Summer: 2–7.

Bricker, W. A. (1967). Competence as a key factor in the study of children's deviant behavior. In *Mind Over Matter*, ed. L. Morgan, Jr., pp. 16–23. Nashville, TN: Tennessee Department of Mental Health.

Dewald, P. A. (1994). Principles of supportive psychotherapy. *American Journal of Psychotherapy* 48(4):505–518.

Erikson, E. H. (1963). *Childhood and Society*. New York: Norton.

Freud, A. (1953). Some remarks on infant observation. *Psychoanalytic Study of the Child* 8:9–19. New York: International Universities Press.

Gold, P., and Richmond, L. J. (1979). Counseling parents of learning disabled children. *Elementary School Guidance and Counseling* 14(1): 16–21.

Jernberg, A. M. (1979). *Theraplay.* San Francisco: Jossey-Bass.

Jernberg, A., and Booth, P. (1999). *Theraplay: Helping Parents and Children Build Better Relationships through Attachment-Based Play.* San Francisco: Jossey-Bass.

Morrow, T. Jr. (1974). Flexibility in therapeutic work with parents and children. *Bulletin of the Menninger Clinic* 38(12):129–143.

Walton, W. T. (1993). Parents of disabled children burn-out too: counseling parents of disabled children on stress management. *International Journal for the Advancement of Counselling* 16:107–118.

6

Bringing the Sibling into Theraplay: A Family Systems View

DOUG LOWETH

An innovation in Theraplay was created to respond to the needs of one family after Theraplay had begun with the mother and daughter in a conventional way. This innovation was designed to address not only the emerging needs of a second child in the family, but also the broader patterns of family interaction.

Theraplay has borrowed from several sources and has been practiced in different forms in response to the needs of particular clients and families (Jernberg 1979). It was built on the child-focused therapies of Austin DesLauriers and Viola Brody, and borrowed from family-focused therapies as well. Jernberg cites Jay Haley for his emphasis on the directive role of the therapist, and Salvador Minuchin's use of in-session manipulation of family interactions. Jernberg (1979) identifies the Theraplay activities that can be used with parents to improve their interactions with their child. She states, "Parents are worked with as intensely as was their child heretofore [in the areas of] their particular conflicts" (p. 163). But Jernberg does not address family systems issues except through the parent–child dyad or parent-parent–child triad in therapy.

Writing ten years later, Jernberg (1989) reaffirms the importance, demonstrated by family therapy, of the involvement of parents, of taking into account the strengths and needs of all family members in treating a child, and of the need to include parents directly in the treatment. Even so, she does not discuss siblings or whole families in assessment or treatment. She cites only two research efforts other than those by the Theraplay Institute, and states, "Research into the effectiveness of family Theraplay is still in its infancy" (p. 393). A literature search failed to locate any sources that discuss applications of Theraplay that include siblings or whole family units. The only exception to this is in informal accounts of this agency (Blue Hills Child and Family Services in Aurora, Ontario).

Nevertheless, it is important to consider the impact of Theraplay with one child on the behavior of other children in the family. Families are systems whose behavior tends to follow recognized patterns, so that change in one part of the system leads to changes in other parts (Compton and Galaway 1984). Symptoms shown, or behaviors expressed, by a member of a family can be of sufficient importance for the stability of the family that when one symptom bearer stops showing certain behaviors, the same behaviors will be resumed by another member. This is particularly evident when the symptomatic behaviors are shown by siblings (Minuchin and Fishman 1981). In the case described below, such a transition occurred.

There are several possible courses of action to be taken depending on how one views the behaviors of the second child. As in other forms of single-child therapy involving the parents, there is a tendency for the second child to want to share the attention that the child in treatment receives, and parents can be directed to respond to this either by including the second child in the therapeutic tasks carried out in the home (Eyberg and Boggs 1989) or more simply by spending time with the second child alone. This assumes, however, that the locus of treatment is the child in treatment, not the family structure as a whole.

In this case we believed, after reviewing the initial course of treatment, that the behaviors of the second child could be understood as equally symptomatic of the same underlying family stressors as those of the child in treatment. The dramatic switch between the children, in which the child in treatment abandoned, but the sibling adopted, the disruptive behaviors that had led their mother to seek help, prompted us to reformulate the goals of therapy and to continue with the children together.

SUBJECTS TREATED, PRESENTING PROBLEMS, AND TREATMENT SETTING

Ms. Jones, a divorced mother in her late thirties, sought treatment for her 7-year-old daughter, Nicole, who was showing disruptive, out of control, and tyrannical behaviors in the home. Ms. Jones described the family as "walking on egg shells" in an attempt to modify Nicole's behavior, or at least cope with it.

The household also included a son, Robbie, 9 years old. Ms. Jones also had a steady relationship with Mr. Greene, in his mid-forties. At the start of treatment he was not living in the family home. They intended to marry, but both adults were moving slowly in making arrangements in consideration of the children's need to adjust to the change. The children continued to visit their father regularly. The marriage had ended several years before. Their father was aware of the treatment and was helping to pay for it, but was not involved. Mr. Greene had children of his own who lived with their mother.

Ms. Jones reported she had given Nicole adequate attention early in life but this had been interrupted because Ms. Jones had experienced depression serious enough to require hospitalization. During the time she spent coping with the depression and her marriage breakup, she reported she had withdrawn her attention from Nicole. She said that she felt guilty about this deterioration in their relationship and that her withdrawal had led to Nicole's current behavior problems. Nicole was a bright, athletic, highly verbal, and engaging child. Her mother described her as a high achiever.

While his behavior was not disruptive, Robbie also had difficulties. In contrast to Nicole, Robbie was shy and awkward. Mother told us that he had experienced repeated rejection by their father, who favored Nicole, and that Robbie leaned heavily on Mother, behaved in an overly dependent way, and lacked self-confidence. Robbie was reported to be having trouble coping academically. Severe sibling rivalry was also cited as a problem.

Mr. Greene and Ms. Jones were both recovering alcoholics. Ms. Jones spoke positively of their recovery program and the support they enjoyed from their group. Ms. Jones had been in private individual therapy for some time. It was in this setting that she had initially developed the view that the dynamics of her relationship with Nicole were at least partly the result of inadequate or damaged attachment.

The treatment setting was a therapy room with an adjacent observation room in a children's mental health agency in Ontario, Canada. The supervisor was a consulting psychologist to the agency, and a Theraplay trainer. Two trainees, one male and one female, worked directly with Nicole, while the supervisor interpreted for Ms. Jones and Mr. Greene behind a one-way mirror. Having a male and a female therapist allowed the team to reflect the composition and roles in the household, and the female therapist was designated to take the lead in the Theraplay room, with the male therapist playing a supportive role.

Indications for Theraplay and Treatment Goals

We believed that Theraplay was indicated by the presence of attachment issues between Ms. Jones and Nicole. Ms. Jones's identification of these issues as key factors in Nicole's behavior made this an especially good choice, as Ms. Jones was supportive of an intervention that would "bring us closer together."

The goals of therapy were to strengthen Ms. Jones's capacity to provide structure for Nicole, to promote a more positive nurturing relationship between her and Nicole, and to bolster her feelings about herself as a parent. We believed these goals would be best served by working directly with Nicole, having Ms. Jones and Mr. Greene first observing for four sessions and then joining Theraplay for four sessions.

Progress of Treatment

Nicole initially tried to resist the therapists' lead and to take control, but she was easily redirected. She readily accepted the nurturing activities, including some of the more regressive ones, which was a surprise, given how maturely she acted.

In the course of treatment Nicole's behavior in the home began to change, reflecting Ms. Jones's increasing capacity to provide structure for Nicole at home, and in turn leading to reports from Ms. Jones that she was feeling more positive about her parenting and about her relationship with her daughter. However, while Ms. Jones reported more compliance in Nicole's behavior, she also reported that Robbie had begun to display noncompliance and other behaviors previously shown almost exclusively by Nicole. The behaviors identified as a target of therapy appeared to be transferred from one child to another.

Theraplay Innovations

After the eighth regular session with Nicole, in which there was a therapist and cotherapist, Robbie was integrated into the Theraplay sessions and the number of sessions was extended by four. This was done to ensure that Robbie could receive some measure of the intervention that had made it possible for Ms. Jones to make inroads with Nicole's behavior, and also to work directly on sibling rivalry issues. The female therapist worked with Nicole on one side of the room while the male therapist worked with Robbie on the other.

While the treatment team had prior experience with siblings in Theraplay, the present case used an innovative method in that a sibling was brought into sessions partway through treatment. (Robbie had not been regarded as being in need of treatment at the start of Nicole's treatment.)

It should be emphasized that before Robbie was brought into Theraplay, Nicole's behavior appeared stable, and the relationship she shared with her mother appeared closer and more nurturing. We believe this helped give Nicole a secure base so she could tolerate the second child entering and sharing the attention in Theraplay from parent and therapists.

In each session the two children entered with both therapists, one male and one female. Following a welcome routine each child moved with one therapist to carry out the Check Up tasks. (In these the therapist goes through a playful and nurturing "inventory," checking to see that the child has brought all his or her hands, fingers, ears and so on, and how much his or her smile, or height, or biceps have grown since the last meeting. The therapist may also attend to any "boo boos" or hurts that may be found on hands, arms, or face, and take care of them with powder, soothing, or band-aids, all the while engaging closely with the child, saying something such as, "There's a little bump here on your finger. That must have been sore. What do you say we take care of that before we get started?") Following this, the children were brought together for several tasks, after which the parents would join for several activities. Wrapping up, the "feeding" task (in which the therapist typically feeds everyone in the circle in turn, sometimes adding a few words, such as "Dad, I really liked how playful you were today. Thanks."), and the "Good-Bye Song" were always carried out with all four family members and the two therapists.

Theraplay tasks were selected, created, or modified to work on developing fairness in the way the parents managed both children, assertiveness for the second child (first child's goals remained the same), and mutuality between the children to offset their rivalry.

Evaluative Methods

In addition to the clinical impressions of the therapists, and Ms. Jones's and Mr. Greene's impressions, the team used the Marschak Interaction Method (MIM) to evaluate the treatment. The MIM, described in Chapter 3, is used with all clients, before Theraplay and after.

With the entire household together for five tasks, we observed that Ms. Jones interacted significantly more with Robbie, and Mr. Greene with Nicole, than before treatment. After treatment their interactions in general were more lighthearted and less guarded. Mr. Greene took on a clearer coparenting role. He and Ms. Jones discussed how a task would be carried out while the children listened. Prior to treatment Ms. Jones and Nicole had shared this discussion while Mr. Greene and Robbie listened. All four engaged in the subsequent discussion as to which favorite game to play. (In the first Marschak most of the discussion about the game took place between Ms. Jones and Nicole.) Strikingly different was Robbie's role in this task. Before treatment he had been verbally drowned out by Nicole; afterward, he led off the game and even explained a point of the game while all the others listened.

The most revealing differences in the second set of tasks, with Ms. Jones and the two children, was in the seating. Before treatment, Nicole sat for this set between Ms. Jones and Robbie, with Robbie far away. After treatment, Ms. Jones sat between the children, drawing Robbie closer in and engaging him in discussion. The second Marschak revealed less overtly competitive behavior between the children. Robbie appeared more purposeful, and therefore on more even terms with Nicole. After treatment both children spent time on Ms. Jones's lap in this set. Before treatment neither had done so.

In a set of tasks with Ms. Jones and Nicole alone, the mood appeared lighter after treatment, with less challenging from Nicole and more physical closeness between Nicole and Ms. Jones. The rather aggressive challenges Nicole had presented before treatment were replaced by gentle ones. The most revealing difference was in the task called "Baby Memories," where the parent tells the child about when the child was a baby. Prior to treatment Nicole sat apart from her mother, with arms crossed. Later she sat on Ms. Jones's lap, with her arms around Ms. Jones's neck. In their voices as well there were distinct shifts from the first Marschak. Nicole appeared to take on a baby-like manner in her voice and walk; Ms. Jones's voice, possibly in response to this, was warm and melodic, as in telling a story to a very young child.

Many differences appeared in the set of tasks for Ms. Jones and Robbie. Robbie appeared after treatment to be more assertive. He kept more distance from Ms. Jones at times, but in ways that suggested a sense of independence, almost cockiness, that was absent on the first Marschak. Ms. Jones appeared after treatment to be less indulgent of Robbie, consistent with how one might treat a capable 9-year-old. When they did "Baby Memories," Robbie seemed distinctly less enchanted after treatment, did not reach out awkwardly to Ms. Jones as before, and (like a 9-year-old boy?) played with his feet while his mother talked about when he was a baby. Silent throughout most of her storytelling in the first Marschak, Robbie here asked several questions, questioned one of her statements, and added a comment of his own, reminding his mother that he likes lizards.

Overall Observations

There were three significant observations that spoke to the value of the innovation. First, the introduction of Robbie into Theraplay appeared not to precipitate a return to previous behaviors by Nicole; the gains made in the first eight sessions appeared to hold, both in the sessions and at home.

Second, Ms. Jones appeared to generalize quickly to both children the approaches she had begun trying with Nicole, which was consistent with the goals of Theraplay, particularly giving more direct and deliberate nurturing gestures to both children.

Third, in a short time Robbie appeared to become more assertive in positive ways. In particular, he had previously been observed to speak and otherwise communicate quietly and hesitantly when an assertive gesture or statement would have been appropriate, such as when expressing a desire for recognition and when asked to state choices. By the end of Theraplay Robbie was using a clearer, louder, and more inflected voice. Nicole continued to be cooperative, happy, affectionate with her mother, and tolerant and pleasant with her brother. Both children enjoyed the sessions, and Nicole stated she wished she could come more often.

FUTURE RECOMMENDATIONS

Theraplay will continue to be thought of, appropriately, as a powerful intervention for use with a parent–child dyad or parent-parent–child triad. It is less often thought of as a powerful intervention in a family system. Theraplay with more than one sibling present in sessions can help address sibling issues, or issues that affect both children, and this should be considered actively when the treatment goals of Theraplay are devised. Theraplay can be tailored to the needs of a parent and child in such a way that it supports actively the treatment needs of the whole family.

REFERENCES

Compton, B. R., and Galaway, B. (1984). *Social Work Processes*, 3rd edition. Chicago: Dorsey.

Eyberg, S., and Boggs, S. R. (1989). Parent training for oppositional-defiant preschoolers. In *Handbook of Parent Training: Parents as Co-Therapists for Children's Behavior Problems*, ed. C. E. Schaefer and J. M. Briesmeister, pp. 105–132. Toronto: Wiley.

Jernberg, A. M. (1979). *Theraplay*. San Francisco: Jossey-Bass.

——— (1989). Training parents of failure-to-attach children. In *Handbook of Parent Training: Parents as Co-Therapists for Children's Behavior Problems*, ed. C. E. Schaefer and J. M. Briesmeister, pp. 392–413. Toronto: Wiley.

Minuchin, S., and Fishman, H. C. (1981). *Family Therapy Techniques*. Cambridge: Harvard University Press.

7

Treating Family Violence through Theraplay

SHERRI BLANCHARD
AND
JOHN BREUER

This chapter discusses the theoretical and clinical model of Theraplay as we apply it at Blue Hills Child and Family Services (in Aurora, Ontario). There are no two families for which the exact same Theraplay treatment strategies would apply; rather, treatment must be tailored to the unique needs, desires, and abilities of the various family members.

Theraplay was chosen for the family described below because the parents were having discipline problems with all three children—two boys, ages 7 and 10, and a girl, age 11. This family was referred by a social worker at a local hospital, who described the youngest child as the worst tyrant he had seen in his practice.

In the initial meeting, the mother reported severe behavioral difficulties with all the children, citing the youngest as the most aggressive. The father indicated that he was aware of the difficulties encountered by his wife, but insisted that the children listened to him. The parents often disputed the severity of the problems and were quite hostile with one another. In addition, each parent frequently blamed the other for the difficulties the family was experiencing.

Theraplay sessions are usually attended by both parents (whenever possible) and the referred child. However, in this case all three children were included. Each had his or her own Theraplay therapist, and Theraplay was carried out simultaneously with all of them in the same room. Each session started with a child and his or her own therapist in a corner of the room doing individual Theraplay. Toward the latter half of the session all of the children and their therapists came together to work on positive relationships with one another and on sibling rivalry issues through the use of group Theraplay activities.

In the discussion with the parents after each Theraplay session, empathy, listening to feelings, and mutual problem solving would be emphasized. It was hoped that by practicing these traits with each other through the twelve weeks of Theraplay, both the mother and father could then unite in their parenting approach to their children.

THE LINK BETWEEN ATTACHMENT AND AGGRESSION

A few research studies address the link between attachment and aggressive behavior. This research is pertinent to this family because of the inadequate attachment and bonding observed between parents and children and the aggressive and hurtful behaviors that occurred from parents toward children, from children toward parents, and among the children.

In a recent literature review, Lyons-Ruth (1996) states that in high-risk families, poor attachment often leads to avoidant infant behavior that is displayed in a disorganized form; that is, these children lack a consistent strategy for meeting their needs for comfort and security when under stress. She says that several studies now document a relation between disorganized attachment and childhood aggression.

According to research cited by Solomon and colleagues (1995) 71 percent of preschool-age children and 83 percent of 7-year-olds who exhibited disorganized attachment patterns also exhibited above-normal levels of hostility in the classroom. The disorganized attachment behavior seen in these children resulted in the absence or breakdown of behavioral and regulatory strategies.

Quality of attachment and its relationship to aggression was also studied in 12-month-olds and 18-month-olds and their mothers (Bates et al. 1985). This study assessed a sample of ninety-six children with the "strange situation" (see Chapter 4) (Ainsworth et al. 1978) and classified them into two insecurely attached groups (anxious/avoidant and anxious/resistant) and one securely attached group. The children were followed up at the age of 4½ to 5 years at their preschool or day-care setting. When observed during free play and teacher-directed play activities, the children who were verbally aggressive and who engaged in fighting and bullying other children were much more likely to have been classified as insecurely rather than securely attached as infants.

Robert Karen (1990) reports that children who experience inconsistent and unresponsive parenting growing up are often full of unresolvable conflict, and they tend to victimize other children and engage in delinquent acts.

In an unpublished research study conducted at the Blue Hills Child and Family Centre, the authors found a significant decrease in the aggressive behavior scores on the Auchenbach Child Behavior Checklist for a sample of twenty-five children who were treated by the Blue Hills Theraplay Service (Munns et al. 1996).

Another study analyzed the dyadic play of preschool children who were best friends. In those pairs in which both children had been rated as securely attached on a questionnaire completed by their mothers, play was harmonious, as the partners negotiated with one another peacefully. In those pairs in which one of the two had been rated as insecurely attached, a great deal of verbal aggression and grabbing of toys was noted (Park and Waters 1989).

Steinhauer (1995), a professor of psychiatry at the University of Toronto, states,

> If our children don't have good attachments in their families and if they end up learning not to trust and to relate trustingly to others, they will grow into adults with chronic relationship problems. . . . We need families and especially fathers, who realize that parenting is an active and not just a passive process. . . . Having an involved father has been shown to increase children's school achievement and decrease problems in control of their aggression. [pp. 33–37]

Touching has been shown to be crucial to the development of normal socializing in humans, and anthropological studies of body contact in different cultures have linked low levels of infant touching with high levels of violence. If we feed the basic "skin hunger" babies are born with, would the result be happier, better integrated children who would feel loved and reassured as adults and less inclined to alienation and violence? Theraplay tries to accomplish this result by helping families learn to enjoy each other through nurturing touch, especially in those cases where touch has been associated more with discipline through corporal punishment than with affection.

THE TREATMENT CASE

Parental and Marital History

Jane, the mother, was the middle child of three siblings. She described her family of origin as very chaotic, and as a child she experienced a lack of affection and attention. She recalled feelings of abandonment, especially when her older sibling, with whom she was very close, moved from the family residence. Jane reported that there were very traditional roles in her family, and she related incidents of physical beatings by her mother, including one incident when her mother slapped her so hard across the face that she broke a tooth. At the time of therapy, she continued to be close to her siblings but was still somewhat estranged from her father, despite an initial closeness with him following the death of her mother.

Bill, the father, worked in his father's business. He was the oldest child in his family. He recalled a warm and close relationship with his mother but not with his father. For punishment Bill said he was frequently hit with a belt by his father and locked in a dark cellar for a few hours at a time. This sort of discipline was used prior to his teenage years, after which emotional rejection became the primary means of punishment. He remembered frequent strife between him and his father in his teenage years, due to his father's controlling personality. Bill also recalled that in adolescence he felt he was unable to connect with other people, and he felt a sense of not belonging. He went on to explain that he presently has a close relationship with his father yet still feels very controlled by him. As they work together in the business, this control is constant because his father knows what Bill is doing every day. Today Bill still fears emotional rejection by his father and continues to struggle to be a valued son. While Bill maintains family relations with his one brother, who is also in the family business, he no longer sees his sister.

In their relationship Bill and Jane experienced many difficulties and had sought marriage counseling on two previous occasions. Bill had been married before and this was Jane's first marriage. She reported that she met Bill and had a relationship with him when he was still in his first marriage, and that this is often used against her by Bill during their fights. When this was explored further, Jane reported that Bill called her a "whore" and a "slut," knowing that she often expressed these feelings about herself in the initial stages of their relationship. Jane reported that she also experienced rejection by Bill's family and that she did not meet them until after the birth of their first child. Despite the initial rejection, Jane did build a close relationship with Bill's mother prior to her death. However, her relationship with Bill's father is still strained and at times the source of many arguments. Bill reported that he does not have a close relationship with any members of his wife's family and finds them pushy and interfering in their relationship.

In discussing the marital difficulties, Jane became very tearful and upset. This was often tempered with an intense anger and frustration toward her husband for his lack of support and understanding. She stated that they have always had difficulties agreeing and have always been quite argumentative. Bill indicated that he is frustrated with Jane because she is not firm enough with the children and will contradict him when he disciplines them. He said that their arguments escalate to yelling and name calling. At these times Bill will leave and not return for some time. His actions often leave his wife and children upset and unsure if he will return at all. When this happens, the children show their insecurities by directing their anger toward their mother. Jane often becomes overwhelmed and unable to cope.

Jane reported that two years ago Bill hit her in the face and kicked her. This violence occurred during an argument that started with Jane reneging on preparing a meal for an important holiday to which Bill had invited his father. Jane simply did not show up and had made no alternate plans for the family's meal. When she finally came home Bill was so enraged that he assaulted her. Bill had little understanding of why this episode would enrage him to this extent. One possible explanation was Bill's intense need for his father to see him as a success and his fear of his father's disapproval. Jane called the police and Bill was then charged and convicted of assault. He remained in jail for two days. The initial court order restrained Bill from having contact with Jane. After a short period of time Jane and Bill began seeing each other and she had the restraining order amended. As part of Bill's sentencing, he was required to attend a group for abusive men. Following this counseling, they entered into marital counseling for a year. Both stated this counseling had not been successful.

Presently, Jane and Bill report no further physical violence, but they have verbal arguments that escalate to yelling and screaming. They do little together and have very few friends. Bill indicated that they have not been able to leave the children with a baby-sitter because they are so difficult to manage. He further indicated that even the occasional visits with relatives are often strained. Bill still uses the threat of a strap (waves a belt in front of the children) when he disciplines them.

Intake Interview and First MIM

In the first interview with Bill and Jane, it was observed that there was still an intense level of hostility between them, although both said they wanted to remain in this relationship. Bill was still quite angry, upset, and overcontrolling with his wife. Jane appeared to be very depressed, resigning herself to being unable to change their situation. She frequently cried and often made statements that reflected strong feelings of guilt. With regard to managing the children, both parents undermined each other's attempts at discipline and would often resort to physical punishment. Moreover, Jane was inconsistent with expectations. Presenting problems as seen in the intake interview and first MIM revealed a lot of parent–child conflict, inadequate bonding, great difficulty with being gentle and nurturing with the children, and chaotic parental leadership and authority. There was a need for structure so that the parents could provide some predictability and have some degree of control with their children.

The marital relationship had been laden with arguments, violence, one-upmanship, and lack of support for each other. Theraplay would provide them with a different role model, one of gentleness, nurturing, and looking out for each other's needs. In the discussion with the parents each week after the completion of the half hour of activities, empathy, listening to feelings, and mutual problem solving would be emphasized. It was hoped that by practicing these traits with each other through the twelve weeks of Theraplay, both the mother and father could then unite in their parenting approach to their children.

In the first interview the parents were also asked to give a history of the difficulties with each of their children. The oldest child, Jackie, a girl, age 11, had been diagnosed as developmentally delayed and was assessed as performing at a 7-year-old level. The family had received speech therapy and occupational therapy services for her in the past. Jackie was described as a difficult infant who was unable to adjust to a sleeping routine and cried frequently. She was described by Jane as stubborn, easily frustrated, and short tempered. Jane was observed to be very concerned with her daughter's fitting in with her peers. There were frequent arguments between mother and daughter over clothing and Jane did not allow Jackie to choose her own clothing for fear she would be made fun of at school. Jackie was also encopretic but the source of the encopresis was behavioral and not due to her developmental delays. She was affectionate with both her parents, but Jane indicated that she often found the affection overwhelming and would ask her daughter to stop.

Through the intake process and the first MIM, it was observed that Jackie had few social skills and very low self-esteem. She would have a tantrum when she did not get her own way. While Jane reported that Jackie was not aggressive, it was observed that she would hit out at her siblings even when unprovoked. Jackie was teased a great deal by the youngest child. She seemed to have very little power in this family and was often scapegoated. It was noted in the first MIM that Jackie sometimes acted negatively to get attention. Other times she quickly withdrew when scolded or, in contrast, would hit out at family members despite seemingly little provocation.

Trevor, age 10, demonstrated few maladaptive behaviors on the first MIM compared to other family members. He was the healthiest emotionally, although he was parentified. During the MIM he was observed to control his siblings in a quiet and subtle way, occasionally enticing his younger brother into doing something he wasn't supposed to do. He seemed to derive pleasure from teasing his siblings or getting them into trouble. Of the three children, he seemed most at ease in his interactions with adults and accepted nurturing with little difficulty. The parents described him as a sensitive, very cooperative child. When frustrated Trevor resorted to crying rather than acting out aggressively. Jane informed us that Trevor was very concerned with the family's difficulties and, on one occasion, confided to her that he tries to be good so that his family will stay together. The parents often discussed their own upsets and difficulties with Trevor. This left him feeling a sense of responsibility and very conflictual in his relationship with each parent. The parents reported that Trevor has some night fears and will not sleep on his own.

Greg, age 7, was the precipitating factor in the parents' request for Theraplay. He was described as violent, and he refused to listen to parental directives. Greg was known to swear, destroy property, and hit his mother when disciplined. On other occasions, Greg had threatened his mother with a knife. He also at times called his mother a "whore" and a "slut," just as his father had done in the past. There were daily temper tantrums at home and Greg insisted on sleeping in his parents' bed at night. He was intensely competitive with his older brother and had no trouble reducing his sister to tears through his aggression. Jane indicated that Greg has always been very independent and difficult to handle. Greg met all his developmental milestones at a normal age, and the parents reported that he exhibited no behavioral difficulties at school. Greg suffered from asthma and eczema. His asthma was controlled through the use of Ventolin and a vaporizer.

At the time of the intake it was observed that Greg controlled all family members. He was impulsive and insistent on having his own way, defying parental directives. Bill indicated that Greg exhibited a lot of his own personality traits, and at times each parent seemed somewhat to enjoy Greg's acting out, particularly when his aggression was exhibited to the other parent.

Treatment and Progress of Children in Theraplay

The following is a summarized version of the highlights of the Theraplay activity sessions illustrating some of the issues, difficulties and progress as seen with each child.

Jackie made many self-derogatory comments in the first session and was reluctant to take any risks. She initially refused to accept challenges and used many defeatist statements such as "I can't." She lacked self-confidence when it came to playing with her siblings during group games. At times she played too aggressively and, as a result, needed to have firmer limits and structure. She was eager for and comfortable with the closeness of the therapist. As therapy continued, she became less guarded and more spontaneous in her expressions and her feelings.

However, she demonstrated no closeness with her siblings, such as, for example, by hugging them. She also was very rough in nurturing activities with her parents, for example, when she lotioned her mother's hands. Toward the end of therapy, she was showing more self-confidence, as seen in her becoming very involved in the family Theraplay instead of taking a backseat to her brothers. She was more spontaneous in the expression of her feelings and was trying to connect playfully to her brothers.

Trevor sometimes would intentionally get Greg in trouble by teasing him or challenging him to break the rules or tease Jackie. He also tended to make rude remarks about his sister. However, he seldom if ever misbehaved directly himself. Rather, he got his siblings into trouble in underhanded ways. Trevor was the most relaxed child and looked forward most to the Theraplay activities, participating well. There was less change noted in Trevor's behavior over the twelve Theraplay sessions than in his siblings'. This is probably due to the fact that his behavior was more appropriate at the start. However, he did increase his demonstrations of affection, especially to his mother, and seemed to develop more empathy with his younger brother.

Greg presented the most challenges to the therapists. He tried to rule the Theraplay sessions through his temper tantrums in the same way he ruled the family. He was always ready to taunt his sister and competed over everything with his older brother, including where to sit in the circle for the Theraplay activities. He had low frustration tolerance and was distractible and demanding; for example, he wanted to go first all the time. He frequently tried to control the activities by suggesting alternate activities, by resisting holding hands in the group, by refusing to join the circle, and by being aggressive—hitting, kicking, and pulling his sister's hair. Paradoxically, as he became more relaxed in the sessions, he also tested more limits; he needed to be restrained for over 15 minutes before the fifth session began and then only agreed to do a few activities in the waiting room, rather than going into the playroom.

Greg also had a great deal of difficulty accepting nurturing from the therapists. It became necessary to try to engage him in a lot of different kinds of Theraplay activities so that he would accept nurturing initially from the therapists and then later from his parents. Gradually he did become more relaxed and able to do such things as accepting a freezie (frozen, sweetened, colored water that the child sips from a plastic straw) from the therapist while lying in his arms. He exhibited more testing of limits after his parents joined the Theraplay in the sixth session. He wanted to lead activities and to cheat or flout the rules. It became evident that although his father could have positive interactions with him, his interactions with his mother usually ended in conflict. He exhibited a great deal of avoidant behavior with her, frequently struggling to get away from her when she playfully tried to engage him. It was therefore decided after the twelfth session to have Greg and his mother come by themselves for three more sessions to work on closer bonding. This goal was not wholly achieved. Although they interacted in the Theraplay activities together, Greg often resisted his mother's approaches, by whining, struggling, or hitting her. Theraplay was discontinued when the clinic closed for the summer.

Over the course of the twelve sessions of Theraplay, there was some decrease in sibling rivalry and conflict. As part of each Theraplay session, along with the activities each child did individually with the assigned therapist or with the parents, there were a number of activities that were done as a sibling group. While we saw a great deal of one up-manship, teasing, and aggression between them in the beginning, toward the end the children seemed more able to be gentle with each other and were beginning to look out for each other. Also, when one child was acting out or refused to participate, the others were less likely to copy or pay attention to this behavior, electing to participate with the therapists in the activity instead.

Treatment and Progress of Parents in Theraplay Activities

Throughout the assessment, the mother appeared anxious, tense, withdrawn, and passive. There seemed to be some underlying depression. She was very demanding of her children, but exhibited very little control over them. She became anxious and angry easily when faced with any resistance from her children. She was also very competitive with them and sometimes behaved like a peer rather than their parent. She was also uncomfortable with nurturing activities, and some avoidance of these activities was noticed. During the powdering of hands activity she squirted powder on the children's chests on top of their clothes rather than on their hands.

The father had more control over the children and was more re-laxed. He favored Greg, the youngest child, over the others. He was also more comfortable nurturing his children than was his wife.

Between the parents there was little eye contact, no touching, and no nurturing. All verbal exchanges were tense and at times the parents were sarcastic. They clearly were frustrated with each other, and did not support each other during interactions with the children. This was definitely a strained marital relationship.

As the parents began their participation in the Theraplay sessions, a significant focus was placed on nurturing each one as an individual. In the sixth session, the parents were beginning to demonstrate some spontaneous affection and enjoyment with each other and with their children.

Treatment Progress and Results
in Family Counseling with Parents

Bill and Jane often sought to meet their own individual needs, even if at times they conflicted with the needs of their children. Neither of them made expectations clear to the other and each would end up furious with the other. Apparently, this pattern was continually exhibited during the course of their marriage. At the time of therapy the marital discord had created such an unstable environment for the children that a number of the parent counseling sessions focused on the marital con-flicts.

In the initial sessions Bill and Jane often resorted to attacking and blaming each other. They felt their needs were not being met by the other, and each felt misunderstood. The initial parent counseling ses-sions focused on encouraging them to begin listening to each other without reacting in a defensive manner. We began by having them use "I" messages when communicating their upset feelings rather than using blaming "you" messages.

It was apparent that neither of them felt loved, understood, or appreciated. Both had very low self-esteem and felt insecure regarding the partner's affections. So we coupled the listening techniques with having them begin praising and recognizing the positive qualities in each other. This was further emphasized through the family Theraplay, during which the parents were supported in demonstrating affection to each other, such as by lotioning each other's hands. This second task area was very difficult, particularly for Jane. She had a lot of unresolved feelings of hurt, rejection, and anger that made it difficult for her to believe Bill was making attempts to change.

Jane would also make statements that she knew would incite Bill's anger. Bill's retaliatory behavior would serve to reaffirm her belief that he would not change. At the same time, she also exhibited a degree of power over Bill's emotions and this may have been her attempt to gain control in the relationship. On one occasion when Bill had given Jane a compliment—"You're important to me"—her response was to immediately criticize him for taking so long to express his appreciation to her—"It took you fourteen years to finally say that." Bill was very upset by this response and said it reaffirmed his belief that their relationship would not change. It was difficult for Bill to understand Jane's feelings toward him and Jane took Bill's defeatist attitude as a sign that he was not willing to make changes. As a result, in the same session, Bill was asked to repeat his compliment to Jane, and the therapists helped her this time to hear the words Bill was saying. The task of complimenting each other was incorporated in all of the remaining therapy sessions.

In the fifth session Bill and Jane were beginning to demonstrate more affection toward each other. Their ability to be affectionate and complimentary was occurring in a more spontaneous manner and was beginning to carry over outside the weekly sessions. As the conflict declined between them, they reported that their children's problem behaviors had also begun to diminish. Bill and Jane were now feeling more confident in arranging for a baby-sitter and began spending some evenings out.

As Bill and Jane seemed more confident in their relationship, we began to address some of the child management issues. One of the key indicators that this couple wanted to be together was their decision to stop their youngest child from sleeping in their bed and to establish a bedtime routine with all the children. This attempt to maintain a bedtime routine was met with mixed results. Bill was starting to participate in the parenting; however, he often intervened in a very intense and angry manner. Jane responded by giving in to the children and thus undermining Bill's attempts to parent. Moreover, the parents would then both feel hurt, and they engaged in taking revenge on each other.

At this time it was important to have the parents begin examining their individual reactions to their children and how this created conflict between them. Jane began to explore her intense guilt feelings and her anticipation of failure, and how these feelings impeded her ability to be firm with her children. The therapists identified areas of success in order to begin building Jane's self-esteem and her ability to parent. They also focused on Bill's anger and temper outbursts, and examined their impact on his children and wife. Both parents also needed help in intervening early with their children before they became angry. Bill and Jane were able to begin discussing expectations and rules for their children. They were also reporting that they had begun to verbally support each other more in front of their children. As Jane felt more supported and encouraged by the changes occurring, she was able to assume a firmer role with them. As Bill's ability to intervene using less anger and aggression increased, Jane was less likely to undermine him. During this time the family went away for a vacation, and the parents reported this was the best vacation they had ever had as a family.

Both Jane and Bill had begun to make important gains in both their relationship and their ability to parent. However, unless they received therapy for their individual issues, the previous patterns in this relationship would likely reemerge. This relationship would be further complicated by the fact that the children were still exhibiting some behavioral problems at the end of Theraplay, and the need for continued parent counseling remained. It was recommended that the family participate in a home support program wherein a worker goes into the home for child management and parent counseling purposes, to help consolidate some of the gains they had made. As well, individual therapy was recommended for each parent. The parents did follow through on getting a home worker, and Bill returned to his support group. Jane continued with her support group as well, but neither sought individual counseling as had been recommended. Theraplay follow-ups were discontinued because the parents felt they were getting enough support from their home worker and that things were going fairly well.

REFERENCES

Ainsworth, M. D. S., Blehar, M. C., Waters, E., and Wall, S. (1978). *Patterns of Attachment: A Psychological Study of the Strange Situation*. Hillsdale, NJ: Lawrence Erlbaum.

Bates, J. E., Maslin, C. A., and Frankel, K. A. (1985). Attachment security, mother–child interaction, and temperament as predictors of behaviour-problem ratings at age three years. In *Growing Points of Attachment Theory and Research*, ed. I. Bretherton and E. Waters, pp. 146–167. Monographs of the Society for Research in Child Development, serial no. 209, 50(1–2). Chicago: University of Chicago Press.

Karen, R., (1990). Becoming attached. *Atlantic Monthly*, February 1990, pp. 35–71.

Lyons-Ruth, K. (1996). Attachment relationships among children with aggressive behaviour problems: the role of disorganized early attachment patterns. *Journal of Consulting and Clinical Psychology* 64(1):64–73.

Munns, E., Jansen, D., and Berger, L. (1996). *Theraplay and the aggressive factor.* Unpublished research study, Blue Hills Child and Family Centre, Aurora, Ontario.

Park, K. A., & Waters, E. W. (1989). Security of attachment and preschool friendships. *Child Development* 60:1076–1081.

Solomon, J., George, C., and De Jong, A. (1995). Children classified as controlling at age six: evidence of disorganized representational strategies and aggression at home and at school. *Development and Psychopathology* 7:447–463.

Steinhauer, P. (1995). Effects of family stress on children. Paper presented at the monthly meeting of the Empire Club of Canada, February. In *Empire Club Addresses 1994–95*, pp. 17–33. Toronto, Ontario: The Empire Club Foundation.

8

Theraplay with Failure-to-Thrive Infants and Mothers

CONNIE BERNT

Theraplay as an intervention has been successfully used in working with environmental or nonorganic failure-to-thrive infants (FTT) and their mothers. In the late 1980s, Theraplay was adapted for use with two young children diagnosed as FTT and their mothers in a birth to 3 years of age early intervention center (Bernt 1990). The FTT population is especially suited to this form of intervention in the areas of attachment and autonomy. This chapter discusses FTT, its etiology and models of interactive factors, and the adaptation of the Theraplay model to FTT. Two case studies are described.

WHAT IS FAILURE TO THRIVE?

The environmental or nonorganic failure-to-thrive syndrome has been defined as a severe deficiency in weight gain in the absence of physical disease. Feeding disturbances account for approximately 1 to 5 percent of the pediatric hospitalizations, of which half have no apparent predisposing medical condition (APA 1994, Berwick 1980). Failure to thrive is the common generic term for young children who do not gain weight. In the psychiatric literature, failure to thrive has been described under different diagnostic categories and is not a separate entity.

The current *Diagnostic and Statistical Manual (DSM-IV)* (APA 1994) has two categories relevant to failure to thrive: a new category, feeding disorder of infancy and childhood, and the previous category reactive attachment disorder of infancy and early childhood. The *DSM*'s defining characteristic of infant and childhood feeding disorders is a failure to eat adequately, with significant loss of weight over one month, an often-used definition of failure to thrive. Causative factors may rest in the child, in the parent–child interaction, or in the parent psychopathology. The reactive attachment disorder is characterized by lack of social relatedness and may involve eating disturbances. Pathological parental care is a necessary factor to diagnose reactive attachment disorder.

Relevant to the current study, the Theraplay cases presented below are examples of severe disruptions in the mother–child relationship. Because of the children's inability to gain weight and because of the lack of evidence of organicity, the diagnosis was feeding disorder of early childhood. Multiple factors such as infant regulatory difficulties, parent–child relationship problems, parent psychopathology, and environment stress contributed to the syndrome. In addition, these children presented with social-relatedness problems characteristic of reactive attachment disorder. The traditional failure-to-thrive diagnosis, not listed in *DSM-IV*, may well be an extreme form of eating disorder characterized by poor weight gain and poor social relatedness. Because of the severity of the condition, the infant or child is more often seen in a hospital setting, rather than a pediatrician's office.

ETIOLOGY

The current *DSM-IV* classification highlights the etiological ambiguity of the failure-to-thrive syndrome. Little or no weight gain for one month and early onset of FTT are behavioral manifestations, the markers for the condition. As noted above, the *DSM-IV* classification does not use social relatedness of the child as the defining characteristic of the syndrome. The parent–child interaction may contribute to the feeding disorder but is not considered the primary etiological factor. However, children with insufficient weight gain, previously classified as FTT and thus a feeding disorder, frequently display the defining characteristic of reactive attachment disorder in their inappropriate or absent social relatedness. Thus the child traditionally labeled FTT could have the characteristics of a feeding disorder and a reactive attachment disorder. The overlapping labels contribute to the ambiguity regarding causative factors of FTT. Is the feeding disturbance central or is the social unrelatedness due to a disruptive mother relationship central to the phenomenon?

Research suggests that FTT is a broader, heterogeneous category that may involve many subtypes. Factors in the child, the maternal relationship, and the family have been studied. The family description of the FTT child is that of a troubled home with chronic stressors, which include poverty, unemployment, illegitimacy, and marital discord (Jacob and Kent 1977, Leonard et al. 1966). Frequently there is no male in the household (Gagen et al. 1984, O'Regan 1986) or the parental relationships are conflictual, violent or disengaged (Alderette and Degraffenried 1986, Newberger et al. 1986).

Drotar (1991) suggests that the family financial situation and child-rearing beliefs affect the availability and allocation of food. For example, if funds are low, a parent might add water to the formula to stretch resources. Family conflict and disorganization contribute to maladaptive caregiving patterns. Besides economic stressors, families often have few support networks (Forrister 1985). Although the prevalence is highest among lower socioeconomic classes, FTT also occurs in middle-class families (Provence 1983). Lack of food is not the distinguishing factor in FTT.

Characteristics of the child also impact on the development of failure to thrive. Findings are conflicting, suggesting frequent but not exclusive incidence of poor child health, complications of pregnancy and delivery, lower birth rate, prematurity, unplanned pregnancy, and physical disabilities (Gagen et al. 1984). Polan and colleagues (1991) found that FTT children expressed less positive affect in the feeding and nonfeeding situations as well as more negative affect in feeding than normally growing children. They suggest the lowered affect may reflect the FTT children's lowered physical vigor or a depressive state. The children's behavior may well be an outcome of a disturbed feeding situation. The authors speculate that aversive early feeding experiences may lead to a negative feeding cycle.

Maternal characteristics and mother–child interactions have also been assessed. The description in the literature of mothers of FTT children is highly diverse, and includes such descriptors as young, immature, lonely, a single parent, low self-esteem, and the inability to give nurturance to a child. High incidence of mental retardation and character disorders have also been described (Fishoff et al. 1971, Jacob and Kent 1977). Other researchers have described mothers as either depressed or hostile to their infants. Histories of depressed woman suggest negative relations to their own mothers (Haynes et al. 1984) or a maternal history of caregiver instability and crisis during childhood (Gorman et al. 1993).

Adding credence to the depression hypothesis, FTT mothers, compared to controls, showed lower incidence of vocalization, mutual gaze, and contingency behavior with their infants (Senter 1993). Mothers of nonorganic failure-to-thrive infants were found to be less nurturant and more neglecting than parents of controls (Black Hutcheson et al. 1994). They provided less intentional and matter-of-fact touch in feeding (Polan and Ward 1994).

In the FTT literature on maternal hostility, mothers were seen as depicting their children as "bad" or "out to get me." Fraiberg (1980) states that mothers see the children as extensions of their bad self or negative transference figures. Older FTT infants and toddlers are often reported to be in conflictual relationships with their mothers (Chatoor et al. 1985). Conflict and negativism are understandable given the frequent history of violence and abuse in the mothers' lives (Weston et al. 1993).

Clearly the personality of mothers of FTT infants and their interactional styles present considerable variability. Drotar and colleagues (1990) found FTT mothers were a heterogeneous group with different maternal styles. This study and those cited above have moved researchers from linear models of causality, such as maternal deprivation, to transactional models based on theories of infant development, mother–child interactions, family systems, and psychodynamic conflicts in the mother. Researchers concur that FTT is a unique situation in which varying factors within the mother, child, and the environment influence the disruption in the caregiving relationship. Yet as an outcome of many variables or as a defining characteristic of the syndrome, a disturbed mother–child relationship is central in the failure-to-thrive mother-child dyads.

MODELS OF INTERACTIVE FACTORS
IN FAILURE TO THRIVE

Models on the development of failure to thrive have been based on developmental criteria. Chatoor and colleagues (1985) and Lieberman and Birch (1985), for instance, look at stages of infant development devised by Stanley Greenspan (1985) and Margaret Mahler (Mahler et al. 1975) as times in the infant or toddler's life when the mother–child relationship has gone awry.

Four stages of infant development are described as periods in which FTT can arise: (1) homeostasis (first month), (2) attachment (2 to 6 months), (3) separation and individuation (6 months to 3 years), and (4) emerging internalization (18 to 30 months). The fourth stage is added as an overlapping category by Lieberman and Birch (1985).

Disorders in homeostasis occur around the infant's task to achieve a balance between internal state and external stimuli. An infant with a medical condition such as colic or prematurity may be more difficult to soothe, and it may be more difficult for the parents to read his or her cues. As a result the infant may be under- or overstimulated, leading to feeding problems. In the second stage, disorders of attachment, the infant becomes increasingly aware of and attached to his caregiver. Although the child may contribute to the problems, the problems generally center around the mother's issues. The mother in this dyad may suffer from depression, social isolation, and lack of emotional and economic support. Mother's own unmet childhood needs may be elicited in her interaction with the infant. Disorders of attachment require emotional nurturance of the mother and stimulation and nutrition for the child as intervention strategies.

In the third stage, separation and individuation, the child becomes more aware of him- or herself and the environment. Children move away physically (by crawling and walking) and assert their own needs and wishes. Struggles around feeding may occur because the mother does not read the child's signals, distrusts the capacity of the child to self-regulate, and/or experiences her own distress around autonomy and individuation. The child actively participates in the battle. Treatment centers on parental guidance and focuses on the maladaptive feeding patterns.

In the fourth stage, emerging internalization, the child builds on the autonomy begun in the previous stage. The child's increasing capacity to internally represent self and other in his or her mind can turn an interpersonal struggle into an intrapsychic conflict. The eating struggle can be symbolically represented in the child's mind. Consequently, both the mother's and the child's conflicts about assertion, power, and autonomy can become involved and played out in the battles around food.

Using the above models of development, FTT can be seen as a *DSM* diagnosis of feeding disorder. Whatever the age of onset, problems around feeding and eating are paramount. In early development, the child's medical condition can interact with the environment to develop a feeding problem. In feeding disorders during the attachment phase, infants exhibit failure to respond in social situations characteristic of reactive attachment disorders–inhibited type. Later onset, at the stage of separation and individuation, may also entail problems of attachment. The children may be attached, but in an ambivalent and insecure manner. They may display features of the disinhibited type, such as indiscriminate sociability. Reactive attachment disorders do not have to center around feeding issues. However, children with feeding disorders frequently display nonattachment, or insecure and ambivalent attachments.

THERAPLAY WITH THE
FAILURE-TO-THRIVE POPULATION

Theraplay is a therapeutic intervention used to enhance the parent–child relationship. The playful interchanges used in Theraplay develop a positive attachment and affective communication between the dyad. In fact, Theraplay is in many ways a re-creation of an ideal early mother–infant relationship. The emphasis on eye contact, vocalization, close physical contact, and sensory stimulation are precisely the missing factors in the failure-to-thrive mother–child dyad.

The two case studies presented below are examples of disruptions of the dyadic bond occurring at different developmental stages. Laura developed FTT in her first month due to an organic condition. The feeding problems persisted into the attachment stage, following negative reports to the mother regarding the child's potential. Eric developed FTT in the separation–individuation phase. The relationship between mother and son was highly ambivalent. Both these mother-infant dyads lacked positive closeness and intimacy.

The methodology for this study of two mother–child pairs was a pretest and posttest using the Marschak Interaction Method (MIM) (Jernberg et al. 1988) administered and videotaped before and after ten sessions. Another MIM was administered at the completion of ten additional sessions. Two independent observers, familiar with the MIM, rated each member of the dyad on discrete behavioral units. For example, the mother was scored on variables such as "touches baby," "holds baby," and "smiles at baby." The child was scored on such attachment variables as "looks at parent," "smiles," and "touches parent."

In administering the MIM, the author instructed the mother to carry out an activity described on each of ten cards. Activities used included items such as "Play Peekaboo with the baby," "Sing a song to the baby," "Feed the baby," and "Leave the room without the baby for one minute." The hypothesis for the study was that FTT was foremost a disruption of the mother–child relationship. Using the Theraplay intervention, mother and child would increase attachment, nurturance, and intimacy, as measured on the MIM. These factors are positive relationship aspects. In addition to the MIM, children were weighed weekly and the Bayley Scales of Infant Development were administered before and after treatment.

CHANGES IN THE TRADITIONAL THERAPLAY TECHNIQUE

The typical Theraplay modalities, centering on structuring, challenging, engagement, and nurturance, were all part of the interventions with the FTT child and mother. However, with feeding difficulties so central to this particular population, nurturance was stressed in the play sessions. The activities stressed physical contact, soothing, and caregiving. Powdering, lotioning, singing songs, kissing body parts, playing facial games, and hiding food on Mom for the child to find were the activities focused on, with many variations. These activities directly promote attachment and intimacy. Laura's mother's distance and depression and Laura's withdrawal suggested nonattachment and thus the need for nurturance and connection through nurturing activities.

For Eric, who was developmentally and chronologically older, attachment was also a primary issue. In this mother–child dyad, lack of
nurturance was evident. However, power struggles around separation
and independence were also played out between mother and child. With
this pair, ways to connect and to move apart, and likenesses and differences, were included in games such as tunnels, rides, crawls to Mom,
and comparisons of facial features and body parts of mother and son
(see Appendix for description of activities in this chapter). Nurturing
activities, such as those done with Laura, were also stressed, with the
hope of creating a positive attachment that allowed autonomy and
individuation.

In addition to the emphasis on nurturing activities, the mothers
were included from the first session as participants, rather than as
observers as in traditional Theraplay. The rationale for their inclusion
immediately was to provide them the opportunity to experience playful, caregiving activities that they may have lacked from their own early
years. By receiving nurturance themselves, it was hoped that the mothers could then pass on that playfulness and care to their child. For example, the therapist would play patty cake with the mother before doing
it with the child. She put lotion on the mother's hands as well as on the
baby's hands and body. And she provided food for the mothers and the
children.

Following each Theraplay session, the therapist met with the mother
to discuss the session or any other areas of concern. Food was also provided at this time for the mothers. The child and siblings were supervised
by other staff, allowing the mothers to have time for themselves. In this
way, mothers were also nurtured and attended to in the setting.

CASE 1: LAURA

Presenting Problems and History

At 11 months of age, Laura was referred to an early intervention center by a hospital because of failure to thrive. She was the second, unexpected, identical twin, born two months prematurely. Following a
normal delivery of her twin, Laura was delivered by cesarean section.
Her mother, Cheryl, was 23 years old at the time of the birth. Laura
weighted 2 lbs. 10 oz. Because of the prematurity, low birth weight,

and need for a ventilator, Laura and her twin remained in the hospital for six weeks.

The home situation was, like many cases of failure-to-thrive infants, rife with financial and psychological stressors. Cheryl lived on public aid with her three other children, boys age 5 and 2½ and Laura's twin. Cheryl moved frequently, living with relatives and intermittently with an abusive boyfriend. The four children had three different fathers. An additional stressor, besides the birth of ill twins, was the death of Cheryl's father suddenly of a heart attack.

At 3 months of age, Laura was hospitalized because of an organic failure to thrive due to an esophageal reflux, suprasternal retraction, and closure of the larynx during inspiration. A laryngotracheomalacia, in which tracheal cartilages are softened, was recommended to open the trachea. Although this procedure went well, Laura was returned to the hospital shortly afterward because of meningitis. Cheryl later reported that the doctors told her Laura would be severely impaired. Essentially, Cheryl took her child home to die.

Hope for this child and investment in helping her waxed and waned. Laura was seen by center staff consisting of an occupational therapist, an educator, and a speech therapist in the child's home beginning at 11 months of age. Staff reported the child was often left lying in a corner covered with a dirty blanket. Cheryl began missing appointments and dropped out of the program. Several months later, she returned to the same early intervention center. Instead of home-based services, she was seen at the center-based program where she received the same services as previously: occupational therapy, education, and speech. In addition, Cheryl and Laura began Theraplay sessions. Laura was then 17 months of age and weighed only 12 lbs. 6 oz. Cheryl attended regularly, coming with her child on the Center bus. After two months, she sent Laura on the bus alone, leaving the bus attendant to care for her child. Following a session in which Laura came to school congested and dehydrated, a report of medical neglect was made, with the mother's knowledge, to the Department of Children and Family Services (DCFS). Cheryl told the staff wistfully, "Yes, take her to the hospital."

Subsequent to the hospitalization, in which Laura gained 5 lbs., she was released to her mother's care under court supervision. The court mandated attendance at the center and intervention with a therapist. A DCFS homemaker was provided for child care and training the mother in housekeeping skills.

Beginning Interventions

Cheryl presented as a depressed, overwhelmed, child-like waif. She was pregnant again, in her seventh month, but she hardly showed. She was positive about the homemaker, a mature, warm woman who accompanied her to the center. Laura was then 24 months old.

At the time of her first meeting with the therapist, Cheryl had moved to an apartment next door to her mother, with her four children and the father of her expected baby. Cheryl stated that she thought Laura looked like Laura's father, a man no longer involved with Cheryl or the children.

Although quiet and reserved, Cheryl was willing to participate in the MIM assessment. Her emotional tone was subdued and serious. She looked at her child at times, touched her softly, and spoke to her quietly. In the game of Peekaboo, Cheryl showed a beginning animation and playfulness. Laura, in contrast to her low-keyed mother, cooed, smiled, and squealed.

One particular task was difficult yet revealing. The task directed the parent to "Tell the child about when she or he was a baby, beginning 'When you were a baby.'" Cheryl hesitated and then responded softly, "You was real small. You had a lot of problems when you was a baby. I could hold you in one hand. You only weighed two pounds." Her voice broke, she looked away and became quieter. Later, Cheryl persisted in feeding her despite her apparent sadness and tearful expression and Laura's tendency to spit out food.

In many ways, this mother showed affection for her baby in her quiet gentleness. Cheryl and Laura's painful history together was apparent in the MIM interchange. At this time, Cheryl was too depressed to nurture her child. Laura was a severely delayed child with a mental age of 3 months on the Bayley Scales of Infant Development.

Treatment: Initial Sessions (Sessions 1 to 10)

Cheryl and Laura were seen for twenty mother–child sessions. For two months after the MIM, Cheryl attended sporadically before becoming engaged in Theraplay. Because Laura responded to kinesthetic movement and vocalization, activities were included that provided this kind of sensory stimulation. Because of the doctor's and mother's concern about Laura's vision, close facial games were also part of the treatment plan. However, it later became evident that Laura's vision was intact.

The treatment procedure was to include mother and child on the mat with the therapist for 20 minutes followed by a 20- to 30-minute individual session with the mother. The therapist was also with the mother during the child's lunchtime feeding in the classroom.

The session format began with Laura playing a game with the mother, such as patty cake. Then the therapist engaged Laura in the task until she was animated and gave the child back to Cheryl, at the height of the child's responsiveness. Laura engaged quickly with coos, smiles, and later a belly laugh.

In the beginning, Cheryl was nonverbal, distant, and preoccupied. After a few weeks she became a little more playful and talked softly to Laura. She became more affectionate over the next few weeks and showed pleasure in Laura's accomplishments, such as pulling a string on her sweatshirt.

In the individual sessions with the therapist, Cheryl did not initiate conversation and responded tersely to questions. She did enjoy the milk and cookies served to her and seemed to want the therapist's interest. Following the birth of a healthy baby boy, Cheryl talked without emotion about her labor and delivery. However, her relief at having a normal child was apparent. Cheryl took pride in her new "fat" baby boy. She began to take better care of herself, fixing her hair and clothes, took interest in the children at the center, and expressed pleasure in Laura's weight gain. Her mood vacillated between quiet contentment and sadness.

Treatment: Sessions 11 to 20

The second MIM, after ten sessions, did not indicate any changes in quantitatively assessed behaviors. However, Cheryl talked more to Laura and became animated on the peekaboo task. Her response to "Tell the child about when she was a baby" was more hopeful. Cheryl said, "You had lots of problems, you was in a coma for a long time. You sure got big now. You're a little better now." Cheryl was also a little better now. At the end of the MIM, she also showed the therapist Laura's new ability to push up on her legs.

The next ten Theraplay sessions were similar to the first session activities with some variation for novelty. Laura showed mild gains in motor skills and responsiveness. She tracked people at a distance, turned her body from prone to supine, and brought her hands to mid-line. She made her own sounds and imitated vocalizations. Mother's mood was brighter and she even initiated new games of her own. She showed excitement about Laura's new "tricks."

Cheryl remained reserved but responded more fully to the therapist's interest. She displayed pride in all her children, including Laura. She shared her initial sadness over the dismal prognosis of the doctor's regarding Laura's future. She was delighted that Laura's vision appeared normal, and made plans for special education services. Cheryl even discussed the sadness around her father's death. Another striking change was her interest in expanding her own horizons. She looked for part-time employment and considered beautician training.

The third MIM did not show significant quantitative changes. However, certain qualitative changes were evident. Cheryl repeated her story to Laura about the past with less sadness and even smiled. She seemed ready to move on with her life. Cheryl fed Laura for longer periods of time. Although the mood of the tape was subdued, Cheryl showed good feelings about her little girl.

Cheryl did not attend the program again. Likely, she anticipated the end of Laura's involvement in the program following her third birthday and needed to separate herself from the therapist and staff. After some months' delay, she enrolled Laura in a special education program. Cheryl was now working full time in the evenings.

Summary

Cheryl and Laura fit many of the environmental characteristics of failure-to-thrive mother–child dyads. Cheryl was young, poor, and burdened with five children. Laura's father had been abusive to the older boys and possibly to Cheryl, although she denied any problems with the man. With two children under 5, Cheryl gave birth to premature twin girls. Laura was the unexpected second who required her mother to have a C-section after a normal delivery of the first twin. The MIM suggested Laura's small size was a blow to her mother's self-esteem.

Further complicating her attachment to this child was Laura's resemblance to her abusive father. During the course of all these traumatic events, Cheryl lost her own father unexpectedly.

From the beginning, Laura was an organically vulnerable child. Her tracheal obstruction produced a physical failure to thrive. If she had received corrective surgery, she might have developed normally like her twin. However, with the development of meningitis and the dire reports of the doctors, Cheryl appeared to give up hope. She brought her child home to die. The child's condition appeared to foster the onset of depression in the mother.

Laura's appearance at 18 months of age was of a classic non-attachment failure-to-thrive child. She was well below the third percentile in weight and height. Although extremely malnourished, she used all her energy to avoid social engagement by turning her head and avoiding any gaze and interaction.

The combined interaction of factors in the child, the mother, and the environment contributed to the development of FTT. Theraplay facilitated the connection of mother and child. The activities allowed mother and daughter to interact in positive ways. The encouragement of eye contact between the dyad also elicited sadness from Cheryl. Her physical encounters with Laura made it hard to avoid or deny her grief.

Cheryl used the therapist as a role model and nurturing figure. By nature, Cheryl was quiet. The playful interchanges helped draw her out of her isolation. The therapist's interest in, nurturing of, and enthusiasm for the child appeared to raise Cheryl's self-esteem and positive feelings for her child. And the positive feedback and interactions from the child helped Cheryl find enjoyment and satisfaction in her little girl.

CASE 2: ERIC

Presenting Problems and Developmental History

Eric enrolled in the center at 22 months of age. He was referred by the hospital following a pediatric workup for poor weight gain. Eric came to the attention of the pediatrician because of his sister Debra's admission to the hospital at 4 months of age with hyponatremic seizures secondary to water intoxication. His mother, Barbara, admitted watering the baby's formula when her public aid funds ran low.

During the two-week hospitalization, Eric did not gain weight until the last two days following a formula supplement. He ate little food. His weight and height were below the third percentile for his age. Developmental tests at 20 months and at 22 months indicated overall delays of two to five months. Eric's lowest scores, five months below age expectancy, were in gross motor areas.

Eric lived with his mother and sister, who was one year younger. The family lived with a maternal aunt who was guardian for Barbara's social security (SSI) benefits. Barbara, an obese 20-year-old, was diagnosed as developmentally delayed. She was childlike and eager to please the staff. Barbara would sit and play with the toys and read simple books to herself.

Because of Barbara's intellectual limitations, her reports of Eric's developmental milestones were likely inaccurate. She reported that prior to hospitalizations Eric would not eat; he would spit out food he took in his mouth. At the center, Eric ate voraciously, requiring staff to limit food to avoid sickness. He spent much time in the housekeeping corner making food for everyone to eat. He played with dolls, alternating nurturing and aggressive acts. Despite his aggressiveness with other children, Eric was appealing and well liked by the staff.

Relevant history for Barbara included sexual abuse by her father from age 14 to age 17. Barbara admitted Eric might be the product of incest, and the aunt reported that Barbara's boyfriend was exonerated of paternity by blood testing, leaving the likely possibility that Barbara's father had impregnated her. Barbara had reported the incest to the authorities. The father was arrested, allegedly beaten by the police, and died of a heart attack. The family ostracized Barbara because of her abuse report.

Initial Interventions

Barbara was delighted about being videotaped for the MIM and eager to show herself and Eric. The pervasive theme of the interchanges was Barbara's need to be seen as a "good" parent and Eric as a "good and bright" child. This impression was further validated by Barbara's comment to Eric at the end of taping: "You did just perfect." She was unattuned to his discomfort and ignored his mild protest or verbal comments. When Eric did not immediately respond, Barbara raised her voice until he complied. The tasks were not mutual and interactive. Eric had to perform without her guidance or assistance. Barbara was more interested in the camera than in looking at Eric.

Barbara's vocal animation and pleasure in the Eric was elicited in the task "Tell the child about when he was a baby, beginning 'When you were a baby.'" She said, "Did you suck your bottle, did you know how to hold your bottle?" In contrast, Barbara perfunctorily gave a cookie to Eric in response to "Feed the child." She quickly moved on to putting on his shoes.

Eric faded in and out of connectiveness with his mother. His lack of concern at her departure in the task "Leave the room" suggests poor connectiveness. He enjoyed the playfulness of some activities and complied when Barbara demanded that he respond. He seemed to have learned to manage on his own.

This dyad displayed low levels of intimacy, closeness, and synchrony. Barbara saw Eric as an extension of herself, who would prove her worth. Her strengths were her capacity to be playful and her desire to be a good mother. Her perceptions of Eric's being bright were significant in terms of her own recognition of herself as "slow."

Treatment

Because of serious disruptions in the family constellation that resulted in Eric's placement in a foster home, Barbara and Eric were seen for only nine sessions together. Eric was seen individually for Theraplay in the mother's absence and following foster home placement.

The mother–child sessions stressed nurturing and playfulness. As with Cheryl, both mother and child were included in the sessions from the start. Barbara enjoyed the games. It was evident she had never learned simple songs, such as "This Little Piggy," or played Peekaboo. Despite encouragement and the recognition Barbara received from Eric in running to her, hugging, and other interactions, Barbara showed difficulty staying focused when the therapist attended to Eric.

Most problematic was Barbara's reluctance to have the therapist feed Eric, complaining he was getting "too many cookies." Once she was able to accept food for herself, Barbara stopped her protest. Her dislike of feeding the child seemed related to her own neediness and difficulty sharing and seeing Eric given to, concretely and symbolically.

Positive aspects of mother and child's behavior were frequently commented on by such statements as "Mom knows just the games you like, Eric," and "Eric sure knows how to hug his mom." Physical resemblances and positive features were also conveyed to mother and child. Eric and Barbara seemed to enjoy the activities.

In individual sessions, Barbara focused on her struggles with Eric to behave. Ways to manage him were discussed as well as role playing, with Barbara playing Eric. Although she could recognize she did not like to be yelled at or coerced, Barbara did not change her behavior during the time of treatment.

Parallel to Eric's struggles for autonomy, Barbara began to develop a more independent lifestyle. She started to look for an apartment for herself and the children and proudly displayed her food stamps. She began to bring lunches for the children and proudly served cake provided by the center for Eric's birthday. Although she came irregularly, Barbara showed attachment to the therapist and staff. With other parents, she advised them to be playful with their children rather than teach the ABCs.

Several factors led to neglect and abuse reports to the Department of Children and Family Services (DCFS)—her poor attendance, Eric's lack of weight gain and poor health, and marks on Debra's legs. Eventually, DCFS took custody of the children after finding Barbara in her own apartment without food or furniture.

Second MIM

Because of the turmoil in the household and the concern that Barbara would be unavailable, the second MIM was administered after nine sessions instead of ten. The tone of the taped interactions was one of sadness, seriousness, and depression. Quantitatively, behavioral changes were not found. Some key qualitative differences were noted. Barbara picked up Eric and attempted to soothe him when distressed. She did not bully him, but rather tried to encourage him when he said no. She gave him all the cookies instead of withholding them as she had done previously. On the task of telling the child about being a baby, Barbara did not mention the bottle, but talked about Eric's push for autonomy in crawling and walking.

The day of the MIM was clearly a bad one for Barbara and Eric. She was fighting with her aunt and being pressured to move out of the household. Debra was showing her own increased independence in walking. Barbara may well have been experiencing several losses in her life, displayed by her sadness in the MIM.

Summary

Many external factors limited Barbara's ability to remain in Theraplay and achieve maximum benefits from the intervention. A supervised, positive living situation and homemaking skills are two additional supports that would have enhanced Barbara's capacity to parent. Barbara was like many FTT mothers in that she was young, single, immature, and low in self-esteem. Further compounding her capacity as a parent was her mild mental retardation. Her history of sexual victimization contributed to her ambivalent attachment and feelings about Eric. Eric's purported resemblance to his father, who abused Barbara, likely added to her mixed feelings regarding him. Barbara lacked family and societal support systems. Despite the many personal and environmental stresses, Barbara managed to feed her daughter Debra, who was physically growing.

From the sketchy history, it appears that Eric was a normal infant. Barbara's preoccupation with bottle-feeding on the MIM suggests she could nurture Eric until he moved away from formula and became more independent in feeding. Additional weight is added to this hypothesis by the subsequent birth of a third child, a boy, who was taken into foster care at 11 months by DCFS. This boy was malnourished and refused to be fed anything but a bottle, but he would eat finger food himself. The onset of FTT for Eric and his brother was at the separation-individuation stage of development. Eric, unlike Laura, was related to mother but indiscriminate in his selection of people to connect with socially. He engaged anyone who would respond to his needs.

Even in the limited time frame of nine sessions, there was an indication of shifts in the parent–child dyad. The therapist worked on the behavioral aspects of the relationship by modeling, reinforcement, and direction. Eye contact, physical closeness, and intimacy stressed in the games, indicators of attachment, were showing shifts in a positive direction.

Nurturance of the mother was crucial for Barbara to experience first hand, such as what it felt like to be cared for in a supportive manner. Direct feeding of Barbara helped her to begin to give food unambivalently to her children. In this way, the therapist became a mother to the mother.

Barbara became attached to the therapist, attempted to feed Eric better, recognized his cues more often, and allowed more autonomy. She attempted to become more independent in her own life. Continued treatment would have addressed the issue of Eric's parentage. Eric, for his part, used Theraplay to develop his curiosity and autonomy. His aggressiveness decreased and he eventually adapted to his new foster home and school.

INNOVATIONS IN THE THERAPLAY MODEL WITH FTT

Theraplay shows promise as an intervention for the FTT mother and child. As an intervention, it addresses a central issue in FTT—the disturbed dyadic relationship. Modified to meet the needs of this population, Theraplay can address the poor synchrony in the relationship.

Both case studies point to maternal, child, and environmental factors that put these children at risk. For Laura, the onset of FTT was caused by organic factors in the first month of life. Unfortunate physical factors led this mother to give up on this child and led to nonattachment and malnourishment. For Eric, the onset of FTT occurred as he began to separate from his mother. The Theraplay model allowed the therapist to meet the needs of the child in the context of the activities. For example, more active games involving moving toward and away from his mother were stressed for Eric. Games involving vocalization and kinesthetic movement were used for Laura. Both children benefited from the Theraplay games.

The focus in Theraplay was on the here-and-now mother–child relationship. Theraplay games involved mother and child in positive, constructive ways. Of the four types of Theraplay activities–structuring, challenging, engagement, and nurturing—nurturing the child and the mother were central in the two cases.

The crucial factor in increasing the mother's response to the child was the nurturing of the mother. This involved feeding, touching, lotioning, and singing to the mother. Before she could attend to the child's needs, she needed to be cared for herself. For both mothers, the therapist was a new, caring attachment figure, someone they could look to for emotional support, a nurturing figure, and a role model. The emphasis on preverbal, early childhood games engaged the mothers quickly. They had the opportunity to experience directly the playful interactions missing in their own childhood. Improved child interactions and the positive regard and nurturance of the therapist enhanced self-confidence and self-esteem. The other severe environmental factors, such as disturbed family relationships, poverty, isolation, and poor social networks, were not addressed in this study.

Further development of Theraplay techniques with the FTT dyads will illuminate particular techniques that are most effective in developing the mother–child relationship. Including mothers in Theraplay in the beginning sessions, focusing on nurturing and giving directly to the mothers in concrete and symbolic ways, is a promising beginning to addressing the needs of this population. Theraplay as a treatment that addresses the relationship aspect of FTT with an intensive strategy in combination with other support services shows positive potential for this heterogeneous population.

REFERENCES

Alderette, P., and Degraffenried, D. F. (1986). Non-organic failure to thrive syndrome and the family system. *Social Work* 31(3):207–211.

American Psychiatric Association. (1987). *Diagnostic and Statistical Manual of Mental Disorders*, 3rd ed., rev. Washington, DC: Author.

———. (1994). *Diagnostic and Statistical Manual of Mental Disorders*, 4th ed. Washington, DC: Author.

Bernt, C. (1990). *Theraplay as an intervention with failure-to-thrive children and their mothers*. Doctoral dissertation, Chicago School of Professional Psychology.

Berwick, D. M. (1980). Nonorganic failure to thrive. *Pediatrics in Review* 1:265–270.

Black, M., Hutcheson, J., Dubowitz, H., and Berenson, H. J. (1994). Parenting style and developmental status among children with nonorganic failure to thrive. *Journal of Pediatric Psychology* 19(6): 689– 707.

Chatoor, L., Dickson, L., Schaefer, S., and Egan, J. (1985). A developmental approach to feeding disturbances: failure to thrive and growth disorders in infants and young children. *Zero to Three* February: 12–17.

Drotar, D. (1991). The family context of nonorganic failure to thrive. *American Journal of Orthopsychiatry* 61(1):23–34.

Drotar, D., Eckerle, D., Satola, J., and Pallotta, J. (1990). Maternal interactional behavior with organic failure-to-thrive infants: a case comparison study. *Child Abuse and Neglect* 14(1):41–51.

Fishoff, J., Whitten, C. F., and Pettit, M. G. (1971). A psychiatric study of infants with growth failure secondary to maternal deprivation. *Journal of Pediatrics* 79:209.

Forrister, D. K. (1985). Child maltreatment subsequent to failure to thrive: the ecological approach. *Dissertation Abstracts International* 46:3157A–3158A.

Fraiberg, S. (1980). *Clinical Studies in Infant Mental Health: The First Year of Life*. New York: Basic Books.

Gagen, R. J., Cupoli, J., and Watkins, A. H. (1984). The families of children who fail to thrive. *Child Abuse and Neglect* 8(1):93–103.

Gorman, J., Leifer, M., and Grossman, G. (1993). Nonorganic failure to thrive: maternal history and current maternal functioning. *Journal of Clinical Child Psychology* 22(3):327–336.

Greenspan, S. (1985). *Clinical Infant Reports: Report no. 1, Psychopathology and Adaptation in Infancy and Early Childhood: Principles of Clinical Diagnosis, Prevention and Intervention*. Madison, CT: International Universities Press.

Haynes, C., Cutler, C., Gray, J., et al. (1984). Hospitalized cases of nonorganic failure to thrive: the scope of the problem and short-term lay health visitor intervention. *Child Abuse and Neglect* 8:229–242.

Jacob, R. A., and Kent, J. T. (1977). Psychosocial profiles of families of failure to thrive infants: preliminary report. *Child Abuse and Neglect* 1:469–477.

Jernberg, A., Booth, P., Koller, T., and Allert, A. (1988). *Manual for the Administration and the Clinical Interpretation of the Marschak Inter-*

action Method (MIM): Preschool and School Age. Chicago, IL: Theraplay Institute.

Leonard, M. F., Rhymes, J. P., and Solnit, A. J., (1966). Failure to thrive infants: a family problem. *American Journal of Diseases of Children* 3:600–612.

Lieberman, A. F., and Birch, M. (1985). The etiology of failure to thrive: an interactional developmental approach. In *New Directions in Failure to Thrive: Implications for Research and Practice*, ed. D. Drotar, pp. 327–351. New York: Plenum.

Mahler, M. S., Pine, F., and Bergman, A. (1975). *The Psychological Birth of the Human Infant.* New York: Basic Books.

Newberger, E. H., Hampton, R. L., Marx, T. J., and White, K. M. (1986). Child abuse and pediatric social illnesses: an epidemiological analysis and ecological reformulation. *American Journal of Orthopsychiatry* 56(4):589–601.

O'Regan, M. K. (1986). A comparison between mothers of failure to thrive and thriving infants on measures of social support, stress, depression, anxiety, intergenerational factors, and mother–infant interaction. *Dissertation Abstracts* 46(10):3159A.

Polan, H. J., Leon, A., Kaplan, M. D., and Kessler, D. B. (1991). Disturbances of affect expression in failure to thrive. *Journal of the American Academy of Child and Adolescent Psychiatry* 30(6):897–903.

Polan, H. J., and Ward, M. J. (1994). Role of the mother's touch in failure to thrive: a preliminary investigation. *Journal of the American Academy of Child and Adolescent Psychiatry* 33(8):1098–1105.

Provence, S. (1983). Struggling against deprivation and trauma: a longitudinal case study. *Psychoanalytic Study of the Child* 38:233–256. New Haven, CT: Yale University Press.

Senter, S. A. (1983). Mother–infant interaction with non-organic failure to thrive children. *Dissertation Abstracts* 43:3569A.

Weston, J. A., Colloton, M., Halsey, S., and Covington, S. (1993). A legacy of violence in nonorganic failure to thrive. *Child Abuse and Neglect* 17(6):709–714.

9

Treatment of a Sexually Abused Child in the Context of Sibling Theraplay

SUSAN WOOD

Theraplay is a form of treatment that seeks to re-create for a child the type of experience that infants receive through healthy interaction with their parents (Jernberg 1993). The infants' emotional needs are fulfilled and they feel safe and nurtured. The message to the infants is that they are valued and loved.

When a child is sexually abused, she is not only physically violated, but her emotional well-being is severely compromised.* The child internalizes feelings of being devalued and she no longer feels safe. Frequently, she is confused about what constitutes caring and affection and she may engage in inappropriate attention-seeking in a misguided attempt to have her nurturance needs met.

Theraplay can offer the child who has been sexually abused an experience in which she is nurtured and unconditionally accepted the way an infant would be in a healthy parent–child relationship. Touch-

---

*For the sake of brevity, this chapter will refer to the child as a female, even though it is clear that male children can be abused as well.

ing is limited to appropriate positive interaction between the adult and the child, and structured activities in which the adult provides acceptable boundaries help to provide a measure of safety. Unlike Theraplay which is done with other client populations (for example, autistic children), the activities chosen would not be as intrusive or challenging.

In the past, Theraplay was not generally used to treat sexually abused children. There were concerns that it could be too physical and intrusive, possibly retraumatizing the child by triggering memories of the abuse.

Some of the leading experts in the field of working with sexually abused and traumatized children (Hindman 1991, James 1994), however, have strongly advocated the use of appropriate positive physical touching as part of the treatment for these children. Beverly James (1994) has pointed out that children who experienced hurtful or inappropriate body contact need to be exposed to positive physical touch so that they can learn through experience that touching can be safe and enjoyable. Jan Hindman (1991) has described the need for safe, non-sexual touching in this way:

> Touching is the primary vehicle for trauma in sexual abuse. Therefore, it is an important treatment process to incorporate non-sexual touching into treatment protocols in order to continue implementing the sanctuary or safe environment in the healing process. Touching is a wonderful behaviour between human beings and certainly there is a professional obligation to provide safe non-sexual touching when absolutely no commitment is involved. Learning to touch in the safety of the therapeutic environment may be one of the most important components in therapy for victims. . . . The desensitization of inappropriate touching will occur as safe touching is a common factor in the therapeutic environment. . . . Without the modality of touching, skin memories will remain powerful and recovery will be limited. [pp. 170–171]

Children who have been sexually abused often develop sexualized behavior that can be threatening to adults. "This can lead adults who come in contact with the child to be physically rejecting of the child at a time when the child's need for physical reassurance is likely to be great" (Smith 1995, p. 78). It has been suggested that the adult not only limit the sexual behavior of the child but also replace the behavior with appropriate touch (Gil 1991, Smith 1995); Cynthia Monahon (1995) has advised that parents can help their traumatized children by providing soothing and comforting touch, as the child's need for comfort intensifies after a trauma. According to Ann Jernberg (1993), nurturing activities "make the world feel safe, predictable, warm and secure. . . . And just as the parent nurtures, soothes and comforts the infant, so does the Theraplay therapist" (p. 255).

Incest survivor Deborah Lipp (1992) has described her experience of motherhood after being sexually abused as a child. She has stressed the fact that her experience of abusive touch led her to feel uncomfortable about touch and yet she longed to be able to nurture her own child. She stated, "I'm afraid I don't know what the right kind of touch is. . . . Because of these early experiences [of incest survivors], to love appropriately, to touch freely and easily, have been beyond their reach since childhood" (p. 116).

Dr. Clyde Ford (1993), who has done somatic therapy with survivors of sexual abuse, makes use of therapeutic touch and movement as part of the healing process. It is his contention that verbal therapy is often not enough, as experiences are frequently processed physically and emotionally.

> Early emotional life is physical, not verbal. We learn by being handled. Bonding, separating, feelings and needs and their fulfillment are first experienced through the body. How, when, and why we are picked up, put down, held close, or pushed away determine the quality of our early emotional existence. What we learn then, for better or worse, forms the template of our subsequent emotional life. What we learn then governs the functional and dysfunctional patterns of our relationships as children, adults, and parents. . . . And what we learn then, we learn through our body. [p. 22]

Psychologist Peter Favaro (1995) believes all children require positive touch in order to develop attachment and intimacy skills. The requirement for nurturing physical touch is seen by author Ashley Montagu (1986) as a basic human need.

There is evidence to suggest that there are many beneficial therapeutic effects to providing nurturing touch in a variety of situations. Tiffany Field, director of the Touch Research Institute at the University of Miami Medical School, found that premature infants who were given 45 minutes of massage per day (i.e., three 15-minute periods per day for ten days) gained 45 percent more body weight (i.e., an average of 8g more weight per day) than those who did not receive the massage, and that in general they were more active and alert and were discharged from the hospital six days earlier (Auckett 1989, Latona 1997). Baby massage has been widely practiced throughout the world for centuries. Frederick Leboyer (1976) has described the ancient art of baby massage as practiced in India. He states, "Being touched and caressed, being massaged, is food for the infant. Food as necessary as minerals, vitamins, and proteins" (p. 17).

In 1983, Dr. Edgar Rey and Dr. Hector Martinez, neonatologists from Bogota Colombia, also discovered that premature infants that were carried on their mother's chest, where they could receive skin-to-skin contact, had a dramatic 40 percent reduction in their mortality rates. Ray and Martinez referred to this type of mother–infant contact as "kangaroo care." They also found that not only did the infants fare better physically, but the mothers became more bonded to their babies (Ludington-Hoe 1993).

Studies conducted by the Touch Research Institute on older babies and on children and adolescents between the ages of 7 and 18 have also demonstrated the beneficial effects of touch on their physical and emotional development. It is now an accepted part of natural healing for children to incorporate the element of positive touch. (Weber 1994). In the opinion of Tiffany Field, "Touch is as essential to the growth and well-being of a child as diet and exercise" (Latona 1997).

CASE DESCRIPTION

A sexually abused girl, age 9, and her 8-year-old brother were referred for Theraplay treatment. The children lived with their mother, Marjorie, a single parent. She requested treatment because of difficulties managing the behavior of the children and excessive conflict between the siblings. The daughter, Carol, had been expressing through acting out her distress over the previous sexual abuse by her mother's ex-husband. The referring source had been concerned about the mother's tendency toward roughness with the children.

Marjorie, the mother, described a family history that was somewhat abusive and in which she felt neglected. She was placed in foster care at 10 years of age and remained there until she was 15, at which time she left to live on her own. She had her first child at the age of 21, but the child was taken from her by the Children's Aid Society and was made a ward of the state when he was 2 years old. Two years later, Marjorie had her second child, Carol, who remained in her care. Carol's father left when she was born. Marjorie's third child, Chad, was born approximately a year and a half later. Chad's father left Marjorie upon learning that she was pregnant.

Marjorie married three years after the birth of Chad. She and her husband had a conflicted marital relationship in which Marjorie was physically abused. They separated as a result of the physical abuse when Carol was 6. After the separation, Carol disclosed to her mother that her mother's husband had sexually abused her. During the course of the Theraplay treatment, Carol also disclosed a second incident of sexual abuse in which she was fondled by a male friend of the family. Marjorie was distressed about her inability to protect her daughter and felt that she lacked the confidence to impose limits in situations that could be potentially abusive to her children.

Theraplay Treatment

The treatment took place at a children's mental health center. Carol and Chad were seen together for the theraplay sessions for two reasons: (1) There was a long waiting list for treatment, and therefore treatment needed to be expedient as well as effective. (2) Sibling conflict was identified as one of the presenting problems, and it was felt that this issue could be best dealt with by seeing the children together.

Prior to beginning the Theraplay sessions, the family was seen for a Marschak Interaction Method assessment (see Chapter 3). The assessment revealed that there needed to be a strengthening of the mother–daughter relationship. It was evident that there was a healthy relationship between mother and son.

Carol resorted to acting-out behaviors to gain attention and yet at times rebuffed her mother's attempts to provide affection. She and her mother tended to engage in power struggles, and then Marjorie, feeling disempowered, would become somewhat harsh and punitive. It also appeared that Marjorie's anticipation of defiant behavior from Carol led her to be reactive and negative rather than attending to moments when Carol was cooperative.

Carol was assigned a female therapist and Chad was assigned a male therapist. The therapists worked individually with each child in sepa-

rate corners of the room and then would come together for group activities later in the session. For the first few sessions, Marjorie observed
the play through a one-way mirror with an interpreting therapist who
explained to her the nature of the activities and the reasons they were
being implemented. Marjorie was later included in the play. Initially
she was given a lot of direction as to how to interact with the children,
and the activities were chosen by the therapist. Later, she initiated much
more of the play and she selected and led more of the activities during
the sessions.

Treatment Goals

The goals for the Theraplay were to promote a healthy attachment
between Marjorie and Carol and to have Marjorie learn to set limits
and boundaries with the children without resorting to punitive behaviors. It was important to provide the family with a safe environment in which to express playfulness and affection. Another important feature of the Theraplay was to assist the family in distinguishing
touching behaviors that were inappropriate (i.e., those that were either too rough or too intimate) from those that were positive, healthy,
and nurturing.

Treatment Methods

During the Theraplay sessions, the therapists provided nurturing activities for both of the children, such as powdering of hands and feet
and lotioning of hands. While Chad participated in these activities without any difficulty, Carol was able to identify those that made her feel
uncomfortable, and the therapist modified the activities to suit her needs.
Carol's therapist was also able to continue to provide nurturing and
positive touch for Carol, which she was comfortable with, on several
occasions throughout the Theraplay.

During Marjorie's involvement in the Theraplay, she was included
in the nurturing activities both as a provider and a recipient. Activities
such as playing Beauty Salon and Duck, Duck, Goose, Hug were chosen, as well as having Marjorie rock the children in a blanket (see Appendix for description of activities). Feeding was included both during

the sessions and afterward during family discussions. It appeared to be very important to this family to fulfill their basic need for nurturing so that they could then be free to move on to other issues of concern for them.

During the sessions, Carol needed assistance to distinguish nurturing, "good" touch from that which was either too rough or too intrusive (i.e., "bad" touch). One instance in which this was very apparent was during a structuring game of Stacking Hands. Carol attempted to use this activity as an opportunity to ruffle the male therapist's hair. Both therapists limited this activity and assisted her in substituting more appropriate touching within the confines of the game. In another instance, the children wanted to add tickling as a dimension of the game Simon Says. Carol wanted them to be able to tickle each other's arm pits. Again, this activity was limited with a very brief explanation and a suggestion given as to a more appropriate manner in which touching could be incorporated in the game (e.g., touching each other's shoulders).

Both children were provided the opportunity for regression by having the Theraplay therapists gradually introduce a bottle. While Chad demonstrated only a passing interest in this activity, Carol was extremely enthusiastic. Marjorie was initially quite hesitant about this; however, she was assured that Carol's need would subside over time. When Marjorie became involved in the sessions, she gave the bottle to Carol while singing a lullaby. This allowed both Carol and her mother to remember and re-create what they recalled had been a safe and pleasant time for them. Carol requested having a bottle at home. Marjorie complied, and later Carol spontaneously gave up the bottle after satisfying her basic need for it.

Structuring activities, which included games like Red Light, Green Light, Stacking Hands, and Simon Says, (see Appendix) were included in the Theraplay to assist the children in learning to take direction from adults. Later this leadership was transferred to their mother, as she led these activities during the sessions.

The children often needed to have their behavior limited and structured due to sibling conflict and rivalry, but also, as previously mentioned, the need stemmed from Carol's experience of sexual abuse and her inability to distinguish appropriate boundaries. The hands-on nature of the Theraplay also afforded the opportunity to educate Marjorie about appropriate boundaries and limit setting.

Treatment Progress and Outcome

This family made excellent progress in the Theraplay treatment. Marjorie was able to persist in her attempts to nurture Carol even though, at times, Carol was rejecting of her affection. Marjorie found that if she left Carol alone for a few minutes and then tried again to approach her, Carol was more responsive. Carol and Marjorie began to express spontaneous physical affection with one another and generally there was increased closeness between them. The relationship between Carol and Chad subsequently improved as Carol began to feel less threatened by the relationship between Chad and her mother. Marjorie began to demonstrate increased confidence in setting limits with the children and she was able to redirect them rather than resort to punishment. She was also clearly more nurturing than she had been before the Theraplay, and she was able to relax and have fun with them.

The progress shown by this family was, to a great extent, enhanced by their level of motivation and their commitment to following through on the suggested activities they undertook at home. During family discussions, however, it became apparent that when the reserves of the family were depleted due to additional stresses, tensions between Marjorie and Carol reescalated. There were occasional instances in which Marjorie was somewhat neglectful of the children and Carol felt fearful that her mother might abandon her. It also became clear that the family continued to experience some feelings of deprivation, and Marjorie found herself reverting to becoming harsh with the children when she felt depressed. The area of greatest progress in this family was in their willingness to discuss these issues with one another. Marjorie began to consider the possibility that she could use some further assistance with parenting skills.

Carol initially refused any individual treatment for the sexual abuse. By the end of the Theraplay she was willing to consider having follow-up treatment in the form of individual therapy.

SUMMARY AND FUTURE RECOMMENDATIONS

In the past, therapists have been reluctant to make use of Theraplay with sexually abused children. However, this method of treatment has many advantages when used appropriately. It provides a new experience of appropriate and caring physical touch to the child. By its very nature it is unconditionally accepting of the worth of the child and does not seek to have the child develop any insight beyond the fact that he or she is a worthwhile human being who deserves to be loved and cared for. Because it is experiential and physical in nature, it offers the opportunity for the child to heal on a basic emotional level.

Inclusion of the nonabusing parent in the Theraplay treatment offers both the parent and the child a chance to repair their relationship by allowing them to remember times when they used to feel close or to create an attachment that may have been somehow disrupted very early in the child's life. In both cases, the parent and child can experience one another differently without any demand that they focus directly on the sexual abuse. At the same time, the trust and nurturing that are eroded by sexual abuse can be dealt with directly, in a very fundamental way, by the Theraplay treatment.

It is recommended that therapists who wish to use Theraplay with the sexually abused child remain sensitive to the needs and comfort level of the child throughout the course of the treatment. The therapist should remain flexible and open to altering activities as necessary. In choosing activities with the sexually abused child, it is important to consider the pacing of the therapy and to be careful not to include activities that would be too intrusive or that the child might not yet be ready for.

The innovative use of Theraplay with the sexually abused child offers an exciting alternative to current treatment strategies and easily complements the modalities of treatment currently available for these children. Most important, it offers them and their families an enjoyable experience.

REFERENCES

Auckett, A. (1989). *Baby Massage: Parent–Child Bonding through Touch*. New York : Newmarket Press.

Favaro, P. (1995). *Smart Parenting*. New York: Contemporary Books.

Ford, C. W. (1993). *Compassionate Touch: The Role of Human Touch in Healing and Recovery*. New York: Simon and Schuster.

Gil, E. (1991). *The Healing Power of Play: Working with Abused Children*. New York: Guilford.

Hindman, J. (1991). *The Mourning Breaks*. Ontario, Oregon: Alexandria Associates.

James, B. (1994). *Handbook for the Treatment of Attachment-Trauma Problems in Children*. New York: Lexington.

Jernberg, A. (1993). Attachment formation. In *The Therapeutic Powers of Play*, ed. C. E. Schaefer, pp. 241–264. Northvale, NJ: Jason Aronson.

Latona, V. (1997). Focus on . . . the power of touch. *Healthy Kids Magazine*. Worldwide Web site: htp://www.dc.enews.com/magazines/healthykids/archive/100195.1html

Leboyer, F. (1976). *Loving Hands*. New York: Knopf.

Lipp, D. (1992). Mothering after incest. *Mothering Magazine*, Spring, pp. 115–121.

Ludington-Hoe, S. (1993). *Kangaroo Care: The Best You Can Do to Help Your Pre-Term Infant*. New York: Bantam.

Monahon, C. (1995). *Children and Trauma*. New York: Lexington.

Montagu, A. (1986). *Touching: The Human Significance of the Skin*. New York: Harper & Row.

Smith, G. (1995). *The Protector's Handbook: Reducing the Risk of Child Sexual Abuse and Helping Children Recover*. London: Women's Press.

Weber, M. (1994). *Natural Health and Healing for Children: How to Provide Drug-Free Care at Home and When to Call the Doctor*. Rocklin, CA: Prima.

B. Working with Multifamilies

10

Dual Family Theraplay with Withdrawn Children in a Cross-Cultural Context

GLEN MANERY

CULTURAL FACTORS

Theraplay has been an effective treatment for a wide range of clientele varying in terms of age, culture, and presenting problem. There is comparatively scant literature about Theraplay and even less about its potential as a cross-cultural helping tool. This chapter presents a case of Theraplay with two Chinese-Canadian kindergarten girls (Tara and Mary) and their parents, and discusses why it was a good treatment choice. Dual family Theraplay was a never-before-tried permutation of the typical single family Theraplay format. This format allowed the clients to be seen sooner and had the added therapeutic potential of group dynamics. Tara, Mary, and their respective families were good candidates for this innovative form of Theraplay. The girls were close in age and had similar presenting problems so treatment strategies could be similar and complementary. Both girls attended the same school and had similar cultural backgrounds so bringing these two families together was an opportunity to foster a sense of community and support between them that could continue after therapy. The case of Tara and Mary also illustrates (1) how Theraplay is compatible in many ways with the values of Chinese and Asian culture, and (2) how Theraplay is better suited in many ways to cross-cultural therapy in general than mainstream, traditional psychotherapeutic approaches. Most Western psychotherapy approaches have limited success with minority populations. "Western models of counseling have major limitations when they are applied to certain special populations and minority groups such as Asian and Pacific Islanders, Hispanics, Native Americans, and Blacks" (Corey 1991, p. 55). The limitations of mainstream, traditional Western psychological approaches begin with their ethnocentric value assumptions, some of which are the following:

1. The standard for normality is based on the Western, white middle-class male.
2. Individuals rather than systems of individuals are the basic building blocks of society.
3. Independence is desirable and dependence is undesirable.
4. Everyone depends on linear thinking to understand the world around them.
5. Counselors need to change the individuals to fit the system and not the system to fit the individual (Pedersen 1988).

Outside the context of Western society, these assumptions stand out in sharp contrast to many of the values of the rest of the world. Since the United States and the West dominate the world of psychology (Leach 1997), the unfortunate result is pervasive cultural bias in counseling and psychotherapy and avoidance of mainstream Western mental health services by culturally different clients (Corey 1991). Although relatively new and little known, Theraplay has helped a broad range of people, from inner-city black children in Chicago Head Start programs, to German children with speech problems, to autistic adolescents, to the elderly, and, as will be shown here, to Asian-Canadians.

At the outset of her book *Theraplay*, Jernberg (1979) declares that Theraplay is based exclusively on observations of mother–infant interactions in the mid-twentieth century United States. By noting this limitation, she avoids the pitfall of the first assumption cited above. This marks a culturally relative stance in which the cultural values of the therapist are not judged superior or inferior to those of the client.

Jernberg advises that the prototypical mother–infant relationship in the United States (and the West) may differ greatly from what is considered healthy in other cultures. For example, in Papua New Guinea, Kaluli mothers avoid eye contact with their infants while talking to them because their culture associates gaze with witchcraft (Uzgiris 1996). Theraplay therapists are expected to be aware of the influence of culture in therapy and to modify treatment accordingly (Jernberg 1979). Although cross-cultural issues are not a focus in the training of a Theraplay therapist, a culturally relative sensibility permeates Jernberg's writings. In this chapter, a broad definition of culture is adopted that includes the whole way of life of a people (Burton and Dimbleby 1995) and all the things that people value and enjoy about their history (Sue and Sue 1990).

Asian-Canadian and Chinese-Canadian Demographics

With regard to counseling and psychotherapy with Chinese-Canadians, Kong (1985) recommends being aware of the general characteristics of Chinese-Canadians but warns against looking for "typical" Chinese characteristics in clients. Asians are a very large and diverse group composed of at least fifty-three different ethnic groups including Chinese, Filipinos, Vietnamese, Japanese, Koreans, Cambodians, Laotians, Indonesians, Thais, Malaysians, and others (Pagani-Tousignant 1992). Although "Asian" and "Chinese" are not interchangeable terms, there are common cultural threads running through most Asian-Canadian communities, including those of Chinese-Canadians, that distinguish them from the dominant culture (Kong 1985). The ties with the past are often so strong that "Chinese individuals who grow up in environments far removed from the Chinese milieu and who may not read Chinese still retain some degree of Chinese character and behaviour" (Kong 1985, p. 185).

In Canada, Chinese-Canadians constitute the overwhelming majority of Asian-Canadians. In 1991, Canada was home to approximately half a million Canadians of Chinese heritage (Department of Multiculturalism and Citizenship Canada, Citizenship Registration and Promotion 1991). In 1985, 80 percent of Chinese-Canadians had immigrated to Canada within the previous twenty years from all over the world. They represent a wide range of educational, linguistic, economic, occupational, and cultural backgrounds. In Toronto, for example, within the larger community of people from Hong Kong and mainland China there are communities of Chinese immigrants from Central America, the Caribbean, South Africa, India, Singapore, Vietnam, Taiwan, England, and other European countries (Kong 1985).

Asian and Chinese Collectivism

A distinctive characteristic of Eastern cultures is the emphasis on the collective. In the West, the focus is on individualism, which emphasizes independence, autonomy in choice and action, and social assertiveness (Tafarodi and Swann 1996). In the United States, in particular, people generally value individuals who are autonomous and rational, who exercise freedom of choice, and who pursue self-realization, self-control, self-respect, self-reliance, self-esteem, and self-determination, all in a linear, progressive fashion (Lam 1997). Developmental psychologists have traditionally sanctioned the notion that human development is a movement toward autonomy and that this is a healthy, universal process (Jacobvitz and Bush 1996). One must keep in mind that these are values. Traditional Asians and Chinese view themselves as part of a social network with a specific role in relation to others (Lam 1997). Asians traditionally emphasize social interdependence, connectedness, and mutual deference or compromise (Hall 1976, Tafarodi and Swann 1996). Therapists need to pay attention to the differences between individualist and collectivist cultural values if they are to avoid difficulties in therapy (Sue and Sue 1990).

The Importance of Family

The fundamental unit in Asian and Chinese culture is the family. "Think about the family and not about yourself" is advice handed down in Asian families (Sue and Sue 1990). Many Chinese people's identities and needs are inextricable from their family/kinship network (Sue and Morishima 1982, Sue and Sue 1990, Yee and Hennessy 1982). The traditional Asian family encourages group loyalty and dependence (Yee and Hennessy 1982) and children remain emotionally and financially attached to their parents (Lam 1997). Many Asian clients see decision making as an interpersonal rather than an intrapersonal process (Sue and Sue 1990). Therapy, therefore, should involve as many family members as possible (Pagani-Tousignant 1992).

Family involvement is encouraged in Theraplay. In addition to parents, significant others such as siblings, extended family, teacher, and principal can be encouraged to join the therapy process (Jernberg 1979). Theraplay's emphasis on family and community involvement is consistent with Asian, Chinese, and many other traditional cultural values. Leach (1997) states, "Since many non-Western cultures focus on collectivistic values it benefits all of psychology to study attitudes and behaviours from a contextual framework" (p. 166).

Interpersonal Sensitivity

Harmony is maintained within the traditional Asian family by extreme sensitivity to the feelings of others. Direct confrontation, disagreement, and criticism are deliberately avoided. Candor is considered impolite, a sign of lack of intelligence or lack of civility (Yee and Hennessy 1982). Emotional control is valued in Chinese culture and is associated with maturity and wisdom (Sue and Sue 1990). A study in California (Young 1972) reported that Chinese-American mothers were more likely than other mothers to describe their children as shy, self-effacing, and over-controlled (Sue et al. 1983). The withdrawn behavior of the girls in the case described below may be due to this cultural characteristic. However, according to Rubin and Both (1991), there is some evidence in the psychological literature linking school children's withdrawn behavior to troubled relationships with their parents. Troubled family relationships do in fact play a part in the case described below.

Shame and Saving Face

According to Yee and Hennessy (1982) both shame and guilt occur in most cultures but are manifested to a different degree in Asian and Western cultures. Traditionally in the West, individuals typically feel guilt if they do something wrong. In traditional China, shame is the most common emotional reaction to one's own misbehavior because it reflects badly upon the status of family and community and so people learn to act very cautiously (Sue and Sue 1990, Yee and Hennessy 1982). Therapists unfamiliar with these cultural details may erroneously see their clients as inhibited, lacking in spontaneity, or repressed (Sue and Sue 1990). Shame is so salient that family problems are tightly held secrets and professional help is sought only as a last resort, when their problems are extremely serious, or when family and community resources have become exhausted (Pagani-Tousignant 1992, Yee and Hennessy 1982).

Language Barriers

Asian and other cultures tend to be turned off by the cultural and verbal barriers posed by talk therapies. Traditional counseling often requires a lot of verbal input from the client while the counselor plays a less active role. However, many Asian and Chinese clients have been raised not to speak until spoken to. Also, there may be language barriers that force clients to choose simple words that fail to express complex thoughts and feelings (Sue and Sue 1990).

For many Asians, people's attitudes, actions, and feelings speak louder than their words. As a result, therapists ignorant of Asian cultures may often see Chinese clients as resistant to psychotherapy when in fact they may be speaking volumes through subtle nonverbal cues (Yee and Hennessy 1982). It has been claimed that fundamental family functioning occurs at the nonverbal level (Keith and Whitaker 1981). Theraplay's focus on physical, concrete, here-and-now experience, play action, and facial and bodily expression gives it an advantage over more traditional approaches in cross-cultural situations because it is unclouded by the abstractions of verbal language. Active intervention styles may be more important than cultural similarity in building rapport between therapist and client (Pedersen 1988). It is also claimed that interpersonal play collapses cultural and social class boundaries and reduces defensiveness much more than "the esoteric complexities of professional helping language" (Keith and Whitaker 1981, p. 252).

However, it is well known that nonverbal communication is rich and complex and can be exclusive. Hall (1976) noted the following: "Far from being a superficial form of communication that can be consciously manipulated, NVC [non-verbal communication] systems are interwoven with the fabric of the personality and into society itself, even rooted in how one experiences oneself. . . . Non-verbal systems are closely tied to ethnicity—in fact, they are of the essence of ethnicity" (p. 82). If nonverbal communication systems are culturally distinct, one may wonder how Theraplay therapists can meaningfully engage a culturally different client at the nonverbal level. This is a difficult and important question that warrants further research. In partial answer, there is evidence to suggest that basic human emotions (joy, anger, sadness, fear, shame, guilt, envy, and depression) are readily identifiable across cultures (Csikszentmihalyi 1997, Stern 1977). Since Theraplay operates at a very primal, neonatal level it may be said that the Theraplay therapist is trained to be sensitive to very basic and powerful human emotions and nonverbal cues.

Visual and Physical Contact

While Theraplay's emphasis on nonverbal communication may be helpful for some Asian clients, its emphasis on visual and physical contact may present other obstacles for them. Asians "rarely touch in public or in the therapy setting, and direct, prolonged eye contact is considered disrespectful" (Pagani-Tousignant 1992, p. 9).

The debate over whether touch is beneficial or appropriate in psychotherapy is still unresolved but many adult clients in psychotherapy have reported benefits from appropriate, genuine, sensitively timed physical contact with their therapist (Horton et al. 1995, McLaughlin 1993). In a patient survey by Horton and colleagues (1995), over two-thirds of the respondents indicated that "touch communicated or reinforced a sense that their therapist genuinely cared, and that the safety created by this bond helped them open up, go deeper, and take risks" (p. 454). Many respondents (47%) reported that touch communicated the therapist's acceptance or positive regard for them despite their doubts about their own self-worth. Many remarked that they trusted touch more than words. In general, some level of trust and intimacy is required in the therapy relationship for clients to perceive therapist touch as enabling them to communicate on a deeper level (Horton et al. 1995).

It has been pointed out that touch is associated with healing in most cultures (Horton et al. 1995). Interestingly, Japanese mothers, "do more lulling, carrying, and rocking than American mothers; they try to soothe and quiet their infants and tend to communicate with them physically rather than verbally" (Uzgiris and Weizmann 1977, p. 99). In Theraplay, visual and physical contact are emphasized because it is assumed that healthy parenting involves many kinds of contact between parent and child. Physical and visual contact are therefore not contraindicated for therapy with Asians but must be approached with delicacy and respect.

Power Relations in the Traditional Asian Family

Authoritarian and patriarchal family structures are traditional in Asian culture (Kong 1985, Pagani-Tousignant 1992, Sue et al. 1983, Yee and Hennessy 1982). Children must demonstrate filial piety (Kong 1985) to their parents by showing them respect and unquestioning obedience. Starting at an early age, children's behavior is guided by prior approval from authority figures in the family and this continues throughout life (Sue et al. 1983, Yee and Hennessy 1982). Women traditionally have a secondary role to men (Yee and Hennessy 1982). Pagani-Tousignant (1992) notes that wives defer decision making to their husbands.

Child-Rearing Practices

Despite their formal relationships, traditional Chinese parents are quite permissive with their very young children and become much more authoritarian as the children get older (Sue et al. 1983). They do, however, encourage early independence in academic achievement and task-oriented behaviors such as eating alone, dressing, and going to bed unassisted (Sue et al. 1983). Young (1972) found that, compared with Caucasians, Chinese-American parents in California expected their children to interact with peers at a later age, but had similar expectations for academic achievement and self-care tasks (Sue et al. 1983).

In contrast, Theraplay espouses an authoritative approach. Baumrind's (1967) research into parenting styles in the United States found that children of parents who have an authoritative style tend to be more independent and higher in social and cognitive competence. Authoritative parents (and Theraplay therapists) set and enforce clear standards, expect mature behavior, and encourage reciprocal communication and mutual recognition of rights. Authoritarian parenting, on the other hand, is associated with children who are less independent and socially responsible. Parents with authoritarian styles try to control and evaluate the behavior and attitudes of their children according to an absolute set of standards. Children of permissive parents are more likely to be immature, impulsive, dependent, and socially irresponsible. Permissive parents make few demands for mature behavior, tolerate and accept their child's impulses, and use as little punishment as possible.

Despite differences in values with regard to child rearing between Theraplay and traditional Asian culture, the two are not entirely incompatible. For instance, authors claim that Asian-Canadians expect and prefer a direct, active, and authoritative approach in a psychotherapeutic setting (Pagani-Tousignant 1992, Sue and Sue 1990).

Achievement Pressure

Research indicates that, compared to non-Chinese-American parents, Chinese-American parents generally have higher academic expectations of their children and exert more pressure on them to work hard and to achieve (Pagani-Tousignant 1992, Sue and Morishima 1982, Sue et al. 1983). This pressure to achieve is a tool for survival and is motivated not by individual needs but by a need to bring security and prosperity to family and community. This can result in emotional problems for the children. As Sue and Morishima (1982) state, "Having internalized values in high achievement, an individual may be constantly self-critical and dissatisfied despite relatively high levels of success. Moreover, persons who perform in a mediocre manner or who fail to achieve may feel a deep sense of shame or alienation" (p. 78). "Asian-American students who get excellent grades tend to have lower self-esteem than other minorities who are academically less successful, because proportionately their goals are set even higher than their success" (Csikszentmihalyi 1997, p. 24). Achievement pressure was a factor in the case described below.

The Problem of Authority in Cross-Cultural Therapy

Although Asians generally prefer a more directive, authoritative therapist, many minorities tend to be wary of therapists and counselors in general, seeing them as agents of the establishment who transmit and function under Western values (Sue and Sue 1990) with the purpose of assimilating them into the dominant culture. Proponents of the theory of social constructionism stand for the empowerment of less empowered minority individuals (Leach 1997) and have challenged traditional hierarchical psychotherapeutic approaches that arbitrarily "elevate the status of the therapist's interpretation" (Paré 1995, p. 10). Social constructionism is primarily concerned with communal meaning and espouses the "exploration of the world as it is co-constructed by therapist and client" (Paré 1995, p. 10). Social constructionism is seen as a force in multicultural counseling and psychotherapy (Leach 1997, Paré 1995).

Theraplay's hierarchy of authority and mentoring (Koller and Booth 1997) may seem to contradict social constructionism and appear to be a hindrance to truly effective cross-cultural therapy. A closer look finds that Theraplay, like social constructionism, does not operate under the illusion of therapist neutrality. Based on the idea that mother and infant actively and significantly influence each other (Jernberg 1979), Theraplay sees the therapist and the client as actively influencing each other. The following description of attunement by Stern (1977) illustrates mutual influence in mother–infant relationships as soon as one hour after birth:

> Mother and infant, like all humans, socially interact in a split second world. Our social behaviors flash by and are perceived more rapidly than we generally imagine. The average maternal vocalization or facial display or movement lasts well under a second. So do the corresponding baby behaviors. . . . Frequently . . . there is not enough time between the onset of each partner's behavior to think in terms of a response (the time between onsets is less than known reaction times). [And so] the two partners can begin to act at the precise same instant. . . . When the mother and infant are acting synchronously, and well under [known] reaction time[s], then we are forced to think that they are following a shared program. A better analogy for this model is the waltz, where both partners know the steps and music by heart and can accordingly move precisely together. . . . [p. 85]

This contradicts Piaget who theorized that unequal power relations between adults and children lead young children "to abandon their own ideas for those [of the adult] without examining or verifying the ideas" (Rogoff 1993, p. 129). Theraplay is consistent with social constructionists who see child development as a collaborative process between children and caregivers. Rogoff and colleagues (1992) state, "It is important to recognize that children may be sources of information, as adults attempt to understand their intentions in ongoing social interaction, and infants may actively attempt to influence adults' understanding of situations to promote the infants' own goals" (p. 324). Child development is seen as a process facilitated by guided participation and apprenticeship, involving caregivers, the community, and, by extension, the culture (Rogoff 1993). In this process, "ideal partners are not equal, but the inequality is in skills and understanding rather than in power" (p. 129). Consistent with this, the Theraplay therapist takes the role of a coach, temporarily occupying "[t]he top position in [the] hierarchy . . . followed by the parent(s), and then by the child" (Koller and Booth 1997, p. 223). Ultimately, therapists have the responsibility to empower the client and to be aware of, and avoid unintentionally exploiting, power differences.

Synchrony and Theraplay

One mental health implication of Asian and Chinese extreme sensitivity to the feelings of others is that, in a therapeutic relationship, a traditionally oriented Asian may not tell a therapist the truth out of a desire to protect the therapist's feelings (Yee and Hennessy 1982). In Theraplay, however, intellectual truth is not as important as the attunement or synchrony between therapist and client. As between mother and infant, facial expressions, vocal patternings, body movements, and postures serve as meaningful guides to the coordination of action between therapist and client. They are as crucial to infant development (Uzgiris 1996) as they are to client development in Theraplay.

The reciprocity of synchrony in Theraplay is a non-linear process. Perhaps the ultimate indicator of the level of synchrony between therapist and client in Theraplay is the successful use of paradox. Paradox exists when the therapist, for example, turns an aggressive push from a child into a challenging game and growth opportunity. It can also experienced as shared humor or a mutually happy turn. Paradox must be used sparingly and with great care and attention to the emotional state of the child and how the therapeutic relationship is developing. The non-linearity of synchrony and the use of paradox in Theraplay contrasts with traditional mainstream Western psychology's conception of therapeutic process. It is likely that the non-linear characteristics of Theraplay are compatible with traditional Chinese values based on Buddhist and Taoist beliefs in the circularity of nature (Sue and Sue 1990).

Cultural anthropologist Edward T. Hall (1976) recognized that the capacity for attunement, or synchrony, is present regardless of culture. He described synchrony as "panhuman." In Theraplay, synchrony and attunement is the essence of play. Although early caregiving patterns may differ across cultures, play is an integral part of parent–child and peer relations in many societies (Roopnarine and Johnson 1994). Relevant to the case presented in this chapter, one study reported that "Chinese children's play activities were similar to those observed among Euro-American children" (Pan 1994, p. 47). We all share a sense of play and playfulness and this is part of why Theraplay works with people from a variety of backgrounds.

Flow and the Problem of Motivation

Motivating passive and withdrawn clients to engage in therapy is a challenge. Play is perhaps the most potent aspect of Theraplay because it is engaging and intrinsically motivating (Ellis 1973). Mothers, who say their experiences with their infants have been among the best in their lives, describe them as including such feelings as concentration, absorption, deep involvement, joy, a sense of accomplishment, spontaneity, abandon, and exhilaration (Csikszentmihalyi 1993). Such experiences have been optimal or flow experiences (Csikszentmihalyi 1993). People who have experienced "flow" had "the feeling that, instead of suffering through events over which they had no control, they were creating their own lives" (p. 176). The flow experience is characterized by a "sense of discovery, the excitement of finding out something new about oneself, or about the possibilities of interacting with the many opportunities for action that the environment offers" (p. 177). Theraplay's self-perpetuating fun between therapist and client occurs as it might in an ideal reciprocal mother–infant relationship. In this relationship each person is eager to please the other and each shows pleasure in return. The gratefulness at having been given so much pleasure leads to ever greater efforts to please (Jernberg 1979).

The similarities between the flow and Theraplay experience are intriguing because they describe what I believe to be the active ingredients of the therapeutic moment in Theraplay. Martin Seligman (1995), who says the study of flow is "the most exciting development in the psychology of positive affect in recent years" (p. 307), describes flow in the following way:

> When does time stop for you? When do you feel truly at home, wanting to be nowhere else? This state is called flow and it is the highest state of positive emotion, a state that makes life worth living. Flow occurs when your skills are used to their utmost—matched against a challenge just barely within your grasp. Too little challenge produces boredom. Too much challenge or too little skill produces helplessness and depression. Flow cannot be achieved without frustration. A life without [some amount of] anxiety, frustration, competition, and challenge is not the good life; it is a life devoid of flow. [pp. 43–44]

An optimal balance of structure, challenge, intrusion and nurturance is as key to Theraplay as it is to the flow experience. I believe that this aspect warrants further research. The similarities between flow and Theraplay, based on the ideas of Jernberg (1979) and Csikszentmihalyi (1993), are listed in Table 10–1.

Table 10–1. Similarities between flow and Theraplay

Elements of Theraplay	Elements of flow
Responsive to cues given by the client; structure	Unambiguous feedback
Provision of minimal frustration; challenge	Sense of potential control (matching skill and challenge)
Focus on the here and now	Merging of action and awareness (focus on the present)
Fun (can lead to loss of self-consciousness)	Loss of self-consciousness
Fun (can lead to an altered sense of time)	Altered sense of time
Growth toward treatment goals, nurture	Sense of growth
Fun (intrinsically motivating)	Autotelic, worth doing for its own sake

The similarities are especially significant to the cross-cultural issue because, according to Csikszentmihalyi (1993), "flow appears to be a phenomenon everyone feels the same way, regardless of age or gender, cultural background or social class" (p. 177). If this is true, then Theraplay can be a flow experience (both fun and growth producing) for children of any cultural background.

In studying flow in families, Rathunde (1988) found that families that created a playlike atmosphere also raised children who were more self-motivated. Such families create an "organized, rulebound environment that structures a child's attention in ways that enhance the playlike quality of experience that is enjoyable in itself" (p. 343). He referred to such a family as autotelic. Rathunde also states that parents who facilitate play are also fostering an autotelic context because "play is considered by many thinkers to be the paradigmatic self-rewarding (or autotelic) experience" (p. 359). The corollary of this is that Theraplay can infuse an autotelic dynamic in the family and foster a self motivating environment. As seen in Table 10.2, the five features that characterize an autotelic family are remarkably similar to the five principles of Theraplay. This table is based on the ideas of Jernberg (1979) and Rathunde (1988).

Pagani-Tousignant (1992) argues that alternatives to the traditional approaches must be tried for the sake of effective cross-cultural counseling and psychotherapy. She urges therapists to break the rules, take risks, and try new techniques. Adamson (1981), in his review of Ann Jernberg's *Theraplay*, said that Theraplay is a "philosophical concept of therapy significantly different from most existing traditional therapies

Table 10–2. Similarities between autotelic families and Theraplay

Features of an autotelic family	Principles of Theraplay
Perception of choice (or feeling of freedom at the moment)	Playfulness, fun
Clarity of rules, roles and expectations	Structure
Centering of attention	Intrusion/stimulation
Commitment/trust	Nurturance
Challenge	Challenge

From Rathunde (1988) and Jernberg (1979)

to the extent that it is both challenging and provocative" (p. 406). It is my contention that unique aspects of Theraplay make it appropriate for work with people who are culturally different from the therapist and was a good choice of treatment for the following case.

ASSESSMENT

Initial Interview with the Chongs

Six-year-old Mary Chong was referred for Theraplay by the school psychometrist for extremely shy and withdrawn behavior in her kindergarten class. She had neither spoken nor interacted with the teacher or her peers in the class during the three months she had been in school. At home she was apparently very active and talkative. Mr. Chong showed the therapists a videotape of Mary in the family living room hamming it up for the camera and directing her older sisters in an impromptu skit.

Mr. Chong was in his mid-fifties and Mrs. Chong was in her mid-forties. Mr. Chong was born in Hong Kong and Mrs. Chong was born in mainland China. They both were educated to the secondary school level. The family immigrated to Canada in the early 1970s. They had three children (two older girls followed several years later by the birth of Mary).

Mrs. Chong's primary role was the care of her children, while Mr. Chong tended to his business ventures. Mr. Chong, however, was having business troubles and was in the process of applying for unemployment insurance. Both parents had siblings whom they visited monthly. They made infrequent social visits with friends.

Chinese was Mr. and Mrs. Chong's first language and Jamaican patois was their second. Mr. Chong had lived in Jamaica. Both had some difficulty communicating fluently in English, but Mrs. Chong occasionally interpreted for her husband. It was noted that when she was asked a direct question, Mrs. Chong would often make a deferential gesture toward her husband. If he did not respond, she would make a tentative response.

Mary's parents described her academic performance as very slow and commented that she was not paying attention to the teacher. They also reported that, at home, Mary resisted their attempts to teach her to write.

During the initial interview, the counselors observed that the parents could not seem to tear their eyes away from Mary. Mr. Chong in particular seemed preoccupied with her and removed from the adults' conversation. The parents manipulated their daughter's limbs for her, for example, moving her arms as if she were a doll or a puppet to get her to wave to the therapists. When the therapist addressed Mary, the parents became quite tense, quickly crowding around her and imploring her: "Answer, Mary, answer! Speak! Speak!"

Initial Interview with the Yus

Five-year-old Tara Yu attended the same school as Mary, but was in a different class. The two were not playmates. The school psychometrist also referred her for extremely shy and withdrawn behavior in her kindergarten class. The Yus described Tara's behavior at home and with relatives as happy, noisy, and bright.

Mr. Yu was born in China. In the late 1960s, when he was 8 years old, he moved to Canada with his mother and seven siblings. Mrs. Yu was born in Hong Kong and moved to Canada in the late 1970s with her family (mother, father, and two sisters). Both Mr. and Mrs. Yu were university trained and both were working professionals. Mr. Yu was a manager. They met at work and married in the late 1980s. They had two children: Tara and her 3 year-old brother. Mr. Yu was the more talkative of the couple. Both were fluent in English. They had many supportive relatives whom they visited regularly.

During the interview, Mrs. Yu seemed tentative and skeptical, while Mr. Yu appeared to be more at ease.

The primary need expressed by both the Yus and the Chongs was for their children to speak in class.

Marschak Interaction Method (MIM)

The Marschak Interaction Method (MIM) was conducted with each family separately in the observation/therapy room, observed and videotaped by three therapists and their supervisor. The MIM activities for the families are listed in Table 10–3.

Table 10–3. Marschak Interaction Method activities used for two families

MIM activities for the Chongs	MIM activities for the Yus
Mom, Dad, and Mary together:	Mom, Dad, and Tara together:
1. Exchange hats	1. Exchange hats
2. Build something with blocks	2. Puzzle
3. Feed each other	3. Feed each other
4. Sing a familiar song together:	4. Play a familiar game
Dad leaves room. Mom and Mary together:	Dad leaves room. Mom and Tara together:
5. Squeaky toys	5. Squeaky toys
6. Draw something together	6. Draw something together
7. Mom leaves Mary alone in room for one minute	7. Mom leaves Tara alone in room for one minute
8. Powder each other	8. Powder each other
Dad returns and Mom leaves room. Dad and Mary together:	Dad returns and Mom leaves room. Dad and Tara together:
9. Piggyback ride	9. Piggyback ride
10. Puzzle	10. Teach something new
11. Dad leaves Mary alone in room for one minute	11. Dad leaves Tara alone in room for one minute
12. Comb each other's hair	12. Comb each other's hair

Pretreatment MIM Observations

The Chongs

Many of the activities between Mary and her father ended abruptly. Mary seemed to draw away from her father as he physically pulled her toward activities. During the exchange hats activity (for descriptions of MIM activities, see p. 190 and for Theraplay activities see Appendix), Mary indicated that she wanted the police hat, but her father took it for himself. "Look at Dad," he said, looking at himself in the mirror. During the feeding each other activity, Mary refused to allow her father to feed her, and only tentatively fed him at his urging. During the singing of a familiar song together, Mary's father implored her,

"Sing louder!" while tugging on her arm. During the abrupt piggyback ride activity, Mary's body seemed to stiffen. She did not use her hands to hold on to her father. Instead, she held her hands out as if they were sticky and she did not want to get her father's shirt dirty. She did, however, crack a slight smile during the ride. Mary had some difficulty with the puzzle activity, but completed it by herself. Mr. Chong remained silent during this activity. When it was time for him to leave the room, he did so abruptly without explanation. Mary sat impassively and waited. He returned after 40 seconds. When it was time to comb each other's hair, Mr. Chong combed Mary's hair first. He commented, "What a pretty girl" and smiled. Mary appeared tentative when it was her turn to comb his hair.

There was little eye contact between Mary and her mother. When Mary pointed to the next instruction card saying, "This one," and tried to help read it, Mrs. Chong pushed her hand away to read it herself. During the squeaky toys activity, both took a toy and Mrs. Chong began moving her toy closer to Mary's in a playful way. Mary moved her toy away and Mrs. Chong left her to play with the toys by herself. During the drawing activity, they both worked on their own drawings. Mother and daughter sat slightly closer together than father and daughter had. Following the instruction card, Mom abruptly left the room. Mary waited impassively in her seat. Mom returned after 30 seconds. Mary smiled upon her return. The powdering activity was over very quickly.

The relationship between Mr. and Mrs. Chong seemed very formal. The therapists detected no overt expressions of affection, verbal interaction, or eye contact between them. In the feeding activity, Mr. Chong seemed reluctant to feed Mrs. Chong, urging Mary to do it for him.

When Mary had difficulty with tasks, such as building a structure with blocks or getting the cap off a marker, one or both parents quickly completed the task for her.

The Yus

Tara was active and engaging with her parents once she overcame her shyness at being in a strange environment. In contrast to the way she reportedly interacted with her teachers or her peer group, she was quite spontaneous with her parents, especially with her father, who joked with her and teased her affectionately. Throughout the MIM, Mr. Yu did much more parenting of Tara than did Mrs. Yu. Mrs. Yu was more reserved and did not interact as freely with her daughter.

During the hats activity, Mr. Yu's spontaneity with his daughter was evident; Mrs. Yu, in contrast, held back and did not participate as much. Interestingly, all attention was centered on Tara, with no evident parent-to-parent interaction. The most revealing aspect of this activity was the attempt by both parents to make it a learning experience for Tara. They asked her a lot of questions about the hats, such as "Why do fireman's hats have such a long, broad rim at the back?" This seemed to dampen Tara's spontaneity and enjoyment of this activity. Similar questions were asked during most of the activities.

During nurturing activities such as feeding, Mrs. Yu seemed excluded. When she powdered Tara's hands it seemed forced. Mr. Yu and Tara appeared to enjoy the piggyback ride and combing activities. Mr. Yu made the teaching something new activity fun and just challenging enough for his daughter.

Assessment Summary

From the therapists' perspective, it seemed that both families were experiencing troubled relationships with their daughters. In the Chong family, the physical boundaries between parents and children seemed inappropriate. Mr. Chong, in particular, seemed to be excessively preoccupied with his daughter while paying little attention to his wife. There was tension within this family, and their interactions lacked a happy, playful quality. In the Yu family, Mrs. Yu seemed uncomfortable with her daughter. Also, both the Yus and the Chongs appeared to be putting an excessive amount of academic pressure on their children.

Post-Hoc Assessment

The therapists did not have extensive knowledge of the cultural factors when they engaged the Chongs and Yus in therapy other than advice from the case supervisor to try to help the clients "save face." Now, after the fact, we can temper the therapists' original assessment with educated guesses about the cultural factors that may have influenced the Chongs' and the Yus' situations. It seems possible that Tara and Mary were withdrawing socially as a way of coping with feelings of powerlessness and cultural disorientation in the transition to kindergarten. These feelings may have been exacerbated by insecure relationships with their parents. Their parents, in turn, were perhaps sending mixed messages to their girls by putting pressure on them to excel academically yet modeling public emotional restraint and deference to authority. As we shall see in the following section, Theraplay seemed to help both families despite the therapists' lack of awareness of cultural factors.

TREATMENT METHOD

Goal Setting

The therapists chose Theraplay as a treatment in order to encourage the family members to engage each other more playfully and enjoy each other more fully. The therapists also hoped that Theraplay could relieve some of the parental pressures on the children to "perform."

Separate sessions were held with both sets of parents to review the videotape of the MIM session and then discuss goals and foci of treatment. This session was presented to the parents as an opportunity to share observations of what was seen on the videotape. The tape was often stopped at points of interest at the request of either the therapist or the parents. Particular attention was paid to the parents' reactions as they watched the tape. The therapists tried to foster a teamwork spirit by keeping the problem separate from the people. Treatment goals were generated in a dialectical process, where hypotheses were presented nonjudgmentally to the parents by the therapists, and the views of the parents were taken into account.

The treatment goals for both families were as follows:

1. Parents spend leisure time with their daughters in a relaxed, playful way without pressure to perform.
2. Mom and Dad become more relaxed and nurturing with their daughters.
3. Mom and Dad have more fun with each other.

4. Mary and Tara become more outgoing and relaxed in social situations.
5. Parents encourage and facilitate their daughters' opportunities for interactions with other children.

After setting goals, the therapists discussed with the parents the means by which Theraplay would help meet those goals. It was explained to each pair that they and another family would be doing Theraplay together. Without overwhelming the parents with information, some of the basic theory and process of Theraplay was explained to offer a sense of what to expect. They were told that Theraplay can be enjoyable and involve a great deal of physical play, and that the therapists would engage the children, and later the parents, in child-like activities but without any pressure to perform tasks. They were told that they might see their child behave in new and exciting ways, and they might be surprised to discover new aspects of themselves as well. The therapists asked the parents to consider how they, their family, and their friends might react to their children becoming more spontaneous. They were encouraged to share their reactions to Theraplay and to ask questions. In this way, the values of Theraplay were made explicit and the families were invited to express their own values.

Therapists

The therapists were three middle-class, university-educated Caucasians. A male therapist was assigned to Tara and a female therapist was assigned to Mary. A male interpreting therapist was assigned to the parents. A female, Caucasian psychologist supervised the case. Therapists must be aware of their own cultural values and biases and, within reason, make these explicit to the client (Sue et al. 1992).

Therapy Setting

Theraplay took place at the Blue Hills Child and Family Services near the small town of Aurora, Ontario. The size of the playroom was approximately 20 feet by 20 feet, large enough to promote more personal interaction without being claustrophobic. The room was carpeted, warmly lit, and minimally decorated. An observation room, which accommodated sound equipment and a video camera, looked into the playroom through a one-way viewing mirror.

Therapy Materials

Basic play objects were used, but the focus of the play was primarily the people. The materials to be used in the activities were introduced only as needed. Depending on the session, the materials used were balloons, lotion, paper, crayons, bubble blowers, potato chips, feathers, powder, newspaper, Nerf balls, ping-pong balls, cotton balls, and/or blankets.

Session Agendas

The therapists planned each session. Usually twelve play activities were selected according to the child's needs for structure, challenge, engagement, or nurturing. The sequence of activities followed a definite pattern with a beginning, a warm-up, a cool down, and an ending. Typically, sessions began with a welcoming song followed by an inventory in which the therapists checked out the girls for signs of physical growth, tickle spots, new teeth, and so on. Nurturing activities such as lotioning or powdering usually occurred in the middle of the session. Feeding, another nurturing activity, usually preceded a goodbye song that concluded the session. The therapists tried to make the activities flow naturally from one to the other, alternating between challenging and nurturing, gross motor and fine motor, exciting and soothing, competitive and cooperative, and differentiating and merging (Jernberg 1979).

The agenda, however, was always flexible and did not preclude a sensitive response to situational requirements. The prime agenda of the therapists was to achieve a playful, dynamic interaction with the girls for which their participation was vitally important. Strict adherence to the agenda would have suppressed the fun and spontaneity of the sessions. The Theraplay therapist's agenda is custom tailored and relationship oriented (Jernberg 1979). Within the framework of the agenda, the therapists adjusted to the flux of the girls' emotions and behaviors.

After each Theraplay session, the adults sat down to discuss how things were going for them at home and at school and their reactions to the Theraplay sessions. The girls stayed in the same room and were given toys to play with while their parents talked.

Course of Therapy

Eight weekly sessions were scheduled. Each session was to include a half-hour Theraplay session followed by a half-hour adult discussion. The adult discussion was an opportunity for parents and therapists to discuss the content and process of Theraplay, to problem solve behavioral issues at home, and to review and assign homework (Theraplay activities that the families do at home). In the first four sessions, parents observed their children from the observation room. The interpreting therapist explained to the parents what was taking place in the playroom and openly hypothesized about the meaning of the children's behaviors throughout the session. The interpreting therapist drew attention to actions of the therapist (how he/she nurtures, challenges, stimulates, sets boundaries, encourages eye contact, etc.) and to the child's actions and reactions. Beginning with the fifth session, the parents joined in the activities for the last fifteen minutes of each session. As the parents were introduced into the play sessions, the interpreting therapist coached them as they participated. In the later sessions, the parents were encouraged to prepare and lead Theraplay activities of their choosing. In this way, the play relationship with the children was transferred to the parents. Based on the girls' progress and expected improvement, the therapists and parents agreed upon a termination date. Four follow-up sessions at three-month intervals were then scheduled.

Therapeutic Strategies

As is usually done with withdrawn clients, the therapists decided to emphasize challenge, nurture, and stimulation. Structure was de-emphasized. With children who are extremely passive, feel they can make no impact on their environment, and appear most comfortable when they are indistinguishable from the woodwork, Jernberg (1979) advises the following:

> Although the vigorous part of Theraplay—including the therapist's "taking charge"—is not the appropriate way to improve their mental health, the fun part in itself is quite appropriate. In these cases, initiative must be taken by the child, instead of by the therapist. Thus there will be gaiety, eye contact, laughter, and wiggling toes, but wherever possible the child's ideas are followed, rather than the therapist's. These kinds of children need to learn that they are safe and that they can effectively make an impact on others. [pp. 28–29]

The therapists planned to gradually introduce more challenging group activities as the girls manifested a growing sense of empowerment. These activities would be just challenging enough to provide the girls with some minimal frustration, then ultimate success and feelings of accomplishment.

The therapists decided that, in the early sessions, the emphasis would be on building dyadic relationships between therapist and child. Initially, each therapist would interact mainly with their child in separate corners of the room. As therapy progressed, more activities would be incorporated in which both children and both therapists interacted with each other.

SESSION OBSERVATIONS

Treatment consisted of nine sessions with Mary and Tara. Mary continued treatment individually for four more sessions. On the scheduled day of their posttreatment MIM, Mrs. Yu fell ill with the flu. Instead of calling to cancel, Mr. Yu and Tara arrived without Mrs. Yu. The MIM was rescheduled, and instead of sending Mr. Yu and Tara home, an additional Theraplay session was conducted with them.

The Chongs

Session 1

Mary was passive and her arms hung limply at her sides during all the activities. She stood and sat and smiled tentatively but did not participate freely. She did join in the activities but under therapist guidance. She did not speak the entire session.

Session 2

Mary began to show some signs of attachment to her primary therapist, Lisa. She seemed to pay attention only to Lisa, not John, the other therapist, during a group activity (Red Light, Green Light). She smiled and nodded and held up her head. During one activity, she said, "spilled water" (meaning "I spilled the water") which were the first words she had spoken in the presence of the therapists.

According to the parents, Mary was not afraid of, but rather curious about, Theraplay. Before this session she asked her parents, "What's the name of the Aurora place?" She was also telling her parents that she does not like to talk at school.

During the adult discussion, Mrs. Chong was very attentive, polite, and proper, and sat upright. She said she had stopped her habit of asking Mary every day if she had spoken at school yet. Mr. Chong said he understood the therapists when they said the girls, without adult pressure to talk, can come out naturally, like a flower blooming. To reassure the parents that Mary was capable of extroverted behavior, the therapists reminded them of the home video. Mr. Chong, however, seemed unconvinced. He slouched in his chair. He avoided eye contact during the discussion more frequently than the other three adults did. He directed most of his comments to and made most eye contact with the interpreting therapist.

There seemed to be an unhappy tension between Mr. and Mrs. Chong.

At the end of the session, Mr. and Mrs. Chong asked Mary to say goodbye to the therapists. She did not respond immediately and, in seeming desperation, Mr. Chong took her hand and waved it for her. The parents had a way of physically manipulating her body that resembled puppeteers and their marionette.

Mr. Chong was trying to make a connection with the interpreting therapist by making eye contact, by speaking more to him than to the other therapists, and by touching him on the forearm.

Session 3

Mary was still generally passive but began to participate in some of the activities. She kicked the ball a little and held the blanket with both her hands. She was attentive, made good eye contact with Lisa, and appeared to eagerly anticipate the next activity. During the Ping-Pong ball blowing activity, she nodded but did not participate. Her parents were particularly tense as they watched her. This activity was intended as a challenge for Mary to express herself orally.

Mr. Chong reported that he played ball with his daughter at home. He was the quietest of the adults during the adults' discussion. Mr. and Mrs. Chong were both distracted by their daughter. During the adult discussion, they consistently positioned themselves in the seating arrangement to be in constant visual contact with her while she silently played with Tara on the other side of the room.

It was apparent that Mary commanded an inordinate amount of her parents' attention. The therapists' impression was that they adore her as they would a delicate doll.

The Chongs and the Yus brought treats to share with the therapists to celebrate the Chinese New Year.

In the session, the girls spontaneously fed each other during the group feeding activity. Neither of the girls resisted being in the arms of their therapists.

The therapists encouraged the parents to praise and acknowledge even the smallest things that the girls do spontaneously.

Session 4

During Simon Says, Mary mimicked Tara's actions, instead of watching the therapist. During the Play-Doh activity, Mary became very involved, pushing and squeezing with her feet. She smiled throughout the session, but during the blanket rock activity, she put on a very big smile. During feeding time, Mary fed John a chip for the first time.

To stimulate more parental involvement, the therapists engaged them in three Theraplay activities after the children's session was over, including balloon toss, choo-choo train, and feeding. Mr. Chong was the only parent who did not appear to enjoy himself.

Previous attempts to direct the Chongs' attention away from their daughter and toward the adult discussion were unsuccessful. In an "attempt to shift key aspects of the system, such as drawing clearer boundaries between the parent and child subsystems, or breaking dysfunctional alliances" (Fine 1992, p. 3), the therapists used a structural intervention and manipulated the seating arrangement so that the

Chongs would face away from Mary. Likely in reaction to this, Mr. Chong abruptly pulled Mary into his lap. Mary did not appear comfortable there.

Both families reported doing Theraplay activities at home.

Session 5

Beginning with this session, the parents were introduced into the last fifteen minutes of the play sessions.

Leaving the adult discussion to the interpreting therapist and the parents, the primary therapists occupied the children, thus creating a visual barrier between the adults and the children. Again, the therapists were using a structural intervention. Noticing this, Mrs. Chong politely protested, saying, "But I won't be able to see her."

Mr. Chong was much more animated and talkative than usual. He spoke in detail about his experiences in Jamaica. Mrs. Chong hovered and fussed over Mary during Theraplay but in general seemed more relaxed. Mr. and Mrs. Chong said they feel younger as a result of Theraplay.

It was possible that the structural intervention freed Mr. Chong's attention and focused it on contributing to the adult discussion.

Session 6

Mary smiled more frequently. She giggled gleefully during the blanket rock activity. She cuddled more freely with her father. She whispered something to her mother during the session, but she had not yet spoken to the therapists.

Though both children showed small signs of improvement, the therapists predicted that extra sessions would be required. The idea of having a ninth session was broached with both families. They agreed. The therapists anticipated Mary would require extra individual sessions and decided they needed to approach the Chongs about this discreetly and sensitively.

Session 7

Mary's regular therapist was out sick. The supervising psychologist replaced her for this session. Mary did not appear to like the change of therapist. She responded to the replacement therapist by frowning. She seemed afraid to throw the ball and would inertly hold onto it.

The therapists were becoming frustrated in their attempts to establish rapport with Mr. Chong. They were skeptical as to whether the Chongs were carrying out the Theraplay activities at home as they claimed.

Session 8

The therapists tried a new activity, the Jell-O eat, swim, and wash. This entailed feeding each other Jell-O (nurturing), then swimming in it with hands and arms (challenging: letting loose), and then washing it off each other's hands (nurturing). The purpose was to "sandwich" the challenging, messy activity with two nurturing activities to make for easier transitions.

Mrs. Chong expressed concern about Mary still not talking or participating at school. Later, the therapists took the Chongs aside and scheduled four extra sessions.

When encouraged to hold Mary in her arms while hand-feeding her, Mrs. Chong said, "If I do this at home, that's all she'll want!" This was the first time she openly questioned anything to do with Theraplay and represented a growing trust and comfort level. The therapists explained that Mary might at first have a great need to be nurtured in this way. They explained that when her needs for the security of a closer bond have been fulfilled, she would grow out of it and not need it any longer. The therapists explained that if a Theraplay time was clearly defined by the parents and distinguished from regular time, then Mary's expectations would adjust accordingly. (The positive effects of Theraplay, of course, would not be confined to the Theraplay time.)

Session 9

Mary continued her gradual progress.

Session 10

Sessions 10 to 13 were conducted with Mary and the two therapists.

Mr. and Mrs. Chong said that they were doing some Theraplay at home. The activities they reported they were doing were the more challenging kind. The therapists encouraged them to try some of the more nurturing activities as well.

According to Mr. Chong, Mary's teacher said that Mary seemed more comfortable in class but still would not join in any activities. Mary did not take the initiative to do any activities without persistent prompting from the teacher.

With Mary lying in his arms as he fed her a lollipop, Mr. Chong asked her several times to name the color of the lollipop. Again, the therapists encouraged Mr. Chong to simply soothe her, stroking her hair (in essence, nurturing her) instead of asking her questions (challenging her). During discussion time, Mr. Chong asked what he had done wrong. The therapists tried to explain that he could have just focused on being with his daughter instead of asking questions of her.

Mr. Chong was more engaged with the therapists.

Session 11

The Chongs said that Mary was looking forward to this session and became very talkative on the way here. Mary became very involved in the blow me over activity, showing more confidence in oral expression. Mrs. Chong was more relaxed today and laughed during some of the activities. Mr. Chong said he enjoyed the human tunnel activity the most and hand lotioning the least. He said he was uncomfortable with it because he was not used to it.

The Chongs continued to do challenging activities at home such as the pillow push and newspaper punch despite the therapists' advice to include more nurturing activities.

Mr. Chong talked about his worries regarding the impending expiration of his unemployment insurance payments.

Mary was invited to Tara's birthday party.

Mary was showing some small signs of improvement. The Chongs continued to be more relaxed and open.

Sessions 12 and 13

The Chongs reported that over the weekend they met with the Yus for a social visit and that Mary spoke to the Yus. Tara and Mary played together and sang and danced for the parents. Mary's teacher told the Chongs that Mary was more comfortable in the classroom and that she could engage in activities on her own. Mary went to Tara's birthday party and it was a success.

Mrs. Chong said that Theraplay had been very good for Mary.

The two families were supporting each other and progressing toward their goals.

The Yus

Session 1

Tara was passive and tense. Like Mary, she stood or sat but did not move to participate on her own and had to be guided to join in. She did not speak the entire session. Unlike Mary, she did not smile the entire session.

Session 2

Tara was tense and passively went through the motions of many of the activities, but this time with a very slight smile. She was very attentive and answered with nods of her head. She looked to her therapist for approval of her actions. She leaned back into her therapist during an activity. During the Red Light,-Green Light activity, she participated by grasping the other therapist's hand. She did not like having powder on her hands. She participated most vigorously in the newspaper punch and newspaper basketball activities.

After Theraplay, Tara went to her father for a big hug. She closed her eyes and hugged his legs. The therapists got a sense that there was a strong bond between them. The Yus said that Tara told them earlier that "Blue Hills is the best place in the whole world to be!" Mrs. Yu seemed tense; she sat upright and rigid, and wrung her hands. She appeared apprehensive and wary of the therapists. Mr. Yu was more relaxed and accepting. In the discussion, he often interrupted his wife's words, effectively cutting her off. He stated that he was conscious of pressuring Tara and was making a conscious effort to stop it. Mr. and Mrs. Yu acted like a team, supporting each other.

Tara was developing a positive orientation toward Theraplay, and her parents supported it. She was beginning to feel safe with her primary therapist.

Session 3

Tara was attentive to both therapists but more so to her primary therapist, John. She nodded and smiled only slightly. She was quite passive until the pillow pushing activity when she pushed really hard against the pillow. She appeared expectant and, as her mother commented, "She wants to laugh," but seemed to be holding back. At first, she resisted lying on her stomach for the Ping-Pong ball blowing activity but finally relented with encouragement from the therapists. She appeared uncomfortable with the lotioning. At the end of the session, Tara went to her mother for comfort.

The Yus were very talkative and engaged in the adult discussion. They said Tara enjoys physical affection in the privacy of home. They said she initiated a Theraplay activity (paper punch) at home.

The therapists acknowledged the Yus allowing Tara her space during the adult discussion.

The Yus' involvement with Theraplay at home boded well for the success of the treatment. It was encouraging to see Tara reaching out to her mother. The Yus explained that Tara's discomfort with lotioning was probably because she felt it was messy.

Session 4

At first, Tara was "almost smiling." Then, she smiled during the blanket rock activity. Tara put lotion on Mary's hands, but still seemed to be put off by it. Making body indentations in Play-Doh intrigued her. She participated enthusiastically in the newspaper swords activity.

Tara seemed to be steadily progressing, but Mrs. Yu was still skeptical.

Session 5

Mrs. Yu seemed less apprehensive and to be having fun during the Theraplay activities. Mr. Yu, along with Mrs. Chong, hovered and fussed over Mary during the Theraplay activities. The Yus were very supportive of and respectful to the Chongs.

Noticing signs that Tara may be progressing faster than Mary, the therapists reminded the parents that children respond differently to Theraplay and that this was normal and to be expected. Being directly involved in the action relieved some of the tension in the parents.

Support from the Yus contributed immensely to the treatment process.

Session 6

Tara was more relaxed during the inventory activity and clearly smiled during the blanket popcorn activity. During blanket rock she smiled and giggled with abandon. Tara and her parents put lotion on one another's hands in a comfortable and nurturing way. Mr. Yu made hiding Smarties fun for Tara. Tara participated in the human tunnel activity spontaneously and without the need for therapist intervention.

The Yus reported some improvement in Tara's behavior at school, where she made some new playmates. During the adult discussion, she lay down in the middle of the circle and then cuddled with her mom.

Mrs. Yu was more assertive and relaxed. Mr. Yu paid much attention to Mary as well as his own daughter.

Tara continued to show more gains than Mary.

Session 7

Tara enjoyed the inventory activity. She twirled around confidently to show John her new shirt. She smiled earlier in the session than usual. Her smiling continued and she spoke for the first time in Theraplay. She said: "Arm." During the airplane activity, she stretched out her arms as if flying. For the cotton ball touch activity, she confidently closed her eyes. Tara did not seem to like being in her mother's arms for the lollipop activity.

Session 8

Tara enjoyed the lollipop activity, cradled in her dad's arms, although Mr. Yu was a little awkward with it. Mrs. Yu, also for the first time, openly questioned the purpose of a Theraplay activity. She questioned the Jell-O eat, swim, and wash activity. She seemed slightly upset. The therapists explained the purpose of the activity and she was satisfied with the answer.

Session 9

Tara was glum and tentative. The therapists guessed she was sad that this was the last session. She cried when she was accidentally bumped into during the tug of war activity.

Mrs. Yu said, "I've learned how to play with my kid!"

This was the last session with Mary and Tara together. The bond between Tara and her mom was strengthened, thus securing a basis for Tara's growing confidence in herself.

Additional Session with Tara and Mr. Yu

Tara was more relaxed and spontaneous than during the previous session. She and her father enjoyed some boisterous fun together. Mr. Yu was again uncomfortable with the lollipop activity.

Mr. Yu said he thought Tara had done well. He said she was playing more with her cousins and that the teacher was happy with Tara's improvement. She was playing with more kids and was talking to the teacher. Mr. Yu said that Mrs. Yu found cradling Tara in her arms to be difficult. He said he knew that there was a stronger attraction between him and Tara than there was between Tara and her mom. He said, however, that Tara and her mom "interact more now" and they were "connecting in a good way."

The Yus were progressing toward their goals.

Posttreatment MIM Observations

The Chongs

Mrs. Chong appeared less anxious interacting with her daughter. She also better accepted Mary's not meeting her expectations. More physical intimacy was observed between the two. Mr. Chong was more comfortable interacting and nurturing Mary. He also did not pressure her as much to perform as he did in the first MIM. Mr. and Mrs. Chong were more supportive of each other and appeared to have more fun together.

The Yus

In contrast to the first MIM, Tara was more open and spontaneous with her parents, especially her mother. Similarly, Mrs. Yu was more outgoing, confident, nurturing, and playful with Tara. Both parents put less pressure on Tara. However, Mrs. Yu still tended to push her to achieve.

During the hats activity, Mr. Yu initially took control of the interaction. Tara spontaneously teased him when he put on the floppy feminine hat, saying "Daddy-Grandma." There were playful interchanges between Mr. and Mrs. Yu.

During nurturing activities such as feeding, Mr. Yu was playful and Tara spontaneously fed her mother. In contrast to the first MIM, Mrs. Yu included herself in the feeding activity. Mrs. Yu was somewhat uncomfortable and forced during the powdering activity.

Of all the Yus' MIM activities, drawing with Mrs. Yu and Tara lasted the longest. Mrs. Yu kept suggesting things for Tara to include in her drawing, as if striving to achieve a better and better picture. It was also possible Mrs. Yu was buying time in order to think of how she was going to carry out the next activity (leaving the room). When Tara asked why her dad was not in the room, Mrs. Yu appeared flustered and fabricated a story that he was in the washroom when she knew he was in the observation room. Mrs. Yu's reaction likely reflected an insecure relationship with Tara. Overall, Tara and her mother seemed to enjoy each other's company more than before.

As in the first MIM, Mr. Yu and Tara were very animated and free with each other. However, judging by her apprehensive reaction to the piggyback ride turned camel ride activity, Mr. Yu tended to overestimate Tara's comfort with his rough-and-tumble play. Similarly, in the teach something new activity his enthusiastic instruction of how to kick the balloon to keep it from falling exceeded Tara's abilities.

Follow-Up

In the four follow-up sessions the girls continued to show progress. Reports from the parents about their performance at school were positive. Although the parents were still pressuring the girls to achieve, they did feel that their enjoyment of each other as a family was continuing.

DISCUSSION

Mary and Tara and their families made progress toward their goals and grew happier as families. Tara's speedier improvement may have been related to the fact that her parents were more acculturated, or Westernized; they spoke English more fluently, they were graduates of Canadian post-secondary education, and they were both employed professionals. Tara, then, would have experienced fewer cultural conflicts than Mary, whose parents were more traditionally Asian and perhaps not as engaged in Canadian culture. The differences in their rates of improvement point to the possibility that cultural factors played a role in their development.

Consistent with the traditional Chinese cultural characteristics, and to the chagrin of the therapists, the Chongs and the Yus often deferred their most important questions and concerns to the end of the session when the supervising psychologist joined the discussion. Traditional power relations were also manifested when wives deferred decision making to their husbands.

It was noted how uncomfortable the Chongs and the Yus were with some of the messier activities such as lotioning. The therapists assumed that by engaging the clients in messier activities the clients would become less inhibited and more spontaneous, leading to more freedom of expression. It was noted that the Chongs and the Yus were initially quite shy of the physical and visual contact inherent in Theraplay. As they continued Theraplay they seemed to become more comfortable with the physical and visual contact and seemed to enjoy much of it. It was important for the Theraplay therapists not to underestimate the potential sense of urgency that lay beneath their reserved exteriors. Despite their reserve, the Yus and the Chongs showed an earnestness that spoke of deep, genuine concern. Considering the influence of shame in Chinese culture we can only imagine how difficult it may have been for the Yus and Chongs to seek help.

Transition to Kindergarten

For Mary and Tara kindergarten was the first time they had spent so much time away from home and parents. Their reactions to this strange new environment may have reflected the type of attachment they had to their parents since infancy (Ainsworth 1977). Most infants in the United States show "securely attached" patterns of attachment to their mothers (Crain 1992). About 20 percent of infants in the United States exhibit insecure-avoidant patterns of attachment. This means they show little or no emotion when their mother leaves them in a strange situa-

tion or when the mother returns (Crain 1992). Studies show that infants who are insecurely attached to their caregiver tend to grow up
with more emotional difficulties than those who are securely attached
(Crain 1992). In the Marschak Interaction Method (MIM) sessions, both
Mary and Tara showed an unusual lack of affect at being left alone by
their parents in a strange environment. Ainsworth might say that Mary
and Tara were insecurely attached to their parents.

A child's transition to kindergarten affects parents also. Parents are
often surprised by how emotionally difficult it is for them to leave their
child at school on the first day, and they may feel a mixture of emotions. They may celebrate this milestone in their child's growth but may
also grieve it. Parents may have concerns about the child's well-being
in the care of another adult. They may have concerns and expectations
about their child's behavior (Blatchford et al. 1982). This may have been
the case with the Chongs and the Yus.

The kindergarten teacher has the challenge of helping children adjust. Of all the challenging behaviors that children present, however,
social withdrawal is perhaps the most difficult to deal with. Blatchford
and colleagues (1982) report: "Staff feel more able to cope with an overt
reaction from children, no matter how negative. In such cases they can
gauge a child's behaviour in the context of his circumstances and more
clearly see how they might help him. The withdrawn child is, however, something of a mystery and perhaps a threat, and what behaviour
to adopt toward him is not easily specified" (p. 38). If Mary's and Tara's
teachers had had more resources or fewer children in their classrooms,
they might have been better able to attend to the girls' needs, perhaps
making therapy unnecessary.

The adjustment to kindergarten is not easy for any child, but it
can be much harder for the children of immigrants who are faced with
cultural conflicts. It must be very confusing for Asian-Canadian children if the home environment is more authoritarian and the school
environment is more permissive.

It has been reported that Chinese-Canadian schoolchildren generally feel less in control of their environments than do whites (Sue et al.
1983). Mary and Tara perhaps felt powerless at school and reacted by
changing their behavior at home, by resisting their parents' attempts
to teach them to write, and by directing older siblings (as seen in the
home video brought by Mr. Chong). The girls seemed to be behaving in
a passive-aggressive manner, as is "commonly seen in persons in a rela-

tively low power position in which overt aggression would surely lead to reprisals" (Reber 1985, p. 520). Although Mary and Tara were quite shy in the initial stages of Theraplay, they both became quite animated during the more aggressive activities such as newspaper swords. These activities allowed them to be aggressive toward one another in a safe, acceptable, and fun way.

Transition to Canada

For Chinese immigrants, as for many immigrants, adapting to a new life in a strange land can be a stressful process. In particular, rigid family systems often have difficulties dealing with immigration processes and cultural transition (Lalinec-Michaud 1988). Larger disparities between one's own cultural values and those of the host country result in more stressful adjustments (Kong 1985, Sue and Morishima 1982) and higher rates of depression (Shah 1988). Immigrants can experience social disorientation, loss of primary group support, frequent unemployment, and loss of status (Lalinec-Michaud 1988) and problems of alienation, discrimination, distrust, and the persistence of stereotyped ideas (Kong 1985).

The ability of immigrants to adapt to the new culture usually affects the development of their children (Kong 1985). Asian immigrants who maintain the same expectations after moving to the West can run into difficulties with their children who are trying to "reconcile Western values of independence with feelings of filial piety and family obligation" (Yee and Hennessy 1982, p. 62). As Kong (1985) states:

> The children of immigrant parents encounter special problems, and many do not have the resources or assistance to resolve them. These children inherit two different sets of heritages, which engender difficult conflicts. The responsibility of having to live up to the expectations of two cultures and two societies is an awesome one. Often, these children are confused and frustrated about what identity they should assume, and which behaviour mode they should adopt when they find themselves in varying life situations. [p. 188]

The emotional consequences for Asian-Canadian children are feelings of anxiety, loneliness, rejection, social isolation, passivity, and being at odds with social situations and school systems (Ho 1992, Sue and Morishima 1982, Sue et al. 1983).

Limitations of this Case of Theraplay

I believe even one visit from a sibling, extended family member, school-teacher, or some other significant person would have enhanced the case of the Chongs and the Yus. Unfortunately, due to time and staffing constraints, these other involvements were not pursued. Nevertheless, the innovative dual-family format extended the treatment beyond the family triangle so that two Asian-Canadian families were involved. In a sense, then, therapy was extended to a community. The two families did, in fact, become friends and sources of support for each other. It is possible that this format reduced some of the stigma associated with seeking professional help because both families had a problem in common.

A disadvantage of the dual-family format was the probability that the parents were initially more guarded and perhaps each family was afraid of letting the other know of their specific problems (face saving). As was noted in session 10, Mr. Chong became more animated and engaged in therapy without the Yus present. Also, the Chongs may have compared Mary with Tara and felt ashamed or distressed that their daughter was not progressing as fast. It is possible that if we had seen the Chongs separately, restraint and shame would have been minimized and Mary would have progressed faster.

An advantage of seeing two families of similar cultural backgrounds simultaneously is that it gives therapists clues to distinguish between cultural and idiosyncratic origins of behavior. While it is normal for an Asian-American family to be enmeshed (Berg and Jaya 1993) the therapists noted that Mr. Chong and his daughter were much more enmeshed in their relationship than any other duo. Both the Chongs treated Mary as if she was a puppet or a doll, but it was Mr. Chong who could not tear his eyes away from her. In session 2, Mary's first and only words to the therapist for many more sessions to come were "spilled water." These words indicated at least two possible issues: self-esteem issues (because she called attention to her "mistake") and control issues (because she expected that the therapists would do something about it for her, because she was incapable). Such expectations would not have been inconsistent for Mary given her relationship with her parents and especially her father. If her caregivers constantly hovered over her, the therapists thought, Mary had little need or opportunity to initiate action herself. It seemed that the relationship was reinforcing Mary's "passive-aggressive" or "I'm helpless . . . do it for me" manner of interacting with the world.

A structural intervention was used in session 4 (blocking the line of sight between the Chongs and Mary) in an attempt to alter the patterns of interaction between parents and child. Mr. Chong's abrupt reaction to the intervention may have indicated the extent to which the pattern was entrenched between Mary and him. In session 6, Mr. Chong seemed to be more attentive and involved with the adults than before. This may have indicated the success of that particular intervention.

In hindsight, I believe that the structural intervention was unnecessary, inconsistent with Theraplay, and perhaps damaging to therapist–client rapport. First, Berg and Jaya (1993) recommend against using such interventions because of the danger of infringing upon cultural norms of interdependency. Second, while Jernberg's Theraplay and Salvador Minuchin's structural family therapy similarly manipulate the ways in which family members behave with one another (Jernberg 1979), structural interventions lack the elements of fun and spontaneity so essential to the Theraplay approach. The intervention was then inconsistent with the overall Theraplay approach and was perhaps jarring to Mr. Chong. Third, the structural intervention was perhaps unnecessary because the execution of the five principles of Theraplay was likely enough to effect positive change. The play of Theraplay, then, by modeling and reinforcing the features of an autotelic family, may have effected changes in family relationships and facilitated the development of self-motivation in Mary and Tara. As Mrs. Yu said in the ninth session, "I've learned how to play with my kid!"

CONCLUSION

Lee (1997) noted that "the future of counselor training will lie in preparing professionals with a global perspective" (p. 284). Theraplay has an important role to play in our increasingly globally interconnected world. I believe the play aspect of Theraplay is key in bridging cultural gaps and preparing people for a cooperative future. Roopnarine and Johnson (1994) state that "Play, a dominant activity of children in all cultures, is viewed to be both a cause and effect of culture. Play is an expression of a particular culture; play is an important context or vehicle for cultural learning/transmission, as well as an indicator and reflection of child development" (p. 5). Huizinga in 1950 wrote that "Play is older than culture" (p. 1) and "Pure play is one of the main bases of civilization." (p. 5).

Keith and Whitaker (1981) believe that play expands one's reality. Theraplay may be an alternative to mainstream psychological approaches which fall short of promoting respect and appreciation for different constructions of reality evolving out of different contexts (Lerner 1989). Theraplay is consistent with many of the values of multicultural counseling theory. Theraplay is sensitive to cultural differences, structured and brief, focused on activity versus talk, and it promotes family ties and the reciprocal, creative process of human development. Given Theraplay's apparent success with diverse populations, it is surprising that workers in the field of multicultural counseling and therapy have not taken notice.

MIM ACTIVITIES

Exchange Hats
Type: Playful
Materials: Four or five dress up hats
Procedure: Parent is instructed to exchange hats with other family members

Squeaky Toys
Type: Playful
Materials: Two or three small squeaky toys
Procedure: Parent is instructed to play with squeaky toys with child

Drawing
Type: Playful
Materials: Two pieces of 8.5" X 11" drawing paper, coloring pencils
Procedure: Parent is instructed to draw anything together with child

Powdering
Type: Nurturing
Materials: One container of baby powder
Procedure: Parent is instructed to put baby powder on child's hands

Feeding
Type: Nurturing
Materials: Potato chips
Procedure: Parent is instructed to have family feed each other

REFERENCES

Adamson, W. C. (1981). Review of the book Theraplay: A New Treatment Using Structured Play for Problem Children and Their Families. *Journal of Marital and Family Therapy* 406–407.

Ainsworth, M. D. S. (1977). Attachment theory and its utility in cross-cultural research. In *Culture and Infancy: Variations in the Human Experience*, ed. P. H. Leiderman, S. R. Tulkin, and A. Rosenfeld, pp. 49–67. New York: Academic Press.

Baumrind, D. (1967). Child care practices anteceding three patterns of preschool behavior. *Genetic Psychology Monographs* 75:43–88.

Berg, I. K., and Jaya, A. (1993). Different and same: family therapy with Asian-American families. *Journal of Marital and Family Therapy* 19(1):31–38.

Blatchford, P., Battle, S., and Mays, J. (1982). *The First Transition: Home to School*. Windsor, GB: NFER-Nelson.

Burton, G., and Dimbleby, R. (1995). *Between Ourselves: An Introduction to Interpersonal Communication*. London: Arnold.

Corey, G. (1991). *Theory and Practice of Counselling and Psychotherapy*, 4th ed. Pacific Grove, CA: Brooks/Cole.

Crain, W. (1992). *Theories of Development: Concepts and Applications*, 3rd Ed. Englewood Cliffs, NJ: Prentice Hall.

Csikszentmihalyi, M. (1993). *The Evolving Self: A Psychology for the Third Millennium*. New York: HarperCollins.

——— (1997). *Finding Flow: The Psychology of Engagement with Everyday Life*. New York: Basic Books.

Department of Multiculturalism and Citizenship Canada, Citizenship Registration and Promotion. (1991). *Canadian Citizenship Statistics*.

Ellis, M. J. (1973). *Why People Play*. Englewood Cliffs, NJ: Prentice-Hall.

Fine, M. J. (1992). A systems-ecological perspective on home-school intervention. In *The Handbook of Family-School Intervention: A Systems Perspective*, ed. M. Fine and C. Carlson, pp. 1–17. Boston: Allyn & Bacon.

Hall, E. T. (1976). *Beyond Culture*. Garden City, NY: Anchor Press/ Doubleday.

Ho, M. K. (1992). Asian-American students: family influences. In *The Handbook of Family-School Intervention: A Systems Perspective*, ed. M. J. Fine and C. Carlson, pp. 75–85. Boston: Allyn & Bacon.

Horton, A. H., Clance, P. R., Sterk-Elifşon, C., and Emshoff, J. (1995). Touch in psychotherapy: a survey of patients' experiences. *Psychotherapy* 32(3):443–457.

Huizinga, J. (1950). *Homo Ludens: A Study of the Play Element in Culture*. Boston: Beacon.

Jacobvitz, D.B., and Bush, N.F. (1996). Reconstructions of family relationships: parent–child alliances, personal distress, and self-esteem. *Developmental Psychology*, 32(4):732–743.

Jernberg, A. M. (1979). *Theraplay*. San Francisco: Jossey-Bass.

Keith, D. V., and Whitaker, C. A. (1981). Play therapy: a paradigm for work with families. *Journal of Marital and Family Therapy* 243–254.

Koller, T. J., and Booth, P. (1997). Fostering attachment through family Theraplay. In *Play Therapy: Theory and Practice—A Comparative Presentation*, ed. K. J. O'Connor and L. M. Braverman, pp. 204–233. New York: Wiley.

Kong, S. L. (1985). Counselling Chinese immigrants: issues and answers. In *Intercultural Counselling and Assessment: Global Perspectives*, ed. R. J. Samuto and A. Wolfgang, pp. 181–189. Toronto: C. J. Hogrefe.

Lalinec-Michaud, M. (1988). Three cases of suicide in Chinese-Canadian women. *Canadian Journal of Psychiatry* 33(2):153–156.

Lam, C. M. (1997). A cultural perspective on the study of Chinese adolescent development. *Child and Adolescent Social Work Journal* 14(2): 95–113.

Leach, M. M. (1997). Training global psychologists: an introduction. *International Journal of Intercultural Relations* 21(2):161–174.

Lee, C. C. (1997). The global future of professional counseling: collaboration for international social change. *International Journal of Intercultural Relations* 21(2):279–285.

Lerner, H. G. (1989). *The Dance of Intimacy*. New York: Harper & Row.

McLaughlin, J. T. (1993). Touching limits in the analytic dyad. *Psychoanalytic Quarterly* 64:433–465.

Pagani-Tousignant, C. (1992). *Breaking the Rules: Counselling Ethnic Minorities*. Minneapolis, MN: Johnson Institute.

Pan, H. W. (1994). Children's play in Taiwan. In *Children's Play in Diverse Cultures*, ed. J. L. Roopnarine, J. E. Johnson, and F. Hooper, pp. 31–50. Albany, NY: State University of New York Press.

Paré, D. A. (1995). Of families and other cultures: the shifting paradigm of family therapy. *Family Process* 34:1–19.

Pedersen, P. (1988). *A Handbook for Developing Multicultural Awareness*. Alexandria, VA: American Association for Counselling and Development.

Rathunde, K. (1988). Optimal experience and the family context. In *Optimal Experience: Psychological Studies of Flow in Consciousness*, ed. M. Csikszentmihalyi and I. S. Csikszentmihalyi, pp. 342–363. New York: Cambridge University Press.

Reber, A. S. (1985). *The Dictionary of Psychology*. London: Penguin.

Rogoff, B. (1993). Children's guided participation and participatory appropriation in sociocultural activity. In *Development in Context: Acting and Thinking in Specific Environments*, ed. R. H. Wozniak and K. W. Fisher, pp. 121–152. Hillsdale, NJ: Lawrence Erlbaum.

Rogoff, B., Mistry, J., Radziszewska, B., and Germond, J. (1992). Infants' instrumental social interaction with adults. In *Social Referencing and the Social Construction of Reality in Infancy*, ed. S. Feinman, pp. 323–348. New York: Plenum.

Roopnarine, J. L.,and Johnson, J. E. (1994). The need to look at play in diverse cultural settings. In *Children's Play in Diverse Cultures*, ed. J. L. Roopnarine, J. E. Johnson, and F. Hooper, pp. 1–8. Albany, NY: State University of New York Press.

Rubin, K. H., and Both, L. (1991). Dyadic play behaviors of children of well and depressed mothers. *Development and Psychopathology* 3(3): 243–251.

Seligman, M. E. P. (1995). *The Optimistic Child: A Revolutionary Program that Safeguards Children Against Depression and Builds Lifelong Resilience*. Boston: Houghton Mifflin.

Shah, A. A. (1988). Cultural disparity and lack of social anchorage in the host country as contributing factors toward reactive depression in immigrants. *Pakistan Journal of Psychological Research* 3 (3–4): 11–21.

Stern, D. (1977). *The First Relationship: Mother and Infant*. Cambridge, MA: Harvard University Press.

Sue, D. W., Arrendondo, P., and McDavis, R. J. (1992). Multicultural counseling competencies and standards: a call to the profession. *Journal of Counseling and Development* 70:477–486.

Sue, D., Sue, D. W., and Sue, D. M. (1983). Psychological development of Chinese-American children. In *The Psychosocial Development of Minority Group Children*, ed. G. J. Powell, pp. 159–166. New York: Brunner/Mazel.

Sue, D. W., and Sue, D. (1990). *Counseling the Culturally Different: Theory and Practice*. New York: Wiley.

Sue, S., and Morishima, J. K. (1982). *The Mental Health of Asian Americans*. San Francisco: Jossey-Bass.

Tafarodi, R. W., and Swann, W. B. (1996). Individualism-collectivism and global self-esteem: evidence for a cultural trade-off. *Journal of Cross-Cultural Psychology* 27(6):651–672.

Uzgiris, I. C. (1996). Together and apart: the enactment of values in infancy. In *Values and Knowledge*, ed. E. S. Reed, E. Turiel, and T. Brown, pp. 17–39. Mahwah, NJ: Lawrence Erlbaum.

Uzgiris, I. C., and Weizmann, F. (1977). *The Structuring of Experience*. New York: Plenum.

Yee, B. W. K., and Hennessy, S. T. (1982). Pacific/Asian American families and mental health. In *Perspectives on Minority Group Mental Health*, ed. F. U. Munoz and R. Endo, pp. 53–70. Washington, DC: University Press of America.

Young, N. F. (1972). Independence training from a cross-cultural perspective. *American Anthropologist* 74:629–638.

11

Multiple Family Theraplay

JAMIE SHERMAN

RESEARCH

Traditional family therapy has focused on a family systems approach within a single family setting. Therapeutic intervention in this form is often long-term and slow in developing because it doesn't duplicate society, relies on egocentric descriptions of problems, and only partially influences the child–parent relationship. Multiple-family group therapy may assist in overcoming some of these problems (Szymanski and Kiernan 1983). Treating families in a multiple-family group has proven effective in a number of studies in helping families develop coping strategies. Families affected by Huntington's disease benefited through the mobilization of hope and altruism and a lessening of the sense of isolation and helplessness in coping with the illness (Murburg et al. 1988). Similar benefit of networking and support were found in studies with schizophrenic clients who showed a lower risk of relapse in a multiple-family group setting (Mcfarlane et al. 1993). A study of residential schizophrenic patients revealed that any form of short-term therapy could be useful in producing a positive systemic change as long as it makes use of a multiple-family group setting. The key elements of change in a multiple family setting are information about the mental illness, a supportive and nonjudgmental atmosphere and participation by several families and by both parents and patients (Mills and Hansen 1991). In the absence of a multiple-family grouping, family satisfaction decreases (Bauer-Anstadt 1984).

The use of Theraplay in the treatment of childhood dysfunction has become a strong and emergent force in the mental health profession, and is now starting to make inroads in related fields. Traditionally, Theraplay is conducted with individual families (Jernberg 1979). More recently, professionals have found Theraplay to be useful in a variety of settings and styles. Phyllis Rubin and Jeanine Tregay (1989) encourage the use of Theraplay beyond the traditional approach:

> A Theraplay group makes a family out of your class. It can develop greater understanding between the children, more awareness of each child as a unique and special individual with both strengths and weaknesses, and can increase the children's tolerance of differences. In becoming a healthy family, the children will learn to get along with others, to stand up for themselves as well as others, to care about each other, to be honest about their feelings, and to support others with constructive criticism, empathy, and nurturing. [p. 24]

The notion of developing a sense of family among unrelated individuals was explored by Rubin (1995) at a shelter for homeless women (see Chapter 12). She introduced the concept of multiple family Theraplay at this setting in an attempt to improve the playfulness of mothers and children because "the women felt undermined as mothers by homeless life in general and that mother–child attachment had suffered early-on. . . . The mothers said that Theraplay groups helped them learn that it was okay to play with their children" (p. 5).

A Theraplay group for women in a public housing program also explored the notion of the healthy family. These women didn't receive nurturing when they were children and subsequently found it difficult to develop close relationships with their children and other adults. Three facilitators brought ten women together in a group known as "Family Magic." The facilitators said the women "didn't know each other initially, became more coalesced, had more fun together, were more enthusiastic and involved than other [Family Magic] groups" (Leslie and

Mignon 1995, p. 6). Interestingly, these women chose not to include their children in these activities because they didn't want to destroy the fabric of the group. The authors, however, were hopeful that the increased playfulness the mothers demonstrated with each other would also lead to increased playfulness with their children.

Some of the problems a child faces are manifestations of familial dysfunction, represented in both the parent–child and sibling dynamics. Therefore, it is necessary to treat the family as a group whenever possible and, as multiple family therapy has demonstrated, the treatment of more than one family simultaneously may benefit the intrapersonal and interpersonal dynamics of each family involved in treatment. This approach offers the opportunity to address issues of individual pathology as well as peer interaction and family dynamic. This chapter focuses on a dual, two-child family treatment that was conducted at the Blue Hills Child and Family Services in Aurora, Ontario.

SUBJECTS AND HISTORY

The De Niros were a two-parent family with two boys, William and Thomas, aged 11 and 4½. Bill, the father, worked full time, and Maria, the mother, held two part-time jobs during the evenings and on weekends. As a result, they relied heavily on Maria's parents for support and baby-sitting. Tragically, Maria's father, who had been suffering from a terminal illness, died just prior to the commencement of the Theraplay sessions. The children were very close to their grandparents and were affected by their grandfather's death, particularly Thomas, who was so traumatized that his mother resorted to traveling with a cell phone in case he needed to speak with her. Bill, who was physically abused as a child and tried very hard as an adult to connect with his kids, found it difficult to care for both children at the same time while his wife was working, so William would often sleep over at his grandparent's house while Thomas stayed home.

William presented as a polite, outgoing, and charming preteen. He was very creative and enjoyed entertaining, which he demonstrated during the Marschak Interaction Method (MIM). His wide smile and confident manner, however, were not indicative of his underlying emotional turbulence. William had very strong feelings of rejection, at home as well as at school. His ostracism at school, coupled with his percep-

tion that everybody idolized his brother, left him with feelings of inadequacy and jealousy, which manifested in aggression toward his
brother, emotional distancing from his father, and verbal and physical
abuse toward his mother. He experienced difficulty at school, had few
friends, and was described as awkward and a social outcast. Thomas
was a quiet, shy, and somewhat withdrawn 4½-year-old boy. He had
very striking facial features: large brown eyes and a gentle smile. Thomas had a very low tolerance for frustration and quickly dissolved into
tears if he didn't get his way, as evidenced by his near tantrum during
the Marschak.

The Kelly family was headed by a single mother, Judith, who grew
up in a large reconstituted family. She recalled being left to fend for
herself as a middle child, and having feelings of loneliness. She had an
8-year old girl, Heather, and a 7-year old boy, Simon. The children's
contact with their biological father was kept to a minimum because
Judith felt he was irresponsible and manipulative. She had kicked him
out of the house two years ago because of his gambling and drug ad-
dictions. Judith relied heavily on her mother and stepfather for be-
fore-school care of the children, as she had a daily one-hour commute
to work. She would pick up the children from day care in the early
evening and race home to make dinner, complete household chores,
and conduct bedtime routines, while trying to maintain equal time
for each child. Both Simon and Heather were constantly embattled and
vying for the attention of their mother, placing strenuous demands
on her time and energy. Due to the tremendous responsibility she
assumed after her separation, Judith found it difficult to divide her
time equitably. Sometimes she appeared to favor Simon and was more
forgiving of his misbehaviors. This often resulted in sibling fighting
and protestations. Brazelton (1992) writes that jealousy over perceived
differences in attention, and subsequent parental guilt and intervention over the eventual sibling squabbling, forms the basis of most
sibling rivalry.

The Kellys lived in a low-income housing development. Judith was
very protective of her children and didn't let them play outside unsu-
pervised. She was reluctant to arrange for playmates because they had
no friends in the area, and their close friends lived too far away.

Heather was a somewhat sullen and withdrawn child who had a
poor self-image and very low self-esteem. She had benefited from a
remedial program for a reading disability. Simon was a highly active,

impulsive, rough child. He was experiencing a great deal of difficulty at school behaviorally and academically and was in a behavioral modification program designed to help him establish self-control and improve his attention while completing school work. Simon had difficulty playing with peers and didn't get along well with his teachers.

WHY THERAPLAY WAS CHOSEN

The families were referred to Blue Hills because of the behavioral difficulties their children were experiencing at home and school. The family history and MIM for these two families brought to light five common areas of dysfunction (1) a tenuous family attachment for at least one of the children, (2) a shortage of time for the family to spend together; (3) control issues, specifically around setting limits and boundaries; (4) sibling rivalry; and (5) coping strategies. As mentioned earlier, the parents had jobs and thus were not home for extended periods of time. In addition, the parents had difficulty setting appropriate limits and held different expectations for their children, which resulted in intense sibling rivalries. These issues led the parents to question their ability to manage their children, which led them to Theraplay.

The following goals were set for these families: (1) to increase parents' nurturing of children; (2) to increase parental control over children in a consistent manner; (3) to build self-esteem for parents and children; (4) to reduce intensity of sibling rivalries; (5) to increase positive, playful family time together. Perhaps the greatest strength both families had was their potential for playfulness.

INNOVATIONS

The therapist team attempted to conduct family Theraplay within a multifamily, multisibling setting without compromising the process of connection between client and therapist. To accomplish this goal, a number of criteria had to be met. Minimizing distractions, establishing control, developing pacing, defining boundaries, and establishing an environment of trust were key elements. These elements are discussed within the context of individual activities, group activities, and counseling sessions.

To establish and maintain structure and routine, one activity menu was devised for the group as a whole, even when the clients were doing individual activities. This served a dual purpose. First, it allowed the clients to focus solely on their own schedule without being concerned with what their sibling was doing, and second, it allowed the therapists to proceed at the same pace. Although the latter point reduced the spontaneity of some therapists, it was vital for the continuity of the session. Appointing one therapist to set the pace during activities removed the guesswork from when to shift activities. The leader took into account the pacing of each activity within the dyads, as well as the overall session time.

Another important consideration was how to create effective space for each dyad. To minimize distractions, the therapists sat in a corner of the room with their clients facing them. This became relevant during the first session as one therapist mistakenly reversed the setup, allowing her client to survey the entire room. This made for a dubious opening for the first few minutes, as she had to fight for his attention. Additionally, each child and therapist sat on his or her own pillow. This marked the physical and emotional boundary for the children by establishing the area where they received most of their nurturing.

Group Theraplay sessions with children have proven very effective in improving communication and social skills and reducing aggression (Rubin and Tregay 1989). In the present families the benefit these children derived from participating in group activities was crucial to their development. The therapists modeled appropriate interaction styles for the children and mediated on behalf of them. This resulted in increased self-esteem, community spirit, empathy, and playfulness. During the seventh session, Simon, an impulsive child with a lack of awareness of others, was concerned there weren't enough chips for the other children. Demonstrating an increased capacity for empathy and fairness, he counted out an equal number of chips for everybody.

The parent counseling sessions proved to be slow in developing during the initial stages because the parents were uncomfortable sharing personal information with another family. However, once they realized the benefit to be gained from listening to another family's experiences, and sharing their difficulties, they quickly warmed to the idea. The combination of professional and peer advice was very effective for both families.

TREATMENT PROGRESS

The first four sessions were divided into three segments: group activities, individual activities, and more group activities. Therapists and clients entered the room as a group and the therapists welcomed everybody together. The dyads then separated into their separate corners where Inventory and Lotioning Hurts on the children's hands and arms were done along with several other nurturing and self-awareness activities. This was the time available to each therapist to bond and connect with his or her client. Time was left during the last few minutes for two or three group activities with goals such as communication, social skills, and sibling interaction, and a goodbye song and hug. The last four sessions were divided into four segments: group activities without parents, individual activities, family activities, and whole-group activities with both sets of parents participating.

The first two sessions proceeded somewhat cautiously because it took longer for a large group to build an atmosphere of trust. As a result, the sessions included nonthreatening, engaging activities such as Hand Outline, Silly Bones, and Mirroring (where client and therapist simultaneously copy the body actions of each other) (see Appendix for description of activities). During these introductory sessions most of the activities, including feeding, were done in dyads. However, more engaging and nurturing activities, such as Handprints, Washing and Powdering Hands and Feet, and Popcorn Toes, were introduced as the level of trust and comfort increased. Concurrently, individual activities were decreased and group activities were increased because the children had bonded well with and trusted their therapists. A barometer for this change was William, who had issues regarding control and parentified behavior, but had become quite compliant.

During the fourth session the therapists built on the high trust level by engaging the children in a very effective cradling activity. Three events were crucial to the success of this session. First, there was a slow buildup of intrusive activities leading into the highly nurturing cradle. Second, just prior to cradling the children, the therapists turned their backs to the center of the room so each dyad was facing the corner. Third, this session represented the first time the children were fed as a group. This acted as a catalyst for group cohesion as the children displayed more empathic and prosocial behaviors.

The fifth session was the first time the parents entered the room. There was a noticeable difference in the children's behavior because, upon seeing their parents, they displayed behaviors more typical of home life. Now the role of the therapist was to transfer the connectedness that was built up over the previous four sessions to the parent–child relationship. To accomplish this the therapists split the room in half, with each family engaging in family-oriented activities aimed at developing the nurturing abilities of parents and decreasing the conflictual relationship of the siblings. As opposed to the initial sessions, when the therapists slowly built up a sense of trust and confidence, the parents were encouraged to be as engaging as possible in order to send this message to their children: "I love you and I enjoy being with you because you are important to my life." As a result, the kids hid under the blanket with their therapists. From those initial squeals of anticipation until the parents, in mock surprise, peeled back the covers, came an emotional transfer of this connectedness. The blanket swing (in which each child had a turn being swung in a blanket by parents, therapists, and other children) was an actual physical and symbolic transfer of this relationship, and from this point on the therapists gradually diminished their leadership role and handed over more responsibility to the parents.

One other area of concern was maintaining continuity during the hello and goodbye songs. This was a problem during the first session as the song was not practiced and resulted in a flat beginning. The song was firmed up the next session as the lead therapist called out the starting point. This allowed the therapists and the children to sing in sync, and energized the group at the start and finish of each session.

After a few separate activities, both families met in the center of the room. Everybody participated in a game of balloon toss, to burn off energy and bond as a group. This continued in one more intimate group activity, and then in feeding chips to everyone. From this point on the therapists continued to encourage nurturing and engagement of their children during individual family time and increased the number of group activities involving both families together where structure and playfulness were stressed.

The parent counseling sessions needed to develop slowly because unfamiliarity among adults also leads to discomfort and uncertainty. The first parent counseling session was the first moment that the parents of these families were asked to interact with each other. The family history, MIM and MIM feedback sessions were all done separately beforehand. While the parents spent time with each other in the observation room watching the first session unfold, there were two interpreting therapists acting as buffers between the two parties. The parent counseling sessions allowed the parents to concentrate on hearing and speaking to each other for the very first time.

However, this relationship also needed to be nurtured and soothed to the point where the parents would freely exchange information and not hold back regarding their own self-image and hidden concerns. For these sessions to work properly, the parents needed time to "check out everybody." They needed to know, just as their children did, that this was a safe place to question one's thoughts and uncertainties without fear of reproach or meeting with disapproval. Until all the adults felt this secure base, they were not going to take many risks. The parents were all very tentative during the first few sessions, responding with extremely safe answers, directing their discussion to the authority figures, and choosing not to explore their own personal family dysfunctions in the presence of strangers.

The parents began to loosen up as the sessions proceeded. Their body language become more inviting, and they began to make more consistent eye contact with all members of the counseling sessions, not just the lead therapists. This trust building was coincidental with the entrance of the parents into the therapy room. For parents who themselves lacked proper doses of nurturing and feelings of self-worth as children, it was not surprising that they would gain a sense of trust and confidence in a place that greatly valued these ideals. Quite naturally, the parents began to open up with more confidence and spoke more accurately about their family situations. Perhaps even more valuable was the open dialogue in which all three parents, especially the two mothers, engaged.

PROBLEMS AND SOLUTIONS

Although significant progress was made with these families, the sessions had difficulties. There were problems that arose during the course of the Theraplay activities that could not have been foreseen in the planning stage. Given the size of the room and the number of people in it, it was understandable that in a few instances therapists encroached on the territory of other dyads during individual activities. An example follows, where dyads were engaged in Ping-Pong Ball Blow while lying on the floor facing each other.

All four pairs were in their respective corners, having a great deal of fun, when one pair's Ping-Pong ball got loose. Instead of immediately returning to their spot, the therapist carried the activity within 2 or 3 feet of another pair, at which point she picked up the ball, returned to her spot, and asked her client to return to his, which he did gleefully. Rather surprisingly, the other pair was not disturbed in the least because the client had his back to the action and was so engrossed in the activity he did not see the disturbance. The most amazing part of this episode was that the client who ignored the encroachment was the most impulsive and hyperactive of the four, so if *he* wasn't affected by the disturbance then probably nobody would be. After discussing the issue, the therapists resolved to be very conscious of not repeating the episode, ensuring that future activities would be controlled more effectively.

The pacing of the individual activities became problematic. As mentioned earlier, the lead therapist was responsible for setting the pace. However, the therapists also had to judge it according to the acceptance level of their own client, leading to confusion as the therapists fell out of sync with one another. This was corrected by sticking to the schedule and, if somebody fell behind, dropping activities as necessary. Although this format did not allow for a great deal of spontaneity on the part of the therapist, it did keep everybody on the same agenda.

Also problematic was pacing during the family activities. Occasionally one team become more engrossed than the other team because of therapeutic issues being addressed. The inherent difficulty was when one family finished before the other; the idle family would then observe the participating family. In the case of these particular families, the De Niros enjoyed themselves more and had more spirit and vitality than the Kellys. The Kellys were drawn to the playfulness of the De Niros, which led to issues of self-image. It was essential to have a repertoire of activities in which to engage the idle family while they waited for the participating family to finish.

One concern that arose occasionally was the therapists' lack of awareness of the mood and feelings of their clients during group activities. On one occasion the group participated in a high-energy activity, which had everybody exchange places on the carpet, followed by a group hug. One therapist was unable to position himself beside his client during the hug, and the client, who was playful and cooperative throughout the session, suddenly became somewhat withdrawn. It became obvious to the team after reviewing the incident on video that some fast-paced activities could leave a child feeling isolated if his therapist wasn't nearby. As a result the therapists became much more aware of positioning and placement during the group activities.

RESULTS

The results for both families were quite positive. The De Niros developed insight into their family dynamics and made significant gains. The parents were much more nurturing of their children and of each other. The feeding activities alone were illustrative of a family that gave freely to one another, was sensitive to each other's needs, and relied on each other. Even during the first MIM there were indications that this group of people held a deep-seated sense of family. The Theraplay treatment, and the willingness of this family to continue these activities at home, allowed this playfulness to manifest in positive ways. Bill and Maria were very supportive of each other, projected an outward connectedness, and a complementary relationship. As a result, they were more confident in their parenting style and had a much better self-image. William no longer displayed signs of a parentified child, as he handed over control to his parents.

Some areas of concern were Thomas's tantrums and William's rejection of his father. It was predicted that Thomas's behaviors would dissipate as his parents developed consistency in their approach to him. Dad had some insight regarding the resentment and rejection William felt. William was resentful of Thomas because he interfered in the private time between William and their father, and felt his father preferred to spend time with Thomas rather than him. Bill allowed Thomas to interfere because, as he said, "He is so young. What can I do?" If Bill did assign a time out, Thomas wouldn't sit still. Bill was overwhelmed because he handled a great deal of the child-rearing duties while his wife worked. He was also confused because when he did arrange for private time with William, sometimes his son was either uninterested or chose to spend time with his friends instead.

Maria felt a sense of guilt over not spending more family time together because she worked evenings and weekends. She had decided to
put her real estate career on hold in order to spend more time with her
family. While this represented a tremendous financial sacrifice, she
understood and appreciated the gains the family had made by spending time together. The sacrifices they made now would lead to greater
payoffs later in life.

The gains made by the Kelly family included a closer relationship
between Judith and Heather, Simon's improved social skills during
group activities, and insight gained by Judith regarding the source of
her children's conflictual relationship. Despite this insight, Judith still
found it difficult to change the inconsistency with which she treated
her children. When the observation was made that she controlled and
rejected Heather far more than she did Simon, she agreed and noted that
her own mother had made the same observation. However, she found
it difficult to limit Simon because of his behavior and said it was easier
to let him go unchecked at times. She felt sorry for Simon because of
his learning difficulties and tended to forgive his misbehaviors.

Judith was very protective of her children and experienced a high
degree of denial regarding Simon's behaviors. Our suggestion that Judith
pursue a complete psychoeducational assessment for Simon to investigate the nature of his potential learning difficulties was met with resentment. She did, however, mention that she was going to take him
back to her doctor for another assessment at the school's behest. It was
our opinion that Simon reacted in a negative manner to stressful academic situations (being uncooperative, sulky, easily distracted, etc.);
consequently, his learning difficulties needed to be addressed before
expectations were set for his behavior.

Ultimately, the gains made by the De Niros exceeded those made
by the Kellys because Judith continued to deny many of Simon's difficulties, preferring to blame his school environment for his problems.
The De Niros made key revelations and significant changes during the
course of the Theraplay by understanding the effect of their behavior
on their family dynamics. However, during the second follow-up session with the Kellys, the therapists noted a dramatic improvement in
the sibling relationship. When this was pointed out to Judith during
the counseling session, she concurred and noted that she encouraged
her children to rely on each other for help and support while she attended to domestic responsibilities. This encouraged a greater bond be-

tween Simon and Heather, reduced the intensity of their sibling rivalry, and reduced Judith's levels of anxiety and stress.

FUTURE DIRECTIONS

In using the multiple-family Theraplay it is important to match the families based on demographics. The demographics and variables to be considered are the number of parents, ages of parents, ages of children, nature of clients' dysfunction, and parenting styles. In the present case, a single mother was included with a married couple—not an ideal combination—because of waiting list constraints. When considering possible combinations, it is important to account for as many of the unknown variables as possible. An important factor is the degree to which the parents get along with each other.

Following is a list of strategies one might consider when conducting this form of Theraplay. During the entrance and welcome song, it is advisable to include a group activity as an icebreaker to establish cohesion within the group, introduce the clients to each other, and loosen everybody up for the individual activities. Although this reduces the number of activities during individual, family, or group time, it will have positive long-term effects. In addition, it may be effective to maintain two or three activities during individual activity time, beyond the fourth session. This would help the therapists maintain and consolidate a strong bond with their client, and, perhaps more important, relax the children for their parents' entrance.

It is important to account for individual preferences. For instance, some children may completely reject lotion but be more tolerant of powder. If the activity calls for a back massage, but one client is ambivalent about the intrusive nature of the activity, then for her alone the activity could be changed to tracing letters on the back, which is just as intrusive but disguised in the form of a challenging activity. The net result, then, is that the activity doesn't have to be exactly the same for each client, but rather can be modified according to individual needs.

Another benefit of this approach is that siblings often argue when they deem their relationships with their parents to be inequitable or attention to be unequally distributed. This offers therapists an opportunity to give each child the same amount of attention, but to vary the activities as a way of saying, "You don't have to do exactly the same thing in order to be appreciated. You are different from your sibling and have different preferences. Don't feel as though you have to emulate your sibling precisely in order to receive the same love and attention from adults." The parents can then apply this strategy at home during times of intense sibling rivalry.

Since the therapists and their clients sometimes only spend 10 to 15 minutes of the therapy session together building their relationship before the group activities start, the bond is not going to develop between the therapist and client at the same rate as it would during individual Theraplay sessions, where the entire session is devoted to individual activities with the client. To compensate for this slower developing relationship, one may want to consider a twelve–session (or longer) course of treatment rather than the traditional eight sessions.

SUMMARY

Theraplay has proven effective in a number of settings using a variety of styles. This chapter demonstrated the effectiveness of multiple family Theraplay with two siblings in each family. The purpose of this form of Theraplay is to address the concerns of each individual child while simultaneously improving social skills and peer interaction styles through the improvement of the family atmosphere. When Theraplay started for these families, the parents were not nurturing their children enough, the children were experiencing intense sibling rivalries, the children were unmanageable, and the families were not spending much playful time together. The goals for these families were to increase parents' nurturing of children, increase parental control, build the self-esteem of parents and children, reduce intensity of sibling rivalry, and increase family playfulness. Theraplay sessions included individual, family, and group activities. These families showed significant improvement in nurturing style, parental control, family playfulness, confidence, and interaction levels. The siblings also showed a significant decrease in the intensity of their rivalries.

Due to the lack of time therapists spend with their clients alone during Theraplay sessions, it takes longer for the therapist and client to connect, as opposed to the bonding during individual Theraplay sessions. As a result, future Theraplay involving multiple families and multiple siblings might consider a twelve-week course of treatment as opposed to the traditional eight weeks.

One of the great attractions of Theraplay is that professionals from nearly every spectrum of the mental health profession have found a common form of therapeutic treatment in which most individuals, regardless of their background, can contribute effectively. Psychologists, nurses, special education teachers, social workers, child-care and residential workers, and others are able to pool their resources in a multidisciplinary effort with the goal of improving family relationships.

ACKNOWLEDGMENTS

I wish to acknowledge the collaborative effort of the therapy team—Dr. Evangeline Munns, Carmen Presutti, Stephanie Vickers, and Marcel Wegman—who helped to make the course of treatment for these families fun and successful.

REFERENCES

Bauer-Anstadt, S. (1984). Method for the study of the effectiveness of attendance in the multi-family group on overall client treatment in a day hospital setting. *International Journal of Partial Hospitalization* 2(3):219–232.

Brazelton, T. (1992). *Touchpoints*. Reading, MA:Addison-Wesley.

Jernberg, A. (1979). *Theraplay*. San Francisco: Jossey-Bass.

Leslie, E., and Mignon, N. (1995). Group theraplay for parents in a public housing programme. *The Theraplay Institute Newsletter*, Fall, pp. 6–7, Chicago.

Mcfarlane, W., Dunne, E., Lukens, E., et al. (1993). From research to clinical practice: dissemination of New York State's family psychoeducational project. *Hospital and Community Psychiatry* 44(3):265–270.

Mills, P., and Hansen, J. (1991). Short-term group interventions for mentally ill young adults living in a community residence and their families. *Hospital and Community Psychiatry* 42(11):1144–1150.

Murburg, M., Price, L., and Jalali, B. (1988). Huntington's disease: therapy strategies. *Family Systems Medicine* 6(3):290–303.

Rubin, P. (1995). Multi-family theraplay in a shelter for the homeless. *The Theraplay Institute Newsletter*, Fall, p. 5, Chicago.

Rubin, P., and Tregay, J. (1989). *Play with Them: Theraplay Groups in the Classroom*. Springfield, IL: Charles C Thomas.

Szymanski, L., and Kiernan, W. (1983). Multiple family group therapy with developmentally disabled adolescents and young adults. *International Journal of Group Psychotherapy* 33(4):521–534.

12

Multifamily Theraplay Groups with Homeless Mothers and Children

PHYLLIS B. RUBIN

Shelters for homeless women and children provide logical settings as well as special challenges for Theraplay groups. One can intuitively see that play and nurturing would be of therapeutic benefit to children who have suffered the disruption of losing their home. They have had to cope with seeing their mothers deal with the stress of being or becoming homeless and must now live with their family in a place that is not their own. Their mothers, having lost some degree of privacy and control over their daily lives, are stressed as they adjust or resist adjusting to the demands of shelter life (Goodman et al. 1991, Rubin 1996). Having lost their connection to home, kinfolk, and personal possessions, stressed homeless mothers are often unable to provide their children with the types of stimulating and affectionate parent–child interactions that promote self-esteem and cognitive development (Koblinsky et al. 1997).

Some researchers have concluded that the experience of homelessness impairs a mother's ability to parent (Banyard and Graham-Bermann 1995, Hausman and Hammen 1993, Koblinsky et al. 1997). Because of financial limitations, frequent moves, and the need to leave possessions, mothers who become homeless tend to have few toys, books, or other stimulating materials with which their children can explore, manipulate, and gain mastery (Koblinsky et al. 1997). Such mothers, more focused on survival needs, tend to spend less time teaching their children or taking them out in the world to learn first-hand about their environment. The concomitants of homelessness—stress, emotional depletion, and the hypervigilance necessitated by crowded conditions and loss of privacy—decrease a mother's ability to nurture and respond to her children. Women often feel disempowered and undermined as mothers by shelter staff (Banyard and Graham-Bermann 1995, Rubin 1996). Tensions increase when mothers criticize others' children and when mothers, to ward off their disapproving peers or the shelter staff, criticize their own children (Hausman and Hammen 1993). Relationships between the mothers, between mothers and staff, and between parent and child quickly become impaired.

According to this argument, the child, suffering from the loss of adequate parenting and the disruptions inherent in sheltered life, manifests learning and social-emotional problems. Such conclusions imply that, were these families not homeless, the quality of the parent–child interaction might be better, and children might show normal cognitive and emotional growth. There is substantial evidence, however, that the mental health needs of homeless women and children predate the situational stress related to the homelessness. Research into the early lives of homeless women has revealed chronic experiences of separation, loss, and abuse known to be associated with insecure attachment. Homeless women are more likely than housed poor women to have been separated from primary caregivers during childhood as a result of marital separation, divorce, death of a parent, substance abuse in the family, or removal from the home due to child abuse (Bassuk 1986, Bassuk et al. 1986, Goodman 1991a, Shinn et al. 1991). They may have lived for significant periods of time away from their immediate family, with relatives, foster parents, or in mental hospitals. So likely are homeless women to have suffered physical and sexual abuse in childhood and/or adulthood (Bassuk 1990, Bassuk amd Gallagher 1990, Bassuk and Rosenberg 1988, D'Ercole & Struening 1990, Goodman et al. 1995, Wood et al. 1990) and to manifest symptoms of posttraumatic stress disorder that developed prior to the first episode of homelessness (Browne 1993, North and Smith, cited in Browne 1993), that violent victimization can be considered normative in this group (Goodman et al. 1995).

Children of these mothers tend to have developmental delays in language and fine and gross motor coordination, severe anxiety, depression, and academic problems (Bassuk et al. 1986, Fox et al. 1990). Although they need more stimulation and interaction, these children get less. Lenore Rubin observed, "The greatest issue for them is their mother's depression. They don't get played with, or talked to, and as a result, they get left behind" (Hirsch 1986, p. 10).

Apparent in these parent–child relationships are the long-range effects of the mothers' early traumatic history superimposed upon the trauma of the present homeless experience (Goodman et al. 1991). Clearly, both mothers and children are suffering. Attachment theory (see Chapter 4) can help us understand the needs of the mothers and the needs of the children, and can inform decisions regarding interventions.

ATTACHMENT THEORY

The development of attachment is an innate process that occurs between child and caregiver, the function of which is to ensure the child's safety and survival (Bowlby 1982). Four categories of attachment have been differentiated according to the child's experience, when distressed, of the availability and responsivity of the caregiver (Ainsworth et al. 1978, Bowlby 1973, Main and Hesse 1990, Main and Solomon 1986).

Insecure attachment patterns in children are linked to early separation from or loss of primary caregivers, and also to violence and neglect, which are traumatic conditions that pervade the histories of women who become homeless. Chronic maltreatment, whether in the form of neglect, emotional/physical/sexual abuse, or depression of the caregiver, constitutes a cumulative trauma that can have the same effect as actual separation from, or loss of, the parent (Khan 1963). Studies have shown that maltreated children are more likely than nonmaltreated comparison groups to develop insecure relationships characterized by combinations of avoidant, resistant, and confused behaviors toward the attachment figure (Carlson et al. 1989, Cicchetti and Barnett 1991, Crittenden 1988).

Improving the quality of attachment between parent and child is paramount because it serves as the basis for the child's future relationships. In a process termed "the intergenerational transmission of at-

tachment" (Bretherton 1990, Van Ijzendoorn 1992), children inter-
nalize the meanings, feelings, and behaviors that characterize interactions with caregivers and develop mental templates of relationships as
either secure, ambivalent, avoidant, or victimizing. Beginning in childhood and continuing into adulthood, we seek to elicit and re-experi-
ence the model of relationships that we hold within ourselves. Our early
model is often highly resistant to change because it operates unconsciously (Bretherton 1985), and because we actively seek relationship
partners who help us recreate the model. Thus, traumatic childhood
experiences not only negatively affect the child's relationship with his
or her mother, but shape relationships in adulthood with peers, supe-
riors, and also with one's children. A striking characteristic of homeless women is their lack of trust in others (Dail 1990, Goodman 1991b,
Rubin 1996). Not only is the pervasive lack of trust a hallmark of insecure attachment, but it is consistent with the sense of betrayal experienced by those who have suffered interpersonal trauma (Finkelhor
1987). Homeless women are more likely than their housed counter-
parts to name their minor children as their primary supports in a time
of crisis (Bassuk and Rosenberg 1988, Wood et al. 1990), describing
the inverted parenting relationship—children acting as caregivers to
their parents—that characterizes anxious attachment (Bowlby 1973).
Clearly, homeless children are reaping from their mothers the legacy
of anxious and painful attachments. Both generations need treatment.

TRAUMA, POVERTY, INSECURE ATTACHMENT, AND HOMELESS MOTHERS

Two descriptions of the effects of trauma will help us recognize the
impact of separation, loss, and abuse on parent–child attachment in
homeless families. The American Psychiatric Association's *Diagnostic and
Statistical Manual of Mental Disorders* (1994) specifies posttraumatic
stress disorder symptoms associated with childhood maltreatment that
are consistent with insecure attachment: "impaired affect modulation;
self-destructive and impulsive behavior; dissociative symptoms; somatic
complaints; feelings of ineffectiveness, shame, despair, or hopelessness;
feeling permanently damaged; a loss of previously sustained beliefs;
hostility; social withdrawal; feeling constantly threatened; impaired
relationship with others" (p. 425).

Bessel van der Kolk (1987) describes the consistent symptomatic pattern observed in traumatized individuals. The pattern includes extreme variances in affective state ranging from hyperarousal to numbing/constriction, disrupted ability to use available support systems, feelings of depression and despair, suppression of feelings, difficulty controlling feelings of anxiety and aggression, distorted perceptions and judgment concerning the trauma, a sense of helplessness and feeling unable to make an impact on others, profound loss of trust in others, and difficulty with intimate relationships.

In a small qualitative study of homeless mothers conducted in the shelter receiving the Theraplay Group, I found that all ten subjects were insecurely attached and had chronic experiences of from four to eleven different types of trauma suffered in both early childhood and adulthood (Rubin 1996). Consistent in the histories of all ten subjects was the trauma of separation—often multiple separations—from at least one primary caregiver, and physical abuse, mainly in the form of harsh discipline. All of the women had suffered chronic maltreatment by parents or caregivers. I assessed the current adult attachment style of this group using Bartholomew and Horowitz's (1991) four-category model and by the subjects' communications about attachment. The attachment style most frequently identified in the subjects as either prominent or problematic was the dismissive style—paralleling the avoidant attachment of childhood—characterized by devaluing need and presenting a staunchly self-reliant stance toward the world. Avoidant/dismissive attachments develop from the childhood experience of the caregiver responding in a rejecting and hostile manner to the child's distress. Thus rebuffed, these children learn to survive and maintain their tenuous connection to the caregiver by repressing neediness and signs of vulnerability (i.e., suppressing attachment behaviors). The shelter staff described these now adult, dismissively attached women in terms consistent with both traumatization and insecure attachment: the women did not trust others to treat them in a caring, compassionate way (loss of trust, feeling constantly threatened); they appeared emotionally beaten, unmotivated, and undisciplined (helpless, hopeless, and despairing; unworthy of care); they demonstrated a poor sense of self and other, and lacked the ability to make responsible personal and parenting decisions (permanently damaged, distorted perceptions and judgment); moods ranged from depressed and withdrawn to irritable, hostile, and potentially violent toward not only their children but also other homeless women living with them in the shelter (impaired affect modulation, extreme variances in affective state, difficulty controlling feelings and emotions).

As mothers, these women were unable to respond sensitively to their children, were psychologically unavailable to them, and tended to use power-assertive discipline and physical punishment. The mothers rarely played with their child, talked mainly to direct, control, and limit, and did not seem to have the energy or desire to engage in pleasant physical or verbal interaction. They tended to be easily irritated and offended by their child's normal behavior, and often expressed feelings of helplessness and hopelessness by discharging or displacing anger and frustration onto the child. Children were expected to care for younger siblings and to meet their mothers' needs, such as bringing one's own diaper to mother for changing. This parenting style is characteristic under conditions of chronic poverty and economic hardship (McLoyd 1990), conducive to many negative outcomes including insecure attachment. The strain of living in poverty produces parents who are likely to be anxious, irritable, and depressed, to have inadequate social supports (Belle 1983), to have restricted access to adequate health care, and who are likely to have been exposed to, or victims of, violence. Absorbed either within themselves or with basic survival needs, they do not have the energy to be patient and accepting of their children. Psychological distress in parents, via poverty, abuse, or other sources, becomes a pathway to insecure attachment (Graham-Bermann et al. 1996). Treatment that can address the needs of poor or homeless mothers and their children is clearly indicated.

THE SETTING

I approached a small shelter for mothers and young children to offer a parenting group and ultimately guide a multifamily Theraplay group. Women 18 years or older, pregnant or with children under age 6, could reside at the shelter for up to two years. Although each family had its own apartment that afforded a significant degree of privacy and autonomy, the women were required to participate in various activities throughout the day, including completing shelter chores and attending group sessions led by volunteers and some staff members. Not only did mothers and children experience a loss of control of their day, but the women often felt undermined as parents because the shelter imposed the daily schedule, and staff often disrupted the mother's position of authority vis-à-vis her children. The parenting group, of which the multifamily Theraplay group was a part, was one of the programs the shelter provided for, and required of, its residents. Women approached the group cautiously and were skeptical of the leader, the discussions, and the activities.

Residents of the shelter were all women of color, predominately African-American, reflecting the racial group hardest hit in major metropolitan areas by harsh economic conditions and the lack of affordable housing. The women ranged in age from 18 to 25. While in the shelter, they were all functioning as single mothers with from one to five children. Some mothers had their youngest children with them, but had lost custody of older children for reasons such as substance abuse. (Known substance abusers had to participate in treatment outside the shelter.) The shelter attempted to screen out women known to have been in treatment for severe psychiatric disorders. Regardless, there was almost a constant sense of tension present. Anxiety was always imminent, with residents' anger flaring both at staff and at their own children. Residents resented being controlled and directed by staff and complained about staff's interference in parental decisions. Some women tended to withdraw from interaction with other residents, showed a chronically sad expression, and rarely spoke to their children—manifestations of the depression that accompanies victimization, oppression, and homelessness. Other residents manifested a cocky and controlling style involving talking, bragging, and dominating the conversation or the group. These women tended to explode when challenged, characteristic of the dismissive adult relationship style so problematic for homeless women. A number of mothers exhibited a combination of poor judgment and poor impulse control. Some were prone to violent outbursts and had threatened other residents. These women usually were asked to leave the shelter. A few of the women, however, demonstrated good judgment, a cooler head, and a welcome degree of patience and humor with their children.

The children ranged in age from infancy to 6 years. Some children appeared of normal intelligence, but others were judged to have developmental disabilities. Some had significant speech and language delays. Many had behavioral problems including excessive displays of anger and aggression, oppositionality, separation problems, and fears.

OBSERVATIONS OF PARENT–CHILD INTERACTION

Consistent with research, the interactions between parents and their children indicated the presence of insecure attachment in the present relationship. There was little if any play between mother and child. The mothers acted primarily as limit-setters and punishers, rejecting their children when they expressed a need for attention. Although the mothers claimed to have toys for their children in their apartments, they rarely brought to the group materials with which their children could play. Even in the apartments, toys were not visible, and children were always delighted when I brought any small plaything during my visit. When toys were available, the mothers did not respond or interact with their children and did not model how to appropriately play with the toys. When offered a toy, children would sometimes sit passively or hesitantly accept it with an expression that seemed to question whether it was okay to play with it. Some parents had such extensive needs of their own that they either ignored or rejected those of their children. These mothers watched, but did not respond to, their crying children, or slept as their baby began whimpering as it lay by her side on the couch.

Depressed, angry mothers, passive, preoccupied mothers, understimulated children suppressing the need for help—these descriptions suggest gross failures of attachment. Theraplay, with its attachment-fostering qualities, was indeed an appropriate technique to use.

THERAPLAY AS ATTACHMENT FOSTERING

Theraplay, with its focus on increasing the frequency of active, positive, and attuned engagement between adult and child, is an intervention that works directly to improve attachment quality. Family Theraplay provides an opportunity to structure, challenge, engage, and nurture not only the child, but his or her parents as well (Jernberg 1984), serving as a vehicle for addressing early unmet parental needs. For these reasons, Theraplay was chosen as the treatment modality for this homeless population that demonstrated the pervasive development of insecure attachments in at least two generations.

The five dimensions of Theraplay (structure, challenge, engagement, nurture, and playfulness) can be seen as therapeutic compensation (Jernberg 1993) for the experience of past losses, separations, abuse, and neglect. When able to confidently take charge, mothers— as do Theraplay therapists—structure the physical life and contain the emotional life of their children. This provides for the child's safety as well as the tools for developing self-control. Children whose mothers are physically or psychologically unable to provide structure are deprived of this organizing function. These children are more likely to feel physically and emotionally out of control in a world they experience as overwhelming and chaotic. We could expect them to be either overactive or withdrawn and frightened, sometimes controlling, and very likely aggressive. Providing structure would help them calm down, increase their sense of safety, and reduce acting out and aggression. Challenging experiences, provided by mothers or through Theraplay, encourage the child to develop competence and confidence within a dyad or group. This dimension would compensate for the legacy of hopelessness and powerlessness born of chronic poverty, alienation, and abuse. Engaging or intrusive interactions draw one out of oneself, and increase interest in and attention to the outside world and to others. This dimension counteracts depressive tendencies and helpless passivity that can contribute to problems of attention, concentration, and learning. Children with such symptoms are likely to experience cognitive and academic difficulties. The nurturing dimension directly heals the hurt child and establishes or reestablishes the child's trust in caregivers, other adults, and peers. The newest dimension—playfulness—offers a joie de vivre that lifts depression and engages the child in interaction with others.

THERAPLAY INNOVATIONS

I intervened with the mothers in two ways. First, I met with them as a group for one hour to discuss parenting issues. These sessions were not didactic or particularly structured, with the women bringing up their concerns about their children, and the group discussing various parenting strategies and helping mothers track back the sequence of events that might have led to a negative episode. During the last half hour, mothers joined their children in the playroom where we all participated in a multifamily Theraplay group under my guidance. The goals of the group directly addressed the attachment needs of the mothers and children, seeking to strengthen the mothers' role as parents-in-charge and the children's role as play-oriented—roles directly undermined by shelter living. Although the groups were loosely structured, the emphasis was on supporting the family unit and increasing positive interactions between family members. There was little effort to relate the content of the mothers' parenting group to the parent–child Theraplay group. Although in Theraplay we always put parents in charge of their children, the therapist typically takes an active role in initiating and structuring the activities. Similarly, in Theraplay groups, the leader is always in charge. One innovation in this case was for the leader to facilitate, that is, to bring materials, to model, and to support positive interactions within dyads, triads, and groups. Group activities moved flexibly from a focus on family interaction to peer interaction. The other major innovation was making this a multifamily group.

The goals of the Theraplay group were (1) to acknowledge and strengthen the family unit, (2) to provide opportunities for positive playful interactions among family members, (3) to provide opportunities to nurture children and mothers, (4) to provide child-centered materials and games that might carry over into the home, and (5) to bring fun and spontaneity into the lives of the families. Thus, sessions were designed to develop family cohesion and interaction, increase positive interactions between children, and provide nurturing experiences for all participants.

Focus on Family Cohesion and Interaction

Because the mothers felt that their authority as head of their family was continually usurped by the structured format of the shelter and by individual staff members, I structured the Theraplay groups so that mothers would be in charge of their families and the family unit would be the primary focus for interaction. The hello song focused on welcoming each family, rather than individuals. We covered each family with a large blanket and, to the tune of "Frère Jacques" or "Where Is Thumbkin," sang:

Group: Where is (mother's name)'s family?
                                Where is (mother's name)'s family?

Family (taking blanket off):	Here we are! Here we are!
Group:	We're glad you came to play. We're glad you came to play.
Group (shaking hands with each member):	Hello, (name of a family member). Hello, (name of other family members).

(Continue until all family members have been welcomed.)

During each family's turn to be welcomed, children relished and mothers seemed sometimes embarrassed by the positive, admiring attention they received from group members. Welcoming children always loved running up to the uncovered family and shaking hands. Some of their mothers readily joined in while others only watched, unable to serve as models of joyful interactions for their children. Because this was a multifamily format, the withdrawn mothers and their children had more positive models to observe and to imitate. Sometimes, timid children of reserved mothers would hesitantly join in the welcoming when they saw their peers and other adults enthusiastically participating.

Each mother then lotioned her children and could receive lotion from her children. This will be further described in the section on nurturing mothers and children.

Because many of the children were in the zero to 6 year range, very simple games were used to promote children and mothers interacting with one another. I followed the suggestions of Mary Alice DaCosse, who has worked frequently with large and diverse groups (DaCosse, personal communication, December 1992). She advocates for brief groups consisting of one to two very simple and quickly executed activities sandwiched between a welcoming and closing, a framework that can expand as the group becomes more cohesive, soothed, and empathic. Thus, rather than a series of activities in which all were expected to engage in a structured, turn-taking manner typical of school-based Theraplay Groups (Rubin and Tregay 1989), I offered one or at most two games, showed the children how to do them, and let them loose to play together with parents or peers with my support. I kept materials simple and cheap so that the children could keep them and the mothers would not be unduly tense at home lest the child lose or break the toy. Using everyday materials also showed the mothers that they had at hand toys that could engage their children in positive, cognitively enhancing play. The goal was to increase the frequency of parent–child interaction. These stressed and depressed mothers, however, might be more available to their children if their children could play with each other and thus give the mothers some respite. These simple toys, then, addressed the children's need for stimulating manipulatives for solitary, peer, or parent–child play.

Out of cardboard and old shoebox pieces, I cut long rectangular peekaboo cards. Some were simply rectangles from which you could peek from behind. Others had a peekaboo hole cut at one end. On one side of the board, I drew a happy face so the person looking for the peeker would have an appealing target on which to focus. We also used the inside tubes from toilet paper or paper towels to peek through. I would bring enough of these for each child and each mother and ask the mothers to give them to their children. I would then model how to play and encourage mothers and children to interact together. If the children seemed only to be interacting with their mothers, I suggested that the mothers encourage siblings to play with the toy together in order to broaden their play world. Children were also free to interact among themselves. Coming up from the playroom with these toys, I always showed staff members what we had done. I was delighted when staff members asked for peekaboo cards for themselves. The staff's interest in interacting with the children represented the potential for the children to experience increased trust and engagement with the world at large.

Mothers made sock puppets from old small socks, drawing a face on the foot of the sock with a permanent marker. There were enough socks for each child and each mother. The children approached these sock faces and began to talk to them. We made hand prints with powder on darkly colored construction paper, one large paper to each family for mounting on the wall of their apartment. The mothers were delighted with this apparently new way to appreciate the uniqueness of themselves and their children. One mother whose baby had been sleeping was briefly upset and disappointed that she would not get his print because he was squirming. While she held him, I helped powder his foot so that she could have her family's "parts" for display. The response of the mothers to this activity showed that their need for narcissistic valuing and admiring had not been sufficiently met. They needed such experiences every bit as much as their children to develop a healthy internal sense of themselves as special, as worthy of care, and as fun to be with. It was this early childhood, body-centered activity that gave the mothers the sensory, holistic grounding they needed—one of the most basic of hands-on experiences.

At Christmastime, I brought ribbon, tinsel, seasonal stickers, Christmas wrapping paper, and other assorted decorations with which mothers could adorn their children. The mothers had a wonderful time uniquely decorating their children and giving themselves matching stickers on their cheeks, foreheads, and chins. I took Polaroid pictures of each family and presented it to each mother. The mothers really enjoyed it, clearly having more fun in this activity than their children!

I brought "warm fuzzies" (pom-poms made of yarn) for each family and staff member, and everyone passed gentle touches around the circle. We used the paper from old phone books to squeeze into balls so children could throw them into "baskets" made by their mother's arms (Morin 1993). To emphasize the family as a unit, I brought small mirrors so each family could admire themselves sitting together. Typical of the multidimensional nature of Theraplay activities, these interactive games were primarily playful, engaging, and/or challenging while simultaneously involving aspects of structure and/or nurturing.

Focus on Positive Interactions Between Children

We played other typical Theraplay games as well, such as Cotton Ball Tickle, Ring Around the Rosie, saying hello and goodbye while rolling a ball to each other, and each taking a turn to hug a stuffed animal (see Appendix for description of activities). The children took turns in small groups, riding in or pulling a plastic laundry basket with a rope tied to it. Participants took turns to cover their faces with scarves and be found by other group members. I did not insist on families playing together in these activities. If parents just wanted to watch, that was accepted. The objective was for the children to engage in playful interactions with each other and reduce the aggressive and attention-getting behaviors that were triggered during periods in which age-appropriate play was not allowed.

Focus on Providing Nurturing Experiences
for Mothers and Children

After welcoming families, the mothers checked their children for hurts
and lotioning needs. Each mother had a small lotion bottle for her family.
Sometimes I would help put lotion around a hurt on a child. I took every
opportunity to admire the smoothness and to smell the sweetness of
mothers and children alike, and to encourage each to similarly admire
the other. Children were more ready to be admiring and curious with
each other than the mothers were to them, or they to their mothers.

In addition to the lotioning activity, I brought treats in small plastic bags for each family to share at the end of each group. I handed these
bags to each mother, putting her in charge of nurturing her family. As
is typical of Theraplay, treats are actually fed directly into the mouths
of the person getting fed. This creates the most primal of nurturing
experiences. Most of the mothers were able to feed their children, and
the children quickly began to feed each other and their mothers as well.

OUTCOMES

During the group sessions, mothers and children made eye contact,
and both accepted from, and gave to, each other. When a child avoided
eye contact, I gently coached and sometimes modeled for the mother
how to attract her child's gaze toward her. The peekaboo games directly elicited mutual eye contact between peekaboo partners. The
children, given a vehicle for, a model of, and permission to play, initiated contact with their mothers, some of whom were passive and
barely responsive. Mothers were observed to smile in spite of themselves, and to finally respond to their child who stood in front of them,
waiting expectantly with imploring eye contact. Both children and
mothers seemed to gain some tolerance for sociability as a result of
being in a group that modeled the norm of playful interaction. Mothers
at times appeared to be embarrassed playing childish, "silly" games
with their children. With other mothers and me as models, however,
they eventually joined in.

One mother was notable in hoarding the treats from her children,
eating them first, eating more than she gave away, and asking for more
to take to her apartment "for the kids." The neediest of the mothers, it

was difficult for her to do anything positive with her four children, who showed a range of disturbances including aggression, severe speech and language delay, and withdrawal. Instead of insisting that she give up her supplies to her children, I addressed her needs by bringing ample treats, refilling her bag when necessary, and allowing all the mothers to take extra treats to their apartments. Although the other mothers knew that she wanted the treats for herself and made deprecating comments quietly, I did not confront her, but made it permissible in the group for mothers to be needy and use the treats as they wished. Not long after this, the other mothers stopped making critical comments. My acceptance of this woman's neediness allowed them to tolerate and accept it as well. In a group of women with dismissive characteristics, this might be considered a major achievement!

When I asked the mothers what they might have gained from these Theraplay groups, they said that they had learned that play was okay to do, and that they felt more comfortable playing with their children. They also had observed their children cooperatively playing the games we had done in our groups. This pleased the mothers because it freed them to meet their own needs, and allowed them to see that their children could occupy themselves constructively.

PROBLEMS ENCOUNTERED IN A MULTIFAMILY FORMAT

So depressed were some of the mothers that they lacked the energy to initiate positive interactions and play with their children. When I looked toward them to encourage their participation in an activity, they sat virtually expressionless, shook their heads no, and passively watched their children. For these parent–child dyads, it seemed that the group could help by allowing the mother some respite and the chance to see her children in a positive light. For such mothers, however, there was also the danger of a negative reaction to being allowed to sit-out the activity. First of all, their children turned to other adults (often me) for interaction. While some mothers may experience this as support, others could experience this as a threat to their relationship with their child as well as a usurping of their parental role. Feeling depressed already, they could interpret this as confirmation of their inadequacy as mothers.

Another difficulty in attempting to strengthen a sense of family was that children tended to be parented by other shelter mothers. Depending on the dynamics within the group of shelter mothers and the friendships that developed, some mothers would take over the parental functions (structuring as well as nurturing and play) of others, and children would seek interactions (nurturing as well as play) from mothers other than their own. This phenomenon would indicate the need for processing this dynamic as well as appreciating that a child's connection to this extended family would be experienced as a loss when families leave the shelter.

Some mothers appeared embarrassed when expected to play with their children. With truncated childhoods of their own, they may have had little experience of being played with by a caring adult. Playful mothering is not likely to be within their mental model of the parent–child relationship. Because they felt needy and too close to their child-like wishes and urges, the idea of playing could threaten their fragile facades of adulthood. Care must be taken to re-parent and re-play with these mothers in a way that allows them to accept it.

Mothers also tended to be reluctant to nurture their children and sought to avoid intimacy and physical contact with them. This is consistent with dismissive attachment characteristics, which include a conscious devaluing of interpersonal neediness as well as the protective avoidance of touch in cases of unresolved physical abuse. This pattern suggests a repressed or suppressed attachment system in need of activation. The mothers have learned that neediness results in rejection and hurt, and that survival depends on denying need and depending only on oneself. They must protect themselves and their children from becoming too attached to people because others are not dependable. Consciously, these women would say that their culture does not believe in coddling children who must grow up and survive in a cruel and uncaring world. Finding ways to speak to and meet the needs of the hurt child/parent, is the healing that is needed.

FUTURE RECOMMENDATIONS

Theraplay, whether single- or multifamily, is an ideal treatment approach that addresses and can begin to heal insecure attachments. It seems crucial, however, with such populations and in such settings where family disruption has been, and is, endemic, that a focus on the family unit be maintained. Living as residents within the rules of the shelter staff, homeless mothers should be expected to be very sensitive to their dependent and subordinate position, and to resent the loss of authority and autonomy in relation to their children and staff. Theraplay, therefore, should be framed in a way that puts homeless women in charge of their families.

For this difficult population in which the mothers need reparative parenting experiences just as much as their children, yet would be likely to reject it if given directly, providing Theraplay for the children could be an effective way to re-parent the parent. There are a number of factors to consider, however, when planning how to present this experience to homeless mothers. I did not address the goals of my Theraplay group with the parents in my group. They seemed to accept it as an extension of our free-form parenting session and did not interpret its purpose as anything other than an opportunity to play with their children. Maybe for this reason, there was little overt resistance except from those depressed and lethargic mothers who remained passive during group. For some groups, however, Theraplay may be more readily accepted if the dimension initially emphasized is structure rather than nurturing. I will suggest two rationales that support such an initial focus. Valuing structure is consistent with the cultural and instrumental norm of power-assertive discipline and the eschewing of coddling and, thus, would more likely fit the mothers' worldview. Parents of oppressed minorities tend to have learned too well that children must obey without the luxury of autonomous protest, and that one ill-timed spontaneous moment could lead to mortal danger. Offering techniques to parents for helping children listen and respond better could set the foundation for a positive parent–therapist alliance. Another important consideration would be the attachment styles of the parents. It is likely that the more dismissively attached the parents, the more they will both devalue neediness in others (their own children as well as other parents in the group) and actively defend against their own. Thus, an obvious focus on nurturing could be threatening for such a group and could hinder the development of trust.

In addition to initially emphasizing the importance of structure, play also may be a useful rationale to use with very defensive parents. Most, although not all, will likely agree that children need to play. Learning to play cooperatively and appropriately may be a goal that would

benefit both children and parents because children who play well together will be less demanding of their mothers. Extending this goal to
its corollaries in later childhood, adolescence, and adulthood is also likely
to be meaningful to this population. Playing well in childhood trans-
lates into better social and (often) academic functioning in school, and
to working and living cooperatively with others in adulthood. It means
developing the capacity for maintaining relationships, the lack of which
contributed to the mothers having had to resort to a homeless shelter
for support. Framing the goal of the group in this way may allow
parents to get in touch with the sadness and loss of such support and
relationships in their own lives and mobilize them to be proactive to
ensure that their children will have better experiences.

Nurturing is the most basic of the Theraplay dimensions and warrants attention, even if it is de-emphasized in the beginning stage of
the group. Homeless women are likely to have had either a lack of
nurturing experiences, or few, insufficient, or disrupted nurturing relationships, of a degree that will keep them emotionally crippled as
parents. Often, they do love their children but are simply unable to
express it through nurturing (Evangeline Munns, personal communication, 1997). Inadequately nurtured, these mothers would likely say
that they felt their parents' power-assertive discipline to be nurturing,
that their parents' autocratic restrictions were experienced as love and
care. Thus, many in this population feel that children should be "tough-
ened up" and "grown up"—as was demanded of the mothers—and that
these defensive characteristics are crucial to survival in a hostile world
where few have the resources to provide adequate care. We also know,
however, that these women may be afraid to express love for their child
through nurturing because such an interaction would put them in touch
with their own feelings of vulnerability, which they had to ward off in
childhood. Clearly, it is imperative that we find ways to nurture these
parents and begin to sensitize them to their own childhood deprivation.
One approach might be to use the idea that the parent is in charge not
only for structuring but also for nurturing activities. Parents could first
experience the Theraplay therapist's taking charge of nurturing them,
and then be coached to take charge of nurturing their own children.

To increase the effectiveness of such a Theraplay group, a 45 to 60
minute parent session is recommended, preferably before the group.
Although having a pre- and postgroup parent meeting would be ideal,
separating parents and children at the end of the group could feel like

another disruptive experience. A pregroup meeting would serve a function similar to that of the interpreting therapist behind the one-way mirror. Initial meetings would focus on the mothers being introduced to the Theraplay dimensions, particularly structuring techniques, and would allow mothers to practice ways of taking charge of their child in a positive and playful manner. Parents could role-play the activities for the session or might role-play a problem situation that a mother brings up for discussion, providing additional opportunities to re-parent the parents. Each pregroup meeting might also include a review and reactions to the last session, the mothers' observations of their children during the group, as well as insights into their own reactions and behaviors. Because sharing insights about themselves requires significant trust in others, such a process may not be achieved in many groups with homeless women. The leader must model the acceptance of each others' comments and disclosures, and encourage mothers to think about how they might help their child based on what they are learning in the group.

Because shelter living is, by definition, temporary, these women and children will be faced with more separations when families move out. Whether abrupt or planned, whether these relationships are close or conflictual, such changes should be processed with the mothers and the children and can be incorporated into Theraplay group activities.

Having the ability to videotape the Theraplay group would be invaluable. Portions of the video of the previous group could be shown during pregroup meetings to identify positive interactions and behaviors, and to better understand the triggers for problematic interactions and behaviors. Taping would require parental consent.

A range of methods of monitoring outcomes is appropriate. One could develop a scale with a description of behaviors characteristic of secure attachment that could be readily observed in child play or during the group. Mothers, or the Theraplay therapist, would rate the child before beginning the Theraplay group, and again after a predetermined period of time, or when the family leaves the shelter. Table 12–1 gives an example of such a scale. Mothers could be involved in determining the positive behaviors or descriptors used in the scale. The Theraplay leader would have to ensure that the behaviors are realistic and age appropriate, and could help frame the description of the behavior in secure attachment terms. This would provide mothers with a constructive framework for observing their child's behaviors and guiding parenting practices. Another method would be to observe and/or videotape each family together, playing a variety of games, similar to the Marschak Interaction Method (MIM) format (Jernberg 1991). In addition to the usual lotioning and feeding activities, families could play with a nerf ball together, play peekaboo, play a favorite game, and read a book together. A posttest family playtime would be videotaped at a later period. Mothers could be given a family picture taken during their playtime with a description of the positive interactions observed.

Table 12–1. Multifamily Theraplay groups with homeless mothers: assessment

NAME _____ DATE _____

Assessment of theraplay progress

Behavior	Never — Sometimes — Frequently					
Establishes eye contact.	1	2	3	4	5	6
Touches others appropriately.	1	2	3	4	5	6
Is caring toward others.	1	2	3	4	5	6
Accepts nurturing when appropriately given.	1	2	3	4	5	6
Is verbally assertive.	1	2	3	4	5	6
When child needs help, comes to mother or accepts help from her.	1	2	3	4	5	6
Plays cooperatively with peers or siblings for reasonable length of time. Reasonable time for child's age: _____	1	2	3	4	5	6
Can be comforted by parent when in distress.	1	2	3	4	5	6
Takes turns willingly during cooperative play with peers.	1	2	3	4	5	6

SUMMARY

Family Theraplay and multifamily Theraplay groups are appropriate and valuable in settings for homeless families. Theraplay can provide healing experiences not only for distressed and stressed children, but for their parents as well. These are generations of people who are not simply experiencing situational stress, but are suffering from the legacy of poverty, abuse, and loss that results in the type of attachment history predictive of conflictual relationships, poor social support, depression, cognitive delays and poor academic functioning, and parenting practices that re-create insecure attachments. They will need continued comprehensive support if they are to truly heal and thrive, not simply survive. Theraplay is one way of reaching and beginning to heal the rejected, abandoned, and hurt child, and parent.

REFERENCES

Ainsworth, M. D. S., Blehar, M. D., Water, E., and Wall, S. (1978). *Patterns of Attachment: A Psychological Study of the Strange Situation*. Hillsdale, NJ: Lawrence Erlbaum.

American Psychiatric Association. (1994). *Diagnostic and Statistical Manual of Mental Disorders*, (4th ed.). Washington, DC: Author.

Banyard, V. L., and Graham-Bermann, S. A. (1995). Building and empowerment policy paradigm: self-reported strengths of homeless mothers. *American Journal of Orthopsychiatry* 65(4):479–491.

Bartholomew, K., & Horowitz, L. M. (1991). Attachment styles among young adults: a test of the four-category model. *Journal of Personality and Social Psychology* 61:226–244.

Bassuk, E. L. (1986). Homeless families: single mothers and their children in Boston shelters. *The Mental Health Needs of Homeless Persons* 30:45–53.

——— (1990). Who are the homeless families?: characteristics of sheltered mothers and children. *Community Mental Health Journal* 26(5):425–434.

Bassuk, E. L., and Gallagher, E. M. (1990). The impact of homelessness on children. *Child and Youth Services* 14(1):19–33.

Bassuk, E. L., and Rosenberg, L. (1988). Why does family homelessness occur?: a case control study. *American Journal of Public Health* 78:783–788.

Bassuk, E. L., Rubin, L., and Lauriat, A. (1986). Characteristics of sheltered homeless families. *American Journal of Public Health* 76:1097.

Belle, D. (1983). The impact of poverty on social networks and supports. *Marriage and Family Review* 5(4):89–103.

Bowlby, J. (1973). *Attachment and Loss. Volume II: Separation, Anxiety and Anger*. New York: Basic Books.

——— (1982). *Attachment and Loss. Volume I: Attachment*, 2nd ed. New York: Basic Books.

Bretherton, I. (1985). Attachment theory: retrospect and prospect. In *Growing Points of Attachment Theory and Research*, ed. I. Bretherton and E. Waters, pp. 3–35. *Monographs of the Society for Research in Child Development* 50 (1–2, No. 209).

——— (1990). Communication patterns, internal working models, and the intergenerational transmission of attachment relationships. *Infant Mental Health Journal* 11(3):237–252.

Browne, A. (1993). Family violence and homelessness: the relevance of trauma histories in the lives of homeless women. *American Journal of Orthopsychiatry* 63(3):370–384.

Carlson, V., Barnett, D., Cicchetti, D., and Braunwald, K. (1989). Disorganized/disoriented attachment relationships in maltreated infants. *Developmental Psychology* 25(4):525–531.

Cicchetti, D., and Barnett, D. (1991). Attachment organization in maltreated preschoolers. *Developmental Psychopathology* 3:397–411.

Crittenden, P. (1988). Relationships at risk. In *Clinical Implications of Attachment*, ed. J. Belsky and T. Nezworski, pp. 136–174. Hillsdale, NJ: Lawrence Erlbaum.

Dail, P. W. (1990). The psychosocial context of homeless mothers with young children: program and policy implications. *Child Welfare League of America* 69(4):291–308.

D'Ercole, A., and Strening E. (1990). Victimization among homeless women: implications for service delivery. *Journal of Community Psychology* 18:141–152.

Finkelhor, D. (1987). The trauma of child sexual abuse. *Journal of Interpersonal Violence* 2(4):348–365.

Fox, S. J., Barrnett, R. J., Davies, M., and Bird, H. R. (1990). Psychopathology and developmental delay in homeless children: a pilot study. *Journal of the American Academy of Child and Adolescent Psychiatry* 29(5):732–735.

Goodman, L. A. (1991a). The prevalence of abuse among homeless and housed poor mothers: a comparison study. *American Journal of Orthopsychiatry* 61(4):489–500.

——— (1991b). The relationship between social support and family homelessness. *Journal of Community Psychology* 19(4):321–332.

Goodman, L. A., Dutton, M. A., and Harris, M. (1995). Episodically homeless women with serious mental illness: prevalence of physical and sexual assault. *American Journal of Orthopsychiatry* 65(4): 468–478.

Goodman, L., Saxe, L., and Harvey, M. (1991). Homelessness as psychological trauma: broadening perspectives. *American Psychologist* 46(11): 1219–1225.

Graham-Bermann, S. A., Coupet, S., Egler, L., and Mattis, J. (1996). Interpersonal relationships and adjustment of children in homeless and economically distressed families. *Journal of Clinical Child Psychology* 25(3):250–261.

Hausman, B., and Hammen, C. (1993). Parenting in homeless families: the double crisis. *American Journal of Orthopsychiatry* 63(3):358–369.

Hirsch, K. (1986). Childhood without a home: a new report on the youngest victims. *The Boston Phoenix*, January 21, p. 10.

Jernberg, A. (1984). Theraplay: child therapy for attachment fostering. *Psychotherapy* 21(1):39–47.

——— (1991). Assessing parent–child interactions with the Marschak Interaction Method (MIM). In *Play Diagnosis and Assessment*, ed. C. E. Schaefer, K. Gitlin, and A. Sandgrund, pp. 493–515. New York: Wiley.

——— (1993). Attachment formation. In *The Therapeutic Powers of Play*, ed. C. E. Schaefer, pp. 241–264. Northvale, NJ: Jason Aronson.

Khan, M. (1963). The concept of cumulative trauma. *Psychoanalytic Study of the Child*, 18, 286–306.

Koblinsky, S. A., Morgan, K. M., and Anderson, E. A. (1997). African-American homeless and low-income housed mothers: comparison of parenting practices. *American Journal of Orthopsychiatry* 67(1): 37–47.

Main, M., and Hesse, E. (1990). Parents' unresolved traumatic experiences are related to infant disorganized attachment status: Is frightened and/or frightening parental behavior the linking mechanism? In *Attachment in the Preschool Years*, ed. M. T. Greenberg, D. Cicchetti, and M. Cummings, pp. 161–182. Chicago: University of Chicago Press.

Main, M., and Solomon, J. (1986). Discovery of an insecure-disorganized/disoriented attachment pattern. In *Affective Development in Infancy*, ed. T. B. Brazelton and M. W. Yogman, pp. 95–124. Norwood, NJ: Ablex.

McLoyd, V. C. (1990). The impact of economic hardship on black families and children: psychological distress, parenting, and socioemotional development. *Child Development* 61:311–346.

Morin, V. K. (1993). *Messy Activities and More*. Chicago: Chicago Review Press.

Rubin, P. (1996). *Understanding homeless mothers: the dynamics of adjusting to a long-term shelter*. Doctoral dissertation, Illinois School of Professional Psychology, Chicago.

Rubin, P. B., and Tregay, J. (1989). *Play with Them: Theraplay Groups in the Classroom*. Springfield, IL: Charles C Thomas.

Shinn, M., Knickman, J., and Weitzman, B. (1991). Social relationships and vulnerability to becoming homeless among poor families. *American Psychologist* 46(11):1180–1187.

Troy, M., and Sroufe, L. A. (1987). Victimization among preschoolers: role of attachment relationship history. *Journal of the American Academy of Child and Adolescent Psychiatry* 26:166–172.

van der Kolk, B. A. (1987). The psychological consequences of overwhelming life experiences. In *Psychological Trauma*, ed. B. A. van der Kolk, pp. 1–30. Washington, DC: American Psychiatric Press.

van Ijzendoorn, M. H. (1992). Intergenerational transmission of parenting: a review of studies in nonclinical populations. *Developmental Review* 12:76–99.

Wood, D., Valdez, R. B., Hayashi, T., and Shen, A. (1990). Homeless and housed families in Los Angeles: a study comparing demographic, economic, and family function characteristics. *American Journal of Public Health* 80:1049–1052.

13

Theraplay Innovations with Adoptive Families

NORMA FINNELL

The children treated with Theraplay at the Children's Home Society are often in the process of being adopted. Most of them have resided for treatment at the Children's Home Society in Sioux Falls, South Dakota. The Children's Home Society is a forty-two-bed inpatient treatment center for children with severe emotional/behavioral problems, and it also has a 12-bed assessment unit. In addition, approximately fifteen to twenty-five children are placed for day treatment, which includes work with them and their families.

The Children's Home Society philosophy is one of helping family members develop healthy relationships with one another. The center provides individual, group, and family therapy.

Theraplay is integrated into many of the children's treatment plans because it is very helpful with a variety of their social-emotional difficulties. However, Theraplay is specifically used with adoptive families, especially sibling groups, because of the obvious need for healthy attachments to develop.

This chapter focuses on how Theraplay has been used with sibling group adoptive placements following more traditional individual

Theraplay with adoptive children in their families. New ways of adapting Theraplay to the needs of adoptive children are described. In addition, suggestions for working with multiple families using Theraplay methods are discussed.

Historically, Theraplay has been used with the individual child and his parents. This traditional method is used with adoptive parents and their new child, with the primary focus on building an attachment between parents and their adoptive child. One of the innovations used is to include other siblings as well, both biological and adoptive, in the family Theraplay session, so the adopted child is incorporated into the whole family system. There are typical stages that a child goes through in the adoptive process, which will be discussed later. Theraplay activities can be helpful in all of these stages and examples are included at each stage.

The children were 4 to 14 years old. Due to parental neglect or abuse, court action had resulted in termination of parental rights. The majority of the children were victims of sexual and/or physical abuse and almost all of them had failed in previous foster care placements and were removed. Consequently, most of them had suffered from reactive attachment disorder and/or posttraumatic stress disorder. These severe psychiatric disorders cause disruptions in families because of extreme behaviors, which all of these children demonstrated. It is significant to note that most of the children had received other forms of treatment unsuccessfully and were unable to cognitively address their problems at the outset. The nurturing that normally occurs early between parent and child was absent, and the children desperately needed those early bonding experiences.

For the majority of the children, therapy took place within the context of residential treatment while the children were in residence and during aftercare outpatient treatment. During this time they were transitioned into adoptive or foster families, and Theraplay was used with all of the children and families to facilitate successful transition. Prior to their involvement in family work, most of the children had received individual Theraplay. Professionals working with these types of children are encouraged to learn Theraplay because children who are placed for adoption at an older age often have not had their early emotional needs met, resulting in difficulties in forming attachments. Theraplay is used to fulfill some of those early emotional needs and helps the child learn to accept positive relationships with others, resulting in more openness in accepting a new adoptive family.

WHY THERAPLAY?

The work of Ann Jernberg (1979), has shown that many children, especially younger ones, are usually unable to cognitively process the problems they experience. If they can be engaged in discussions about their past, they learn to say words, but just talking about their serious difficulties in relationships usually does not significantly change their ability to relate with others. Extreme abuse and/or neglect results in attachment problems and other serious symptoms, and because it is known that children learn best by experience, Theraplay is a treatment of choice. Just as one would not simply talk with babies about how they are going to learn to love somebody, older children with special needs also need to experience the caring of adults in order to realize that it is possible for them to be loved unconditionally.

One of the unique aspects of Theraplay is that it goes back to promoting basic attachment feelings between parents and children through specially designed nurturing activities. At times this includes regression, and adoptive parents need to realize that in experiencing this regression children may start accepting the unconditional love and babying that they either previously did not receive or would not accept. Theraplay provides a playful way to help parents give that nurturing, very much as they would with a new baby. As the children accept this nurturing and other components of Theraplay, their basic attachment feelings emerge. If in a regressive state they allow the adult to meet their needs, they have taken the first step toward accepting their parents as caregivers, which is the basis for attachment.

It has been found that children who are simply handed over to their adoptive parents often display extreme behavior problems. Many times this is because age-appropriate behavior is expected when, in fact, these children have never had the loving nurturing that parents give to infants and young children. Until the children accept this nurturing, they are unable to progress past that developmental stage because they need the basic foundations of attachment, such as being held, cuddled, powdered, lotioned, and provided with good unconditional care. Instead of focusing on trying to encourage the children to change negative behavior patterns that have emerged, children are taught to experience and feel the unconditional love that parents give their infants. As they learn to accept this, they begin to develop attachment behaviors and find that they want to belong in the family.

Children who are placed for adoption following court action, because of abuse, often require immediate attention because their extreme behavior makes potential parents afraid to keep them. The parents feel as though their life is topsy turvy because of the chaos that results. Often they respond to misbehavior by applying extreme consequences, thinking that a severe enough consequence will change the behavior, but it does not.

One reason Theraplay is useful with older children is that adoptions are like marriages (Donley 1983). Because the children are old enough to have some understanding of what is going on, both parents and children need to make a decision about their commitment in the relationship. This does not imply that children choose their families, but they can choose whether or not to make an emotional commitment. Theraplay assists in this process. Both parents and children have a previous history that needs to be shared and understood, and they need to get to know each other. To sit and talk becomes boring for children, but Theraplay activities make it fun and interesting for parents and children to get to know each other and develop a common set of experiences that build the foundation for a family. The family needs to learn to talk and play together, and Theraplay discourages resistance by engaging family members in fun, experiential activities that promote attachment.

In the beginning, it is often helpful to structure simple activities. These can be based on what a parent might do with a new baby, such as checking the child over and noting the color of his eyes and hair, checking fingers and toes, finding out how strong the child is, and identifying unique and special characteristics about him. There are then many activities that parents and children can do together. Initially, adoptive children are treated on an individual basis with their parents, and when the children are responding satisfactorily to their parents, other siblings are included in family Theraplay as well. Other siblings who have had behavioral or emotional problems may also have needed individual therapy prior to the family functioning together.

Theraplay activities that are helpful in working with parents and children include the following: (see Activities List, pp. 252–256 for a description of all activities cited in this chapter).

1. Theraplay inventory or checkup
2. How Are We the Same Game
3. Good Touch Train

4. Getting to Know You Game
5. Trace shapes, letters, or numbers on the back of other family members
6. Prompt family members to identify inherent positive qualities about each other
7. Help children make lists of ways to make their parents happy

The therapists' repertoire of activities is limited only by their imagination in helping parents and children get to know each other. It is critical that the therapist direct the activities so that the parents remain focused on the inherent qualities of the children, not simply on the clothing they wear or other external qualities. We want parents to recognize their children's physical strengths, their special talents, and physical and emotional characteristics that the parents can learn to enjoy. Because these children may have lived in many homes over a period of years, they find that as they enter an adoptive placement their life changes yet again. The parents and children need to learn one another's preferences and how to function cohesively as a family.

RESEARCH SUPPORTING THE USE OF THERAPLAY

The successful use of Theraplay with adoptive children is supported by the work of Jernberg (1979, 1983, 1990). She has shown that Theraplay can be an effective way for adoptive children and parents to develop attachments. However, controlled research using Theraplay with adopted children is currently lacking.

Donley (1983) states that parents and children need to find ways to share their personal histories and to develop common interest. Theraplay is an action-oriented program that invites and excites parents and children to do this sharing. Often, it is done in a noncognitive way, which makes it much more successful for children who are cognitively or emotionally delayed.

THERAPLAY INNOVATIONS

As the adoptive process takes place, parents need to consider the upcoming changes. Often it is helpful to use Theraplay with them in role playing what it might be like to have the new child in their home. Both parents and children need to realize that they are basically "shopping" for a child or a parent and that it is reasonable to consider their first visits as a trial. In the past, children were often presented to parents and told that these people would be their new family. This could be very frightening and intimidating and gave the children no feeling of control or choice about this family. Adopted children need to feel a sense of control, as they often had no control up to this point in their lives.

New parents working with their new child need to learn how to take charge without fighting control battles. Theraplay does this by utilizing enticing games that help the child realize that this relationship can be safe and fun, and help the child feel better about him/herself. Theraplay is geared for success, and the Theraplay therapist recognizes when the child needs to win, and builds in ways for the child to be successful.

While Theraplay historically has been used on an individual basis at the Children's Home Society, it has been found also to be very useful with families as the adoption proceeds. When children are fully receptive to their parents in Theraplay, it is time to make the clinical decision of including one or more of the biological or other adoptive siblings. It then begins to simulate group Theraplay, but can become more intimate because family members can learn more personal things about each other. For example, Theraplay activities can teach positive touching through activities such as a Good Touch Train, which gives children and families the opportunity to experience healthy touching in a supervised and supportive fashion.

As other children are added, sometimes behavior problems occur because of competitiveness. Mother, May I is a good activity to help children enjoy following their parents' directions. Creative Theraplay rewards children with a hug when they have complied with a game in a fun way, and this also encourages intimacy. It is especially fun with sibling groups and their parents, or in multifamily therapy groups, which will be discussed later.

Throughout all of the activities, prompting family members to identify the inherent positive qualities about each other facilitates interaction, intimacy, and bonding. The therapist is directive in asking a parent or child to do things in specific ways and is direct in coaching them through the completion of the activity.

To promote reciprocity, a goal of Theraplay is to help children make lists of ways to make their parents happy. This was particularly helpful for a boy who had previously announced, "Moms have no place in my life." This child made his list with the help of his therapist, and his mother was delighted to find it taped to a place where he would often be reminded of it. She then realized how he had been reaching out to her, a new experience for both of them. It is sometimes helpful to do this privately between therapist and child so that the parents do not know the child is intentionally developing ways to please the parents. This is done in conjunction, of course, with helping parents find ways to please their children.

THE EIGHT PROCESSES IN ADOPTION

In their extensive work with adoptive children and families, Reitz and Watson (1992) identified seven key processes that affect adoptive families:

1. Entitlement
2. Claiming
3. Unmatched expectations
4. Shifting family systems
5. Separation, loss, and grief
6. Bonding and attachment
7. Identity formation

An eighth process, the search is also important, because children eventually ask about their biological parents. As the adoption process commences, consideration must be given to which of these processes are relevant. This list can also be helpful in identifying problems. Theraplay is useful in addressing problems, especially in bonding and attachment. But Theraplay activities can be utilized to solve problems in any of these processes. Following are specific activities that address the eight processes:

Entitlement

Parents must be helped to recognize that they have the emotional and legal right to parent their children. While the court confers the legal rights, "the emotional right grows out of the parents' increasing comfort with their roles as mother or father to the child" (Reitz and Watson 1992, p. 125). The Theraplay game called Mother [or Father], May I is a variation of an old childhood game, Captain, May I; it allows parents to be in charge. It encourages the playful practice of cooperation and helps with later disciplinary issues.

Claiming

An adoptive family and an adopted child must mutually come to feel they belong to each other. Typical Theraplay activities in this stage include having parents identify what is unique and special about their child and how the child is similar to the parents. While Theraplay often looks for specific and individual differences, in this stage it is important to notice similarities in how the child looks or acts like the family. An example of a Theraplay game is Follow the Leader. The child is taught, again in a playful way, to copy what parents do and to behave like them.

A Theraplay activity that has been successful with larger families is the How Are We the Same? game, a nurturing game in which family members powder one another's hands and then make hand prints on a large piece of colored construction paper. This game helps them point out similarities and differences to each other as a fun way of getting to know each other.

As the children learn to belong to their new families, it is important for the family to develop new rituals, such as holiday and birthday traditions. One idea is look–alike clothing or T-shirts for each family member announcing, "I am a [family surname]."

Unmatched Expectations

Both parents and children may be mourning the loss of their dreams. The parents may have dreamed of a perfect or different child than the one they received. The child may have wanted a different family composition or richer parents, or other differences. Now they need to begin to create a common history, which can be done through photo albums and telling their personal stories to each other. Some of this sharing needs to be cognitive, with guidance from a therapist.

A Theraplay activity helps parents and children identify their specific likes and dislikes. The therapist picks a topic, and the parent and child identify things they like and don't like in that topic. The therapist picks the topic of colors; the parent says, "I like purple," and the child says "I like red." If the topic is food, the parents say, "I like pizza," and the child says, "I like pizza." They can then celebrate their likes and dislikes and recognize how they are the same and different in various ways. As they create the common history, they are able to relinquish their dreams and enjoy the pleasure of falling in love with their new parent or child.

Shifting Family Systems

It is inevitable that when adoptive children enter a family, everything changes. The balance in the family is changed, routines and rituals are different, and everyone must make adjustments.

In the Theraplay activity In Our Family, parents and children are asked to identify things they want in their family: "In our family, I want. . . . " The Theraplay therapist can direct them to think of things they can get now such as lots of hugs or lotion on their hands.

With large families many group Theraplay activities can be used. In one, all family members except one form a circle holding hands. The other person is outside the circle and attempts to get in while everyone in the circle attempts to physically prevent him/her from doing so. This points out how difficult it is for someone new to enter the family and builds understanding about ways to help each other in the process. The game is then replayed, with at least one person willing to help the "outsider" get into the family circle. Another Theraplay activity, Circle Magnets also helps family members learn to join together and function as a team.

Separation, Loss, and Grief

This part of the adoptive process is critical for parents and children. Parents may be grieving the loss of a child or despairing about their infertility, while the child is grieving the loss of previous caregivers, including biological parents. Typical Theraplay activities emphasize nurturing, where parents rock, lotion, and powder a child in a way the child will accept. This helps children recover from the losses they experienced. Because children who have suffered losses often misbehave, it is important to get the child into the parents' hearts quickly. This positive, shared experience helps them all through the difficult times to come. Older adoptive children have often never received the basic nurturing experiences that promote feelings of attachment, so it is critical that they learn that adults can care for them in basic nurturing ways that communicate unconditional acceptance.

An exciting Theraplay game is Hide and Seek. The child hides, often under a blanket, and the parents then search for her. While she is in hiding, the parents can lament the loss of the child and name the specific characteristics of the child they are looking for. The delight of being found is exciting for most children.

It is important for parents and children to share their sadness. If a child begins to cry, it is critical that the parent simply hold and comfort him without expecting any talk. Because as new parents they want the child to be happy, the tendency is often for them to try to cheer them up. However, it is most effective if they are helped to see that the child needs to grieve, and that by holding and comforting him they are a help. Theraplay can focus on having parents and children take turns naming sad things that have happened in their lives and share each other's sadness. Theraplay often has parents rock the children in their arms, sometimes singing a special song about them, sometimes feeding them a lollipop, or allowing them to drink from a baby bottle.

To deal with separation, a transitional object is often used, and something symbolic such as a written contract about the parents' commitment to the child is very powerful. A book called *The Kissing Hand* (Penn 1993) is an example of a therapeutic way to handle separation problems as children claim their new parents and don't want to let them go.

Attachment

In this area, traditional Theraplay is the treatment of choice. It promotes attachment by replicating what a normal mother might do with a younger child, especially nurturing. Other examples include rocking the child in a blanket or in the mother's arms while singing a special song about him/her, feeding a favorite food, playing beauty salon, or perhaps engaging in Donut Dare. The nurturing activities are designed to involve positive touch, which builds self-esteem and unconditional acceptance. Therapists are advised to learn traditional Theraplay methods to help with bonding and attachment, which are the crux of parents and children accepting each other and learning about each other. The child is allowed to regress, although not required to engage in regressive behavior.

Theraplay considers the emotional age (often that of a younger child) rather than the chronological age of the child, and his needs are met accordingly. Examples of activities include having the child try the parent's lap out for size in a playful way and then asking the parents to sing a song to the child after identifying all of the unique and special characteristics that they notice about him. The therapist guides the parents to notice the child's positive qualities and this helps them fall in love with each other.

With sibling groups, it is best to have the parents use Theraplay individually with each child first, then move to family Theraplay activities. The previously mentioned Getting to Know You Game is very powerful in the bonding and attachment stage. Other ideas are limited only by the therapist's creativity and imagination.

Parents adopting children will benefit from learning the three R's, C's, and P's in developing attachment:

The three R's:	Rules
	Rituals
	Routines
The three C's:	Conversation
	Contact
	Cuddling
The three P's:	Patience
	Persistence
	Play

Identity Formation

Theraplay activities are used to recognize what is different about the child from the parents and other family members. Theraplay activities include comparing size of hands, color of eyes, and other ways in which the child is physically different. The child is helped to recognize her own unique qualities. In the game Fast Hands, parent and child take turns placing their hand on the table and one tries to quickly tap it before the other pulls it away. There are variations of this game, such as thumb wrestling or arm wrestling. The parent can then celebrate the child's abilities and focus on her uniqueness.

Search

The search for a child's past is almost inevitable, and adoptive parents need to recognize that this is normal. Early Theraplay pays off during this stage because the child is connected emotionally to the parents, and they need not be threatened by his search. Parents can assist the child in recovering a lost history.

Although not a standard Theraplay activity, Hearts makes the point about children loving their biological and adoptive families. The parent is asked to draw a small picture of a heart on a large piece of paper. Then the children are told that when they were born they were only able to love themselves. A second heart is drawn around the outside of the first heart and the child and parent determine together who the child learned to love next. Succeeding hearts list all of the people that the child has learned to love in his life. A final large heart lists the adoptive family. The game points out that the child has room in her heart to love many people. Full credit for this activity is given to a joyful loving adoptive mother who created it.

Family Theraplay continues to be important during the search stage. Families need to have fun activities to do together that promote the ongoing, established interactive patterns they have developed to make a connection with their child. By this stage, the child is usually older, and Theraplay activities include keeping physical connection, making eye contact when talking, and showing love through daily demonstration of care and concern.

BEHAVIOR PROBLEMS

During the eight processes described above, behavior problems almost always develop. As the parent brings these behavior problems into

therapy, it is most helpful if the therapist considers the possible antidote that will meet the need without the child demanding it. These
antidotes are then used to create Theraplay activities that can be done
in therapy. Following are some examples:

Running away: Parent and child play variations of tag.

Lying: Parent and child play "true/not true." Parent makes a concrete statement such as "My shirt is blue" and child is asked
to respond with "true" or "not true."

Hoarding food: Give the children canned goods to keep in their rooms.
They may open them with permission.

Opposition: The parent says a word and the child says the opposite.

Stealing: The child is given an object to guard and take responsibility for. Compliments and praise are given for doing so successfully. A dollar bill is a good item to use.

Aggression: Fast Hands and other ways for the child to demonstrate strength, such as arm wrestling or thumb wrestling,
are important. Paper Punch or Sword Fight using rolled newspapers are safe ways to display aggression. Pushing and pulling games of strength give the child a feeling of self-worth
and self-control.

Encopresis: Water play and play in activities that are messy such
as clay or chocolate pudding are the best antidote.

Enuresis: Water play and particularly play with soap bubbles is
delightful to the child. Regressive bonding activities of holding and nurturing create the feelings of unconditional acceptance the child so strongly needs.

Proactive thinking on the part of the parents and the use of Theraplay to promote positive feelings is always more successful than angry
reactions.

MULTIFAMILY THERAPLAY

It has been found that adoptive families often have much in common
with one another, and thus it can be useful to work with several families at a time. There are many Theraplay activities that can be done with

a group, such as Human Knot and Good Touch Train. Another activity involves all members standing in a circle shoulder to shoulder. The therapist uses a bottle of lotion to write each person's initial on an outstretched hand. All group members then place their hands together and help each other rub the lotion in. With multiple families, many noncompetitive games, especially those involving nurturing, are met with success.

To organize and facilitate multifamily Theraplay, a number of families, usually three to five, are invited to participate. Co-therapists lead the sessions, which are scheduled over a period of several consecutive days. Part of this time is spent discussing therapeutic issues, but Theraplay plays an important part in promoting family fun and bonding. Opening ceremonies include each family lighting a candle together and discussing their hopes. Near the end of the session a fun activity is Find Your Parent. Closing ceremonies include each family's members sitting on a quilt with their candle lit, identifying things they enjoy about their family.

TREATMENT PROGRESS AND CURRENT STATUS OF FAMILIES TREATED

Beginning with one child five years ago until the present, approximately fifteen to twenty children and families have learned Theraplay at our center. All of the families treated have thus far maintained their adoption. One child is currently receiving treatment for posttraumatic stress disorder symptoms she is experiencing as she matures and recalls past traumas. However, her parents have no intention of disrupting the adoption and consider her "our child." Many of the families are very open in admitting there are days when they question why they had accepted this challenge, but all of them have indicated their desire to maintain their relationship and continue to develop their families. They all need much support, and often just an encouraging phone call helps remind them that if they engage their children in Theraplay activities together, many of the behavior problems will dissipate.

All of the families involved in this type of treatment have made steady progress. Adopting older children, especially sibling groups, is never easy, and many problems are encountered. Old behaviors appear, particularly during stresses in the child's life. However, if the initial steps are done well, and Theraplay has been used to begin the attachment process, the families generally do well. When these problems occur, it has been found helpful to return to Theraplay and give focused attention to the individual child, and then again have the entire family involve themselves in Theraplay activities.

Parents adopting sibling groups need good advice and encouragement. When behavior problems occur, they need help. However, even more important, they need to consider the child's needs and to find Theraplay activities that they can use to meet the needs so that the child does not resort to negative behavior. It is important that parents be helped to remember that Theraplay can be the basis of a relationship. When this is done, parents have been extremely cooperative. Parents have also benefited from receiving small doses of Theraplay from the therapist. Having the therapist notice a new haircut, special smile, or great giggles can enhance parental self-esteem. They, too, enjoy unconditional acceptance! Having the therapist point out things they have done exceptionally well and how they are inherently good as parents has often facilitated the parents' continuing efforts.

A critical sign that the Theraplay activities are helping in building relationship is when the children ask, "Can we do these activities at home?" Parents are then encouraged to do the activities at home and to come up with their own specific family activities that are based on intimacy and playful interaction.

Treatment progress can often be measured by looking for signs of attachment. Following is a list of attachment behaviors that begin to develop as the child settles into the family. When the child does these things, fewer behavior problems are reported.

ATTACHMENT BEHAVIORS

1. Makes eye contact spontaneously
2. Voluntarily seeks physical contact
3. Accepts physical contact when parents initiate it
4. Obeys willingly
5. Obeys grudgingly but without rage
6. Imitates parents' behavior
7. Demonstrates separation anxiety; protests parents' absence
8. Confides in parents

9. Admits mistakes
10. Seeks comfort during stressful times
11. Accepts comfort during stressful times
12. Indicates acceptance of family rules, beliefs, and values
13. Shows preference for specific caregivers
14. Clings

PROBLEMS ENCOUNTERED AND SOLUTIONS

Children who have experienced abuse and neglect can have severe behavior problems. Even the best-prepared parents struggle with the children's belligerence, intentional enuresis, lying, stealing, aggression, and hysterical behavior. Sibling groups who have been through extreme trauma together are often found to have a pattern of very wild and hysterical behavior that they stimulate in each other. It presents as silly and giddy, but borders on hysterical because it is extreme and the children appear unable to stop themselves. The solutions often lie in helping the parents determine what the children want and need, and helping them find a therapeutic way of responding.

Solutions to problems are facilitated by giving parents support and affirming their personal belief that they are good parents. They benefit from opportunities to vent their frustrations, and it is often necessary to help them find other adoptive parents with whom they can discuss them. They need encouragement to take care of themselves. They also need encouragement to recognize things they cannot change, and decide whether they can live with them. In Theraplay, these parents need as many laps as there are children. With each child on a lap receiving Theraplay, the hysterical pattern is interrupted and the children become calm.

Respite services have been one of the major ways to solve problems. Even the most loving parents can tolerate extreme behaviors for only so long. When the children take a short vacation to a treatment facility, another foster family, or extended family, it gives the parents a chance to reflect on their own needs and solutions to problems. They also often find themselves missing the child, which is very important.

One of the best approaches to problems is to review with the parents the eight processes of adoption and determine which are the most problematic. Then they can be helped to determine a way to meet the children's needs through Theraplay activities. It is often important to focus on individual Theraplay activities with a parent and child, but then move into including the entire family to promote cohesiveness in playful activities.

TREATMENT RESULTS

With support, all of our families are maintaining the placement and have rarely indicated intention of disrupting it. They have all been helped to realize that parenting adopted children is a lifelong process and that there are ongoing struggles. They have learned that whether received by birth or through adoption, children will present problems which need to be solved.

The early work of Theraplay has increased attachment feelings and helped parents fall in love with their children. Once the child is in their hearts, they are able to survive the difficult times. They all report that they benefit from using the Theraplay activities at home, and the activities help them feel closer to the child. The parents indicate that they need their therapist in order to maintain confidence in themselves and to be assured that their judgment is correct. They have done best when encouraged to problem solve and come up with their own solutions rather than depending on the Therapist to find a solution.

Even when things are going well, it is most helpful for the family to have regular Theraplay checkups where the entire family comes in to assess not only problems but positive physical and emotional growth.

FUTURE RECOMMENDATIONS

Therapists should help parents realize at the outset that not only the parents but also the children have a role in making this relationship work. Children who are more than a few years old have often developed many behavior problems and very clearly know how to get out of a situation they do not like by demonstrating bizarre behavior, which will drive parents away. If, at the beginning, parents and children have gotten to know each other's preferences and personal history, the adoption process has gone quite well.

At the beginning, Theraplay should be used with parents and children individually, and then with the entire family to help the children accept the regressive nurturing that they did not receive as infants. Many parents do not naturally do this, and although it may feel uncomfortable to them at first, it is important that the therapist coach them in holding the child and engaging him with eye contact so that he can learn to accept tender nurturing.

It is recommended that the therapist very actively involve the entire family in Theraplay activities together to meet each other's needs and to recognize that other family members have needs.

SUMMARY

Adoption is an attachment process, and Theraplay can help. Many parents naturally engage their children in Theraplay activities and this is very useful. However, specifically designed therapeutic activities that help parents and children develop intimacy is critical.

Entire families can be involved in Theraplay, which helps all family members learn about each other and how to interact with each other. This helps the child take root within the adoptive family and feel like a true family member.

Multiple families can work together to help each other in facilitating the attachment process. Often, extremely disruptive children need many adults for a short period of time to help them through their difficulties and for them to realize that the adults can manage them. Multiple family work can be time- and cost-efficient as well as very effective.

When attachments develop, children learn to confide in their parents and develop trust, and behavior problems subside.

ACTIVITIES LIST

Theraplay activities particularly suited for adoptive children are as follows:

1. *Theraplay Checkup*: Parents notice unique and special characteristics of the child: special freckles, dimples, wiggly toes, and other inherent qualities.

2. *How Are We the Same Game*: Parents and children look for physical characteristics that are the same, such as curly hair, color of eyes, or a special smile.

3. *Good Touch Train*: All group members stand in a row, one behind the other. Each member is asked to give the person in front of him or her a good touch on the back, and that person is asked to respond with comments or moans and groans about whether the touch feels good.

4. *Getting to Know You Game*: Parent or therapist identifies a topic, such as food, color, and activity, and parents and children identify their specific preferences.

5. *Trace Shapes, Letters, or Numbers*: Parents and children write letters, shapes, or numbers, especially those they know the child will like, on each others' backs and try to guess what the shape or letter it is.

6. *What's Neat about You*: Therapist prompts parents to identify inherent positive qualities about the child.

7. *Happy Parents' List*: Children and parents identify what makes parents happy, with the emphasis on things such as hugs, that can be practiced in the therapy session.

8. *Mother/Dad, May I?*: Parents are at one end of the room, children are side by side at the other end of the room. Parents take turns giving the children a direction, such as three giant steps, and before the children can do it, they must say, "Mother/Dad may I?" and the parents give permission.

9. *Circle Magnets*: Every family member is separated into his own space, and the therapist begins singing a song, preferably about the family. As the singing continues, the family gets closer and closer together until there is a group hug at the end.

10. *Donut Dare*: Parent holds a donut on his finger and family members take turns taking a bite out of it, with the intent of not breaking through to the hole, at which point the donut falls off.

11. *Paper Punch*: Parent holds a sheet of newspaper outstretched and children are asked to demonstrate their strength by punching through the paper with their fist.

12. *Human Knot*: All members of a group stand shoulder to shoulder and grasp two extended hands, which do not belong to

the person next to them. This forms a knot and they are helped to untangle the knot without letting go of hands.

13. *Find Your Parent*: Parents and children are asked to walk around while the therapist sings a song. When the singing stops, children are encouraged to see how quickly they can find their parent's lap.

14. *Foot/Hand Prints*: Parents and children compare size and shape of hand prints, which are drawn or made with baby powder.

15. *Pudding Finger Paint*: Parents and children participate in making a picture with flavored pudding and can enjoy licking it off each other's fingers.

16. *Marshmallow Taffy*: Parents and children take several marshmallows and, using their thumb and forefinger, squish the marshmallow and begin stretching and pulling it until it becomes taffy. They may enjoy feeding it to each other.

17. *Blowing Bubbles*: Parents and children get their hands wet and add liquid soap. By putting their hands together and then spreading their palms apart slightly, they can blow big bubbles together.

18. *Child Walks on Hands*: Parent holds child's feet and guides child in showing her strength by walking as far as possible on her hands.

19. *Finding Tickles*: Gently, parents find tickle spots behind ears, under knees, and in other special places.

20. *Bean Blow*: Parents and children each have a straw and are asked to blow an object such as a bean or a cotton ball back and forth to each other across a line.

21. *Human Tunnel*: All of the group members, except one, are on their hands and knees side by side. The remaining person can crawl under the tunnel to the end, and then another person gets a turn.

22. *"Row, Row, Row Your Boat"*: All family members sit in a circle with their arms on each other's shoulders. They sing "Row, Row, Row Your Boat" and, at the end, everybody leans back onto a pillow or joins in a group hug.

23. *Feeding Activities*: A critical part of regressive activities important in forming attachment is feeding. Family members are encouraged to find creative ways to feed each other fun treats provided by the therapist.

24. *Tug of War*: Parents and children engage in a simple tug of war using a bandanna or short rope. Therapist structures the teams to create desired alliances.

25. *Pretzel Dare*: Parents and children hold a pretzel on their fingers and see who can get the most bites out of it before it breaks.

26. *Licorice Eating Contest*: Parents and children begin eating a long strip of licorice with one person at each end. When they get to the middle, their noses touch.

27. *Hiding Food*: Parent has child close eyes and hides small special treats on him in safe and fun places. Child then finds the food, and parent feeds it to him.

28. *Bubble Gum Dare*: Parents and children chew bubble gum and see who can make the biggest bubble.

29. *This Little Piggy Went to Market*: Parent discovers child's toes and plays "This Little Piggy" by saying, while touching each toe from biggest to smallest, "This little piggy went to market, this little piggy stayed at home, this little piggy had roast beef, and this little piggy had none; and this little piggy cried, wee, wee, wee all the way home." While saying "wee, wee, wee," parent's fingers climb gently to child's tummy for a soft tickle. To personalize this, parent then varies the scenario to discover things about the child. For example: "This little piggy had big brown eyes, just like you; and this little piggy had a special dimple on his chin, just like the one I see on your chin; this little piggy had soft curly hair, like your hair" and so on, discovering the unique and special characteristics about the child in a very personal way.

30. *Peekaboo*: Parent covers child's eyes and delights in finding child's eyes between her fingers, or covers child's face gently with a blanket and delights in finding her.

31. *Newspaper Basketball*: Parents and children roll up pieces of newspaper and compete in making baskets through a hoop they have made by holding their arms in a circle.

32. *Balloon Toss*: Parents and children bat a balloon back and forth to each other and see how many times they can pass it back and forth without it touching the floor or anything in the room except a person.

33. *Follow the Leader*: Parents and children take turns leading the

rest of the family in walking or moving about the room in fun and interesting ways.

REFERENCES

Donley, K. (1983). *Opening New Doors: Finding Families for Older and Handicapped Children*. London: British Agencies for Adoption and Fostering.

Jernberg, A. (1979). *Theraplay*. San Francisco: Jossey-Bass.

———. (1983). Therapeutic use of sensory-motor play. In *Handbook of Play Therapy*, ed. C. E. Schaefer and K. J. O'Connor, pp. 128–147. New York: Wiley.

———. (1990). Attachment enhancing for adopted children. In *Adoption Resources for Mental Health Professionals*, ed. P. V. Grabe, pp. 271–279. New Brunswick: Transaction.

Penn, S. (1993). *The Kissing Hand*. Washington, DC: Child Welfare League of America.

Reitz, M., and Watson, K. M. (1992). *Adoption and the Family System*. New York: Guilford.

14

Adults and Children Together (ACT): A Prevention Model

JANET ZANETTI

CHARLES O. MATTHEWS

RICHARD P. HOLLINGSWORTH

JUSTIFICATION

Research and clinical experience over the past fifty years has demonstrated that effective intervention with young children must address the environment of the child. "Even in those cases where the child's problems seem to originate because of biological characteristics, such as difficult temperament, or neurological defects suspected in autistic, hyperactive, or developmentally impaired youngsters, many of the problem behaviors seem to be intensified by the interaction patterns between parent and child" (Eyberg 1988 p. 35).

Depending upon the orientation of the professional, intervention might be in the form of individual therapy of the parent or the child, family counseling, or a psychoeducational approach involving parent skills training. Delivery of care may take place in the office of the clinician, in the family home, or in the community educational center.

In many instances, however, parents most in need of help for themselves or their children are least likely to seek it. Insufficient information about the availability of services, lack of adequate resources to obtain services, or a failure of personal commitment to continue in services may keep families from obtaining help.

Community programs are needed that utilize an outreach model of treatment/training and that involve a partnership of parents and professionals. Mental health services delivered in the educational setting provide a multidisciplinary approach that supports the child in a familiar environment. The goals of these programs can be preventive or remedial.

The purpose of this research study was to investigate the effects of a six-week training program, ACT (adults and children together), on parents and children in the Head Start program in Virginia Beach, Virginia. In this research study, ACT was intended as a preventive intervention for parents and children not currently using a clinic's services.

ACT is a structured intervention of play activities designed to replicate patterns of healthy interaction between parents and children during the first developmental stage of life. This period, between birth and 18 months of age, concerns the developmental tasks of attachment and separation which are critical for ego development and subsequent social adjustment (Ainsworth et al. 1978, Bowlby 1969, Erikson 1963).

ACT has been adapted, by the researcher, from Theraplay, which was developed by Ann Jernberg (1979). ACT focuses on four basic developmental needs identified by Jernberg: structuring—delineating time and space; nurturing—the pleasure of contact; intruding—stimulation and arousal; and challenging—competitive confrontation.

ACT differs from the Jernberg model in several ways:

1. Dyads consist of parent and child instead of clinician and child.
2. Sessions include multifamily dyads.
3. Techniques are not individualized; all participants receive structuring, nurturing, intruding, and challenging activities.
4. Training time is limited to six weeks.

POPULATION

ACT, like the original Theraplay, is intended for families that are participating in Head Start, a community-based early childhood program for children of ages 3 to 5. The goals of the Head Start program are to bring about academic readiness in children and to promote social competence in their families. Parental training is a significant component of the program.

Developed in 1965 by a planning committee of fourteen professionals in medicine, early education, and mental health, Head Start has served over 13 million children and their families. Funding for the program has come primarily from the federal government. All the families enrolled in the program have low income or receive public assistance, as mandated by Head Start legislation.

Edlefsen and Baird (1994) report on changes they have observed in the disadvantaged pre-school population which they serve. "First, children are arriving with fewer intellectual, social, and emotional school-readiness skills. Second, pre-school children have a precocious knowledge of life issues and experiences that they lack the emotional and cognitive ability to understand and integrate. Third, the inability of parents to show interest or participate in their child's educational experience has become increasingly apparent" (p. 567). School-based services, which utilize a multidisciplinary team approach, offer a viable model for early intervention.

SUPPORTIVE RESEARCH

The current study utilized the theoretical position of Erik H. Erikson (1963) in an examination of parent–child interaction. Erikson's psychosocial theory, regarding personality development, has been cited by scientific, clinical, and education groups over several decades. It is on stage one of the Erikson model, which he called trust versus mistrust, that the current study is focused. This developmental stage, which occurs roughly between birth and 18 months of age, concerns the tasks of attachment and separation and is primarily a period of sensorimotor development.

Research has shown that successful resolution of the attachment–separation stage of life depends upon the quality of the interaction between parent and child. When the responses of the caregiver are appropriate to the infant's temperament and needs, secure attachment results (Ainsworth et al. 1978). But secure attachment involves more than the satisfaction of physiological needs. Consistent and responsive interaction in familiar rituals is also an important part of the attachment bond

(Erikson 1963). The infant who is securely attached establishes trust in the availability and consistency of the caregiver and will risk separation in order to explore his or her environment and to establish other relationships (Feiring 1984). When responses of the caregiver create understimulation or overstimulation of the child, anxious or avoidant behavior may result. Developmental progress may be inhibited unless corrective emotional experiences, which address the tasks of this lifestage, are provided.

Since the 1960s, a variety of interventions have emerged to remediate family dysfunction.

> Encouraged by the emerging psychotherapy research findings indicating the importance of the facilitative conditions for psychotherapy outcome and spurred by an acute awareness of the shortage of mental health personnel, a growing number of workers began to train professional and lay helpers to enhance their interpersonal functioning in term of the facilitative conditions. The facilitative conditions became known as skills, and systematic skills-training programs emerged. [Levant 1983, p. 29]

Levant compared several client-centered family skills-training programs, including (1) Relationship Enhancement (RE), developed by Guerney; (2) Communication and Parenting Skills (CAPS), developed by D'Augelli and Weener; (3) Human Resource Development (HRD) programs, developed by Carkhuff; (4) Microcounseling, developed by Ivey; (5) Parent Effectiveness Training (PET), developed by Gordon; and Personal Development Program developed by Levant and associates. Levant (1983) sums up the objectives of these programs:

> (1) training for treatment in which family members are trained in the application of a form of therapeutic intervention to be applied to another family member . . . (2) training as treatment in which the training of the family member is viewed as the treatment itself . . . (3) training for enhancement in which the aim is either preventing clinical problems or stimulating the development of family members through teaching interpersonal communication and other social skills. [p. 29]

Professionals with a behavioral orientation have utilized parent skills training to instruct parents in the concepts of operant conditioning. Patterson (1975) developed a systematic training program for parents that included instruction in differential attention, reinforcement, and consequences. Hanf (1969) outlined a two-stage model in which she instructed the child's mother in operant behavior-management skills as well as coaching the mother and child together in the therapy session. Eyberg (1988) added to the work of Hanf by integrating the skills used by play therapists as well as behavior therapists. "It seemed that the most rapid and effective way to treat the psychological problems of young children would be to treat the parent–child dyad together, coaching parents directly in the established therapeutic skills used by play therapists and taught by behavior therapists" (p. 33).

The presence of the parent in treatment/training sessions can help to strengthen the child's connection to the family and foster the relationship system that is so critical to the child's psychological well-being (Eaker 1986). It can be reciprocally beneficial to adults and children. Parents can be coached to gain particular skills, and the family can experiment with changes in their interactional patterns within a safe setting (Scharff 1989).

Working with parents and children together can be particularly challenging for professionals who lack a developmental perspective. Early (1994) observes that some therapists have discouraged conjoint family therapy involving young children or unconsciously encouraged disengagement of families already in conjoint therapy "out of a sense of relief" (p. 119). Play can be an effective means of working with families with young children. A range of experiential options are available for use in family play. Vos (1988) defines *experiential* as "any intervention which consists of something other than simple discussion or 'talking about'" (p. 116). She includes art-based techniques such as family drawings and family sculpture, games and tasks, Gestalt-related techniques, guided imagery and fantasy, humor and cartoons, myth and metaphor, photographs, psychodrama and role play, and toys and puppets.

Theraplay is another approach that addresses the needs of both parent and child utilizing the technique of play. Theraplay utilizes the touch and movement natural to early development. It is intended to promote attachment, self-esteem, and trust in others through joyful engagement. Theraplay differs from traditional play therapy in the degree to which the adult assumes responsibility for the activities. Much of the Jernberg model includes techniques adapted from work by Des Lauriers (1962) and Brody (1978), in which body and eye contact and vigorous motor activities are a part of the program. Theraplay adds to these earlier models an emphasis on nurturing.

Golden (1986) reviewed Theraplay as a therapeutic modality to facilitate the development of healthy narcissism in both child and parent. "In the context of the Theraplay sessions, and while observing their child in the Theraplay sessions, parents are helped in developing their own healthy narcissism. They are helped and given permission to feel powerful, important, significant, impactful, and understood" (p. 104).

Robbins (1987) has utilized Theraplay with parent groups to "enhance the parents' capacity to accept and practice healthy self-nourishing behaviors" (p. 6). In this instance, parents participated without their children, using one another as objects of discovery and play. The adults exhibited the same growth in degree of intimacy, trust, and nurturing as is seen in parent–child interactional groups. Playpartners is another adaptation developed by Robbins (1990) for parents and children utilizing the nurturing component of the original model. Dance is incorporated in this program.

Rubin and Tregay (1989) developed Theraplay groups for special education classes, using the classroom teacher, other professionals, and peers as primary objects of play. Their book, *Play with Them—Theraplay Groups in the Classroom*, has influenced others to organize groups in regular preschool and primary classes. Rubin (1995) reports on her use of Theraplay with mothers and children in a shelter for the homeless (see Chapter 12, this volume). Several additional Theraplay models were reported on in the *Theraplay Institute Newsletter* in 1995. Talen (1995) integrated Theraplay techniques into her work in a community-based primary health care project. "Because attachment is a basic need for healthy development, primary health care for young children should address the attachment issues and relationship qualities between children and their caregivers" (p. 1). Talen used a multidisciplinary approach that included teachers, nurses, and students in training. A variety of opportunities were provided for parents and staff to broaden the understanding of health to include interaction aspects (see Chapter 18, this volume). Bostrom (1995) describes a preschool curriculum based on Theraplay that provides a way to help parents understand the needs of their child and to look at their own life and needs as well. Additionally, Bostrom has used group Theraplay to foster attachment in post-institutionalized adopted children. Martin (1995) introduced Theraplay to preschool through third grade teachers in western Virginia for use in their classrooms (see Chapter 17, this volume). "The common element for all of these teachers is the realization that as educators we must give more attention to the social and emotional needs of the children, not in reaction to misbehavior, but in meeting the needs at the developmental level at which they began" (p. 4). Others are incorporating Theraplay into the classroom (Lovejoy 1995) and treatment centers (Moyer 1995, Munns 1995). Theraplay also has been utilized with children impacted by the human immunodeficiency virus (HIV) (Chambers 1995) and pervasive development disorder (PDD) (Bundy-Myrow 1994, Rieff and Booth 1994). Koller and Booth (1997) have written and presented extensively on the techniques of family Theraplay.

BACKGROUND

Before beginning the research study, a pilot program was conducted to assess the effectiveness of ACT for small group training. The activities were formalized into a training package that included video and written representation of the activities.

Facilitators, with bachelor's degrees in counseling and experience in family service delivery, were recruited and trained by the researcher. Training included written instructions of the ACT program and a review of video segments of the pilot group.

Meetings were scheduled between the researcher and the Head Start administrators, supervisors, and teachers to review the concepts and activities for ACT. Written agreements, outlining the responsibilities of the Head Start staff and of the researcher, were obtained. Centers that could provide adequate space and privacy were identified. ACT groups were scheduled at four Head Start centers.

Written notices were sent home with each child at the centers identified for ACT play groups. Additionally, parents were given information about ACT in a presentation, by the researcher, during the regularly scheduled monthly parent meetings.

One additional orientation meeting was held for parents who indicated an interest in ACT. The following points were reviewed:

1. Participation in the study was voluntary.
2. Weekly attendance and follow-up appointments were required.
3. Confidentiality of objective measures was assured.
4. Permission to videotape sessions was needed to ensure equal training between groups.

Participants were fully informed of their right to refuse to answer specific questions on the assessment instruments or to withdraw from the study at any time without penalty of losing their child's place in Head Start. Informed consents were obtained from participating parents.

Families were excluded from the study if no parent or designated caregiver was available; if either adult or child was in crisis or recovering from crisis such as death, divorce, or physical trauma; or if either adult or child was exhibiting psychotic, organic, or drug-related symptoms.

GOALS

Literature on parent–child interactional play suggested the direction for the following hypotheses for the study:

1. Incidents of negative behavior, as measured on the Parent Rating Scale-48 (Conners 1990), will decrease in children who participate with their parents in the ACT program.
2. Levels of stress, as measured on the Parent Stress Index/Short Form (Abidin 1990), will be reduced in parents who participate with their child in the ACT program.

DESIGN

This study utilized a pretest, posttest, time-control group design. Experimental and control groups were formed from a pool of volunteer families. Fifteen families were contained in each group. Only the experimental groups received training in ACT. At the conclusion of the study, control subjects were offered the opportunity to join a play training group.

Training program sessions were held on site, during school hours, to maximize parent and child participation. Sessions were conducted weekly for six weeks. Each session lasted approximately 60 minutes. Groups contained no more than six parent–child dyads. All subjects participated in play activities for the first 30 minutes. Following play, parents had an additional 30 minutes for discussion. Children were supervised by Head Start staff during the discussion time. A total of five six-week training groups were conducted over the duration of one year.

DATA GATHERING

Assessment included objective measures, structured interviews, and observations (see pp. 272 and 273). Objective assessment of adult stress and of children's behavior was conducted prior to treatment and at the conclusion of the six-week training. Adults in experimental and control groups completed both assessments at both intervals. Observation from videotapes of training sessions was reviewed weekly for planning and informal evaluation of parent–child interactions. Structured interviews were conducted with experimental group participants following training.

PROCEDURES

For the initial session of ACT, a large space in the room is cleared of furniture and materials. There are no toys—only the participants. In ACT, it is intended that the adult and child become the primary play objects for each other in much the same way that an infant and its caregiver interact.

Participants enter the room together and remain a dyad throughout the session, maintaining touch and eye contact as much as possible. Sessions begin and terminate with participants sitting together in a large circle.

Activities are introduced by the facilitator and vary in a predetermined way, alternating boisterous and calming experiences in both regressive and age-appropriate activities. No specific rules are established, except that participants must remain in the room. Modeling or a few words from the facilitator signal shifts in activities. Participants are encouraged to discover their own patterns and style of interaction within the basic activity.

Each session has a specific beginning, middle, and end routine. Each meeting contains greeting activities, new activities (sessions 1 to 6), review activities (sessions 2 to 6), and closing activities. Following the play activities, children are taken to a separate area for snacks and games. Parents remain for discussion.

Session 1: Structuring

Participants begin by sitting together in the large circle (nest) that has been outlined on the floor with chalk or tape. Dyads are instructed to adopt the "waiting" position with the child sitting or reclining between the parent's outstretched legs. Names are exchanged.

The facilitator begins with a brief introduction about animal babies, citing ways in which the babies are cared for, protected, and taught by their parents. Children are asked if they can remember being a baby. Participants are encouraged to share any early memories of this time. The facilitator describes how a human baby waits to be born, curled up and protected inside the mother. Parents are told to wrap their arms around their "babies," holding them gently but tightly in a ball. The facilitator slowly counts 1–2–3–4–5, then demonstrates how to unfold and stretch.

The facilitator describes a typical first-time meeting of parents and new baby. Parents are instructed to lay their "baby" down gently on the floor and to examine the child, noting color of eyes and number of fingers and toes. Later, parents are encouraged to rock the child in their arms, humming or quietly singing a lullaby. Early games such as peekaboo, pull-ups, and mild tickling are suggested. The session concludes with children assuming the lead in teaching parents a game from the current school program.

Session 2: Structuring (Review) and Nurturing

Parents and children enter the room together. Parents have been instructed to remove the children's shoes before coming to the circle (nest). Facilitator greets each person by name and has them sit in the waiting position. A short period of checkup is encouraged—"Does anyone have anything that they want to share? What do you remember about last week? How did that feel to you?" After a brief discussion, the facilitator begins by asking the dyads to assume the curled position. This signals the start of the reenactment activities. Children practice folding, holding, and stretching after the count of 5.

The facilitator asks the parent–child dyads to redo a few activities such as peekaboo or finger and toe nibbling from the previous week. After about 5 minutes, the facilitator signals a shift in activities by returning to the circle and assuming the waiting position.

The facilitator tells a short story about how different animal parents feed their young. The discussion leads into the feeding of human babies. Mention is made of nursing and bottles, but the enactment utilizes spoon feeding of soft foods such as applesauce or pudding. Children are held in their parent's arms when fed. Eye contact is stressed. The session concludes with children teaching their parents a game from their school program.

Session 3: Nurturing (Review) and Introducing

The facilitator greets participants by name. A short checkup follows: "What's new? What has happened to you since we were together?" The facilitator asks the group to assume the curled position, folding, holding, and stretching after the count of 5.

The nurturing activities from the previous week are reviewed. Nurturing is expanded to include finger foods. Parents and children feed each other bananas or small doughnuts. Playfulness is stressed.

After a brief time, the signal to shift activities is given by the facilitator, who returns to the circle and assumes the waiting position. The facilitator tells a story of animal babies being groomed by parents. Grooming activities, using powder and lotion, are introduced. The children are asked to stretch out on the floor and parents are shown how to apply lotion or powder to hands and arms and feet and legs. The facilitator models slow massage with lotion or powder.

The session ends in the same manner as previous weeks with children teaching parents a current school game. Families take home the individual containers of lotion and powder to use during the week.

Session 4: Intruding (Review) and Challenging

Greeting activities are the same as in previous weeks. Participants sit in the waiting position in the circle for checkup, then assume the curled position of folding, holding, and stretching.

The facilitator reviews grooming activities. Grooming is expanded to include combing hair. Parents and children groom each other with new combs furnished by the facilitator.

The signal to shift activities is given by the facilitator who returns to the circle and assumes the waiting position. The facilitator tells a story of animals growing up, learning to walk and run and to explore their world. Children and parents are asked to reenact the crawling stage, going around the circle on their hands and knees. Verbal prompting establishes a pattern of left–right coordination. Movement progresses to skipping and running around the circle. Directions are reversed. The facilitator stops activities by dropping to waiting position on the circle. Closing activities involve child-taught games as before.

Session 5: Challenging (Review)

Greeting activities include circle, checkup, and then folding, holding, and stretch activities. The facilitator reviews challenging activities from the previous week and expands the dyadic activities to include leg wrestling between parent and child. Group challenges include wheelbarrow and plate balancing races and pillow fights.

The facilitator drops to circle to indicate shift in activities. Discussion follows about how quickly animal babies grow and learn. The facilitator introduces the idea of maturation and leaving the nest (termination). Children and parents use tape measures and bathroom scales to compare their sizes. Body outline pictures may be done if time allows.

Closing activities are the same. Parents are asked to bring baby pictures for next time.

Session 6: Termination

Opening activities include circle, checkup, fold, hold, and stretch activities. The facilitator reviews the idea of growing up. Discussion focuses on how families remember the baby days by sharing baby pictures, keeping favorite toys, and telling stories. Participants compare baby pictures that the parents have brought. A guessing game follows. A comparison of pictures to body outline pictures can be done if these were completed the previous week.

The facilitator signals shift in activities by returning to circle. Discussion follows that explores the idea of remembering the group. Parents and children are encouraged to work on sanding and gluing wooden blocks to plywood bases to form a permanent memory. Closing routine is the same.

RESEARCH RESULTS

1. Results on objective measures, the Abidin Parent Stress Index/ Short Form (PSI/SF) and the Connors Parent Rating Scale–48 (CPRS–48), failed to reach statistical significance. It is important, however, to note that change for most subjects was in the hypothesized direction.
2. Informal assessment of videotapes from this research study showed observable change in both adult and child behavior in the direction of increased eye contact, more positive touch, and greater cooperative interaction. No formal analysis of observational data was performed.
3. Structured interviews conducted with experimental (training group) parents at the completion of the program indicated that all fifteen adult members were interested in continuing the groups. Six of the fifteen control group subjects expressed the intention to join groups. Twelve of the fifteen experimental (training group) parents noted improvement in child behavior; one felt that the play group had made the child worse; and two parents did not see any difference in their child or themselves.

LIMITATIONS OF THE STUDY

There were several limitations to this study. Caution should be applied in interpreting and generalizing outcomes for the following reasons:

1. Sample size was small; although it was within the limits for experimental research, it does not allow firm predictions.
2. Subjects were nonrandomly assigned to experimental or control groups, due to the limited number of volunteers at each center.

3. Both experimental and control groups consisted of volunteer families. Responses may be different for subjects who self-select than for the target population, many of whom would not volunteer.

4. Time between pre- and postassessment may have affected outcomes for some subjects. Training groups employed an open-enrollment policy, which precluded strict adherence to recommended test- retest schedules for two subjects who entered late.

ADDITIONAL INFORMATION

Practical knowledge gained from this study may be of interest to other researchers and practitioners contemplating delivery of community-based mental health services to families in economically disadvantaged circumstances.

1. Attracting and keeping subjects in programs can be challenging. Methods for improving volunteer response in this study included:
   a. Making the initial appeal as interesting as possible.
   b. Stating how the study would specifically benefit subjects.
   c. Recruiting persons known and respected by subjects to introduce the program.
   d. Offering courtesy gifts for participation.
   e. Keeping frequent contact by telephone and written notice (Borg and Gall 1983).

2. Pre- and postassessment tools for volunteer populations need to measure strengths as well as deficits. Assessments should be nonthreatening in tone and not burdensome to the subject in terms of response time.

3. Frequent exchange of information between the professionals is needed to assure optimal service to families. Professionals must plan carefully in advance, be flexible, relinquish private space, and respect the goals of other program components.

IMPLICATIONS FOR FURTHER STUDY

The current study attempted to examine objectively the effects of one time-limited training program, delivered on site, to a small sample of subjects. Continued examination of this model with larger samples, drawn from other populations, and conducted for longer periods of time will be necessary before a full assessment of the effectiveness of the ACT program can be determined.

Outcome measures that are sensitive to dyadic interactions need to be developed and explored. Comparisons of outcomes from self-reports, coded observations, and structured interviews are indicated. Utilization of teacher assessments in combination with parent assessment is strongly recommended for other researchers. Input from the child should be included to strengthen future studies.

Follow-up studies are indicated as well. What long-term benefits can be identified? Does an intervention between parent and child generalize to other family members or to the classroom? What are the implications for parent growth?

Finally, are there specific facilitator skills that promote spontaneity and exploration in group participants? Is modeling more effective when parents and facilitator share a common ethnic background? Is it possible to support attachment between parent and child concurrently with promoting social support?

SUMMARY

Remediation of attachment-separation issues is most often addressed in a clinical setting. Few studies examine programs that offer parent–child interventions in an educational setting. The results of this study should be of interest to both educators and clinicians for several reasons:

1. Change is promoted through healthy parent–child interactions that pose no risk to the participants.
2. Group members learn by observing one another as well as by modeling facilitator actions.
3. Needs of the parent and needs of the child are addressed simultaneously and promote benefits that are reciprocal in nature.
4. On-site training is most likely to be utilized by the families who most need it.
5. Professional resources are maximized in a service delivery that addresses several families at once.
6. Time-limited interventions, which focus on a specific task and are concluded when that task has been mastered, fit the current fiscal demands.

When parents are included with helping professionals, children receive the maximum benefits from their programs. Additional research and development of psychoeducational models that strengthen this partnership is indicated.

STRUCTURED INTERVIEW FOR PARENTS

1. Why did you decide to join the ACT play group?
2. Tell me about your child. What are his/her strengths and weaknesses?
3. What do you remember about your child's early development?
4. What memories do you have of your own early childhood?
5. What did you gain from the program ACT?
6. Do you have suggestions for improving the program ACT?

EXAMPLES OF PARENTAL REACTIONS TO THERAPLAY

Question: What Did You Gain from the Play Group?

A single mother who participated in ACT twice, once for her son and once for her daughter, talked about her own childhood.

> There was a lot of . . . not abuse but neglect. My parents were separated when I was growing up and I always said that I had a mother and a father but not parents. I missed out on a lot. . . . I didn't do the normal things that little girls did. I didn't play with dolls or I didn't learn to jump rope and I still don't know how to ride a bike. I promised myself when I had children of my own that it would be different. I want them to learn how to play.

A single mother of three children explained how she benefited from ACT: "I took it [the training] for myself, too. It guided me. It hasn't been that long since the kids were born but it took me back too to when they were babies." A mother of twins, who has older and younger children, talked about her motivation for coming to ACT: "It gave me a chance to spend time with just one of them. They need to know they are loved. I think every center should have a group." A single mother recalled her own difficult and rebellious years: "I did it for B. and I did it for me. He's the best thing that ever happened to me. He's my anchor. It's important to spend time with him."

REFERENCES

Abidin, R. R. (1990). *Parenting Stress Index Short Form Test Manual*. Charlottesville, VA: Pediatric Psychology Press.

Ainsworth, M. D. S., Blehar, M. C., Watersm, E., and Wall, S. (1978). *Patterns of Attachments*. Hillsdale, NJ: Lawrence Erlbaum.

Borg, W., and Gall, M. (1983). *Educational Research: An Introduction*. New York: Longman.

Bostrom, J. (1995). A pre-school curriculum based on Theraplay. *The Theraplay Institute Newsletter* F:3–4.

Bowlby, J. (1969). *Attachment and Loss: Vol. 1, Attachment*. New York: Basic Books.

Brody, V. (1978). Developmental play, a relationship-focused program for children. *Journal of Child Welfare* 57(9):591–599.

——— (1997). *The Dialogue of Touch: Developmental Play Therapy*. Northvale, NJ: Jason Aronson.

Bundy-Myrow, S. (1994). Group Theraplay for children with PDD. *The Theraplay Institute Newsletter* S:9.

Chambers, C. (1995). Group theraplay with children impacted by HIV. *The Theraplay Institute Newsletter* F:5–6.

Conners, C. K. (1990). *Manual for Conners' Rating Scales*. New York: Multi Health Systems.

Des Lauriers, A. (1962). *The Experience of Reality in Childhood Schizophrenia*. New York: International Universities Press.

Eaker, B. (1986). Unlocking the family secret in family play therapy. *Child and Adolescent Social Work Journal* 3(4):235–253.

Early, J. P. (1994). Play therapy as a family restructuring technique: a case illustration. *Contemporary Family Therapy* 16(2):119–130.

Edlefsen, M., and Baird, M. (1994). Making it work: preventive mental health care for disadvantaged pre-schoolers. *Social Work* 5:566–571.

Erikson, E. H. (1963). *Childhood and Society*, rev. ed. New York: Norton.

Eyberg, S. (1988). Parent–child interaction therapy—integration of traditional and behavioral concerns. *Child and Family Behavior Therapy* 10(1):33–46.

Feiring, C. (1984). Behavioral styles in infancy and adulthood: the work of Karen Horney and attachment theorists collaterally considered. *American Journal of Psychoanalysis* 44(2):197–208.

Golden, B. R. (1986). How Theraplay facilitates healthy narcissism. *Journal of Child and Adolescent Psychotherapy* 10(2):99–104.

Hanf, C. (1969). *A two-stage program for modifying maternal controlling during mother–child (M-C) interaction.* Paper presented at the meeting of the Western Psychological Association, Vancouver, British Columbia, April.

Jernberg, A. (1979). *Theraplay.* San Francisco: Jossey-Bass.

Koller, T., and Booth, P. (1997). Fostering attachment through family Theraplay. In *Play Therapy Theory and Practice: A Comparative Presentation,* ed. K. O'Connor and L. Braverman, pp. 204–233. New York: Wiley.

Levant, R. F. (1983). Client-centered skills-training program for the family: a review of literature. *Counseling Psychologist* 11(3):29–46.

Lovejoy, T. (1995). Theraplay in a pre-school mental health program. *The Theraplay Institute Newsletter* F:8.

Martin, D. (1995). Applications of Theraplay in early childhood classrooms. *The Theraplay Institute Newsletter* F:4.

Moyer, M. (1995). Group Theraplay in a special needs day school. *The Theraplay Institute Newsletter* F:4.

Munns, E. (1995). Theraplay at Blue Hills Play Therapy Services. *The Theraplay Institute Newsletter* F:4.

Patterson, G. R. (1975). *Families.* Champaign, IL: Research Press.

Rieff, M., and Booth, P. (1994). Theraplay for children with PDD/Autism. *The Theraplay Institute Newsletter* S:1–4.

Robbins, J. (1987). Nurturing play with parents. *Nurturing Today* 9:6. S. Grand Maris, MN.

——— (1990). Playpartners. Iowa State University of Science and Technology Newsletter.

Rubin, P. (1995). Multi-family Theraplay in a shelter for the homeless. *The Theraplay Institute Newsletter* F:5.

Rubin, P., and Tregay, J. (1989). *Play with Them—Theraplay Groups in the Classroom.* Springfield, IL: Charles C Thomas.

Scharff, J. S. (1989). Play with young children in family therapy. *Journal of Psychotherapy and the Family*, 5(3–4):159–172.

Talen, M. R. (1995). Community-based primary health care: a new role for theraplay. *The Theraplay Institute Newsletter* F:1–2.

Vos, B. (1988). Guidelines for selecting experiential techniques in family therapy. *Family Therapy* 15(2):115–131.

PART III

Group
Theraplay

15

Theraplay with Physically Handicapped and Developmentally Delayed Children

DEBORAH AZOULAY

Theraplay is a versatile method of play therapy that has been successfully used with special needs children who are challenged by physical handicaps and/or developmental delay. Success requires some modification in the implementation of techniques and the selection of activities appropriate for individual client needs. However, the essence of Theraplay remains. The sessions are structured, physical, and fun. The focus is on developing a positive attachment between the child and an adult as well as on increasing self-esteem and building trust. To accomplish this, Theraplay uses the types of interactions that naturally occur in the healthy parent–infant engagement.

THERAPLAY WITH CHILDREN WHO ARE PHYSICALLY HANDICAPPED AND COGNITIVELY NORMAL

Not much work has been done on the specific application of play therapy to the physically handicapped but cognitively normal. Yet these children frequently cope with pressures unknown to their nonhandicapped peers.

> Physically handicapped children must cope with stresses stemming from frequent hospitalizations, their families' and friends' discomfort with their conditions, and distortions in body image. In addition, there are the realistic restrictions imposed by the particular disability, as well as the usual range of potential psychological problems independent of the handicap. [Saloman 1983, p. 455]

Despite the need for psychological interventions with this group of children, the literature on this subject is not vast. Axline (1969) briefly notes that handicapped children benefit from play therapy if the handicap is the source of conflict, anxiety, and emotional disturbance. The use of the client-centered approach is also mentioned by a few other writers (Cruickshank and Cowen 1948, Saloman 1983, Williams and Lair 1991). An application of counseling is discussed by Thompson and Rudolph (1983). Donovan and McIntyre (1990) discuss their success using a developmental-contextual approach with children with a variety of handicaps. Salomon and Garner (1978) discuss therapy that focused on verbal communication and vicarious experience with a very physically limited child.

As well, little has been written about the use of Theraplay with this population. Jernberg (1979) discusses its application with children who have cerebral palsy and she states that Theraplay can benefit these children when modified and adapted. However, the children discussed are severely physically handicapped, basically nonverbal, and very low functioning cognitively. (The needs of these children will be discussed later in the chapter.)

Yet Theraplay can be an excellent modality for the treatment of physically handicapped children with social, emotional, and behavioral problems. Their development of normal social skills may be impeded by a combination of lack of mobility, poor self-esteem, and an overprotective or overindulgent environment. For some children, traumatic or painful experiences of hospitalization or other medical treatment add to their anxiety and sense of loss of control. As a result these children may have difficulty learning to relate to others in a manner that allows them to be successful, self-confident, and happy. Instead they may seek to control their environment excessively, gain attention through misbehavior, withdraw, refuse to cooperate, or lose faith in their ability to succeed.

The corrective therapeutic experience for these children should create a warm environment that teaches them to develop intimacy with others. It should instill a sense of structure and boundaries, and the acceptance of limits. It must build self-esteem and encourage children to strive to develop to the limits of their potential. Ultimately this is done by creating new patterns of behavior between the child and therapist and then the child and parent.

CASE STUDY 1

Client

Ronnie, a 7-year-old boy, was a paraplegic and used a wheelchair. Cognitively, he was very bright. He had a delightful sense of humor, was basically congenial, and was articulate. He was brought to play therapy services of a mental health clinic by his mother, a single mom.

Presenting Problem

In school and at home Ronnie acted in an erratic fashion, sometimes showing volatile mood swings. He engaged in tantrums and had difficulty making and keeping friends. Underlying this behavior was a strong desire for control and an excessive need to win. Recently Ronnie had engaged in suicidal ideation, telling his mother that he wanted to die. She became alarmed and sought psychotherapy for her son.

Setting

Within the clinic a female psychologist and a male cotherapist engaged in Theraplay with Ronnie. Meanwhile a female interpreting therapist, watched from behind a one-way mirror with Ronnie's mother. There were eight sessions and each consisted of a half hour of Theraplay followed by a half hour of parent counseling. In addition, a pre- and posttreatment assessment was undertaken using the Marschak Interaction Method of observation (Marschak 1960). Ronnie's mother also completed the Achenbach Child Behavior Checklist (Achenbach and Edelbrock 1983) before and after treatment.

Pretreatment Assessment

Observations showed a positive relationship between mother and son. They were affectionate and enjoyed each other's company. However, Ronnie was quick to take control of interactions and his mother frequently deferred to him. Ronnie was anxious and waited tensely when, as part of the Marschak, his mother briefly left the room. In discussion it became clear that Ronnie's mother, who had a demanding career, found it difficult to find consistent time with him.

Treatment Goals

The following objectives were established for treatment:

- to support the positive relationship that did exist between mother and son
- to increase the mother's ability to be in charge
- to decrease Ronnie's need to control and increase his trust in other people
- to increase Ronnie's frustration tolerance
- to build Ronnie's self-esteem and decrease his need to always win
- to promote socialization with peers
- to assist the mother in finding ways to combine the demands of her career with the need to spend more predictable and consistent time with Ronnie.

Theraplay was considered an ideal therapy for Ronnie. It allowed the therapists to provide structuring (thus setting limits) while at the same time nurturing Ronnie (and bolstering his self-concept). Mother's participation gave her a hands-on opportunity to experience these strategies, and parent counseling was used to address generalization of the new patterns of behavior to the home setting.

Innovations

It was necessary to be creative in the choice and use of Theraplay activities. Ronnie was able to use his arms and hands while sitting in his wheelchair. He was also taken out of the chair and allowed to pull himself along the ground for more active games, to his great delight. Suggested activities for work with a physically handicapped and cognitively normal child are found in List A of this chapter.

Therapy was provided for Ronnie, while his mother watched with an interpreting therapist. She had opportunities to directly participate in the Theraplay and was also involved in parent counseling. This combination of services proved effective.

Treatment Progress/Problems Encountered and Solutions

Ronnie was an eager and enthusiastic participant in most of the session and immediately developed a strong bond, especially with the male cotherapist. However, at the start he was also very controlling and argumentative.

From the beginning Ronnie enjoyed the attention and nurturing of activities like Body Parts Inventory and Cotton Ball Touch on his upper body (see List A, pp. 293–295), where he could feel the softness. The therapists thought that the wheelchair would be a barrier to intimacy, so Ronnie was taken out of it for most of each session. Work was done on the floor where Ronnie was able to move around by himself along with the therapists on the floor as well. Therapists imitated Ronnie by pulling themselves with their elbows, in order to move about. The presence of a male cotherapist made moving Ronnie easier. It also provided a male role model for him.

Ronnie particularly liked active games, vigorously engaging in Ping Pong Ball blow while lying on his stomach during the first session. However, when the session finished, Ronnie wanted to continue with another game, and his angry resistance to ending became a temper tantrum. His mother stated that this type of behavior frequently occurred at home and at school.

As the sessions continued Ronnie relished challenging activities and was proud to show his strength and skill by punching through a newspaper and throwing paper balls into a basket made by the therapist's arms. His desire to always win became very evident, however. When a therapist caught him moving as he raced across the floor on his stomach in the game of red light/green light, Ronnie became argumentative and angry. However the therapists firmly insisted he follow the rules and return to the starting position, which he did.

Ronnie continued to test limits but gradually spent less time arguing when he did not win and more easily accepted redirection. He was able to enjoy competitive games like thumb wrestling. Although he was ebullient when he won, he took a loss with good grace.

There were still some times, though, when Ronnie became upset if he didn't win or get his way. Once, when he was caught in the game of Red Rover, he cried and argued that it wasn't fair. He refused to participate in the next game of putting lotion on noses, so the therapists carried on without him.

This was followed by a licorice-eating contest. Ronnie became angry that he couldn't change the rules to allow use of hands and again refused to participate. Again the others played without him. Realizing that his behavior was not gaining him anything and that he was missing out on the fun, Ronnie then participated very well in the remaining activities.

Ronnie's mother joined the Theraplay from the fourth session. She demonstrated a playful spirit and willingness to engage. Ronnie and the therapists hid under a blanket as she "searched" everywhere and finally found them, to Ronnie's delight. Some regressive activities were used, such as rocking Ronnie in a blanket as the adults sang to him and then gently lifting him into his mother's arms. He loved this. Structured games were used as well and Ronnie was required to follow clearly setout rules. Everyone had fun with the race that required pushing a Ping-Pong ball with the nose.

Since Ronnie's mother was involved in the play, she not only watched the therapists handle his tantrums and confidently provide limits but also was able to do this herself with the therapists' support.

Meanwhile, in the counseling sessions that followed the Theraplay, there was an opportunity to discuss the mother–son interaction at home. Mom was encouraged to provide consistent rules, and follow through with consequences. She was assisted in exploring ways of spending more time with Ronnie, doing Theraplay activities at home. The need to promote more peer socialization experiences was also emphasized.

Outcome and Follow-Up

As the therapy progressed, Ronnie's mother reported that she was being firmer with him at home. When the two of them played games she no longer always let him win, as she had previously done. Behavior was somewhat better in school as major incidents of tantrums decreased. Ronnie expressed no more suicidal thoughts.

During the posttreatment Marschak, Ronnie's mother showed the ability to take control in a confident but friendly manner. She followed through on her requests to Ronnie in a pleasant but firm way. He was more cooperative and made fewer attempts to control his mother. The Achenbach checklist completed by the mother also showed that Ronnie's behavior had improved at home in comparison with her pretreatment evaluation.

Ronnie and his mother came for a follow-up session three months later. At this time he had also been placed on medication by a physician, which may have contributed to his progress. However, his mother reported that although Ronnie "had his ups and downs," he remained basically cooperative and did not engage in temper tantrums. He was better behaved at home and school, was able to more easily accept losing at games, and engaged in more peer contact.

THERAPLAY WITH CHILDREN WHO ARE DEVELOPMENTALLY DELAYED

Many approaches have been taken to helping developmentally delayed children learn social skills and appropriate behavior, and experience emotional growth. For these children, gains come slowly and are less likely to result from incidental learning. Progress is often hindered by poor communication skills. Children's lack of awareness and understanding can result in fewer choices for them and a reduction in the variety of experiences available, which, in turn, can mean fewer learning opportunities. These children all too often begin to rely on maladaptive behaviors to gain a sense of control and to interact with others.

Many methods are employed to teach appropriate social skills to developmentally handicapped children. Behavioral strategies are often used (Gresham 1981). An educational or skill training component is part of many teaching programs (Hellendoorn 1994, Nakken et al. 1994, Vaughn et al. 1983). Parent training is recommended (McConkey 1994).

Play therapy also has been used with this population to foster relationships and communication as well as to develop self-confidence. Play has been employed to teach games, rules, structure, and participation in activities using imagination and fantasy.

A variety of different play therapy techniques have been tried. O'Doherty (1989) has used play and drama therapy to re-create early attachment. Client-centered therapy has been employed (Mehlman 1953, Mundy 1957, Newcomer and Morrison 1974). Important work in the use of play therapy with developmentally handicapped children has been done by Leland (Leland 1983, Leland and Smith 1971, 1982). His approach combines several techniques, including behavioral.

Theraplay has been used successfully with developmentally handicapped children also. Rieff (1991) has reported successful use of individual Theraplay in a clinic with infants and toddlers. These children were described as being in the mild to severe range of retardation, with a number of other disabilities as well. Emotional and behavioral problems were also present. Jernberg (1979) discusses work with children with cerebral palsy and with other nonambulatory, cognitively limited children.

We have used individual Theraplay in a school setting with developmentally delayed children, ranging in functioning level from mild to severely handicapped. Many of these children were also physically handicapped and were diagnosed with a variety of medical conditions. Theraplay has proved to be a useful approach when attempting to motivate low-functioning children who are not responding well to traditional teaching methods. Theraplay activities (see List B, pp. 295–297) have been used to increase the children's attention to others, encourage them to respond to a teacher's initiation, and increase their ability to interact with adults.

In addition, we have used group theraplay with developmentally delayed children. Group Theraplay has often been used in schools (Rubin and Tregay 1989) with children who have fairly good physical and cognitive skills. However, good results have also been obtained with more handicapped children.

CASE STUDY 2

Clients

Seven children participated in the Theraplay group: Fatima, Rebecca, Ali, Barbara, Susan, Lea, and Ian. They ranged in age from 4½ to 7 years and in functioning level from mild to severe delay. All were multihandicapped. Two had severe visual problems. Two were beginning to walk and the others were not mobile.

Setting

These children made up a class in a school for developmentally handicapped children. Theraplay was led by a therapist with the support of the class teacher and an educational assistant. Whenever possible, other educational assistants also joined the weekly half-hour session so that a good adult/child ratio would be available. Ten sessions were held.

Rationale for Theraplay

Theraplay is used to help children who are cognitively normal return to activities of infancy and young childhood to relearn early attachment-enhancing interactions that were missed or not learned well. However, Theraplay is also valuable for children who have never progressed past those early levels of development. These children need specific teaching to learn to interact with adults and peers and develop confidence in themselves.

Innovations

This was an application of group Theraplay in a school setting for multihandicapped, developmentally delayed children. We used activities in a combination of one-on-one adult-to-child interactions and group play. The goal was to enhance learning by developing the following skills:

Eye contact
Paying attention to adults and peers
Anticipation of adult response
Understanding cause and effect
Appropriate touching of others
Imitation
Showing and receiving affection
Turn taking
Positive awareness of themselves and their bodies
Peer contact
Verbal and nonverbal communication

Treatment Progress/Problems Encountered and Solutions

Every session started with the familiar song, "Welcome, welcome everyone. Now we're going to have some fun." The song became the signal for the start of Theraplay for the children. Each session ended with the good-bye song and a hug.

From session one, the children enjoyed receiving a personal hello and inventory check. Muscles and smiles were exclaimed over. Hands were powdered and hand prints were made. Then each hand was gently washed in warm water.

From the beginning, some problems were encountered. At first the children were taken out of their chairs for the session, as it was thought this would enhance the development of intimacy. However, since they had difficulty sitting properly, they were very uncomfortable.

In the following sessions the children remained in their chairs, which were placed in a circle. As a result they were more attentive and comfortable. The adults were always either beside the children or in front and facing them, depending on the activity. This proximity was enough to allow for the desired closeness between the children and adults.

Not all the children responded well at first. Ian showed tactile defensiveness and cried loudly whenever he was touched. However, his teacher did touch him, gently and in moderation. Gradually he became used to the contact and stopped crying. By the end of the ten sessions he laughed with enjoyment as he held hands with his teacher and swayed to music or as he experienced a back massage.

Adaptations were necessary because of the lack of mobility of the children. Many active games were introduced with modifications. "Row, Row, Row Your Boat" was played as everyone held hands and moved side to side while still sitting. Since the children were young and relatively light it was possible to lift them for other games. They loved London Bridge as one child was helped to stand and hold hands with another staff member, meanwhile rocking another child inside their combined arms.

Another challenge was the mix of functioning levels in the children in this class. Lea was unresponsive to most efforts, but enjoyed having powder put on her and being cuddled. By the end she was making some good eye contact. Rebecca watched with her big eyes but didn't always initiate either. But one day an educational assistant was rubbing lotion on her and Rebecca responded by trying to rub some on the adult! Fatima loved observing and laughed and giggled when she was included in the fun. Ali anticipated being touched, and beamed when given attention.

On the other hand, Barbara and Susan were capable of much more. They were seated beside each other and encouraged to interact not only with staff but as much as possible with each other. With glee they participated in a cotton ball fight, blew bubbles to each other, and hit a balloon back and forth. They initiated play with each other, took turns and shared.

Feeding was used in each session but somewhat differently from the usual Theraplay activity. In most Theraplay sessions food is placed directly in the mouth of the child as a form of nurturing by the adult. However, the teacher of the class was reluctant to do this since most of these children were at a developmental stage where they were struggling to learn to feed themselves. She did not want to discourage the children from learning what she was trying so hard to teach them. Thus, those children who were able were encouraged to feed themselves as the adult gave out the chips and cheese-flavored treats.

This moment was also used to give the children capable of it a choice of which treat they would like to have. There were those who always wanted chips and others who knew they preferred cheese-flavored treats. Some children did have to be fed, because they couldn't feed themselves.

Some children did not eat regular food and were not interested in feeding at all.

The children all loved music, so music was incorporated into the activities as much as possible. A tape would be turned on, played for 10 seconds, and then suddenly shut off—the signal for everyone to get a tickle. The children waited with smiles for the music to stop.

Results

At the end of each session a rating sheet for each child was filled out by the teacher and educational assistant. The average score for each child was graphed so that progress could be monitored. (See rating sheet (Table 15–1) and an example of a graph (Table 15–2)). All the children in the group showed some progress, although some progressed more than others. It was found that the children who made the most changes were those in the middle range of functioning.

Table 15–1. Assessment of Theraplay progress

NAME					DATE			
Behavior	Never ———— Sometimes —— Frequently							
Establishes eye contact	1	2	3	4	5	6	7	8
Looks at others (10 seconds)	1	2	3	4	5	6	7	8
Touches others appropriately								
Without help	1	2	3	4	5	6	7	8
With prompts	1	2	3	4	5	6	7	8
Shares with others								
Without help	1	2	3	4	5	6	7	8
With prompts	1	2	3	4	5	6	7	8
Shows affection	1	2	3	4	5	6	7	8

(continued)

Table 15–1. (*Continued*)

Behavior	Never ——— Sometimes —— Frequently							
Takes turns								
Without help	1	2	3	4	5	6	7	8
With prompts	1	2	3	4	5	6	7	8
Participates in tasks								
Without help	1	2	3	4	5	6	7	8
With prompts	1	2	3	4	5	6	7	8
Follows instructions								
Without help	1	2	3	4	5	6	7	8
With prompts	1	2	3	4	5	6	7	8
Communicates with words	1	2	3	4	5	6	7	8
Communicates with sounds	1	2	3	4	5	6	7	8
Communicates nonverbally	1	2	3	4	5	6	7	8
Tries to imitate	1	2	3	4	5	6	7	8
Smiles, laughs to indicate pleasure	1	2	3	4	5	6	7	8
Initiates interaction								
With adult	1	2	3	4	5	6	7	8
With peer	1	2	3	4	5	6	7	8
Cooperative play (attends and takes turns)								
With adult	1	2	3	4	5	6	7	8
With peer	1	2	3	4	5	6	7	8
Attends to task (1 minute)	1	2	3	4	5	6	7	8
Attends to task (2 minutes or more)	1	2	3	4	5	6	7	8

Table 15–2: Theraplay Graph: Percentage Score on Teacher's Rating Scale for "Ian"

LIST A: SUGGESTED THERAPLAY ACTIVITIES FOR PHYSICALLY HANDICAPPED AND COGNITIVELY NORMAL CHILDREN

*Some children may not be able to do all of them. The severity of the handicap determines if the children can do these activities.

Activities for Severely Physically Involved Children (Whose Handicap Affects Arms and Legs)

1. Inventory of body parts (to raise self-esteem of child): comment on special features of child, such as shiny brown hair, little dimple on the chin, big strong shoulders.
2. Check hurts and put on lotion or a Band-Aid.
3. Hand outline (drawn on paper).
4. Lie on stomach and blow Ping-Pong balls to each other (or do this across a tray attached to the child's wheelchair).
5. Cotton ball touch: touch sensitive body parts, such as face, with cotton puffs.
6. Hide Smarties on child, as child closes eyes while lying on back; then find the Smarties and feed to child. If child cannot safely eat Smarties, other food items can be used.
7. Say one nice thing about your neighbor.
8. Feed child (potato chips, popcorn, grapes, pudding, or any other food child can eat and likes).
9. Child blows up cheeks, which are "popped" by adult, who presses cheeks with palms of the hands.
10. Honk child's nose, beep ears, etc. Different body parts make different noises.
11. Make shapes on sensitive body parts while child closes eyes; child guesses the shape.
12. Peanut butter/jelly game: the leader says "peanut butter" and others respond with "jelly" at the same volume and tempo.
13. Pass lotion on nose, from one nose to another by rubbing noses.
14. Feather touch on sensitive parts of child's body, such as the face. Child closes eyes and guesses where the therapist is touching.
15. Blow bubbles: therapist blows bubbles and, if physically capable, child tries to pop them.

16. Hum garden: Hold child's hands and everyone begins humming very softly. Gradually the volume of the humming increases and the arms are lifted up at the same time, until the hands are high and the humming is loud. Gradually the arms descend and the humming becomes quieter.

17. Pass a funny face: make a funny face for a neighbor, who then "passes" it to another person.

Children with Movement of Arms and Hands

1. Silly bones: touch body parts, such as therapist's elbow to child's elbow.
2. Pass a message by squeezing hands while sitting in a circle.
3. Powder hands and find a letter on the hand.
4. Call out a name/catch the (nerf) ball: sit in a circle and take turns calling out someone's name and throwing the ball to that person.
5. Stack hands up and down: leader puts one hand on table or wheelchair tray. Neighbor places hand on top of first hand, next person continues, and so on.
6. Popcorn: moving Ping-Pong balls on a blanket, as if balls are kernels of corn popping.
7. Punch through a newspaper: therapist holds a single piece of newspaper tightly as child punches through the paper. Child keeps punching through the paper and then crumbles pieces of the newspaper into small balls.
8. Throw newspaper balls into a "basket" made of therapist's arms.
9. Red light/green light: crawling on stomach for children who can't walk.
10. Lotion hands; slip and grip game: therapist lotions child's hand and then grips the hand as child tries to slip hand out of the therapist's grip.
11. Thumb wrestle.
12. Simon says: modify instructions to fit what child can do. Add a positive touch, for example, "Simon says, give your mother a hug."

13. Cotton ball throw: sit in a circle. On the word "go," throw a cotton ball at someone. This ends in a "free for all" with all participants throwing cotton balls at everyone.
14. Sword fight, using rolled-up sheets of newspaper.
15. One potato, two potato: touch each child with ball as you sing:

One potato, two potato
Three potato, four
Five potato, six potato
Seven potato, more.

The child who is touched when "more" is said gets a hug.
16. Red Rover: moving on stomach.
17. Clapping patterns: sit in a circle; leader claps a pattern and the rest repeat it.
18. Mother, May I: moving on stomach.

With Parent Also in Theraplay

1. Hide under blanket and be found by parent.
2. Blanket rock: child lies on blanket while adults lift corners of blanket and gently rock it while singing a special song about the child.
3. Licorice eating: child and parent eat from opposite ends until they meet in a kiss.
4. Circle magnets: sing, and when song stops all move in closer. Repeat this until participants are close enough for a group hug.

LIST B: SUGGESTED THERAPLAY ACTIVITIES FOR CHILDREN WHO ARE DEVELOPMENTALLY HANDICAPPED AND PHYSICALLY HANDICAPPED

1. Inventory of body parts (to raise self-esteem of child): comment on special features of child, such as shiny brown hair, little dimple on the chin, big strong shoulders.
2. Powder hands; make print of hands.

3. Wash hands in warm water.
4. Try on hat and look in mirror.
5. Cotton ball touch: touch sensitive body parts, such as face, with cotton puffs.
6. Sing or play music, and when it stops give a tickle.
7. Touch body parts—each makes a different sound.
8. Feed child (potato chips, popcorn, grapes, pudding, or any other food child can eat and likes).
9. One potato/two potato: touch each child with ball as you sing

> One potato, two potato
> three potato, four
> five potato, six potato
> seven potato, more.

The child who is touched when "more" is said gets a hug.
10. Peekaboo.
11. Lotion on hands, face, feet.
12. Blow bubbles to the child.
13. "Row, Row, Row Your Boat": as you hold hands and sway; or hold child in adult's lap, facing adult, and rock.
14. "All Around the Garden":

> All around the garden
> Like a teddy bear,
> Upstairs, downstairs
> Tickle you under there. [give tickle]

> All around the garden
> Like a little mouse,
> Upstairs, downstairs
> In your little house. [give tickle]

15. Play music and "dance" by holding child's hands and swaying.
16. Take off shoes and socks and find "lollypop" toes.
17. "Motor Boat": hold hands and move them up and down to the speed.

> Motor boat, motor boat, go so slow,
> Motor boat, motor boat, go so fast.
> Motor boat, motor boat, step on the gas.

Motor boat, motor boat, go so slow,
Motor boat, motor boat, out of gas. [Hands go down]

18. "Itsy Bitsy Spider."
19. Soft touch with material talking about how nice it feels.
20. Put something with color on child's nose and show in mirror.
21. Put on nail polish.
22. Beauty parlor: child looks in mirror while adult brushes hair, puts in ribbon, and so on.
23. Give back massage.
24. Blanket rock: child lies on blanket while adults lift corners of blanket and gently rock it while singing a special song about the child.
25. Place child's hand on paper, draw the outline, and show child.
26. Hide food on child's body and have someone find it and let child eat it; make sure that child can safely eat the food.

Additional Activities for Children Who Are Developmentally Handicapped and Physically Mobile*

*Some children will not be able to do all of them.

1. Nerf ball throw: sit in circle; take turns calling out someone's name and throwing the ball to that person. If necessary, adult helps child catch ball.
2. Duck, duck, goose: sit in a circle. One person walks around circle and touches another person, who gets up. The two people run around the circle in opposite directions and give each other a hug when they meet.
3. Popcorn: move Ping-Pong balls on a blanket, as if balls are kernels of corn popping.
4. Dance to music with a partner.
5. Cotton ball throw: sit in a circle. On the word "go" throw a cotton ball at someone. This ends in a "free for all" with all participants throwing cotton balls at everyone.
6. Squeeze jello with your hands or your toes.
7. Simon says do this: model the actions as you say them; can have the children give someone a hug.

8. Ring Around the Rosy.

9. "London Bridge Is Falling Down": two people—can be a child and an adult—make a bridge with their arms and the others pass under, singing the song. The arms are lowered and a child is caught between the arms and rocked.

10. Blow bubbles: children blow if they can, or adults blow bubbles on to children, who may try to pop them.

11. Clap hands in a simple pattern: children imitate a simple clapping pattern.

12. Patty cake.

13. Magnets: sit in circle and sing; when singing stops, all move closer to each other. This repeats and ends with a group hug.

14. Hello feet: shake hands with feet.

15. Keep balloons up in the air.

16. Choo choo train: form a line, with each person placing hands on the next person's waist, and move. Make sound effects like a train as you move.

17. Blanket tug of war.

18. Pass a touch: sit in circle. One person gives a neighbor a gentle touch and that person passes the touch to the next person, and so on.

19. Stack hands up and down: leader puts one hand on table or floor. Neighbor places hand on top of first hand, next person continues and so on.

20. Call name of someone and exchange places.

21. Blow bubbles in soapy water with straws.

22. Throw crumbled newspaper balls in arm hoop.

23. Motor boat, as in list above but moving in circle.

24. Sword fight with rolled up newspapers.

25. Red Rover.

26. Hum garden: everyone holds hands and crouches down low. Begin humming very softly. Gradually the volume of the humming increases, and participants begin to stand up at the same time. Finally everyone is standing and the humming is loud. Gradually everyone begins to crouch down and the humming becomes quieter.

27. Pass a funny face: make a funny face for a neighbor who then "passes" it to another person.

28. Punch newspaper: therapist holds a single piece of newspaper tightly as child punches through the paper. Child keeps punching through the paper and then crumbles pieces of the newspaper into small balls.

REFERENCES

Achenbach, T. M., and Edelbrock, C. S. (1983). *Manual for the Child Behavior Checklist and Revised Child Behavior Profile.* Burlington VT: University of Vermont, Department of Psychiatry.

Axline, V. M. (1969). *Play Therapy*, rev. ed. Toronto: Random House of Canada.

Cruickshank, W. M., and Cowen, E. L. (1948). Group therapy with physically handicapped children. I: Report of study. *Journal of Educational Psychology* 39(4):193–215.

Donovan, D. M., and McIntyre, D. (1990). *Healing the Hurt Child: A Developmental-Contextual Approach.* New York: Norton.

Gresham, F. M. (1981). Social skills training with handicapped children: a review. *Review of Educational Research* 51(1):139–176.

Hellendoorn, J. (1994). Imaginative play training for severely retarded children. In *Play and Intervention*, ed. J. Hellendoorn, R. van der Kooij, and B. Sutton-Smith, pp. 113–122. Albany, NY: State University of New York Press.

Jernberg, A. M. (1979). *Theraplay.* San Francisco: Jossey-Bass.

Leland, H. (1983). Play therapy for mentally retarded and developmentally disabled children. In *Handbook of Play Therapy*, ed. C. E. Schaefer and K. J. O'Connor, pp. 436–454. New York: Wiley.

Leland, H., and Smith, D. E. (1971). *Play Therapy with Mentally Subnormal Children.* New York: Grune & Stratton.

——— (1982). Play therapy for mentally retarded children. In *Play Therapy: Dynamics of the Process of Counseling with Children*, pp. 313–323. Springfield, IL: Charles C Thomas.

Marschak, M. (1960). A method for evaluating child–parent interaction under controlled conditions. *Journal of Genetic Psychology* 97:3–22.

McConkey, R. (1994). Families at play: interventions for children with developmental handicaps. In *Play and Intervention*, ed. J. Hellendoorn, R. van der Kooij, and B. Sutton-Smith, pp. 123–132. Albany, NY: State University of New York Press.

Mehlman, B. (1953). Group play therapy with mentally retarded children. *Journal of Abnormal and Social Psychology* 48(1):53–60.

Mundy, L. (1957). Therapy with physically and mentally handicapped children in a mental deficiency hospital. *Journal of Clinical Psychology* 13:9–13.

Nakken, H., Vlaskamp, C., and van Wijck, R. (1994). Play within an intervention for multiply handicapped children. In *Play and Intervention*, ed. J. Hellendoorn, R. van der Kooij, and B. Sutton-Smith, pp. 133–143. Albany, NY: State University of New York Press.

Newcomer, B. L., and Morrison, T. (1974). Play therapy with institutionalized mentally retarded children. *American Journal of Mental Deficiency* 78(6):727–733.

O'Doherty, S. (1989). Play and drama therapy with the down's syndrome child. *Arts in Psychotherapy* 16:171–178.

Rieff, M. L. (1991). Theraplay with developmentally-disabled infants and toddlers. *Theraplay Institute Newsletter* F:4–5.

Rubin, P. B., and Tregay, J. (1989). *Play with Them—Theraplay Groups in the Classroom: A Technique for Professionals Who Work with Children*. Springfield, IL: Charles C Thomas.

Saloman, M. K. (1983). Play therapy with the physically handicapped. In *Handbook of Play Therapy*, ed. C. E. Schaefer and K. J. O'Connor, pp 455–469. New York: Wiley.

Salomon, M. K., and Garner, A. M. (1978). The use of play materials in treating a severely handicapped child. *Child: Care, Health and Development*, 4n: 131–140.

Thompson, C. L., and Rudolph, L. B. (1983). *Counseling Children*. Monterey, CA: Brooks/Cole.

Vaughn, S. R., Ridley, C. A., and Cox, J. (1983). Evaluating the efficacy of an interpersonal skills training program with children who are mentally retarded. *Education and Training of the Mentally Retarded* 18(3):191–196.

Williams, W. C., and Lair, G. S. (1991). Using a person-centered approach with children who have a disability. *Elementary School Guidance and Counseling* 25:194–203.

16

Group Theraplay for Children with Autism and Pervasive Developmental Disorder

SUSAN BUNDY-MYROW

Children with autism and pervasive developmental disorder (PDD) are like multifaceted jewels that require a specially designed setting to display their brilliance. They require a secure base, supporting "arms" to lift and position them carefully, and the right kind of light. Theraplay is particularly suited to help these children both attune to and receive "therapeutic light" as well as reflect their own brilliance to others. This chapter reviews the diagnostic criteria of autism and PDD, and identifies particular strengths and learning styles to incorporate in working with these multifaceted children. Next, the components of Theraplay are presented, and examined in light of their therapeutic fit for this population. Modifications are offered. The final section provides a summary of various Theraplay groups conducted over a seven-year period including a parent–child model, heterogeneous groups, and homogeneous dyads and triads. Participants were children in two settings: a private, not-for-profit special education school for children age 3 through 14, and self-contained special education classes within a public elementary school. Cognitive abilities ranged from severe mental retardation to average intelligence.

CHARACTERISTICS OF THE CHILD WITH AUTISM
AND PERVASIVE DEVELOPMENTAL DISORDER

The American Psychiatric Association's *Diagnostic and Statistical Manual of Mental Disorders* (1994) provides the descriptive criteria for diagnosing autism and related disorders. Autism is a specific disorder within the larger class of pervasive developmental disorders. As knowledge has increased regarding the study of autism, it is reflected in each revision of the manual. The fourth edition of this manual (*DSM-IV*) published in 1994, specifies three major areas of qualitative impairment characterizing autism: (1) social interaction; 2) communication; and (3) restricted repetitive and stereotyped patterns of behavior, interest, and activities. Further, onset of the disorder must occur prior to age 3 as evidenced by delays or abnormal functioning in social interaction, language as used in social communication, or representational play. Related disorders such as Rett syndrome or childhood disintegrative disorder must be ruled out (APA 1994).

Reciprocal Social Interaction

Interaction involves an awareness of self and other, acknowledgment of the other, and the intent to share attention with the other. When a child exhibits markedly abnormal or impaired development in social interaction, the deficits are obvious and sustained. The nonverbal behaviors that regulate interaction such as eye-to-eye gaze, emotion-related expression, body posture, and gestures may be impaired. Looking *through* rather than *at* another, maintaining a fixed facial expression, and difficulty anticipating or responding to postural changes of others, such as being hugged or lifted, are examples. Shared attention as manifested by a person's spontaneous attempt to involve another person in one's own experience may be absent. As a child's world expands beyond the primary adults to the emergence of peer relationships, the child with autism may appear to have no interest in establishing friendships or playing with other children. Concepts involving social meaning such as sharing and the reciprocity of giving and receiving are extremely difficult for this child to comprehend. As the child grows older, s/he may demonstrate interest in peers, for example, observing peripherally as other children play, yet lack knowledge of social conventions and the skills necessary for successful interactions.

Communication

The impairments in communication may include the absence of spoken language, delay in language development, and marked difficulty with conversational skills such as initiating and maintaining a topic. The quality of speech itself may be stereotyped or repetitive, with abnormal patterns of pitch, intonation, rhythm, or rate. Children with autism tend not to engage in the simple imitation games of toddlerhood, such as clap hands and pat-a-cake. The child may appear content to play alone, but the development of imitative or pretend play that is generally observed in preschoolers engaged in solitary play may be absent or very limited in the autistic child.

Patterns of Behavior

A challenge reported by many parents of autistic children is the difficulty finding toys and activities to occupy their children. This diagnostic criterion refers to autistic children's restricted number and types of interests, the perseverative quality with which they approach objects and activities, and fixed motor patterns such as repetitive rocking, hand flapping, or pill rolling (as if rolling an imaginary pill with the fingers). What distinguishes the activity of the child with autism from other children is an unusual focus or intensity. For example, the child who drops her fork while in the midst of eating may then continue to drop the fork as if "detoured" from the task of eating. Parents may also report a significantly greater degree of distress from their child than would be expected if a regular car route is changed. A child may also be preoccupied with parts of objects or movement, such as spinning wheels, fans, or repetitively playing a videotape segment.

Additional features may be observed such as altered sensory responses to sound, touch, light, and odors; avoidance of tastes and textures; and sleep disturbances. The child may exhibit unpredictable emotional responses such as lack of fear in a dangerous situation or exaggerated fear in a seemingly harmless situation. The manifestations of the disorder change over time and may vary in intensity depending upon the child's developmental level.

To meet the criteria for autistic disorder, a child must exhibit six or more of the behavioral descriptors in *DSM-IV* with a minimum of two in the area of social interaction and at least one in communication and atypical patterns of behavior. When the criteria for autistic disorder is not met because of later age of onset, atypical presentation, or subthreshold characteristics, a diagnosis of pervasive developmental disorder not otherwise specified (NOS) may be made. Another diagnostic option within the general classification of Pervasive Developmental Disorder is Asperger's disorder. Like Autism, children with Asperger's disorder exhibit impairments in social interactions and restricted patterns of interest. In contrast to autism, the child develops age-appropriate language (i.e., communicative phrases by age 3), cognitive skills, self-help skills, and adaptive behavior (APA 1994, p. 77). To simplify discussion of the range of pervasive developmental disorders, which vary in the degree to which they meet the criteria for autism, the term autistic spectrum disorder is used in this chapter. Given consistent programming and adaptive strategies in social relatedness, communication, daily living, and vocational skills, the child with autism and related disorders can participate with others and optimize his/her capabilities.

THE STRENGTHS AND LEARNING STYLES OF THE CHILD WITH AUTISTIC SPECTRUM DISORDER

Bryna Siegel (1991) has applied Lorna Wing's three-part model of autism to the differential diagnosis of autism and developmental language disorder (DLD). Wing (1981) postulates that the presentation of autism is always evident as a triad of social impairments: in reciprocal social interaction, in language, and in play. Siegel suggests that children with autism can be differentiated from other children on the basis of their social, play, and language levels (constituting verbal IQ), and nonverbal scores (e.g., performance IQ). Unlike the retarded child who demonstrates consistently low scores across all areas, and the child with DLD who primarily shows deficiencies in the language area, the children with autism show a pattern of low scores in the verbal areas of social, play, and language, but elevated scores in performance IQ. In general, the larger the difference between nonverbal functioning and social relating, the clearer the basis for a diagnosis of autism. The scatter within the profile of the children with autistic spectrum disorder suggests differences in these children with positive ramifications for their learning and educational programming.

In view of their relative strengths in nonverbal functioning, the abilities associated with this area ought to be tapped to connect with and increase comprehension, and ultimately increase the independent and adaptive functioning of the child with autistic spectrum disorder. To understand their environment, children with autism can more easily use visuospatial thinking, for example, thinking in pictures and via objects and concrete associations rather than in words alone. The ease with which some children complete puzzles is an example of a facility with part–whole relationships. It is frequently helpful, for example, to let the child see what constitutes the whole of his assignment, be it five cards to match or one page of ten math problems. The child may show particular strengths in memory to recognize information yet have difficulty recalling the answer in a fill-in-the-blank format. Rote memory is another strength, as attested by parents whose children recite, or sing particular parts of a videotape, and predictably carry out a routine as if it is scripted.

People with autism have difficulty organizing and understanding their environment. The following modifications can help children who need to increase their understanding of a social world and decrease the behavioral manifestations associated with anxiety (Cox 1994, Geneva Centre 1995, Quill 1995): (1) Increase the amount of structure by clarifying the physical, visual, and personal boundaries. A context is thus provided and the environment is segmented for greater understanding (Schopler and Mesibov 1995). (2) Provide routines to also increase understanding and, consequently, security and confidence. (Including some variation and coping methods for change may diminish the likelihood of excessive resistance to change.) (3) Provide organizational aids, such as photographs, pictures, and the printed word, that build on the child's visual learning style. When talking to the child, it is helpful to adapt your communication to the needs of your learner. (4) Provide social scripts (visual and written "why's" and "how to's" of social and self-help situations) for clarifying the environment (Gray 1996). (5) Provide individualized sensory supports for the child (e.g., bouncing on a therapy ball prior to a difficult group activity, or "brushing" of arms to assist focusing).

THE THERAPLAY MODEL: CONNECTING TO THE CHILD WITH AUTISTIC SPECTRUM DISORDER

The Theraplay model was first developed through work with autistic and schizophrenic children. In the 1960s, Ann Jernberg was working with Austin Des Lauriers, a psychiatrist at Michael Reese Hospital in Chicago. Des Lauriers observed that the traditional child therapy of the time was ineffective in reaching the inwardly directed child. Needed was a method to make contact with the autistic child in an intensive and persistent way (Jernberg 1979). Viola Brody (1978), the originator of developmental play therapy and a colleague of Des Lauriers, had introduced active physical contact, physical control, and singing into her work. The therapist needed to be memorable. If autistic children think in pictures, as described by Temple Grandin (1995) in her autobiographical work, they would clearly see the face of their Theraplay therapist.

Theraplay's SCIN components—structure, challenge, intrusion (later renamed engagement), and nurturance—provide a good fit for the child with autism (Jernberg and Booth 1999). In spite of a healthy dose of parenting that would provide necessary and sufficient components for the growth of a "neurotypical" child (Gray 1996), the child with autism requires a different focus and level of intensity for relationship development. Whether due to a thin skin, in which the child receives too much stimulation of equal intensity and therefore withdraws protectively, or the equivalence of a thick skin, in which the threshold for the perception of stimulation is not reached, the child with autism does not easily learn that contacting others can be positive and meaningful, not just utilitarian.

The Theraplay therapist must primarily provide the intensity, persistence, and surprise for the child to notice him/her. Thus, intrusion/engagement activities are critical. Structure further provides predictability and security for the child. The child with autism cannot make progress unless his world makes sense to him. The challenge of Theraplay entices the child to stay connected, to participate one more time before withdrawing. Nurturing is important for every child, but for children with autism it entails their discovering what is perceived as comforting; therefore the therapist must use the recommended dose of touch to promote a healthy interpersonal connection.

Individual vs. Group Theraplay

In addition to the combined individual and family Theraplay model discussed in previous chapters, the child may be seen individually without direct parental participation, as in a school setting. The emphasis is on the quality of interactions and the development of positive, growth-enhancing experiences within the therapist–child relationship. Coordination with the school staff to foster opportunities to acknowledge and generalize new patterns of relating are encouraged.

In group Theraplay, the focus is on relating beyond the parent–child relationship. Like the young child who expands his world to include siblings and peers, the Theraplay group includes and extends the parent-child relationship to the larger family and friends.

Both Brody and Jernberg developed group Theraplay models. Brody's model involved several therapist–child pairs in a group setting with initial focus within the dyad and gradual awareness between peers. Jernberg simulated a family in her model by providing two adult therapists with between four and eight children. As noted in Rubin and Tregay (1989), one therapist could speak to the child and the other could respond for the child, as needed. Rubin's groups of children in intact typical and special education settings quickly paralleled the development of family dynamics because the members already functioned as a group. Unlike the individual Theraplay model emphasizing uniqueness, the group Theraplay model focuses on similarities to others, and reciprocity to build cohesiveness. As in the individual Theraplay model, the SCIN components are emphasized in each group activity. The fun is featured, and as in a secure parent–child relationship, the adult guides and takes charge.

How can a Theraplay group be helpful for all the children in a heterogeneous group including the child with autism? Because the group creates a family situation, children express different sides of themselves that may not be readily apparent in the traditionally structured classroom. Rubin and Tregay (1989) noted that often the first signs of underlying problems were seen in Theraplay groups. The behaviors were always present, but the Theraplay atmosphere created in the group fostered new insights as to why the child was behaving in self-defeating ways. The teacher and therapist were subsequently prepared to meet the child's underlying needs via the Theraplay components.

> Harry did his schoolwork quickly but poorly. He worked on every assignment but not to completion. Socially, it appeared at first glance that Harry had appropriate interactions. Yet he tended to get bored easily, and would walk away from games and others (Rubin and Tregay 1989). The main point was that Harry put little effort into either his schoolwork or interpersonal relationships. In effect, he withdrew and isolated himself; he appeared in control as if he didn't need any genuine contact, especially caregiving. The fun of a Theraplay group can challenge a child like Harry to stick together with the others and risk accepting their care and concern.

Bundy-Myrow (1994) describes a heterogeneous group designed ostensibly to assist five children with autistic spectrum disorder increase their group skills and benefit from more socially typical peers. Therefore, while it was not mandated (via the individual education plan) for several of the children to participate in the group, it was clear to their teachers that these children could benefit from a fun opportunity to increase their social interaction skills. The Theraplay group was helpful to both the group of children with autistic spectrum disorders and the nonmandated peers.

> Jenny in particular surprised us. Always wanting attention and frequently testing limits, Jenny was shy when it came to freely accepting the fun and caring attention of her peers and teachers. As she became more comfortable accepting soft touches, surprises with silly soap foam, and sharing a snack in a new fun way, Jenny was better able to share adult attention with others and ask more appropriately for what she wanted.

Regardless of a child's educational classification, be it learning disabled, mental retardation, behavior or communication disorders, or multiply handicapped, the child's social and emotional development are also involved (Rubin and Tregay 1989). When the reasons for behavior are unclear, it is difficult to effectively manage it. Theraplay groups can help to understand the reasons and address the child's pivotal needs to promote positive behavioral adjustment.

FEATURES OF GROUP THERAPLAY FOR CHILDREN WITH AUTISTIC SPECTRUM DISORDERS

- Smaller group size
- Higher adult-to-child ratio
- Particular focus on boundaries and space
- Increased use of visuals
- Repetitive opening and closing sequences
- Modified pace and duration of activities to meet limited attending skills
- Sensory input included in activities
- Initially concrete, hands-on activities (sensorimotor level of play)
- Positive, simple language
- Increased cuing and preteaching
- Use of music—sing directions!
- Focus on basic social skills
- Coordination with educational team to reinforce and generalize skills

GROUP THERAPLAY GOALS FOR CHILDREN WITH AUTISTIC SPECTRUM DISORDER

By definition, children with autistic spectrum disorder exhibit deficits in social relatedness. Theraplay, as a relationship-based approach, can directly address these needs. Examples of group goals are responding to one's name, initiating and returning eye contact, initiating and responding to greetings, increasing tolerance for proximity, decreasing tactile defensiveness, increasing reciprocal interactions of giving and receiving through play, and increasing attending to adults, peers, and group interactions. As a child becomes accustomed to the format of a Theraplay group, with its consistent beginning and ending sequences, goals can be adjusted to promote greater independence. Reduction of physical and verbal prompts necessary for task completion are examples. Making and offering choices, choosing a peer for a paired activity, maintaining safe physical boundaries with others, following adult directives and group rules, and asserting one's needs and preferences in positive ways are some of the possible goals that can be addressed in the group. In general, the higher the functioning of the members, the more direct feedback they can provide to the therapists to maximize the fun in Theraplay.

Favorite Activities

Many games can be modified to meet the Theraplay components. Consider favorite games from childhood. What aspects appealed to you? Was it nurturing? Challenging? Surprising? Predictable? The reader is referred to the following resources for activities: Jernberg (1979), Jernberg and Booth (1999), Rubin and Tregay (1989), and Morin (1993).

Following are several activities that quickly became "oldies but goodies" because of their appeal for the children with autism as well as others. Note that practically any activity can be modified to simplify or increase the degree of challenge. Remember to start each child's turn with a "Ready? Set, Go!" or "1, 2, 3!" to ensure attending, comprehension, and eye contact. In addition, choose an opening and closing song or jingle. Include a "checkup" activity, such as High five Hello, cotton-ball soft touch for boo-boos, and see if child brought his blue eyes and brown curls (see Appendix for description of activities in this chapter). It is also useful for the assistants to keep engaging their child while he is waiting his turn. Every moment is an opportunity to make warm, fun contact!

Games can be organized by the following categories:

Lotion Games

Lotion can be used in opening activities to put around a hurt, and different types of lotion (e.g., perfumed vs. plain) can be presented for the child to choose. Slippery Hand Pull is enjoyed by many children with autism, perhaps in part due to, the firm touch provided. Adult and child sit knee to knee facing each other. Adult grasps child's hand and on the count of three, each pulls the other's hand and counts until their hands release. Compare the difference when hands are softly lotioned. (Let the child receive the lotion; the adult takes charge of the lotion bottle!).

Blowing Games

Children can learn to blow relatively easily by imitating the blowing out of a birthday candle. The advantage of blowing games are that they facilitate eye contact and physical closeness. Cotton balls can be blown across a pillow, or across an aluminum foil runway, simulating a race car. Soap foam can also be blown, and because it is more difficult to direct it creates fun surprises. Bubbles are a traditional favorite and can be used to increase body awareness by challenging the child to touch the bubble with hand, elbow, or foot.

Blanket Games

A soft, sturdy blanket is an essential Theraplay item. Children love to receive a blanket ride in which a child sits in the center of the blanket as adults and peers stand holding the ends of the blanket. All sing "Round and round the mulberry bush, the monkey chased the weasel. The monkey thought it was all in fun when Pop! goes our friend _____ ." On Pop!, the child is raised up from the floor for his amusement. Options: child may select high or low Pop! The blanket can also be used to pass or bounce a ball from child to child creating your own version of Blanket Basketball.

Hiding Games

Versions of Peekaboo are popular across a wide age span. The game can be as simple as hiding behind your hands or a pillow yet as sophisticated as Hide and Seek games. To facilitate sticking together, consider including the formation of a train in the Hide and Seek game, as each child is found. The train will grow as the children hold on to each other with the addition of adult "glue."

Pull Games

In addition to Slip and Grip, children can simulate rowing a boat in pairs, with adult assistance, or as a total group boat. To help the group stick together and provide a more definitive boundary, rubber tubing can be used to form the boat. Another option is to make a stretchy boat from weaver's loops, the kind used to make pot holders. (They hold up fairly well!) Children can also practice moving fast and slow through the game Motor Boat. Traditionally played in a pool, sing the song "Motor boat, motor boat, go so slow. Motor boat, motor boat, go a little faster. Motor boat, motor boat, step on the gass-er. Until we stop! . . . And run out of gas." This game can be played sitting, varying the speed with which the group pulls each other back and forth. When the boat runs out of gas, all bend forward touching the floor in a resting position.

TYPES OF GROUPS

The groups conducted over a seven-year period in two different school settings consisted of homogeneous dyads and triads of autistic children, heterogeneous groups consisting of complete classroom groups or the pullout model, and parent–child groups. *Homogeneous* groups refer to a type of membership in which participants are chosen on the basis of a similar characteristic, in this case, diagnostic category. *Heterogeneous* groups, as described here, refer to membership consisting of children having autistic spectrum disorder among other children with different diagnoses, such as speech delay, mental retardation, learning disabled. Location of the group is another descriptor. A group conducted within the members' classroom, including teaching staff, is considered a *Push-in* model because the service is provided for the entire class as part of the classroom programming. In contrast, a *Pull-out* model involves children leaving their class(es) to participate in a therapeutic service on specified days and times. The last type of group described is a *parent–child, multiple-family* group in contrast to more frequent child groups.

Homogeneous Groups

Small groups of two or three children with autistic spectrum disorder can be very effective when children are ready to expand beyond a one-to-one situation with an adult, yet have short attending skills or become easily overwhelmed by stimuli.

Six-year-old Janie, a nonverbal child, had received individual Theraplay and had accomplished her adult-directed goals. Her eye contact was improved, she loved hugs and squeezes, and anticipated our sessions, which were fun and giggle-filled. Janie was ready to include a friend her own age in her life. This group met one time per week for 30 minutes for the duration of the school year. The second child, Lara, was interested in others for fleeting moments. She would repeat words said to her, and become self-absorbed. Sometimes she appeared confused and worried and would cry. Other times she was happy and would smile in greeting.

Lara quickly began to enjoy the play group with Janie. Janie's assistant gradually let go of her hand to let Janie walk independently down the hall to Lara's class to call for her. Our groups had consistent greeting sequences emphasizing eye contact, handshakes, and "high 5's," use of lotion for soft touches and for boo-boos brought to group. (Note: A grown-up helped Janie direct her dab of lotion to Lara, instead of Janie's mouth.) Activities after the greeting sequence were varied, and the girls also shared a snack. In our good-bye song each week, we held hands singing a modification of the old "Mickey Mouse Song" ending with "We are friends."

Both girls became more attuned to each other. When Lara would see Janie in the hall, she would spontaneously wave and say, "Hi, Janie!" Lara's mood became more consistently happy and her attending during group activities markedly improved. She sang parts of the good-bye song and freely passed items to Janie including snack. It was more difficult for Janie to part with various items once in her possession, but her interest in Lara and the assurance that Lara would also give to her won out. Perhaps most significant, and evidence of the effectiveness of this method for these girls, was Janie's spontaneous move to sit next to Lara during a combined class activity. Previously, Janie had not initiated interactions with any peers outside of group. Lara's class was already seated in the gym waiting for class to start. Janie entered, left her own group, and sat down next to Lara. The girls held hands.

Heterogeneous Groups

These groups have the advantage of providing the child with autistic spectrum disorder with more typical peer modeling from which to learn. For some children, it is sufficient to watch a peer engage in an activity and then be able to imitate it. However, many children require the equivalence of a social script for replication. When the motivating influence of a peer is paired with specific teaching and practice, the child with autism can more easily be primed for his turn.

The Pullout Model

Following is a description of a heterogeneous group of seven boys, aged 10 through 14, who were selected on the basis of their needs to increase positive relating with adults and peers.

> Three of the boys carried diagnoses of autism or pervasive developmental disorder. Social-emotional issues for the other boys included low frustration tolerance and aggression, avoidance, and significant dependence. The group met once per week for 45 minutes during the school year and the summer. Using a pull-out model, the boys left their respective classrooms to join the therapists in a group room. Goals for this group included increasing eye contact, decision-making skills, giving and receiving positive attention, and conflict resolution. All of the members were previously known to the group leaders. Art therapist Janet Ide had worked individually with several of the members, as had this author. Janet's expressiveness with or without the art media, plus her ability to visually illustrate situations with the use of sign language, added significantly to our Theraplay atmosphere. The boys grew trusting of and comfortable with each other. In addition to the Theraplay components of a greeting, game, snack activity, and closing, we built on the boys' verbal skills by adding a "news" component after the greeting.
>
> Isolated Ernie made a friend and accepted help from Stan, who had previously been dependent and childlike. Kyle, a relatively high-functioning boy with autism, decreased his inter-

rupting and began talking *to* rather than *at* others. He also increased his awareness of social rules (and enforced them) by informing a peer if it was not his turn to talk. We were not sure how much Ernie comprehended because he had few conversational skills and his nonverbal expressions were difficult to read. During one session, after the leaders spent time to resolve a verbal hurt between two group members, Ernie surprised us by saying to the guys, "Oh, be a man!" He obviously had been attuned to the discussion and was ready to move on to some fun.

Most sessions took place in a small group room, but we had access to the gym and outside play areas as well. To facilitate the development of interpersonal skills via games, routines were practiced in the smaller room first. When the boys showed sufficient comfort with the directions and rules and could stick together, we played in the less structured, larger gym setting. Further, once a core group of high-valence games and snack activities were learned, each boy took a turn to be our "star of the week," which provided one the chance to choose the game and snack activity. The boys really enjoyed this privilege, and although many wanted to choose every week, they learned to take turns and some learned to encourage particular choices of others.

The Push-In Model

When one or more children with autistic spectrum disorder participate in group Theraplay in their classroom with teachers, therapists, and classmates, a push-in model is being used. These students can benefit from having a history together, and sharing the security and predictability of the structure associated with their class.

For a total of twenty-two weeks, Danny, Ron, and Chris received group Theraplay two times per week for 30-minute sessions along with their three other classmates. A special education teacher and a speech/language pathologist led the group. Each initial session of the week had a new group agenda that was learned during that session and practiced during the second session of the week. (We found that the second time around children could accommodate to relatively new information more readily.) To increase comprehension of the group segments, laminated cards were made, illustrated by picture exchange communication system pictures (Frost and Bondy 1995). These primary-school children learned to anticipate and stick together for four group segments: (1) hello, (2) play, (3) snack, (4) good-bye song. Segments 1 and 4 were consistent and, not surprisingly, learned first. It is interesting to note that rather than promote perseverative behavior, it appeared that the security of this consistent segment promoted more spontaneity and verbal responses. Danny, in particular, grew more confident in his greetings and on two occasions, spontaneously added a funny face, then smiled as we laughed appreciatively.

During paired activities (which were new each week, as these were the game and snack components), the children moved from adult–child dyads, to child–child dyads with adult support. This group enjoyed blowing cotton ball cars along the aluminum foil track to their friends, complete with motor sounds. Games with lotion and those providing tactile input were also winners. Once we learned to anticipate the amount of structure and nurturance the other children in the group needed, we saw the Theraplay atmosphere in action: fun, spontaneous, safe, caring, and motivating.

Parent–Child Groups

There are many variations of groups to involve parents. In discussing parent–child groups, our task force, consisting of administrators, professionals, and parents interested in educational programming for children with autism and PDD, identified several important components. A portion of the group was recommended for parents to interact without their children present to provide both opportunities for information and support from others who might share their joys and concerns. It was also important that the whole family could attend because many parents had to travel long distances, and obtaining child care could be difficult. Therefore, supervision was available for both the child with autism and siblings. The supper hour was identified as a possible time to conduct the group because parents were more reluctant to take their children out later in the evening, and the long Buffalo-area winters were known to be unpredictable. The children already were becoming familiar with Theraplay in that it was included twice weekly in their classrooms. Using this model for the adults would have two purposes: (1) to share the group method, mutual experiences, and change over time with the parents; (2) to establish an atmosphere in which the children could generalize the skills and comfort they were experiencing in school to another setting that included their parents.

> The group was held for nine monthly sessions between the hours of 5 and 7 P.M., and were held at the school that most of the children attended. Ten of eleven possible children and their families became involved in the program over the course of the year and attended Family Night at least once. A core group of five children with their families attended at least two-thirds of the sessions. Two additional families joined after mid-year and attended regularly. The program consisted of approximately 30 minutes of group Theraplay with children, parents, siblings, teachers, related service staff, and aides. (It was most impressive that each classroom team ensured that a familiar team member would attend this optional group.) Supper was provided in the classroom for the children and in a different room for the parents. The children were supervised by two aides. Following the meal, a topic of parental choice was discussed, such as challenges facing the family, or a speaker addressed various topics such as respite services, sleep problems, or devising social stories (Gray 1996) to increase comprehension. At the close of Family Night, parents rejoined their children and departed for home.
>
> As in all Theraplay groups, this group was not without its challenges. Change in routine is very difficult for some children with autistic spectrum disorder, and despite beginning familiarity with the group format, it did not seem right to these children to be returning to school at supper time, and with Mom and Dad. It took two children two to three sessions to comfortably walk into the school and readily join friends and family in the fun of the group. Although it was difficult for all to see the two children cry, we persisted in finding ways to

structure and comfort them. What worked best for Mark was
for co-leader Nan Judd to walk him to his classroom and return to group when he was calm. Devising a social story regarding returning to school for play group was also very helpful to assist Mark's comprehension of this situation. If Mark
and his parents had stopped attending Family Night because
he was initially distressed, they would have missed an important growth experience—one from which this child gained the
confidence and security to give to others and receive nurturance
from his parents and friends, in a new setting. His world of
competence has increased.

Other highlights of this group involved fun on a full group
level as well as dyadic interactions. Ronny was very sensitive
to auditory stimulation and with the excitement (primarily
of the adults) from fun interactions, the room could become
loud before the leaders suggested softer voices. Ronny tolerated
the auditory flux of this environment, and enjoyed the blanket ride, despite the concentration of people and the exuberant
surprise (Pop! Goes our friend Ronny!) embedded in the song.

Max, too, could be overstimulated easily and would bite
his wrist when frustrated. He was particularly hesitant taking interpersonal risks. In the presence of his mom in group,
Max was able to stick together, and experienced being a leader
and great role model for the other members! Over the course
of the eight sessions he attended, he bit his wrist infrequently,
that is, five times. When Norm, a new boy, joined our group
mid-year, Max welcomed him and selected Norm for any
paired activities. The high degree of comfort was reflected in
Max's interactions with Norm, marked by more independence
and reciprocity than previously seen.

Feedback from the regular participants indicated that the
Theraplay group and parent sessions were helpful to both parents and children. While a family format is not for everyone,
and other models such as individual sessions or a home visit
model might be considered, 70 percent of the families that attended at least once were in favor of Family Night continuing.

Regardless of the type of group, once alerted to the fun of Theraplay
groups, the child with autistic spectrum disorder may independently

attempt to set into play a particular aspect of the group. It might be a favorite snack activity, the silly soap foam to clap and make "snow," or the blanket-ride game. The related supplies therefore, can soon elicit intense interest from the members and are best secured in a sturdy bag. One caution remains. If you do not want your "goody" bag to be the focus of your group, sit on it!

REFERENCES

American Psychiatric Association. (1994). *Diagnostic and Statistical Manual of Mental Disorders*, 4th ed. Washington, DC: Author.

Brody, V. (1978). Developmental play: a relationship-focused program for children. *Journal of Child Welfare* 57(9):591–599.

Bundy-Myrow, S. (1994). Group Theraplay for children with PDD. *The Theraplay Institute Newsletter*, Spring.

Cox, R. (1994). *Being me . . . is who I am: positive approaches to treatment in autism*. Paper presented at the Autism Family Support Program, Fairport, NY, April.

Frost, L., and Bondy, A. S. (1994). *Picture Exchange Communication System* Cherry Hill, NJ: Pyramid Educational Consultants.

Geneva Centre for Autism. (1995). Pervasive developmental disorder: diagnoses, movement disorders, and teaching strategies. Workshop presented to the Board of Cooperative Educational Services (BOCES) of Southern Erie, Chautauqua, Cataraugus Counties, NY, March 15.

Grandin, T. (1995). *Thinking in Pictures and Other Reports from My Life with Autism*. New York: Doubleday.

Gray, C. (1996). Gray's guide to neurotypical behavior: appreciating the challenge we present to people with autistic spectrum disorders. *The Morning News*, Winter, pp. 9–13. Jenison, MI: Jenison Public Schools.

Jernberg, A. (1979). *Theraplay*. San Francisco: Jossey-Bass.

Jernberg, A., and Booth, P. (1999). *Theraplay: Helping Parents and Children Build Better Relationships through Attachment-Based Play*. San Francisco: Jossey-Bass.

Morin, V. (1993). *Messy Activities and More*. Chicago, IL: Chicago Review Press.

Quill, K. (1995). *Teaching Children with Autism: Strategies to Enhance Communication and Socialization*. Albany, NY: Delmar.

Rubin, P., and Tregay, J. (1989). *Play with Them. Theraplay Groups in the Classroom.* Springfield, IL: Charles C Thomas.

Schopler, E., and Mesibov, G. B. (1995). *Learning and Cognition in Autism.* New York: Plenum.

Siegel, B. (1991). Play diagnosis of autism: the ETHOS play session. In *Play Diagnosis and Assessment*, ed. C. E. Schaefer, K. Gitlin, and A. Sandgrund, pp. 331–374. New York: Wiley.

Wing, L. (1981). Language, social and cognitive impairments in autism and severe mental retardation. *Journal of Autism and Developmental Disorders* 11:31–44.

17

Teacher-Led Theraplay in Early Childhood Classrooms

DORIS M. MARTIN

In the fall of 1991, a kindergarten teacher with many years of success-ful teaching in the United States and in Germany shared her frustra-tions with her classmates and me in a graduate course that I was lead-ing called "Trends and Issues in Early Childhood Education." The question that Chancey* faced every day was, How could she possibly give the children what they needed and manage to have energy and time left to teach them anything? With a voice full of despair and frustra-tion, she described the personal plights of several of the children in her class. Shawna was suffering the loss of her mother who had been re-cently incarcerated. Joe, who regularly terrorized his classmates with his bullying aggressions, had shown his teacher wounds on his back recently inflicted with a belt by his angry father. Lilly, in contrast, had no friends, showed almost no initiative, and spent much of her day sucking her thumb while sitting alone in her own little dream world. The school counselor had been called in, but was already dealing with

---

*Pseudonyms are used for all the children and teachers.

a caseload beyond what seemed humanly possible. I shared with Chancey my recently acquired copies of Jernberg's (1979) *Theraplay* and *Play with Them* by Rubin and Tregay (1989), and recommended that she try the simply outlined Theraplay session with her class. Chancey's adoption of, success with, and excitement about Theraplay led to my conducting Theraplay workshops and seminars for other teachers in the area.

BACKGROUND

This chapter is the result of my work with and study of Theraplay in regular early childhood classrooms over a three-year period. The teachers with whom I worked had teaching experience ranging from two years to over twenty years. Formal education ranged from a one-year associate degree to master's degrees in early childhood education. Their classrooms represented different types of programs and purposes including 3-year-olds in day care, 4-year-olds in a university laboratory school, kindergarten in a church-operated school, and kindergarten through third grade classes in public schools. The one thing that all of the teachers had in common was a clear commitment to children and a recognition that they and the children in their classrooms would benefit from a more systematic approach to addressing children's emotional and social needs.

Initial training for these teachers involved participation in a full-day seminar that included a review of the principles of Theraplay, a discussion of children's maladaptive behavior, and the underlying needs associated with particular behaviors. A role play of a group Theraplay session incorporated a variety of activities and discussions of the kinds of needs that each session addresses. Videotapes of sessions were discussed as were issues associated with getting started, getting support and approval, and details such as session length and frequency. The teachers were supplied with a variety of activities but were urged to adapt and create activities that best matched the interests and abilities of their own groups. They were also encouraged to use all or any part of the Theraplay session that might prove beneficial in their classrooms. Participants in all training sessions were encouraged to use *Play with Them* (Rubin and Tregay 1989) as their primary resource.

After the teachers had had a period of experimentation in their classrooms, I observed and consulted with them, using videotapes of the sessions. In addition, smaller groups of teachers met to share their tapes and experiences with each other and to discuss questions and concerns that had emerged about the use of Theraplay in classrooms. From this exchange came suggestions for alterations and adaptations for carrying out successful sessions that addressed both group and individual needs. Innovations involved changes in teachers' conceptions of their roles as well as effective alterations to the prescribed structure of Theraplay as presented by Rubin and Tregay. The following section provides a very brief review of group Theraplay and the significance of its use in classrooms. The remainder of this chapter discusses key issues for teachers and the innovations in teaching practices that can accompany the application of Theraplay. Some of the issues are immediately practical while others are theoretical in nature.

The purpose of conducting Theraplay in classrooms is to create a secure environment where children and teachers can come together in a playful and caring community. Group Theraplay sessions led by teachers in regular early-childhood classrooms, preschool through grade three, marks a departure from the traditional role of teachers and the usual curriculum focus of early childhood classes. Theraplay conducted by nontherapists, in a nontherapeutic setting with children who have not been identified as clients, raises new questions and interpretations regarding its use. Goleman (1996) asserts that many families, for a host of reasons, are not providing children what they need to develop emotionally. For these children, school is a place with opportunities for developing relationships with a trusted adult and a relatively consistent group of peers. Conducting group sessions in classrooms provides the benefits of Theraplay to many more children than is possible with use by therapists alone.

Early childhood programs frequently pay lip service to educating the "whole child" and make claims to help children develop physically, mentally, emotionally, and socially. In reality there are few institutions that have directed systematic efforts toward addressing social and emotional development within the organized curriculum (Hyson 1994, Sinclair 1994). The goal for the children in Theraplay is to develop individual competence in contributing to the well-being of themselves and others, and to experience themselves as valued and worthy members of the group. Used in this context Theraplay becomes preventative as well as therapeutic—it is at once both health producing and health restoring.

When schools or child care centers focus systematic attention on children's emotional and social needs, it is often after children have been identified as having problems, that is to say, children with whom their teachers and classmates no longer know how to cope. At this point the resources of a school counselor or outside agency may be called upon for help. However, in some areas counseling services are simply not available. In one state, legislators recently proposed replacing school counselors with reading specialists, ignoring the contribution that counselors make toward children's overall success in learning. In still other institutions behavior problems are dealt with through a series of punishments, with little or no attention given to the unmet needs that fostered the behaviors in the first place. Some schools do make concerted efforts by scheduling the school counselor to provide instruction in classrooms on a regular basis in addition to seeing select children individually or in small groups. These efforts are commendable, but given the growing numbers of children who cannot form healthy relationships with their peers or adults (Garbarino 1995), and the limited time and money available for counseling, as a society we must find additional ways to address the needs of young children. Group Theraplay provided by trained teachers can assure that all children are given the opportunity to be acknowledged and valued by peers and adults within their classroom group.

ORIGINS OF GROUP THERAPLAY

Phyllis Rubin and Janine Tregay (1989) designed the format of the group Theraplay session based on the work of Ann Jernberg. Originally Rubin conducted individual sessions with Tregay's special education class. However, when the number of individuals needing Theraplay expanded beyond Rubin's available time, necessity provoked the invention of working with children in groups. Over the years Rubin and Tregay developed a session format that incorporated a high degree of physical interaction, playfulness, and a strong sense of connection among the individuals. Studies of healthy mother–child relationships reveal that nurture, structure, challenge, and engagement (intrusion) are essential for all children and must be met at some point if the individual is to develop healthy relationships with others (Jernberg 1979). Group

Theraplay provides a framework in which the four basic needs of nurture, challenge, engagement, and structure are all experienced. Through careful observation teachers and counselors identify problem behaviors of individual children. The group leader or leaders use the presenting problem behavior and whatever other resources are available (i.e., communication with the family, student records, etc.) to determine which of these four needs must be addressed. Activities are then selected that offer the greatest potential for meeting those needs. The group Theraplay session begins with the opening song, is followed by "check-ups," a game(s), food share, and closes with a final song(s). Three simple rules are reviewed with the children as often as necessary. The rules for the children are "stick together," "no hurts," and "have fun." A fourth rule, which applies to the teacher only, is, "the adult is always in charge."

THE ADULT IS ALWAYS IN CHARGE

Adherence to this fourth rule establishes the adult as the clear authority, the wise older person who ultimately knows what is best for the child. Jernberg (1979) says, "He [the therapist] does not allow the child to call the shots" (p. 50). The early childhood educator would have little quarrel with this statement; however, in application this rule raises questions for many. The rule implies that children are not permitted to make choices regarding their activities, an idea that runs counter to a child-centered classroom and is seemingly contradictory to the ideals of a democratic classroom. This rule is especially significant in that the trend in early education has been a moving away from an authoritarian model where the adult ruled supreme to a more collaborative system that values and promotes shared decision making and shared leadership. The democratic model for classrooms, however, should not be confused with permissiveness, which is, I believe, what Jernberg is trying to avoid. In the constructivist classroom the adult shares responsibility with the children at the level commensurate with the children's maturation or need; however, the adult is still in charge.

During the Theraplay session the control or power of the teacher is exercised through her ability to discern whether a child's choice of activity reflects a simple desire/interest or whether it is an attempt to challenge the adult's authority. The group leader will need to ascertain whether the granting of an individual child's request that is contrary to the adult's plan is indeed in the child's best interest. For example, one teacher had just announced pretend face-painting as the activity when Tara, a child who almost never expressed a preference for anything, even when asked, whispered her desire to play Duck, Duck,Goose, Hug (see Appendix for all activities in this chapter). Does the adult reward this first display of initiative or does the literal interpretation of the rule that the teacher is in charge result in the child's request being denied? The leader must constantly weigh and balance the needs of the group, its individuals, and the particulars of the situation in making these spontaneous decisions. For me, the adult's being in charge is not to deny a child's power, but rather to find ways to legitimate it within the structure of the session. The teacher, with her familiarity with the particulars of each child, is in an informed position from which to make those decisions. By reflecting on sessions and through careful observations of the class in other contexts, the teacher can determine the best response to each situation.

In a constructivist classroom where children are used to having an adult that is responsive and open to their requests, children may frequently make demands on the teacher for activities that are fun and familiar. However, in this instance if the teacher concedes to the children, she may deny them the greater benefit derived from the activity that the teacher had judiciously selected to address specific needs. The teacher's process of choosing a new activity is not within the capability of young children's understanding, nor are they privy to the underlying purposes for those decisions. By honoring the children's requests the adult may deny her own power as reflected in her ability to reason and carefully select a particular activity. Aside from the power issues related to children's choice, there is the element of surprise that helps to support the adult in the role of being in charge. When the adult is responsible for determining the activity, every child may be surprised and thus be drawn into the activity initially, if for no other reason than curiosity. Asking children what they want to do alters the pace of the session, may invite confusion or even chaos, curtails the fun, and thus constrains the therapeutic value of the session. Security is in knowing the adult is in charge. When the adult is securely in charge, children feel safe to take risks and to play.

HAVE FUN: ISSUES OF PROFESSIONALISM

The group Theraplay rule to have fun provides teachers with still another challenge. The rule applies to both teacher and children, and, furthermore, the leader is to have fun by playing and being playful with the children (Jernberg 1979, Rubin and Tregay 1989). How does a teacher maintain her authority with a group of young children while playing with them? And how does a teacher who plays with the children maintain her dignity as the teacher? Can she be taken seriously as a teacher if she plays with her children? These questions and others must be answered by the teacher for her own satisfaction, and to the satisfaction of the parents, her colleagues, and the administration. This role of playmate and player is not only uncommon, it is also uncomfortable among early childhood educators who have had to fight for the respect for their positions and to distinguish themselves as serious professionals as compared to people who just play with kids all day. Teachers are hired to teach, not to play. Letting go of the traditional role of the teacher may not be as hard for the early childhood teacher as it is for the administration and parents. Professional justification for playing with children can be borrowed from some types of play therapy; however, teachers are not seen as therapists even though much of what they do may be therapeutic. Another professional educator who plays is the physical education teacher. Even here the play is as demonstration and as challenge and is not necessarily "playful." For teachers to justify their play and playfulness, they must look to the child development literature and study of parenting behavior.

Teachers who share a constructivist teaching philosophy may find it easier to accept that the children will receive what they need from a Theraplay session without the leader making the lesson explicit in words. However, even in classrooms where a constructivist approach is followed, teachers will typically react to children whose behavior is disruptive, disrespectful, or even dangerous by discussing the situation with the child. Words are relied on as the conveyer of learning or as the motivator for changes in behavior (Fields and Boesser 1994). For example, the teacher may respond to a child's aggression by saying to her, "That hurt when you hit Alfonso. How would you feel if someone hit you?" Reliance on verbal instruction is seldom sufficient for children whose underlying need to be nurtured is not being satisfied.

To answer the question of the value of play, each teacher must have a justification for carrying out Theraplay in the first place. One teacher who had taught for many years in many different situations eagerly carried out Theraplay as a way to deal with her very challenging group. Nan was naturally playful and embraced the opportunity to enter into play with her kindergarten children. As a veteran master teacher, her play with the children went unquestioned. She invited colleagues, parents, and administrators into her class to observe the difference that these sessions had made with her children.

> The class bully, whose father was sometimes in prison and who abused his children when he wasn't, was able to laugh and participate with his peers during these play sessions. In the atmosphere of playfulness he allowed Nan to wrap him in a blanket and rock him while the group sang lullabies to him. Others wanted their turn. Sonya, whose distrust of the world had all but immobilized her, could not resist the physical challenge to push the teacher over. For Nan, justification came in the changes that allowed her class to become a place where children could have fun learning after they had had fun having fun.

Penny, on the other hand, needed several sessions of feeling in control before she could relax and truly have fun with her children. As she gained confidence in her ability to lead the group, she relaxed and so did the children. As the sessions became more playful, Penny's natural sense of humor bloomed and became part of the playfulness.

> One child, whom Penny had affectionately nicknamed "Prickles," began to demonstrate affection and kindness to her peers instead of her habitual negative responses. She began to let other children play with her outside of the session instead of rejecting them with her jagged criticism. Penny remarked that the Theraplay session helped her to see the soft side of Prickles, perhaps also encouraging the child to give up the protection offered by her prickly behavior. As a result of gentle teasing, Penny and Prickles began to enjoy a shared sense of humor. As Penny's confidence grew so did her awareness and understanding of the value of what she was doing. Her in-

teractions became increasingly playful and nurturing. She was developing new and more intimate relationships with the children.

TEACHING CHILDREN TO TOUCH

Sensitivity to physical contact of any kind and its potential for leading to accusations of sexual abuse and misconduct have contributed to our denying children's needs in what is still a relatively safe place—the classroom. In their haste to reduce liability, some institutions working with children have declared that there will be no touching. Individual teachers have stated that they don't get into that, referring to any physical display of affection.

Yet no touching is anathema to the effectiveness of Theraplay. Jernberg was clear: Theraplay is effective because it meets needs at the development level, not at the chronological level. For example, most healthy 6-year-olds no longer have the need to suck on a bottle and be swaddled in a blanket, although even healthy children may enjoy the experience. However, children who did not receive cuddling from a caring adult when they were infants or toddlers can benefit from these experiences whatever their current chronological age. Six-year-olds are likely to have the cognitive and linguistic skills to discuss their behavior, but until the earlier needs for nurturing are addressed, healthy development will be thwarted.

For the past ten years as a teacher of future teachers I have regularly been asked whether they as students should allow kindergarten children to sit in their laps during practica. The question inevitably is extended to include many kinds of physical contact. In an atmosphere highly charged with suspicion toward potential sexual and physical abusers, these young preservice teachers are questioning whether touching should be permitted. But in Theraplay, touching is not just permitted, it is absolutely encouraged.

The following examples of touching and the use of the "no hurts" rule are illustrated based on an activity that is similar to the familiar children's game Duck, Duck, Goose. In this game, however, "hug" is substituted for "goose." The child whose turn it is walks around the outside of the circle tapping each child on the head while saying "duck." To designate the next player, the child says "hug" instead of "duck."

That child then runs in the opposite direction. When they meet they
give each other a hug.

> Four-year-old Ben walked around the circle tapping each child
> on the head in succession with each tap becoming increasingly
> hard until the teacher reminded him, "Be gentle. Remember our
> rule, Ben—no hurts." He softened and resumed the taps until
> he chose the next child. At 7, Alvin was bigger and stronger
> than most of his peers. He liked to express his power with the
> group by giving bear hugs that were hurtful to other children
> and adults. Other children resisted his affection. In the Thera-
> play session adults modeled gentle hugs and reminded Alvin
> of the no hurts rule. His peers gradually responded with af-
> fection toward him instead of rejection. Six-year-old Lila failed
> to respond to her peers' and the teachers' hugs. One of the
> adults ran with her and standing behind Lila took Lila's hands
> and gently helped her create a circle that included the other
> child.

In this activity, hugging is an integral and deliberately intentional
part of the play. Other Theraplay activities that include touching and
physical contact may be more incidental to the play. Children who
are the victims of sexual and physical abuse need to be approached
sensitively and cautiously; however, they especially need the experience of touch that is nurturing and playful. These contacts are powerful lessons in helping children experience positive touch—touch that
doesn't hurt, touch that doesn't possess, but rather touch that is fun
and nurturing.

AGGRESSIVE AND RESISTANT CHILDREN

Children who resist adult guidance and limitations or who are physically and verbally aggressive challenge the adults who are responsible
for them.

> Three-year-old Anthony's initial resistance took the form of
> refusing to come to the carpet where the group gathered for

Theraplay. This resistance behavior had been part of his response to any kind of whole-group activity and was not directed at Theraplay per se. Anticipating his reaction, the teacher legitimized his need for her attention by making him the leader of the train that wound around the room gathering the other children while singing "Little Red Caboose." Once he was in the group, he did not leave, but he did refuse to participate in most of the activities. The teacher did not give Anthony additional requests that he join them, and in keeping with the rule of "have fun," she did not admonish him for his refusal. She simply observed his behavior and did not react to his resistance by giving it emphasis. One day, when a change in the schedule caused Theraplay to be canceled, Anthony was the one child who noted its absence and told the teacher that he wanted it. It seems that this very special group time had begun to serve as secure base for the rest of the day's activities.

In a therapy session, the therapist could have given Anthony attention using any of a number of playful intrusions or paradoxical challenges. However, with a whole group of children also needing her attention, the group leader had to rely on a deeper understanding of his behavior and the draw of the activities to keep his interest and gradually his involvement in them.

Five-year-old Clark, who typically refused to join his peers in the circle, eventually joined on his own when his curiosity over what was being said during a whispering activity overcame his need to resist. His teacher wisely selected activities that required his immediate presence. She had invited him, and then instead of nagging him to join them she told him that it was fine for him to sit away from the group, but that he could join them if he changed his mind. In this way she respected him and his ability to choose but narrowed the range to two possibilities, coming to the group or sitting nearby. She had legitimated his behavior and at the same time removed the immediate object of his resistance. Furthermore, by choosing playful, fun activities she engaged him despite his practice of resistance.

Jernberg (1979) states, "The Theraplay therapist initiates, rather than reacts to, the child's behavior" (p. 54). In the classroom session where there are many children to attend to simultaneously, the Theraplay group leader's initiations will not always be sufficient to engage all of the children all of the time. Resistant children can be extremely skilled in forcing their teachers into struggles over who is in charge. Their behavior can be experienced as a threat to adult authority and labeled as stubborn, resistant, or defiant. Or their behavior can also be labeled persistent and viewed as a potential strength and a cluster of strategies that children develop in response to a particular context of relationships that may prove unnecessary over time.

STICK TOGETHER: BUILDING A CARING COMMUNITY

The group leader creates a caring environment and carefully models genuine acceptance of each child as she guides the children in doing the same for each other. These positive interactions among the group members within the session are the basis for establishing a group ethos that is inclusive and respectful. Regardless of the relative health of the group, individuals can be helped through the leader's deliberate structuring of playful interactions chosen to meet particular children's needs.

PRACTICAL CONSIDERATIONS FOR GROUP THERAPLAY
Who Gets to Play?

The practice of denying children participation in activities in which they misbehave is a common way for adults to manage children's behavior and to regulate the quality of the experience for other children who do participate according to adult expectations. The problem with this practice is that the children who repeatedly offend are those who most need the experiences of the group. Supporting children in the seemingly simple rule of sticking together may be more difficult than it may first appear. When children are sent away from the group or are otherwise denied participation, they experience rejection, isolation, and perhaps even abandonment, the very opposite result of sticking together, where individuals join together in mutual support. Repeated exclusion from the group reinforces children's preexisting images of being unworthy. Through their own out-of-bounds behavior and the consequential expulsion from the group, these children prove their unworthiness over and over. There may be extreme situations where remaining in the group may be dangerous, but the goal of Theraplay is to have all children participate fully in the whole Theraplay session. The question then becomes, How does the leader support all children's participation?

Leading Theraplay Sessions

The adage that two heads are better than one is applicable to group Theraplay. Having two adults is especially important when leaders are learning to conduct sessions, when children are very young, when the group is large, or when there are children who are aggressive or are likely to leave the group. Though each session should have a designated leader, the leadership can rotate from session to session. With two adults, one leads while the other is free to support children who may find participation a special challenge. Another advantage of having two adults is the addition of a second observer, a second perspective, and the support that each leader can give the other. Assistant teachers, volunteers, or classroom aides can perform the same supporting role. When teachers are experienced in leading the group, finding a time for Theraplay becomes more flexible than if only counselors led groups.

Ideally groups will be led by two or more adults. However, many teachers have led their groups without assistance, depending on the overall emotional and social health of the group, size of the group, and skill of the leader.

Group Size

One teacher of preschool children divided the class of sixteen into two groups. While she led a session with one group, the other half of the class was supervised outdoors by volunteers or played in another area of the room. The mix of children was altered each week so that over time all children had interactions with all the others. Initially this allowed the teacher to separate those children who she suspected might provide the most challenge to the rule that the teacher is in charge. It also allowed her to relax so that she too could enjoy playing with the children. For leaders just starting Theraplay, it is important that they experience success and have fun, just as the rule states.

INNOVATIONS AND ADAPTATIONS IN STRUCTURE

The Theraplay group session as modeled by Rubin and Tregay is centered around checkups and play activities. Verbal discussion occurs almost exclusively in response to children's immediate interactions with each other and the leader. Though Jernberg (1979) describes a role play example in a group session with four children, Rubin and Tregay (1989) have not formally included role play in their format. Perhaps the large group session as designed by Rubin and Tregay omitted role play because of the difficulty it posed for their special population of children. However, some teachers have used the opening ritual song and a game in combination with more traditional talk-based class meetings. The checkups and activities help to develop and foster the kinds of interactions that increase the effectiveness and inclusiveness of class meetings. The class meetings may be led by the teacher or, as in one first grade, the teacher models the role of facilitator for the first eight weeks and then begins rotating the role among the children. Content for class meetings may be determined by posting agendas to which children and teachers contribute items. One kindergarten class made extensive use of role play in posing solutions to interpersonal conflicts. Classroom sessions were ended with a song. As has been observed in many sessions, children spontaneously put their arms around each other and sway to the rhythm of the music, evidence of the emotional warmth evoked by the session.

In Anna's kindergarten class of twenty children, role play was successfully combined with elements of Theraplay. Anna did not have the benefit of a second adult. The sessions began with a song, followed by checkups, a single game/play activity, and discussion that almost always involved role play as a way of problem solving concerns identified by any member of the group including the teacher.

> In one class meeting, several girls stated that they did not like it when the boys looked up the girls' dresses and teased them when they were climbing on the jungle gym. Anna then asked

the whole group to consider what might be done about it. Two ideas were suggested: the girls could always wear pants, or the boys could stay away from where the girls were playing. The girls would not agree to always wear pants; they adamantly stated their desire to wear dresses or skirts if and when they wanted to. Several boys then stated that they would not tease them anymore. Following this session the boys' taunting of the girls dramatically ceased.

In another session Joey indicated his area of interest by copying the word *blocks* onto the agenda sheet. The classroom rule stated that only five children were allowed in the block area at any one time. Joey had left the block area to use the toilet but when he returned another child had entered the area. Joey was told by the second child that he could not return to the blocks because five children were all that could be there. Joey protested.

When Joey described this situation to the group, the children were unable to follow his meaning, so Anna asked the children involved to replay the scene. In this group session, Lamar, a child who was considered developmentally delayed, surprised Anna and perhaps the other children by restating the issue so that the others understood it and then went on to suggest a solution that eventually became the new plan for such situations. This was a child who was in danger of failing kindergarten and was being considered for retention. He had rarely contributed during group meetings. The democratic and accepting atmosphere of the Theraplay session supported this child in expressing himself in front of the whole class with a clarity he had previously not shown.

This scene illustrates what several teachers have described as Theraplay's sessions' propensity to allow them to see children in a very different light. One teacher, in referring to a child whom she had a difficult time appreciating, said "Our interactions in Theraplay have helped me to see the softer side of Angela." Angela was a child that the teacher previously described as a "cactus."

In Lora's third grade class, Theraplay sessions and the rules of Theraplay became the topic of many of the students' journal writings.

Lora's group was very cliquish and tended to isolate some children and deny others the privilege of participating in activities. The rule of no hurts quickly took on significance in the emotional realm. Children who had been ridiculed or rejected not only wrote about the experience, but also brought these incidents before the group during group checkups. The temptation to express revulsion at sitting beside or being partnered with a frequently rejected child receded as children experienced each other as playmates who had fun together during the Theraplay sessions. The teacher focused on nurturing activities such as swinging a peer in a blanket. This activity provided physical challenge and required cooperation at the same time. Children doing the rejecting and those being rejected experienced the careful handling of their peers in a context of having fun. As the sessions continued, their sense of community grew. Children who were among the most hurtful became aware of their actions and developed a new sensitivity toward the class. In conjunction with the play-oriented activities of Theraplay, Lora incorporated a more cognitive activity of journal writing.

CONCLUSION

Childhood education experts agree that creating a nurturing environment facilitates learning and is in keeping with democratic education ideals. In Theraplay teachers are encouraged to suspend the traditional role as dispenser of knowledge and to enter into play with the children. This does not mean that the teacher relaxes her authority, or that anything goes. Far from it. The teacher or leader is ever vigilant in the task of monitoring each child's experience and taking charge in a way that reassures the children that someone older and wiser is in control. This sense of the teacher being in control is essential for creating security and trust among the group members.

Teachers using Theraplay recognize the value of meeting children at their level of development and recognize that the best role for the teacher is what is dictated by the children, not by a particular philosophy or trend. Being child-centered means that the children's needs are addressed, not glossed over, excused, or blamed on their parents. Fears of being suspected of child abuse must be put into perspective, and as educators we must abide by our ethical and professional responsibilities to help children resist abuse through supporting their ability to distinguish and differentiate between touch that is playful and nurturing and touch that is possessive or hurtful.

For children whose basic needs are already being met, Theraplay reinforces healthy attitudes toward self and others, all the while encouraging an ethos of caring and concern for others. For children with deep unmet needs, these sessions provide an intentional context in which adults and peers can begin to meet those needs. Theraplay sessions call for the wisdom and intelligence of the teacher to be creatively and playfully involved in the emotional healing of all the children.

Theraplay is powerful in that it provides a legitimate structure for teachers to address children's very deep and basic emotional needs in an atmosphere of nurturing playfulness. In connecting with children at the level of need, adults can free children of the burdens that prohibit their full and effective participation in a community of learners. Theraplay enables all children to grow in their ability to care about themselves and their peers and the world around them.

REFERENCES

Fields, M. V., and Boesser, C. (1994). *Constructivist Guidance and Discipline*. New York: Merrill.

Garbarino, J. (1995). *Raising Children in a Socially Toxic Environment*. San Francisco: Jossey-Bass.

Goleman, D. (1996). *Emotional Intelligence: Why It Can Matter More Than IQ*. New York: Bantam.

Hyson, M. (1994). *The Emotional Development of Young Children: Toward an Emotion Centered Curriculum*. New York: Teachers' College Press.

Jernberg, A. M. (1979). *Theraplay*. San Francisco: Jossey-Bass.

Rubin, P. B., and Tregay, K. J. (1989). *Play with Them: Theraplay Groups in the Classroom*. Springfield, IL: Charles C Thomas.

Sinclair, C. (1994). *Looking for Home: A Phenomenological Study of Home in the Classroom*. New York: Teachers' College Press.

18

Using Theraplay in Primary Health Care Centers: A Model for Pediatric Care

MARY R. TALEN

PROBLEM STATEMENT

Primary health care practices and well-child checkups have been a cornerstone for disease prevention in medical health care settings. The main focus of these checks has been in providing immunizations, early detection of diseases, and monitoring physical growth and development. While much has been done over the years to intervene early in the physical disease process, little has been done in primary health care settings to address the growing social and emotional difficulties that are surfacing in today's children (Allen et al. 1993, Goldberg et al. 1997, Miller-Heyl et al. 1998, Sturner et al. 1980).

Today, health care providers are faced with an increase in the intensity and frequency of severe child behavioral and developmental problems. The number of children seen in pediatric health care clinics identified as needing behavioral health interventions has significantly increased in the last decade (Lavigne et al. 1993, Merritt et al. 1995, Sturner et al. 1980). Because a growing number of children are being cared for in fragile families that are struggling with inadequate resources and limited social support systems, our health care system needs to implement comprehensive health programs for monitoring and supporting children's psychosocial as well as physical development. As family stresses (substance abuse, violence, social isolation, etc.) are increasing, children's health problems and behavioral disorders have been increasing (American Orthopsychiatry Report 1994). Child abuse, neglect, and abandonment are on the rise. In 1996 over 3 million children were reported as victims of abuse, raising the national rate from 41 out of 1,000 in 1990 to 44 out of 1,000 in 1996 (Children's Bureau 1996). More families are struggling with financial insecurity, limited education, family and community fragmentation, and health problems, along with fewer resources and social isolation. Over 21.6 percent of children under the age of 6 live below the poverty line (U.S. Census Bureau 1997). A growing number of children are without adequate health care, lack basic immunizations, and have had no physical or developmental screenings. Because of these problems, prevention and intervention programs for preschool children that address both physical and psychosocial development have become a national health care priority.

In traditional pediatric health care settings, disease prevention has been the central role for well-child exams. The medical providers have focused on preventing or minimizing the impact of specific physical disorders (e.g., diptheria, pertussis, tetanus, and diabetes). Our current medical health care practices have been extremely successful in eradicating infectious diseases in children (e.g., smallpox, polio), and children afflicted with chronic diseases are benefiting from improved medical management through medications, sophisticated monitoring procedures, state-of-the-art technologies, and other specialty treatments. While we have gained substantially in biomedical intervention, we have lagged behind in psychosocial areas. The focus of disease in our culture has been shifting from biologically or genetically determined childhood diseases to children's social/emotional/behavioral disorders that are now affecting their health (Green 1994). Several reports indicate that pediatricians spend considerable time (25 percent to 60 percent) in well-child care addressing psychosocial concerns of parents about their child's development and activity level, parenting questions, sleeping, eating, or toilet training concerns (Allen et al. 1993, Garrison et al. 1992, Sturner et al. 1980). Coupled with this, several studies indicated that pediatricians consistently underidentify behavioral health problems in children, while the prevalence of childhood behavior disorders is growing (Garrison et al. 1992, Glascoe and Dworkin 1995, Lavigne et al. 1993). Our understanding of health and wellness can no longer be limited to individual physical disease prevention (e.g., immunizations, lead screening) or injury prevention (e.g., seatbelts, poisons), but must be broadened to systemic concepts that include parent–child interactions, family environments, and cultural and community contexts (Anthony and Cohler 1987, Miller-Heyl et al.1998, Roberts 1993, Roberts and McElreath 1992). In addition, the relationship between family dynamics, communities, and health has gained greater prominence in our health research and intervention models (Campbell and Patterson 1995, Prior et al. 1992). However, new developments in understanding the relationship between family and children's psychosocial health have not yet been integrated into our health promotion practices and well-child health exams.

There is also a growing body of research that suggests that healthy, stress-resistant, resilient children develop in the context of supportive family relationships. These healthy relationships include emotional closeness and early secure attachments, parental sensitivity and responsiveness to the child's needs, and a sense of parental self-efficacy and self-competency (Cowen et al. 1990). With sound attachment, the children learn that they are loved, worthwhile, safe, and protected. The caregiver is perceived by the child as an available, predictable source of comfort and support. This primary attachment relationship becomes a secure foundation for the development of age-appropriate cognitive and interpersonal skills, many of which are formed in the preschool years. Successful development of attachment and competency lead to a sense of self-efficacy—a belief that a person can cope with life's pressures and demands—as well as a sense of empowerment—gaining control over and making critical decisions about one's life.

Consistently, it has been the family environment (e.g., maternal stress, family conflict, and violence vs. support, warmth, and shared feelings and thoughts) that have predicted higher health and behavior risk factors for children (Thompson et al. 1993). In addition, the relationship between family factors and health and behavior has been empirically supported (Campbell and Patterson 1995). While well-child checkups have been long recognized as an important intervention for inoculating children against physical disease, we are now faced with the challenge of inoculating children and families with the "antibodies" for psychosocial and emotional disorders.

Health care projects and new clinical practices are being developed that emphasize prevention, focus on biopsychosocial aspects of health, and use multidisciplinary teamwork to accomplish these health care goals (Algranati and Dworkin 1992, Allen et al. 1993, Jones et al. 1996, Kush and Campo 1998, Roberts and McElreath 1992). Improving children's health using a biopsychosocial model has been a priority of our health promotion project. Building on the assumption that children's health is significantly related to the quality of caregiver–child relationships, the nature of these primary relationships are the focus of this project's comprehensive child checkup (CCC) protocol. The foundational premise of this project is that attachment is a basic need for healthy development of young children (Jernberg 1979, Karen 1994). Primary health care for young children should address the relationship issues between children and their caregivers (Karen 1994). Our belief has been that healthy development is significantly related to a child's family functioning and community context. Understanding and fostering healthy children requires that health care providers attend to these interpersonal dynamics that have developed between children and their parents. Promoting healthy relationships and developing early intervention are important avenues for creating a secure foundation for a child's development. This is the time for caregivers to understand the developmental needs of children, to gain caregiving skills, and to develop positive "in sync" relationships with their children (Jernberg 1979, 1993). Providing information to caregivers on normal behavior, providing anticipatory guidance, and enhancing healthy caregiver–child interactions can set the stage for a child's emotional as well as physical well-being, positive self-esteem, and appropriate social relationships.

Based on this foundational knowledge, primary health care and well-child check-up procedures need to include an assessment of the interactional relationship and attachment qualities between child and primary caregivers. By enhancing the attachment qualities, providing developmental information, and supporting parent efficacy and responsiveness, children can develop their stress-resistant potentials and improve their physical and psychological wellness, and parents can improve their effectiveness in meeting their child's needs. The Marschak Interaction Method (MIM) (see Chapter 3, this volume) and the Theraplay method can be used in the health promotion protocols because their concepts mesh well with the goals of biopsychosocial well-child checkups (Jernberg 1979). The Theraplay approach is a natural fit with new ways of thinking about health care and promoting children's health. This is an active, playful, and interpersonal process for assessing and addressing a child's development (e.g., memory, gross and fine motor skills, expressive and receptive language, tactile sensitivity, temperament) and interpersonal relatedness (Bernt 1991, Jernberg 1979, 1993). The Theraplay method (see Chapter 2, this volume), with its emphasis on structure, challenge, engagement, and nurture, offers a robust yet simple model for understanding and describing healthy child development and social relationships within the pediatric health care clinic. The focus of this project has been on prevention, health promotion, and psychosocial wellness for children and their parents. The overall aim of the CCC has been to expand and provide a structure in this health care plan for teaching parents about their child's emotional and social development, supporting and sustaining healthy caregiver–child interactions, and creating a mechanism for early detection and intervention of problems.

INTEGRATION OF THERAPLAY WITHIN PEDIATRIC HEALTH CARE SERVICES

The first five years of the child's life is when families establish a relationship with their primary health care professionals such as nurses, physicians, and physician assistants. Each provider has a unique role in contributing to the comprehensive assessment and plan for promoting and maintaining a child's health (Kush and Campo 1998, Roberts 1993, Shute 1997). During these visits, the health care team takes on a variety of roles and responsibilities. Nursing staff is typically responsible for assessing the child's general development by taking the child's height, weight, and providing a vision and hearing screening. The nursing staff is also trained in providing health education information for parents. For example, injury prevention information about using seatbelts, using sunscreen, or keeping guns in locked cabinets are important pieces of information that the staff reviews with parents. The nurse or physician also inquires about the child's general cognitive and language development and observes the parent–child interaction. The physician's role is to assess the child's physical health and development (e.g., heart, lungs, congenital or developmental anomalies) and to screen the child's oral health, strabismus, hyperlipidemia, bruising or poorly explained injuries or scars from possible abuse, and risk of lead exposure, along with keeping immunizations up to date. All of these areas are important in child health care. The health care providers are involved in screening, education, and intervention to ensure the child's healthy development (Green 1994).

The integration of both nursing and medical perspectives gives families a foundation for understanding and providing for their child's growth and development. However, a comprehensive health promotion plan that incorporates the psychosocial elements of child development is a complex task, and most health care providers have had limited training and few models that provide a structured approach for assessing these strengths and identifying parent–child difficulties (Garrison et al. 1992, Novak 1996, Shute 1997). The vast majority of pediatric practices do not incorporate a behavioral health assessment into their well-child checkups, and often parents' questions about normal developmental issues (e.g., expectations for children based on age) or self-regulatory and self-soothing abilities (e.g., eating, sleeping, calming, toileting) are often short-changed. It is also rare for health providers to devote time to reassure parents about their strengths and resources and address their parenting questions. Behavioral health providers such as psychologists and social workers are also viewed as specialty providers and referral resources for those children who present with more significant behavioral problems and behavioral health disorders such as attention deficit disorders, autism, or separation and anxiety disorders. These behavioral health providers are not usually part of the primary health care team.

Incorporating a behavioral health assessment as part of a health promotion protocol that includes the attachment relationship and the child's social/emotional development is an important addition to well-child care (Roberts and McElreath 1992). Providing specific feedback and information to parents in this area may support and foster the social skills, self-esteem, and resiliency that children need to protect them from other disorders. This comprehensive approach also creates a supportive environment on multiple levels:

- It provides parents with an understanding and appreciation of the unique and individual aspects of their child's growth and development.

- It provides preventive measures, such as anticipatory guidance, early identification, and early intervention in problems that interfere with a child's development.
- It develops positive collaborative attitudes between parents and a multidisciplinary health care team. In particular, it fosters positive experiences with behavioral health providers and a recognition of the unique contributions of psychology, social services, and other disciplines to the overall health care of the child.

A second area of health care is health maintenance for children who have a chronic illness. Those who are diagnosed with diabetes or asthma, sleeping and/or eating irregularities, learning disabilities or attention deficit, or other developmental delays due to physical handicaps are at risk for developing social and emotional difficulties as well (Glascoe and Dworkin 1995, Minuchin et al. 1978, Patterson 1991, Patterson and Garwick 1994). Patterns of interaction that parents and children develop around the symptoms or caregiving dynamics of a chronic illness may complicate the intensity and duration of the disease. In these situations, parents frequently have more contact with health care providers, but generally the relationship factors between parents and children are often overlooked in medical treatment plans. In assessing the health of children with chronic illnesses, it is also important to assess the patient caregiving unit as a whole (Rolland 1993). The child's environmental context and emotional climate in the family has a significant relationship to health risk factors and health maintenance plans (Minuchin et al. 1978, Patterson and Garwick 1994).

While health care providers may be very skilled in addressing the biomedical management of a disease, they usually do not have the knowledge or skills to assess or intervene with parent–child interactions that either support or exacerbate a child's health. For example, one parent had been having regular weekly visits to the urgent care center because her child was having asthma attacks and she could not get him to settle down enough to give him breathing treatments. She complained that her child was unmanageable; he was just too silly and wouldn't sit still. Often in this situation, the child would be given a treatment in the urgent care setting and the family was sent home. The acute symptoms were alleviated but the contextual factors that may have exacerbated the symptoms were not addressed. In this situation, the behavioral health provider was part of the health care team and observed an interaction in which the mother was trying to get the 4-year-old's attention and get him to cooperate with the treatments. As she intensified her requests, he became increasingly silly until she grabbed him and tickled him, playfully attempting to capture his attention. This interaction only escalated the child's silly behaviors so that his breathing became even more labored and restrictive. As the behavioral health consultant observed this interaction, she was able to point out how frustrating his silliness must be for her and that she might feel limited in her options to get him calmed down and help him accept his breathing treatments. Viewing this interaction helped the behavioral health consultant frame the problem as an interactional difficulty and opened new possibilities for the mother. Without laying blame, the behavioral health provider and nursing staff supported the mother in coping with the child's frustrating behaviors. At the same time they were able to model other, more soothing ways to nurture, relax, and engage her child. Theraplay techniques such as rocking and singing a song or applying lotion using long, firm strokes and a deeper, slower voice tone demonstrated specific, concrete tools for her to use with her son that would support him learning relaxing strategies, develop healthy behaviors, and not interfere with his health.

CLINICAL PROTOCOLS AND HEALTH CARE ORGANIZATIONAL ISSUES

The comprehensive child checkup has been an outgrowth of a community-academic partnership. This partnership's mission has been to enhance the delivery of primary health care and develop multidisciplinary, practice models for health care. Our clinical practices have moved away from specialty, hospital-based services and toward community-centered, multidisciplinary teams. The focus of care has shifted toward prevention and primary care and developing biopsychosocial health care plans for individuals, families, and communities. The CCC protocol has been one of these community-academic projects. The checkup was designed to assess the psychosocial development of children and to develop system-based interventions for parents and health providers. The focus of the project was twofold: (1) to assess a child's physical, cognitive, emotional, and social development; and (2) to improve, enhance, and sustain healthy child–caregiver relationships. This prevention and primary care health program was aimed at preventing abuse and neglect, promoting psychosocial family and child wellness, and supporting the emotional and developmental needs of children.

The method for accomplishing these health care goals has been structured around two areas: developing programs *within* the pediatric and/or family health care center, and focusing on interactions *between* children and their primary caregivers (parents, grandparents, foster parents, aunts and uncles). Health care supervision plans and goals are developed within the context of the health care center, and the standard well-child protocols can be expanded to include an assessment of social/emotional/developmental functioning in the context of the child's primary relationships with parents or caregivers (Kush and Campo 1998).

Introducing Theraplay into Primary Health Care Systems

Introducing the CCC protocol into the health care setting was divided into three stages: (1) introduction stage, (2) training, and (3) piloting and revising. Establishing working relationships within the cultural context of the pediatric/family health care center needs to be the first step for implementing a comprehensive biopsychosocial approach for children's health care. Without rapport and a foundational relationship with the health care team, the goals of this project cannot be effectively implemented. This rapport can first be established by behavioral health providers meeting with the health care center's staff of health care providers and learning about their practice plan and health care mission. This introductory phase needs to develop slowly so that the behavioral health consultants build an appreciation for the health care providers' knowledge and skill with parents and child. The initial relationship-building phase centers around the behavioral health consultants' observing the organizational processes, the personal style of each provider, and the relationships between the staff. This observation time provides the behavioral health consultant with an awareness of the strengths and skills of the physicians and nurses, an understanding of the types of problems that the providers encounter, and an appreciation for the treatment and interventions that providers give to fami-

lies. This is also a time for the behavioral health providers to observe
the types of difficulties that children present and the various coping
strategies of parents and providers. The providers often feel overwhelmed
with the emotional needs of the children and the frustrations, stresses,
or inexperience of the parents. Many of the mothers of young children
do not know how to create a nurturing environment or provide appropriate discipline to their children. Children may be excessively shy
and withdrawn or physically aggressive with each other, and may have
been physically restrained or hit by parents. Providers often operate with
time constraints and have limited strategies for helping parents effectively cope with these child development issues.

The introduction stage for the project occurred over a three-month
period. Faculty members, health care providers, and doctoral level psychology providers met with the physicians, nurse practitioners, nurses,
medical assistants, and office staff to learn about the organization while
observing the children's behavior and identifying the challenges that
the staff faced daily. It was also an opportunity for staff and parents
to become accustomed to seeing the behavioral health providers within
the health care center. This rapport-building stage created an atmosphere
of trust and understanding between the providers and behavioral health
staff. This was an important step in establishing the CCC protocol in
the health care center. It gave us the direct experience we needed to
address with credibility the concerns of the staff and parents.

The second step was devoted to training the health care team in
the Theraplay model of child behaviors, attachment, and healthy caregiver–child interactions. The purpose of this training was to teach the
staff about the relationship between social and emotional needs, types
of parental responses, and children's coping behaviors. This training also
helped elicit staff support and understanding of the CCC project. This
training was integrated into two regular staff meetings to accommodate the time constraints of an already busy medical staff. Through role
plays, videotaped examples, and direct experience, the staff became familiar with the children's psychosocial development and the behavioral
outcomes of caregiver–child interaction. The staff was introduced to
different activities for enhancing psychosocial development through
positive relationship building. The MIM assessment and the Theraplay
structure and activities gave the providers a concrete way to assess the
children's ability to respond to structure and rules, give and receive

affection, cooperate with adults and peers, and demonstrate self-awareness and self-confidence, use gross and fine motor skills, and express
themselves. The staff was taught about the foundational concepts of
healthy caregiver–child interactions. The basic concepts—structure,
challenge, engagement, nurture with playfulness—were related to child
behaviors and caregiver–child interactions (Jernberg 1979, 1993). The
training also provided a common ground for identifying and assessing
child problems and building collaborative interventions. The staff learned
how to assess dysfunctional interactions based on the model and observed new ways to relate to children and parents that fostered healthy
development. The health care providers were encouraged to adapt these
principles and strategies to their office visit activities. As part of the
training, they brainstormed new activities that they could introduce
into their physical exams or interventions that would model and support healthy relationship development and provide early intervention
for their children. They were equipped, for example, with new ways to
engage a shy child, and they were exposed to different strategies for
structuring and redirecting the behaviors of the active child. In addition, specific intervention strategies that were identified from the CCC
were also incorporated into the health care plans. Meetings were held
to discuss with the parents and teachers ways to initiate healthy interactions with a child and to support each other in these changes. This
training also helped the staff understand the goals and objectives of the
CCC project. Consequently, they became active participants in and col-
laborators within the project.

The third step was implementing three pilot CCC exams. These
initial procedures were used to identify difficulties and obstacles in administering this project. One area that needed additional attention,
however, was the time management and scheduling demands that occur within a busy pediatric practice. Well-child exams typically take
15 to 20 minutes. Incorporating another parent–child interactional
assessment and feedback altered the scheduling and administrative processes in the center. The additional parent–child interaction assessment
would increase the time another 20 to 30 minutes. In addition, nursing and physician staff was needed to integrate their assessment information and to develop collaborative feedback to the parents. This training seminar provided time for the staff to discuss ways to address these
issues and to incorporate their problem-solving strategies.

The Comprehensive Child Checkup

The checkups were conducted during the second phase of the project. The goals of the CCC were first introduced to the parents at their regularly scheduled physical exams for children who were 3, 4, or 5 years old. Parents were introduced to the purpose of the project through a written brochure that described the process and benefits of the CCC. The brochure described how this well-child health care visit was designed to assess unique aspects of their children's growth and development and enhance their self-esteem and social relationships. The checkup was described as a method that may help detect difficulties before they become problems (e.g., aggressive behaviors, low self-esteem), discover positive aspects of their children's development, and recognize their social skills. This was also an opportunity to receive support, encouragement, and guidance as parents.

Parents who were interested in receiving this well-child checkup volunteered and signed a form giving their consent to participate in this project. The form described the purpose of the CCC and outlined in detail the process of the parent–child interaction and feedback from a behavioral health consultant—either a licensed psychologist or social worker.

The checkup was then conducted in three parts. The first part focused on the standard physical health exam, which was conducted by the nursing and physician team. This included a questionnaire and interview updating the child and family health history (e.g., injuries, illnesses, allergies, immunizations), changes in the family environment (e.g., moves, divorce, changes in child care), assessment of the child's physical health and development (e.g., height, weight, injuries and bruises, vision and hearing screening, physical anomalies, lungs, hearts, etc.), and interviewing the parent about safety precautions and injury prevention. After this process, the nursing staff helped in the family's transition to the assessment of the child's psychosocial development and introduced the behavioral health consultant. The behavioral health consultant spent a few minutes with the family building rapport and identifying the delights and difficulties the parent experienced with the child. The consultant described the procedures of the MIM and explained how observing the parent and child activities would provide important information about their child's social and emotional development. Five prescribed tasks were used for the parent–child interaction. These activities lend themselves to assessing the structuring, challenging, involving, and nurturing qualities between parent and child. The following standard activities were used:

1. Adult and child play with two stuffed animals.
2. Adult teaches child something that the child does not know.
3. Adult ignores the child for one minute.
4. Adult builds a structure with five blocks and asks the child to copy it.
5. Adult and child put lotion on each other.

The parent and child were asked to sit by the desk, and the parent was instructed to read the card aloud and then do the activity with the child, and take as long as they needed for each activity. Material for the activities were placed in a container next to the parent. The behavioral health consultant observed quietly and took notes during the interaction using the MIM checklist form. After they finished the activities, the behavioral health provider asked if the activities gave an accurate sample of how their child behaved with them at home.

After the parent completed activities with the child, the behavioral health consultant excused herself in order to consult with the nursing and physician staff. The consultation between the health care teams members was used to integrate the information from the two assessment sections and to collaborate on specific feedback and guidance for the parents. In most cases, the nurse and behavioral health consultant met with the parent for feedback. During this time the child was given either a healthy snack (pretzels and juice) or a toy to play with to keep him occupied during the feedback time.

First we reviewed the results of the physical development and health screening and the Child Behavior Checklist (Achenbach and Edelbrock 1983). The opportunity to report on their child's strengths and progress helped alleviate parents' fears and provided concrete evidence about their child's development. If a problem was detected, the results usually confirmed what they already suspected. It provided the evidence to say that something was out of sync. One parent, for example, was distraught that her child just did not listen to her and seemed easily distracted and avoidant. We discussed with her that his hearing seemed significantly impaired and that he had compensated well for his deficit. We had observed during the MIM how she had worked so hard to communicate with him in nonverbal ways and we were impressed with the creative, encouraging ways she used to communicate with him. She was visibly relieved that her hunches were confirmed and her parenting abilities were supported. We referred her to the appropriate hearing specialists where she received treatment for him.

After discussing the results on the child's physical development, we reviewed the interaction, specifically focusing on the following areas:

- Support and reinforcement for positive parenting.
- Information to understand their child's temperament, developmental needs, and normal child behaviors.
- Suggestions for enhancing their parenting skills that would match the unique characteristics of their child.

Using information from the clinical interview, we were able to join with parents in their goals and expectations for their child and identify the most difficult situations that their child exhibited based on our comprehensive assessment. Referring to the interaction with parents helped us point out healthy interactions with their child. If a parent gave a positive reinforcing comment to the child during a task, we were able to point out how well the child responded to positive remarks, with comments such as, "Look how your daughter just relaxed and followed your suggestion when you touched her in such a gentle way and used that softer voice. This could be the type of touch she needs to help her learn how to soothe herself and develop better sleeping habits." These types of statements opened up new possibilities for the parents and had a powerful impact on their perception of themselves as competent parents. After hearing about their strengths as parents, they were then receptive to addressing the more challenging interactions. We were able to refer to the more difficult situations with their child and offer alternative responses. For example, it was not unusual that parents' expectations were too advanced for the developmental level of the child. The staff's goals were normalizing the parents' frustration (e.g., "Many parents feel frustrated and irritated when their 4–year-old child seems to ignore them"), providing alternative strategies, and changing the expectations for a child of that age to ones that were more in line with the developmental abilities (e.g., taking the child by the hand and modeling for her the first step in how to put on her coat will be more effective in getting her attention and cooperation). Letting the child observe and learn by doing one step at a time and praising her works best with a child this age.

We also provided all parents at the end of each session with specific recommendations: (1) suggestions for enhancing their child's development and health, which included biomedical (e.g., injury prevention, diet, hygiene, immunizations, etc.) and psychosocial areas (e.g., developmental abilities, social abilities, trust, and self-confidence); (2) suggestions for further assessment or treatment including Theraplay sessions. Parents received a summary sheet of the child's developmental profile and a feedback form that offered suggestions on activities and interactions that would enhance their child's self-esteem, self-regulating, self-soothing, and self-confidence (see Table 18–1).

Table 18–1. Family Wellness Checkup Feedback Summary Form

CHILD'S NAME: _____ DATE OF SESSION: _____

PARENT'S NAME: _____

From our family wellness checkup, the following activities would benefit your child's growth and development.

___1. *Structure*: Activities have a beginning, middle, and end. Activities teach the child to develop self-control. These games and activities teach child to respond to requests. Useful for children who are overactive, undirected, overstimulated, or who want to be in control.

 Suggested Activities: red light–green light, do (activity) when I say the magic word, Mary mack, and follow the leader.

 Recommended Activities: _____

 _____

___2. *Challenge*: Activities that help the child extend himself or herself. Activities promote feelings of competence and confidence. Useful for withdrawn, timid, or rigid children.

 Suggested Activities: Jumping, somersaults, balloon toss, pillow pop-up.

 Recommended Activities: _____

 _____

(continued)

Table 18–1. (*continued*)

___3. *Engagement*: Activities that are unexpected, delightful, and stimu-
lating. Useful for children who are withdrawn, avoidant of contact, or too rigidly structured.

Suggested Activities: I'm gonna getcha, funny faces, face
painting.

Recommended Activities: _____

_____

___4. *Nurture*: Activities that are soothing, calming, quieting, and reassur-
ing. Useful for children who are overactive, aggressive, and act too
grown-up.

Suggested Activities: Rocking, cradling, cuddling, lotioning, feeding.
Soft voices and gentle touches, singing.

Recommended Activities: _____

_____

If parents were interested in addressing the difficult areas with their
children, follow-up Theraplay sessions were also offered. Referrals to
behavioral health services (e.g., Theraplay sessions) were generally well
received because the process of therapy was less foreign and the stigma
demystified. In addition, the problems were well defined and the goals
for treatment were clearly stated. The Theraplay sessions were then
designed to address the problem interactions between child and parent and provide a role model of alternative interactions that would
alter a child's behavior. The treatment followed the format for the
Theraplay approach; see Jernberg (1979) or Chapter 2, this volume,
for a more detailed account of this approach. The protocol for brief
treatment included the following:

1. An initial play session with a therapist and child. The parent
observed the play activities behind a one-way mirror while another therapist discussed the purpose and strategies of the
activities.

2. A play session with the therapist and child with the parent and therapist observing. The parent joins the session at the end for feeding activities.
3. A play session with the therapist and child. The parent joins the middle of the session and is coached and supported by the therapist on new interactions.
4. The parent participates in most of the play session and has more opportunities to practice new interactions that he/she has observed while being supported and encouraged by the therapists.
5. A termination/completion play session with therapists, parent, and child.
6. A follow-up MIM and feedback session for parents.

This protocol for brief intervention provided parents with new role models and resources along with specific ideas for interacting with their child. A case example illustrates this approach.

Case Example

A 34-year-old African-American mother and 36-year-old father with two children, ages 3½ and 6 months, scheduled an appointment for checkups for their children. They had recently moved into the area because of a job transfer and they needed new health providers and a physical exam for the 3½-year-old, since he was registering at a new child care center. During the initial phone call for setting up the appointment, the medical receptionist asked the mother if she would be interested in the comprehensive child checkup. The receptionist explained the purpose and process, and the parent expressed an interest in it, since she was having difficulty with her son's aggressive behaviors and limitless energy at home.

At the initial appointment, the parents were given a description of the CCC project and completed an initial health information form, the Child Behavior Checklist (CBCL), and a consent for treatment form. The nurse met with the children and parents, asked if they had any questions about the CCC process and explained that she would be conducting the first part of the checkup and then would introduce them to the behavioral health consultant for the second part. She also explained that they would put all of the information together and share with them their health assessment and recommendations. The initial developmental and physical health exams indicated that the 3½-year-old was physically healthy and in the upper 95th percentile for height and weight. The CBCL profile indicated that he was significantly advanced in language and cognitive development and had aggressive behaviors. The MIM showed that this mother matched her son's cognitive ability well. She had an exceptional ability to verbally structure, explain, and teach her son new things, such as working a calculator. The father, too, was very verbal and was able to structure and maintain his son's interest in teaching him about how a light bulb worked. However, in the nurturing and involvement tasks, the child became more active and the parents appeared frustrated and unsure of themselves. The mother appeared fearful, timid, and withdrawing when the child became more animated and physically demonstrative. For example, when the mother and son put lotion on each other, the mother quickly ended the interaction when her son tried to put lotion not only on her hands but also on her arms and elbows. The father, on the other hand, would slowly and mechanically put the lotion on and the child became easily bored and distracted and instead tried different ways to squeeze the lotion bottle.

After the biomedical assessment and the MIM, the nurse, physician, and psychologist met briefly to share their perceptions of the child's development and recommendations for promoting the family's health. Primarily, the child was physically healthy and mature in stature. His language and cognitive abilities were advanced for a 3½-year-old, while his social and emotional functioning were delayed in their development and needed more attention.

The feedback from the initial CCC allowed us to reinforce the parents for raising a healthy child who was physically mature and able to perform activities beyond most 3½-year-olds' ability (e.g., advanced vocabulary, jump on one foot) and developing well in his ability to understand the world around him. We also empathized with the parents' frustration and feelings of exhaustion because they had a very bright child. We identified several ways that he was more advanced for his age in his language and problem-solving abilities. We also offered feedback on the aggressive behaviors they experienced with him. We explained that while their son was physically mature and intellectually bright, his emotional development was within a normal 3½-year-old level. We wondered if his advanced physical maturity and verbal abilities led them to overestimate his social and emotional needs. This perspective helped the mother understand why she was having such difficulty coping with her son's high activity level. She also reported that her brother had been physically aggressive with her and she was intimidated by expressions of anger. We suggested nonverbal, nurturing ways for her to engage with and calm her child. We talked about alternative ways that she could help him feel safe even when he may feel out of control. The father was also encouraged to gauge his activities to a younger level to help meet his son's emotional needs—games like Hide and Seek, pretending to make him into a pizza, or blowing bubbles were ways to match his social development with less emphasis on teaching. This family came in for one follow-up session to observe a Theraplay session with the child. The mother was particularly observant of the way the therapist was holding the child closely and using more time and more touch to help him moderate his physical energy level. The behavioral health consultant had a confident style even when the child became more physically active. Observing this approach allowed the mother to change her expectations for her son and to use more nurturing, calming activities that created a sense of protection and safety. The father was also interested in observing playful games that a 3½-year-old enjoys. This opened up new possibilities for him. At the end of this session, the parents were thankful for the opportunity to see and experience new ways to interact with their son. They also reported that they were aware of providing more nurturing and playful interactions with their infant daughter.

CONCLUSIONS AND FUTURE DIRECTIONS: CREATING COLLABORATION IN COMPREHENSIVE CHILD CHECKUPS

Since the focus of this CCC project has been to work within a child's social system and between health care providers, parents, and children, continuity among all the partners is paramount. Linking the family environment and health care supervision plan requires special structured attention. The method for creating this link in the CCC involved two strategies: (1) mutual collaboration between the health and behavioral health care providers on the purpose and structure of the CCC; and (2) consultation between health care providers and parents on their child's overall health, development, and interactional behaviors based on the MIM and the health assessment screenings.

Using the information from these assessments, discussions, and observations, the health care providers were able to plan interventions for the physical and behavioral health needs of the children. In addition, specific intervention strategies that were identified from the CCC were also incorporated into the medical record. Continuity in subsequent checkups could be maintained and parents' competencies reinforced to support healthy interactions with their child.

DISCUSSION AND POSTSCRIPT

The CCC project has been evaluated by the health care providers, parents, and administrative staff. Ten health care staff members, including physicians, nurses, psychologists, social workers and other behavioral health consultants, physician assistants, and office managers participated in the staff training. The evaluations of this aspect of the project have been consistently positive, and plans are being made to train more health care providers in this model. The staff did note that the time constraints and scheduling issues were the biggest obstacles in effectively implementing the project. Future projects like these need to be aware of the time investment, and commitment of the staff is crucial to the success of the project.

The twenty-two 3- to 5-year-old children and their parents who participated in the CCC also evaluated the checkup protocol. They rated how satisfied they were with the services, how useful the information was to them, and how helpful and supportive the health providers were during the CCC procedures. Of these families, ten were very pleased with the project, four were pleased but wanted more information, five found it somewhat helpful but they felt too rushed during the feedback session, and three found that it was not helpful and took too much time. Some parents noted that there was too much information and too little time to have all of their questions answered. Although we have some overall positive evaluations on this program, future research will be needed to determine the overall effectiveness of this primary behavioral health care program and its effectiveness on children's social and emotional development. Another contribution of this program was in applying biopsychosocial concepts to well-child care.

The health care providers were able to incorporate information about a child's behavioral, social, and emotional health into their physical health care plan. It provided a structure for parents and providers to implement interventions that enhance a child's ability to develop a positive self-image, resiliency, and positive social relationships.

Overall, these health care projects can be the beginning avenues for changing how we assess children's health, broadening health care professionals' understanding to include interrelationships and intervening in the interpersonal context for improving children's biopsychosocial health. It is our hope that these projects can continue and expand in other primary health care settings.

REFERENCES

Achenbach, T. E., and Edelbrock, C. (1983). *Manual for the Child Behavior Checklist and Revised Behavior Profile*. Burlington, VT: University of Vermont Department of Psychiatry.

Algranati, P. S., and Dworkin, P. H. (1992). Infancy problem behaviors. *Pediatrics in Review* 13(1):16–22.

Allen, K. D., Barone, V. J., and Kuhn, B. R. (1993). A behavioral prescription for promoting applied behavior analysis within pediatrics. *Journal of Applied Behavior Analysis* 26(4):493–502.

American Orthopsychiatry Report. (1994). *Strengthening Mental Health in Head Start: Pathways to Quality Improvement*. New York: American Orthopsychiatric Association.

Anthony, E. J., and Cohler, B. J., eds. (1987). *The Invulnerable Child*. New York: Guilford.

Bernt, C. L. (1991). Theraplay as an intervention with failure-to-thrive children and their mothers. *Dissertation Abstracts International* 52(2–b):1047–1048.

Campbell, T. P., and Patterson, J. (1995). The effectiveness of family interventions in the treatment of physical illness. *Journal of Marital and Family Therapy* 21(4):545–584.

Children's Bureau. (1996). *Child Maltreatment 1996. Administration for Children and Families*. Washington, DC: U. S. Department of Health and Human Services. http://www.acf.dhhs.gov/programs/cb/stats/ncands96/section2.htm.

Cowen, E. L., Wyman, P. A., Work, W. A., and Parker, G. R., 1990. The Rochester Child Resilience Project: overview and summary of first year findings. *Development and Psychopathology* 2:193–212.

Garrison, W. T., Bailey, E. N., Garb, J., et al. (1992). Interactions between parents and pediatric primary care physicians about children's mental health. *Hospital and Community Psychiatry* 43(5):489–493.

Glascoe, F. P., and Dworkin, P. H. (1995). The role of parents in the detection of developmental and behavioral problems. *Pediatrics* 95(6):829–836.

Goldberg, S., Janus, M., Washington, J., et al. (1997). Prediction of preschool behavioral problems in healthy and pediatric samples. *Journal of Developmental and Behavioral Pediatrics* 18(5):304–313.

Green, M., ed. (1994). *Bright Futures: Guidelines for Health Supervision of Infants, Children, Adolescents.* Arlington, VA: National Center for Education in Maternal and Child Health.

Jernberg, A. M. (1979). *Theraplay*: San Francisco: Jossey-Bass.

———. (1993). Attachment formation. In *The Therapeutic Powers of Play*, ed. C. E. Shaefer, pp. 241–256. Northvale, NJ: Jason Aronson.

Jones, R. N., Latkowski, M. E., Green, D. M., and Ferre, R. C. (1996). Psychosocial assessment in the general pediatric population: a multiple-gated screening and identification procedure. *Journal of Pediatric Health Care* 10(1):10–16.

Karen, R. A. (1994). *Attachment: Unfolding the Mystery Bonds Between Mothers and Infants.* New York: Norton.

Kush, S. A., and Campo, J. V. (1998). Consultation and liaison in the pediatric setting. In *Handbook of Pediatric Psychology and Psychiatry*, vol. 1, ed. R. T. Ammermann, J. V. Campo, pp. 23–40. Boston: Allyn & Bacon.

Lavigne, J. V., Binns, H. J., Christoffel, K. K., et al. (1993). Behavioral and emotional problems among preschool children in pediatric primary care: prevalence and pediatricians' recognition. *Pediatrics* 91(3):649–655.

Merritt, K. A., Thompson, R. J., Jr., Keith, B. R., et al. (1995). Screening for child-reported behavioral and emotional problems in primary care pediatrics. *Perceptual and Motor Skills* 80(1):323–329.

Miller-Heyl, J., MacPhee, D., and Fritz, J. J. (1998). DARE to be you: a family-support, early prevention program. *Journal of Primary Prevention* 18(31):257–285.

Minuchin, S., Rosman, B. L., and Baker, L. (1978). *Psychosomatic Families*. Cambridge, MA: Harvard University Press.

Novak, L. L. (1996). Childhood behavior problems. *American Family Physician* 53(1):257–262, 267–269.

Patterson, J. M. (1991). Family resilience to the challenge of a child's disability. *Pediatric Annals* 20:491–499.

Patterson, J. M., and Garwick, A. W. (1994). The impact of chronic illness on families: a family systems perspective. *Annals of Behavioral Medicine* 16(2):131–142.

Prior, M., Smart, D., Sanson, A., et al. (1992). Transient versus stable behavior problems in a normative sample: infancy to school age. *Journal of Pediatric Psychology* 17(4):423–443.

Roberts, M. C. (1993). Health promotion and problem prevention in pediatric psychology: an overview. In *Readings in Pediatric Psychology*, vol. 14, ed. M. C. Roberts, G. P. Koocher, D. K. Roth, and D. J. Willis, pp. 347–362. New York: Plenum.

Roberts, M. C., and McElreath, L. H. (1992). The role of families in the prevention of physical and mental health problems. In *Family Health Psychology*, vol 17, ed. T. J. Akamatsu, M. A. P. Stephens, S. E. Hobfoll, and J. N. Crowther, pp. 45–65. Washington, DC: Hemisphere.

Rolland, J. S. (1993). Mastering family challenges in serious illness and disability. In *Normal Family Processes*, ed. F. Walsh, pp. 444–473. New York: Guilford.

Shute, R. H. (1997). Multidisciplinary teams and child health care: practical and theoretical issues. *Australian Psychologist* 32(2):106–113.

Sturner, R. A., Granger, R. H., Klatskin, E. H., and Ferholt, J. B. (1980). The routine "well child" examination: a study of its value in the discovery of significant psychological problems. *Clinical Pediatrics* 19(4):251–260.

Thompson, R. J., Merritt, K. A., Keith, B. R., et al. (1993). The role of maternal stress and family functioning in maternal distress and mother-reported and child-reported psychological adjustment of nonreferred children. *Journal of Clinical Child Psychology* 22(1):78–84.

U. S. Census Bureau. (1997). http://www.census.gov/hhes/poverty/histpov/hstpov20.html.

Appendix:
Theraplay Activities

Activity	*How it Works*
1. Airplane	Therapist swoops up child and "flies" her around the room as if she were an airplane.
2. All Around the Garden	Therapist takes child's hand and makes a circle with her finger on the child's palm as she recites: "All around the garden Like a teddy bear One step, two step Tickle you under there" (gently tickle under the chin or some other appropriate spot) or another version: "All around the garden Like a little mouse Upstairs, downstairs In your little house" (give gentle tickle)

3. Arm Wrestling

Therapist and child face each other in a sitting position with their elbows resting at a table and their hands interlocking. On the word "go" or on the word "cherries" each opponent tries to bring down the forearm of the other so it is flat on the table.

4. Balloon Blanket

Start by placing one inflated balloon in a blanket that is held up by everyone in the group. At a signal from the leader a child is told to try to maneuver the balloon to someone else in the group by moving the blanket up and down. Everyone helps him to do this. After a few of the participants have had a turn, add more balloons and the whole group flings the blanket up and down until all the balloons are off the blanket.

5. Balloon Toss

Therapists and family members try to keep one, then two, then three or more balloons aloft without touching the floor. This activity can be started by having one person toss a balloon to another. A variation is to call out a body part (i.e., elbow) where everyone must toss the balloon only with an elbow.

6. Bean Blow

Parents and children each have a straw and are asked to blow an object such as a bean or a cotton ball back and forth to each other across a line.

7. Beauty Salon

With a female child have her sit in front of a mirror and comb her hair. (Put a ribbon or barrette or headband or crown on after combing.) Add a necklace or bracelet. Apply a little makeup if the child is older. If not, make a clown face. Do the latter for young male children as well. If older, apply makeup such as a moustache, heavy eyebrows, sunglasses, a hat, necktie, etc. Throughout, give gentle, caring application of materials and point out the special positive features of the child.

8. Blanket Basketball	See balloon blanket.
9. Blanket Popcorn	Therapist and family members hold corners and sides of blanket. Therapist puts Ping-Pong balls or small Nerf balls or cotton balls into the center of the blanket as if putting popcorn into the pan. Therapist then pretends to put butter into the pan and turns up the heat. As the therapist says "it's getting hotter," everyone flips the blanket up and down a little harder, making the "popcorn" pop up a bit more each time. When therapist says "It's really popping," everyone flips the blanket as hard as they can until all of the "popcorn" has popped out of the pan.
10. Blanket Rock or Swing	One child at a times takes a turn lying quietly in the center of a sturdy blanket. Therapists and family members hold corners and sides of the blanket, raise it gently off the floor, and softly swing it back and forth while singing a song about the child, such as "Rock-a-bye Sally, in the tree top, etc. At the end of the song sing, "When the bough breaks the cradle won't fall and up will come Sally, cradle and all" as the group swings the child into the parents' arms.
11. Blanket Tug of War	Therapist, children, and parents sit in two rows facing each other holding onto a blanket (or rope or towel) between them. Members at the back of each other hold onto the waist of whoever is in front. On the word "go" each line tugs at the blanket trying to get the other side over. Therapist structures the two teams to create desired alliances.
12. Blow Me Over	Therapist or parent and child face each other sitting on the floor, arms and legs outstretched, holding hands throughout. Therapist or parent and child take turns blowing the other one down to a lying position and sucking them back up to

a sitting position. Blowing is just for effect while pushing or pulling with arms facilitates the motion.

13. Blowing Bubbles

Therapist and child take turns blowing bubbles through the bubble wand. Child can chase and burst the bubbles, or each can have a wand blowing bubbles towards each other.

14. Body Outline

Child lies down on a piece of big paper and therapist or parent outlines child's body with a felt pen. Then both fill in features inside the body outline—nose, eyes, mouth, hair, shirt, etc.

15. Body Part Sounds

Touch different body parts, making a funny sound for each, such as "honk, honk," as you touch child's nose, or "erk, erk," as you touch his ears, etc.

16. Body Parts Inventory

Notice all the unique parts of child's body, such as blue eyes with brown flecks in them, a dimple right in the chin, a curl in the hair that goes right behind the ears, strong muscles in the arms (measure with tape measure). At times, therapists can compare child's features with those of his parents.

17. Book Balancing Races

Choose small books that balance easily (or bean bags) and therapist and child balance them on their heads as they have a race to the other side of the room.

18. Bottle Feed

Take child wrapped in a soft blanket in the therapist's or parent's arms and feed the child a bottle with the child's favorite juice, pop, or milk. The adult cradles the child and gently rocks, in time to a lullaby that is sung by the adult. A special song made up about the child may be sung, such as "Twinkle, twinkle little star, what a special girl you are. Hair so soft and rosy cheeks, two bright eyes from which you peek."

19. Bubbles

Parents and child get their hands wet and add liquid soap. By putting their hands together and then spreading their palms apart lightly, they can blow big bubbles together.

20. Bubble Gum Dare — Parents and children chew bubble gum and see who can make the biggest bubble.

21. Check Up — Same as body parts inventory (# 15). This activity is usually done at the beginning of the Theraplay session, right after the welcome song.

22. Choo-Choo Train — Everyone gets in a row behind each other with hands on waist of person in front. The leader winds around the room and pretends to go up and down hills, under bridges, etc. with everyone calling out "choo-choo" and occasionally "toot-toot" as they chug around the room.

23. Circle Magnets — Everyone sits in a circle facing inward with space between them. They sing a familiar song but when leader stops singing, everyone moves a few inches into the circle. The singing is started and stopped and this is repeated until everyone is huddled close into the circle. Everybody gives a group hug at the end.

24. Clap Patterns — Leader claps out various clap patterns and children copy the sequence of claps. Leader starts out with a simple sequence of claps and then makes them progressively more difficult. If therapist is sitting in a kneeling position in front of a child then the clap patterns can include touching different body parts of each other.

25. Cotton Ball Blow — Everyone lies on tummies facing inwards in a circle formation or facing each other if there are only two people. A cotton ball is placed in the center and each person tries to blow it away from himself and towards another person. Holding hands helps to form boundaries for the cotton ball.

26. Cotton Ball Fight — Form a circle or two rows with a pile of cotton balls in front of each person. On the word "go,"

people throw a ball at whoever they want, maybe even calling out the name of the person first. As the game progresses it becomes more free, with everyone pitching balls at everyone else as fast as they can.

27. Cotton Ball Guess or Touch

Child closes eyes. Therapist lightly touches different parts of child's body and child tells therapist what part of body he is touching.

28. Cotton Ball Soothe

Child lies down and therapist gently but firmly touches child with cotton ball around face, shoulders, arms, hands, and on outside of legs and feet without lifting cotton ball.

29. Cotton Ball Tickle

Therapist touches child with cotton ball lightly on tip of nose, and around chin or neck.

30. Cradling

Therapist or parent cradles child in arms while in a sitting position and rocks the child while singing a special song about the child or a lullaby.

31. Donut Dare

Therapist or parent puts finger through hole in donut. All family members have a turn taking a bite from the donut until someone bites through the donut and the donut breaks. That person then breaks up the rest of the donut and feeds it to the other family members.

32. Duck, Duck, Goose, Hug

Everyone sits in a circle with "it" passing behind each person and gently tapping them on the head with the word "duck" or "goose." On the word "goose" the tapped person jumps up and chases around in the opposite direction from "it." When they meet they give each other a hug and then continue running to the empty spot left by the "goose." Whoever gets there last is the next "it" and the game continues.

33. Facial Games

Everyone sits in a circle. Someone makes a face showing an emotion while everyone else guesses what emotion is being portrayed. Everyone takes a turn. In the second round all participants relate an incident where they felt the emotion they had portrayed in the first round.

34. Feeding Activities

Feeding is always included in every Theraplay session. The therapist feeds a chip, seedless grapes, etc. directly into the mouths of the children and parents. Participants can take turns feeding each other. Therapist or parent may cradle a child in his/her arms and feed the child a lollipop, or a baby bottle filled with juice, pop, or milk, while singing a song to the child.

35. Find Your Parent

Parents and children are asked to walk around while the therapist sings a song. When the singing stops, the children are encouraged to see how quickly they can find their parent's lap.

36. Finger and Toe Nibbling

Therapist or parent pretends to nibble child's fingers or toes saying "yummy yum, these taste good."

37. Follow the Leader

Parents or therapists or children take turns leading the rest of the family in walking or moving about the room in fun and interesting ways, one behind the other.

38. Foot Outline

Child places bare foot on a piece of construction paper and therapist outlines the foot with a felt pen. Other members can have their feet outlined on the same piece of paper and outlines are compared.

39. Footprints

Baby powder is dusted on the child's bare foot and then is placed on a piece of dark construction paper and pressed firmly leaving a footprint. This can also be done using finger paints. It can also be extended to having both feet painted and then lifting and holding the child up as he walks up a large piece of paper taped to the wall (wall walk).

40. Getting to Know You Game	Parent or therapist identifies a topic such as food, color, or an activity and parents and children identify their specific preferences.
41. Good-bye Song	At the end of a Theraplay session participants hold hands in a circle and sing a simple good-bye song such as
	"Good-bye Sally, good-bye Johnny, good-bye everyone, we're glad you came today."
42. Good Touch Train	All group members stand in a row, one behind the other. Each member is asked to give the person in front of him or her a good touch on the back. That person is asked to respond with comments or groans and moans about whether the touch feels good.
43. Hand Outline	See Foot outline (# 38).
44. Handprints	See Footprints (# 39).
45. Hand Stack	In circle formation facing inwards, on knees, leader puts a hand palm down near floor. His neighbor places his hand on top of leader's hand. Next person places his hand on top and this continues until all have stacked their hands on top of one another. Then leader takes his bottom hand and puts it on top of the last person's hand and this continues with the stack of hands rising until everyone is on tip-toe. Then reverse order of hands coming down to the floor again.
46. Happy Parent's List	Children and parent identify what makes parents happy, with emphasis on such things as hugs, that can be practiced in the therapy session.
47. Hello Feet	In circle formation sitting facing inwards, with people in socks or bare feet, say hello to each other by touching feet. A variation of this is to have all the feet hidden under a blanket and people take turns guessing whose feet they are touching.

48. Hello Good-bye	In circle formation standing facing inwards the leader throws a Nerf ball (or bean bag) to someone calling out her name—"Hello, Christine." That person catches the ball and says "Thank you, Evangeline." Christine then throws the ball to someone else calling out his name and so on. This is repeated until everyone has a turn catching and throwing the ball, and the ball is returned to the leader. This whole procedure is repeated, only faster this time, with everyone throwing the ball to the same person the second time around. In the third round the leader introduces a second ball following the first. The leader can introduce a third ball and so on depending on the skills of the group.
49. Hide Eyes behind Scarf	In sitting circle formation, one person is blindfolded with a scarf while another person is brought in front of him and he must guess who that person is by feeling his face, head, or shoulders, etc.
50. Hide M & M's	Hide, M & Ms (candies) or raisins on child who is lying on his back with his eyes closed. Then therapist or parent finds the candies and feeds them to the child one at a time. Child's head needs to be elevated with an extra pillow, so he doesn't choke while he is eating.
51. Hide under Blanket	Child hides under a blanket or under pillows and parents find him and give him a hug.
52. Hide-and-Seek Train	Children hide under blankets, in cupboards, in corners, etc., and parents find each child and form a train adding each found child to the train.
53. High Five Hello	Leader spreads out his fingers and touches palm of child with outstretched fingers saying "Hi five."
54. How Are We the Same Game	Parents and children look for physical characteristics that are the same, such as curly hair, color of eyes, or a special smile.

55. Hum Garden	Holding hands in a circle formation, participants kneel touching their heads to the floor and start humming softly and then louder as they raise themselves to a standing position with their arms upraised shouting as loud as they can. Then this is reversed with their humming getting progressively softer as they go back to touch the floor with their foreheads. In the second round, the group chants "We are great" in the same soft-loud-soft sequence.
56. Human Knot or Tangle Untangle	Leader begins by shaking hands with someone in the circle and introducing himself. With his other hand he shakes hands with another person still holding a hand with the previous person. These two people shake hands with others without letting go of hands until everyone is connected and intertwined in a human knot. Then, without letting go of hands, the circle tries to untangle back to original circle formation.
57. I'm Mad, I'm Sad, I'm Glad	In a circle formation a pillow is passed around with the leader starting by pounding the pillow and saying, "I'm mad about. . . . " The pillow is passed around until everyone has said something he or she is mad about. Then the leader starts another round by pounding the pillow and saying, "I'm sad about. . . . " In the third round the leader hugs the pillow and says "I'm glad about. . . . " and passes the pillow to the next person, and so on.
58. Inventory	At the beginning of a theraplay session the therapist makes an inventory of all of the positive features of the child, such as "sparkly eyes, rosy cheeks, big strong shoulders, etc." (Same as "Check Up, #21).
59. Itsy Bitsy Spider	Therapist uses finger motions as he sings this nursery rhyme.

60. Jelly Bean
Toes

Therapist pretends he has found child's toes to be "jelly beans" or "popcorn," etc. Therapist feels each toe while saying to the child, "I wonder what's in here? Do you think it could be jelly beans?" Then the therapist whips child's sock off and exclaims "It is jelly beans, my favorite flavors too!" and pretends to nibble the child's toes.

61. Jelly Toes or
Hands

Squeeze jello with your hands or toes.

62. Licorice Eating
Contest

Parents and children begin eating a long strip of licorice with one person at each end. When they get to the middle, their noses touch or they might give each other a kiss.

63. Lollipop Feed

Parent or therapist cradles the child in his arms while feeding him a lollipop and singing a lullaby or a special song about the child.

64. London Bridge

Parents and child form a train passing under a bridge that therapist have made with their upraised arms while everyone sings "London bridge is falling down, falling down, falling down. London Bridge is falling down, my fair lady oh." On the words "my fair lady oh" the therapists' arms are lowered and a child is caught between their arms.

65. Lotioning
Hurts

Therapist or parent finds "hurts" (scratches, bruises, other marks) on child's hands or feet and gently applies lotion or powder around the "hurt."

66. Lotion on
Noses

Therapist puts lotion on end of his nose and passes the lotion on the next person in the circle by rubbing noses, and so on.

67. M & M Hunt

See Hide M & Ms (#50).

68. Mirroring

Therapist or parent sits or stands facing the child. Therapist moves arms and body in various ways with the child copying everything the therapist does. Then reverse with the therapist or parent "mirroring" the child's movements.

69. Mother, May I	Leader stands at one end of the room while all others stand in a row at the opposite end of the room facing the leader. First person asks the leader, "Mother, may I take two giant steps forward?" (or something equivalent). Leader answers, "Yes you may" (or may not). Each person asks a question starting with "Mother, may I," and if they don't, they miss their turn. If anyone tries to sneak forward when it is not their turn, the leader can send them back to the starting point. First person to reach "Mother" is the leader of the next round.
70. Motor Boat	Hold hands in a circle while moving to the right going slow or fast depending on the words of the song or chant: "Motor boat, motor boat go so slow, Motor boat, motor boat go so fast, motor boat motor boat step on the gas. Motor boat, motor boat go so slow, motor boat motor boat go so fast, motor boat, motor boat out of gas." At this point all collapse on the floor.
71. Musical Chairs or Hoops	Chairs or hoops are scattered around the room. Everyone walks freely while leader sings a favorite song. As soon as the leader stops singing, everyone leaps into a hoop or sits on a chair. Then one chair is taken away and a song is sung again. This is repeated until there is only one chair left, with everyone sitting on top of the person who first sat on the last remaining chair.
72. One Potato Two Potato	In a sitting circle formation, the leader passes a bean bag chanting, "One potato, two potato, three potato, four, five potato, six potato, seven potato more." Whoever has the bean bag on the word "more" is "it" and gets a hug from each of his neighbors, or if it is a small group, then everyone gives him a hug.
73. Paper Punch and Basketball Throw	The therapist holds a newspaper sheet tautly so the child can break it easily in half as he punches through the paper with his fist. Then the child

punches through the half sheet so it becomes two quarter sheets. For older, stronger children, the newspaper can be a double thickness (two sheets). The child punches through a number of newspapers and then squeezes each piece into a ball that is used to toss into a basket holder made by the therapist's arms joined to form a circle.

74. Pass a Funny Face	In a sitting circle formation, a member makes a funny face and his neighbor passes it on to the next person and so on until it comes back to the leader. Everyone gets a turn making a new funny face which is passed on.
75. Pass a Message	In a circle formation the leader whispers a message to his neighbor and this message is passed around the circle until it comes back to the leader who compares it out loud with what he originally said.
76. Pass a Touch	Leader passes a touch to his neighbor who passes it on to the next person. For older children this can be made more challenging by having a person not only passing the touch he has just received, but adding on his own form of touch. The next person repeats all the previous kinds of touches and adds his own.
77. Patty Cake	Leader or parent plays traditional Patty Cake with child.

"Patty cake, patty cake, baker's man
Bake me a cake as fast as you can.
Roll it and pat it and make it with a
B (or initial of child's name) and put it
in the oven for baby (or child's name)
And me."

For older children "Pease Porridge Hot" can be substituted.

78. Peanut Butter Jelly	In circle formation, leader calls out "Peanut Butter" and the group answers "Jelly" in the exact

tone, speed, and loudness that the leader has used. The leader varies his presentation of the words.

79. Peekaboo   With a child lying on the floor, therapist plays "Peek-a-boo" with the child, using child's feet or a pillow to hide behind and then suddenly popping out and saying "Peek-a-boo."

80. Pillow Push   Therapist and child, from kneeling position, each take a large pillow and push against each other in a pushing contest.

81. Pillow Ride   Child is placed on a large pillow and the pillow is pulled by the therapist or parent. Having a child ride on a blanket or in a basket that is dragged across the floor by an adult is also a fun activity.

82. Ping-Pong Ball   See cotton ball blow but substitute Ping Pong balls
    Blow   for cotton balls (# 25).

83. Play-Doh   Make imprints of a child's body parts, such as
    Trophies   fingers knuckles, hands, toes, nose, ear, elbow, etc. using Play-Doh.

84. Pop Cheeks   Child and Parent or therapist fill their cheeks with air and the other person pops the air out by gently hitting the cheeks with the flat of each hand.

85. Popcorn   See Blanket Popcorn (# 9).
    Blanket

86. Popcorn Toes   See Jelly Bean Toes (# 60).

87. Powder Hurts   Same as Lotion Hurts (# 65).

88. Pretzel Dare   Same as Donut Dare (# 31).

89. Red Light,   Leader is at one end of room and the others stand
    Green Light   facing her at the opposite end of the room. When leader turns her back and calls out "Red Light," everyone must freeze and if caught moving by the leader, they are sent back to the starting line. Green Light means people can move forward.

Whoever reaches the leader first is the winner of
the game and becomes the next leader.

90. Riding on a Blanket

See Pillow Ride (# 81).

91. Ring Around the Rosie

Hands held in a circle and everyone moves in one
direction, singing traditional rhyme:

"Ring around the rosie
Pockets full of posies
Husha, Husha
We all fall down" (everyone falls down)

92. Rock in Blanket

See Blanket Rock (# 10).

93. Row Row Row Your Boat

Everyone in a circle joined with hands on next
person's shoulders, sways right and left to beat
of song or forms a chain while sitting in a row,
moving back and forth with hands on waist:

"Row row row your boat
Gently down the stream
Merrily, merrily, merrily, merrily
Life is but a dream"

94. Say One Nice Thing about Your Neighbor

In a circle, sitting position, leader starts by saying one nice thing he likes about the person next
to him. The next person then gives a compliment
to person next to her and so on until everyone
receives a compliment.

95. Silly Bones

Two people facing each other or can be done by a
whole group. Therapist calls out "Silly Bones says
touch our hands." Child and therapist then touch
hands. Leader calls another body part and so on.

96. Simon Says

Played in the traditional way where leader calls
out "Simon says put your hand up" and the
group does this. Leader calls out various other
commands and the group obeys as long as the
command is prefaced with "Simon says." If this

is not done, then the group does not obey. If someone obeys a command not preceded with "Simon says" then that person is "it" and becomes the leader. This can be varied so commands such as "Simon says give your neighbor a hug," or "Simon says say one nice thing about your neighbor," are thrown in.

97. Slip and Grip

Partners lotion each other's hands and then one grips the other's hand while the partner tries to slip his hand free.

98. Stacking Hands

See Hand Stack (# 45).

99. Sword Fight

Roll a newspaper diagonally and tape it to create a "sword." Therapist or partner and child each have a sword and pretend to have a sword fight by whacking each other's swords. This makes a loud sound, but is not hurtful.

100. This Little Piggy

Parent or therapist recites traditional rhyme and then varies it:

"This little piggy had brown eyes, just like you
"This little piggy had rosy cheeks, just like you
"This little piggy giggled, just like you
"This little piggy liked ice cream, just like you
"And this little piggy went wee wee wee all the way home" (give gentle tickle to child).

101. Thumb Wrestling

Face partner with fingers interlocked and thumbs up. Leader says something like "1,2,3,4, this a thumb war." On the word "war" each opponent tries to bend over the other's thumb.

102. Trace Shapes, Letters or Numbers

Parent or therapist faces the back of the child and traces a shape (letters or numbers) on the back of the child with a finger. The child guesses the shape. The parent or therapist rubs off the shape and traces another. In the end give a good back massage to the child. Roles can be reversed.

103. Tunnels

Parents and therapists and siblings form a tunnel by bending over their knees and arms. Child crawls through the tunnel and joins the tunnel at the end while another person crawls through. (This includes adults crawling if they are athletic enough.)

104. Washing and Powdering Hands and Feet

Therapist has a basin of warm soapy water and a dry towel ready to wash the hands or feet of the child after such activities as hand or foot outline where felt pen marks or finger paints can be left on. After drying hands, lotion or powder them.

105. Welcome Song

At beginning of each Theraplay session, welcome the participants by joining hands and singing a song such as

"Welcome, Welcome, everyone, now we're going to have some fun," or "Hello Johnny, hello Sally, hello Tommy, we're glad you came today."

105. Wheelbarrow

Parent or therapist lifts and holds up child's legs while she braces herself on her arms with head up. Child moves forward by "walking" with her hands. Others can form wheelbarrows and a contest can be held racing from one end of the room to the other.

Index